WATCHDOGS OF TERROR

Russian Bodyguards from the
Tsars to the Commissars

Foreign Intelligence Book Series

Thomas F. Troy, General Editor

WATCHDOGS OF TERROR

Russian Bodyguards from the Tsars to the Commissars

Second Edition
Revised and Updated

PETER DERIABIN

UNIVERSITY PUBLICATIONS OF AMERICA

Originally published in 1972. Copyright N 1972 by Arlington House.

Second Edition, Revised and Updated.
Copyright © 1984 by Peter Deriabin.

Library of Congress Cataloging in Publication Data.

Deriabin, Peter, 1921-
    Watchdogs of terror.

    (Foreign intelligence book series)
    Bibliography: p. 435.
    Includes index.
    1. Secret service—Soviet Union—History. 2. Internal
security—Soviet Union—History. I. Title. II. Series.
HV8224.D45   1984   363.2'83'09747   84-11873
ISBN 0-89093-674-9.

Printed in the United States of America.

TO

my American son

my Moscow daughter, AND

my sister who is somewhere in Siberia

"Of all the foes, the most hateful is the friend-foe."

"I believe that sometime, from time to time, the master must without fail go through the ranks of the party with a broom in his hands."

"The method of chopping off and blood letting . . . is dangerous and infectious. You chop off one head today, another one tomorrow, still another on the day after—what in the end will be left of the party?"

Contents

PART TWO

COMMUNIST EXPERIMENTS AND INNOVATIONS

Foreword

For some ten years, I was a Russian counter intelligence officer and bodyguard, serving during the end of the Stalin era, a time when the system of protecting a national leadership had reached a technical perfection still unattained elsewhere in the world.

During that period of difficult and dangerous service, and until several years later when I came to the West after deciding to quit my country of birth forever, my knowledge of the methods of guarding nations' hierarchs was narrowly restricted to Soviet techniques. I knew, of course, that the tsars had their bodyguards, but that information was colored more by propaganda about the wrong-doings of the tsars and their servants than by hard facts about the problems and operations of my predecessors. I also knew that the leaders of other contemporary nations had their bodyguards, but there, too, my range of vision was extremely limited.

Naturally, therefore, after arriving in the West, I gravitated with great thirst toward everything I could hear, learn, or read about Russia, and particularly toward my former work, that of a professional bodyguard. Only emigrés from Communist countries, and especially from Russia, can appreciate the unique ability to gather information which the free world offers, a privilege and a right refused them in their lands of origin, where even the most trivial fact is often obscured, distorted, or denied.

In my preliminary research, I was impressed to find that very little has been written about Russian bodyguards per se, and especially about the roles they have played in perpetuating or overthrowing the reigns of the leaders they had been sworn to protect. Several texts by late chiefs of tsarist bodyguards were all that were available on this specific subject, and these were somewhat disappointing since they tended to apologize for or excuse shortcomings and to romanticize those bygone times rather than to throw light on the specific problems and techniques of their work. Additionally, I was a bit startled to see circulating almost unchallenged in the free world what at best can be described as "apocrypha," books that alleged intimate knowledge about Stalin's bodyguards—claims rendered immediately suspect to the serious reader by the inclusion of references to nonexistent or fictitious personalities. Apocrypha or not, I had to familiarize myself with those books, but decided I would not—could not—include them in the bibliography.

Accordingly, because of such paucity of information from the former tsarist chiefs of bodyguards, and the unintended or willful misinformation about the Communist period, I have relied chiefly on factual histories, of both Russian and Western scholars; on semiromanticized accounts of specific Russian eras and personalities so popular in the West; and on reports of Western authorities of repute. Fortunately, the integrity and ability of pre-Bolshevik historians is beyond question, as is the standing of most Western historians concerned with Russia, and I relied very much upon them for the tsarist times. For the post-Bolshevik era I leaned most heavily upon my own knowledge and experience, but I also most gratefully utilized facts furnished by Western experts listed in the bibliography. And, for the same period, I also examined Communist accounts, but, as could be expected, with few fruitful results, except for occasional miscellaneous factual detail concerning personalities and circumstances which were invariably distorted by embellishments or deletions, or otherwise tailored to fit the mutations of the party line in successive "histories."

This proved to be a fascinating study, despite numerous complexities, contradictions, and some questions I could not resolve. From it, as well as from my service with Stalin's bodyguards whom I joined almost a quarter century ago, I have gained a knowledge of the unique position of the bodyguards of Russian rulers throughout history, a role challenged only by that of the guards of the Oriental despotisms, now long extinct, and possibly by those of the present Chinese leadership. Certainly, no such system of protecting the hierarchs has been conceived of in the West, nor should it be, nor do I think it would ever be countenanced by citizens of democratic societies.

The uniqueness of the Russian bodyguard system, under commissars as well as tsars, appears to be the result of two prime factors. The first of these, based upon the rather indisputable historic fact that all Russian regimes have been despotic, is that Russian bodyguards, no matter how strong and able, effectively protected the ruler only so long as they utilized terror—terror on the broadest possible scale. On the one hand, a maximum application of terror enabled barbarous Ivan the Terrible to survive his deeds; on the other hand, the failure to resort to ruthless terror was the reason that Alexander II, the liberator of the serfs, was assassinated. And Nicholas II, who could have used terror, but did not, instead had it applied against himself. Use of terror by the Communists to maintain themselves is axiomatic from Lenin down to the present.

Equally important to the special role of Russian bodyguards throughout recorded history is their dual function: they have not only guarded the leader by protecting him from his enemies; they have also shielded him by directly liquidating his enemies, real or imagined, usually most bloodily, but always most effectively. Imagine that happening in the U.S.A.: a Secret Service man killing off, or at least imprisoning, all garden-variety political opponents of an American president.

In examining the comparative problems of tsarist bodyguards and those of the Soviet regime, I also noted what appears to be an interesting parallel. For the petty princes of Kiev, Moscow, and other fiefdoms, and indeed for most of the tsars until the early years of the nineteenth century, the chief menace faced by rulers and their bodyguards came from within the palace, from rebellious kinsmen and their allies seeking power. Starting with the reign of Nicholas I, however, and through those of his three successors, intramural palace rivalry had become dormant, and the main threat to the leader originated outside the imperial family, with disaffected nobility, intelligentsia, workers, and peasants. A similar evolution appears to characterize the Communist era. Until the time of Khrushchev, the principal danger for the ruler and his bodyguards also came from within a palace of sorts. Lenin was threatened by hard-bitten revolutionaries of a different political stripe and to a very much lesser extent by surviving tsarists. Stalin was faced with real and imagined fellow Bolshevik enemies, once possible rulers themselves, and had them all, including Trotsky, his most redoubtable foe, liquidated by his bodyguard system. By the time of Khrushchev, however, and his subsequent relatively peaceful removal, the struggle for power appeared to be assuming a less sanguinary pattern, such as occurred during the reigns of the last four tsars; even though struggle for leadership is inherent to communism, for all its talk about "democratic," collective rule. Concurrently, the more ordinary people—writers, artists, scientists, even collective farm bosses—their shackles slightly loosened with the end of Stalin's terror, became restive and therewith came a potentially significant change in the source of threat to the leadership. It is still far too early, of course, even to hazard a guess as to whether these social strata will follow the footsteps of their fellows of the last century, but the pattern is established, at least. Much depends on whether the contemporary opposition is prepared to attain its professed ideals by adding deeds to words.

My study for this book also proved enlightening for me—particularly since I was once a Communist—by exploding much Bolshevik mythology. Remember, that while in my country as a boy and student, and while serving it as a soldier, bodyguard of Stalin, and officer of its secret police, my only knowledge of Russia's political history was gained from glorified texts about Lenin, required reading of Stalin's works, and Marxist-Leninist courses. Only then can one understand first my amazement and later my appreciation in learning that Lenin's adherents played little more than the parts of parlor pinks in the overthrow of the tsars; in finding that the Bolsheviks had profited by decades of preparatory terror by the Socialist Revolutionaries and their predecessors, surfacing comparatively safely only after the hard work had been done for them by others, others whom they speedily liquidated and have always repudiated and denigrated.

Of course my special contribution, and my main story, is that of the Soviet bodyguards and their extraordinary role in the survival of the Soviet system. But they take their place in a long and colorful Russian history that was shaped by internal power fights in high places, in which the bodyguards were always an important factor and often a major actor.

In fact, the role of the bodyguards can hardly be understood without that history. So I begin this book with a sketch of pre-Soviet and Soviet history—the main events and actors. By handling my subject in this way, I have had to remind my readers of things that have been told before by better qualified historians—and I have had to risk some repetition between the two parts of the book. The story of the bodyguards weaves its way, just under the surface, throughout this first part, and comes to the top in the later sections (Chapters IV-VII, the Epilogue, and the Appendices).

The story of the bodyguards tells much about Soviet power today. While Stalin's system—for its sheer size and for the capabilities it directly controlled—may never be equalled, the essentials of his system remain unchanged. It cannot be otherwise: not just the health of the leaders depends on it, but the very survival in power of their system. This is its peak, its summit: here the controllers are controlled.

Finally, this book was intended to contribute to a deeper understanding of the country of my birth, and give some appreciation of the role the security of its leader has played in its history. As the only former bodyguard of a Russian leader, Tsarist or Communist, presently in the West, I also hope it can correct some misconceptions and fill some gaps about how Russia's leaders gained, maintained, or were deprived of power.

My gratitude for literary assistance, valuable comments and suggestions in the preparation of this book goes to Edgar E. Clark.

The author, of course, is to be held responsible for the opinions, statements and conclusions in the text.

PETER DERIABIN
June 14, 1972

Part One

SUCCESS AND FAILURE

UNDER THE TSARS

CHAPTER I

Pre-Bolshevik Bloody Russia

1. KIEV

As a nation-state, the Russians are comparative newcomers to the Eurasian continent. Ethnically, at first they were East Slavs, as differentiated from other Slavs who penetrated west to present-day Poland, Germany, and Czechoslovakia and south to Yugoslavia. The origins of all Slavs are obscure, but they are believed to be pre-Christian era descendants of Persian invaders and thus of Indo-European stock.

In their prehistoric times, the East Slavs are thought to have been a peaceful people, organized into tribes, of which the two principal were the Polyane, or plains people, and the Drevlyane, or forest people. The Polyane concentrated in the rich soil of the steppes of what is now the heartland of the Ukraine. The Drevlyane inhabited the forests and marshlands to the north. From tribal groups, those early Russians broke up into clans and then families as fierce, warlike masses from Asia—the Avars, Huns, Goths and others—overran the area. Those incursions also served to alter the ethnic makeup of the East Slavs.

So far as formation of a Russian state is concerned, however, significant foreign penetration of the East Slav territory did not come until early in the ninth century with the emergence of the Vikings, whose raids terrified much of the settled Western regions of that time. Those Scandinavians, who entered Russia, were known as Varangers (there is a peninsula of that name in today's northeast Norway) and they sought trading passage between the cold waters of the north and the Black Sea to reach the riches of Byzantium. The East Slavs lay athwart the route, along the great rivers between the arctic north and the temperate south.

The earliest recorded Russian history dates from the arrival of the Varangers. It mentions two towns, Kiev on the Dnieper flowing to the Black Sea, and Novgorod, to the north, on the Volkhov emptying into Lake Ladoga. A somewhat legendary account tells of Kiev being founded by a Prince Kiy of the Polyane and of the building of a fortified area on high ground on the west bank of the Dnieper. No detail is given of the beginnings of Novgorod, but that town is believed to have been a flourishing trading center possibly before the founding of Kiev.

Toward the end of the first half of the ninth century, some Varangers en route south passed through Novgorod which was experiencing disorders within the city and raids from primitive tribesmen in the environs. At the request of the residents of Novgorod, a few of the Varangers, who were redoubtable warriors as well as traders, stayed on to guard the town. The leader of this band of Varangers was Rurik, the fabled founder of the Russian Empire. In Rurik's group were two companions, Askold and Dir, who went south to administrate and later seize control of Kiev, where they had found numbers of other Varangers to support them. At about the same time, Varanger forays down the Russian rivers to the Black Sea started, culminating with savage raids on Byzantine towns on the Asia Minor coast.

Meanwhile, feeling either poorly rewarded or tired of his duties, Rurik quit his post at Novgorod and returned to his homeland. For a time, Novgorod enlisted other Varangers as guards but those Scandinavians proved unsatisfactory. As a result, in 862 the town's elders persuaded Rurik and his company to return to their posts to "establish order and unity among them." That marked the beginning of the Rurikid dynasty, which ruled over Russia until the seventeenth century, when Rurik's kinsmen and descendants, weakened by internecine struggle, were succeeded by the Romanovs.

The first Russian Chronicle indicates Rurik was not anxious to return to Novgorod "because of the savage habits of the people" and states that for some time after coming back he maintained his camp several miles away on Lake Ladoga to keep open the return route to his homeland. Nor was Rurik's second tenure without trouble. An opponent named Vadim tried to overthrow him in a dispute over tribute paid the Varangers by the city. Rurik, however, not only won that struggle, but also gained the title of Prince of Novgorod. With that, he sent kinsmen and deputies to the subject towns of Pskov in the west and Belozersk and Rostov in the east to bring them under his control.

When Rurik died in 879, his cousin, Oleg, acted as regent, since Igor, Rurik's son and heir, was a child. Oleg was ambitious and ruthless. In 882, he led a company of Varangers down the Dnieper by river craft. Arriving at Kiev, Oleg invited Askold, Dir, and their chief supporters to join them for a parley. Once aboard, the visitors were murdered to a man. Oleg claimed that the Kiev Varangers had been traitors to the youthful Igor, but the real motive for the murders was to gain control of Kiev and of the water route to the Black Sea, along which Askold, Dir and company had traveled in 865 for a daring and brutal raid on Constantinople. A few years later, Oleg added the town of Smolensk to his dominion and at the end of the ninth century had established the first Russian state: Kiev and its tributary towns of Chernigov and Pereyaslavl in the south; Smolensk, Belozersk and Rostov in the center; and Novgorod, Pskov and Polotsk to the north. And at about the same time, Oleg assumed the title of Grand Prince of Russia and established his capital in Kiev.

In 907, toward the end of his regency, Oleg duplicated the feat of Askold and Dir by fighting his way down the river route to the Black Sea and to Constantinople. Oleg, however, went to the Byzantine capital for trade and a treaty rather than a raid. He had plenty of fighting nevertheless en route, his principal adversaries being the extremely barbaric and vicious Pechenegs, invaders from Asia entrenched in the area of the southern Dnieper. Early—undoubtedly romanticized—Russian accounts of this expedition said 2,000 boats were engaged in it: boats which had to be taken by portage around river rapids by slaves, part of the merchandise being taken to Constantinople.

Igor, Rurik's son, became Grand Prince with Oleg's death in 912 and ruled until he was killed in 945. Igor (his Varanger name was Ingvarr) was more a savage Viking raider-chieftain than a grand prince, leading two forays aimed at Constantinople, which he never reached but thoroughly terrified. Even when the Varangers from Russia came in peace as traders, Constantinople was extremely wary of them. The men of Oleg, Igor, and their successors were never truly

[19]

trusted; they were allowed within the walls of the city in groups of no more than fifty at a time, unarmed and by one specified gate only.

In 941, Igor headed his first expedition south, put defenseless Greek and Asia Minor coastal towns to the torch, killed off their inhabitants by crucifying them or burying them alive, and tortured and killed all priests who fell into his hands by having nails driven into their heads. Before the raiders reached the capital, however, a small but able and courageous Byzantine squadron engaged Igor's advance craft, virtually incinerated them with Greek fire, wiped out Varanger landing parties, beheaded all prisoners, and then chased the remnants of Igor's forces back to the mouth of the Dnieper. Igor himself barely escaped with his life and lost all but a handful of his men.

Nothing daunted, after striking up an alliance with the Pechenegs, he embarked again for Constantinople in 944. Upon reaching the Danube delta, however, his forces and his alliance showed signs of weakness so Igor made peace with Byzantium. A year later, this bloody ruler met his death deep in the Russian forests at the hands of the Slavs. He had just collected his usual annual tribute of furs, wax, honey, and slaves, from the Drevlyane, but wanted more. On his second visit to the forest people, he was caught in ambush and killed.

For a decade after Igor's death, his widow, Olga, ruled the Kiev principality and its subject cities until Igor's son and heir, who later became Svyatoslav I, reached his majority. Olga was a capable administrator; she not only continued to collect tribute from subject territories, but also set up permanent collecting points for the payments. Nor did this woman, who later became the first Russian ruler to accept Christianity, forget vengeance against the Drevlyane who had killed her husband. When Prince Mal of the Drevlyane sent a deputation to Kiev seeking Olga's hand in marriage, she had the envoys buried alive; a second delegation on a like mission she had burned alive. And before Olga settled the score with the Drevlyane, some 5,000 of them were killed by her men.

The brief reign of Svyatoslav (965–72) was one of continuous battle, an attempt to secure commercial riches to the south in which little attention was given to running the Kiev principality. He refused to embrace Christianity because he thought it would make him appear a weakling to his fighting men. In 968, he led his troops south and across the Danube to overwhelm the Bulgarians (then a Mongol people, who had first settled along the Volga in their move out of Asia) and took their capital, Pereyaslavl (Preslav). At the height of that victory, however, Svyatoslav had to hurry home to fight off the Pechenegs, who were attacking Kiev. In his absence, the Bulgarians, with help from Constantinople, regained their country. A good tactician, Svyatoslav met that setback by making peace with the Pechenegs, striking up an alliance with the Magyars on his right flank, and reentering Bulgaria at the head of 60,000 men. He quickly reconquered Bulgaria, then crossed the Balkan mountains to capture the Byzantine city of Philippopolis and butcher 20,000 of its inhabitants. Driving next toward Constantinople itself, Svyatoslav suddenly quit after an advance unit was routed and withdrew back into Bulgaria. The great Byzantine general, Deputy Emperor John Zimisces, pursued the invader there in 971. After a number of bloody and losing battles, Svyatoslav was decisively defeated at Silistra on the Danube. His forces reduced to 22,000 men, the Kiev prince sued for and was allowed honorable surrender, being permitted to leave with his remaining troops on provision he refrain from again molesting Bulgaria and the Byzantine sphere of influence at the mouth of the Dnieper. On his way home, he encountered final disaster. At the Dnieper rapids, his forces were ambushed and massacred by the Pechenegs. Svyatoslav fell in that battle and the Pechenegs' Khan Kurya celebrated victory by drinking from Svyatoslav's skull. According to legend, only one Russian escaped that fray, Svineld, a member of the guard, the sole member of Svyatoslav's army to return to Kiev.

Svyatoslav was not only unfortunate in battle, he was also extremely unwise in providing for his succession. Before leaving for his second Bulgarian venture, he had divided his Russian realm among his three sons, thus originating a system of multiple succession that caused devastating civil wars throughout the land for the next several centuries.

Those troubles started virtually with Svyatoslav's death. His eldest son, Yaropolk I (972–80), was no more than a boy in the hands of rapacious advisers when he became Prince of Kiev. The most nefarious of that court was Svineld, the lone survivor of the Dnieper massacre, who persuaded Yaropolk to do battle with Oleg, a fight in which Oleg was killed. Vladimir, the third son of Svyatoslav, took the prudent course of fleeing to Novgorod where he found refuge and support.

In 980, Vladimir advanced south to Kiev. There, Yaropolk was betrayed by an adviser and murdered and his younger brother became Vladimir I, grand prince. The same intelligence that had led Vladimir (980–1015) to shelter in Novgorod also caused him to become a Christian and so become an early member of the Russian Orthodox pantheon of saints, although he certainly was not a saint, having first happily sacrificed humans before his pagan gods and then, once converted, having killed all his subjects opposed to their prince's new-found faith. Before conversion, Vladimir had carefully sized up the material merits of the four nonpagan beliefs with which he, or his subjects, had had contact. Three he rejected outright: the Hebraic, because Jews confessed to being homeless because of their sins; that of Allah, since Moslems shunned alcohol; and that of Rome, because the Pope was spiritual chief of all temporal rulers. His choice was Greek Orthodoxy, but with Varanger blood still predominant in his veins, he decided to fight for conversion rather than accept it as a gift from a superior: he captured the Byzantine port of Kherson at the mouth of the Dnieper and then sent emissaries to Constantinople with the threat that the Byzantine capital would suffer a similar fate unless Vladimir was given in marriage Princess Anne, the sister of the two emperors then reigning. Constantinople capitulated, Vladimir became a Christian, and Princess Anne married him in Kherson.

The princely carnage that followed Vladimir's death was almost unbelievable. Comparatively, Shakespeare's tragedies about royal internecine struggles are mild, indeed. That great Russian bloodletting can be placed directly at the door of Vladimir, who, as did his father, made the mistake of dividing his realm between sons. And, in Vladimir's case, this error was several times compounded because he had no less than twelve sons.

The eldest son, Svyatopolk (1015–19), later known as Okoyanny ("the Accursed") for his fratricides, succeeded his father by the process of murdering two brothers, favored by the princely bodyguard, since they were born of Vladimir's marriage to Princess Anne. Although the elder of those two youths, Prince Boris, had no intention of opposing Svyatopolk, the latter waited until the bodyguard had dispersed and then sent two Varangers, identified in legends as Eymund and Ragnar, to cut off Boris' head while he was at prayers.

Next, Svyatopolk bribed the cook of Prince Gleb, Boris' brother, to dispatch his second potential rival by knifing him while he was aboard a river craft near Smolensk.

Meanwhile, Yaroslav Mudry ("the Wise"), the ablest of Vladimir's sons, who was ruling in Novgorod, had been having serious trouble in that city because he had made two Varangers (also named in legends as Eymund and Ragnar) commanders of his troops. By night, the people of Novgorod had risen and killed the two Varangers. Enraged, Yaroslav reacted by killing some one thousand of the Novgorod troops he believed were involved in the rising. Almost at that moment, however, he heard of his father's death and Svyatopolk's seizure of power, so he patched up his quarrel with Novgorod, set sail with his bodyguard and the Novgorod troops for Kiev and drove out Svyatopolk.

That victory of Yaroslav proved short-lived. Within weeks, Svyatopolk enlisted the help of his father-in-law, Boris the Brave, King of Poland, and with those Polish forces and allies among the Pechenegs overcame Yaroslav, who retired again to Novgorod. Once back in power, Svyatopolk continued his fratricide. He sent killers after another brother, Prince Svyatoslav, nominal prince of the Drevlyane. Svyatoslav escaped the first attempt, tried to flee to the Western Slav lands of his mother, but was caught in the Carpathian mountains and murdered. At about the same time, Svyatopolk drove yet another brother, Prince Vsevolod, ruler of Vladimir, into fatal exile. Vsevolod fled to Sweden, where he later asked the widow of King Eric to marry him. That queen, known in sagas as Sigride-the-Killer, had Vsevolod burned to death in her palace, the same fate she had meted out to earlier suitors.

By 1019, the people of Kiev had tired of the Polish troops quartered on them and killed goodly numbers. Tired in their turn of being murdered, the Poles withdrew. With that, Yaroslav (1019–54) returned with his forces from Novgorod and drove out Svyatopolk for good. By then adjudged thoroughly insane by his contemporaries, Svyatopolk took to his horse and rode wildly throughout Poland where he died within the year, according to Varanger tales. Russian legend said "the Accursed" again sought the assistance of the Pechenegs who killed him at the exact place he had had Prince Boris murdered.

The reign of Yaroslav Mudry, also called Khromets (the limper) because of a youthful leg injury, was long and, for Russia, relatively benevolent. He gave Russia its first code of laws; he crushed the Pechenegs for good; he extended the state's domains north of Novgorod and west of Pskov. But he, too, was not overly endowed with brotherly love for the surviving sons of his father. He had one, Prince Sudislav of Pskov, falsely slandered and then entombed in a *porub*, a covered pit, to spend twenty-four years in his own excreta, surviving on bones tossed to him like an animal. Nor was Yaroslav's wisdom great about the succession problem. He had hoped to avoid the fratricidal struggles for power that marked the previous reigns and tried to unite his descendants as a family. What he did, however, was to subdivide the realm between five sons and a grandson and give roles of precedence to its various subsidiary cities, thereby multiplying conflict that ended with the elimination of Kiev as the seat of power.

In fact, Kiev survived only little more than a century after the death of Yaroslav. Its decline was caused less by squabbling among the princes than by the invasion of a new group of Mongol-Tatars from Asia, the Kipchak Turks, or Comans, called the Polovtsy by the Russians. The Polovtsy not only repeatedly attacked Kiev, but more importantly, also barred the water trade routes to the south, the very *raison d'être* of Kiev. As a result of that raiding and stoppage of commerce, the princes began abandoning the exposed, open terrain of Kiev in favor of more secure tenures in the cities of the north and especially in the relatively newer settlements in the densely wooded country to the northeast.

The twilight period of Kiev was marked by the reigns of two very good and able princes, Vladimir II, called Vladimir Monomakh because he was the grandson of Byzantine Emperor Monomachus, and Vladimir's son, Mstislav, who ruled from 1113–32. Renowned as the King Alfred of Russian history, Vladimir Monomakh led three campaigns against the Polovtsy, battles which were virtually crusades. He was also a most chivalrous man, coming to the aid of a young knight and minor prince, Vasilko, who had been blinded by his enemies. Except for the weak and cruel Svyatopolk II (1093–1113), in whose house Prince Vasilko had been blinded, the rest of the ten descendants of Yaroslav who ruled Kiev in its final century were just and able men. All except Svyatopolk II refrained from the murderous family feuds so common to their Rurikid predecessors, no doubt because they were too preoccupied with battles for survival with the Polovtsy. But that did not mean that struggle for power among the rapidly multiplying scions of Yaroslav had ended: that never ceased.

The last grand prince to rule in Kiev was Yury Dolgoruky ("the Long Arm," 1154–57), the fifth son of Vladimir Monomakh. Yury gained and retained his throne mainly due to the help of his lieutenant, his second son, Prince Andrey Bogolyubsky (Beloved of God), who combined the qualities of an able soldier and an expert politician.

2. VLADIMIR

With Yury's death, Andrey could have become Grand Prince of Kiev. Instead, he chose to establish himself in Vladimir, some 500 miles northeast of Kiev, far from the princely feuds and free from the increasing ravishings of the Polovtsy. Vladimir became the seat of Russian power and retained that position for the next century and three-quarters. Andrey returned only once to Kiev, in 1169, to storm it, treat its populace as savagely as foreign enemies and install his brother, Gleb, there as his deputy.

The first Grand Prince of Vladimir met his end in 1174, when princely conspirators from the neighboring tributary cities of Rostov and Suzdal caught him at home alone, not only without his bodyguard, but without his sword as well. Chronicles tell that Andrey at first beat off his attackers who left the house "trembling all over," but once outside they heard his groans of pain, so returned and killed him.

Andrey's murder brought Vladimir two years of civil war with its neighbors, Rostov and Suzdal, a struggle won by Vladimir, almost to its own surprise. Early in this war, Vladimir was ruled by Mikhail I (1175–76), Andrey's brother and the fourth son of Yury. When Vladimir became victorious, primarily because of the efforts and sacrifices of its lesser nobility and freemen, it demanded and won what for those times was a considerable degree of independence: establishment of the principle of primogeniture for its ruling family. In installing Yury's fifth son, Vsevolod III (1176–1212), as grand prince, the city took the oath not only to him, but also to his sons.

Vsevolod, known as Bolshoye Gnezdo (Big Nest) because of his many children, distinguished himself only by continuing the princely propensity for feuding by naming as successor his second son, Yury

II (1212–16). By intramural conniving and battling, Vsevolod's first son, Constantine (1216–19), briefly gained the throne only to be overthrown by Yury II (1219–38).

Historically, at least, the resumption of power by Yury II, meant nothing except that he was to be the last native ruler of Russia for the next two and a half centuries. The significance was probably not appreciated by him, but during that reign there moved westward from the heartland of Asia another great wave of barbaric, warlike tribes, perhaps the greatest invasion of Russia of all time.

Those invaders, the Tatars of Genghis Khan, first appeared on the steppes of southern Russia in 1224 in great, sweeping raids and then disappeared as mysteriously as they had come. They returned, however, in considerable force in 1228 and threatened to overwhelm the Polovtsy with whom several of the Rurikid princes were allied by marriage. Rather than see the Polovtsy defeated and absorbed by the Tatars, seven princes and their troops joined battle with the invaders on June 16, 1228, on the banks of the river Kalka, near the Sea of Azov. Initially, the Russians were advancing and the Tatars falling back in retreat, but the Polovtsy fled and threw the Russian rear into disorder. Defeat, in which most of the princes and some seventy of their commanders perished, came for the Russians after three days of battle. The victors, who later were to teach the Russians unity and the techniques of administration and tax collection, gave them a lesson in cruelty on the field of battle. The Tatars built a wooden floor above their prisoners, then crushed them to death by feasting and dancing atop them. Those festivities completed, the invaders once more disappeared into the east from which they had come.

The only educated Russians of the time, the churchmen, understood the menace posed by the Tatars and implored the princes to stop their feuding and rally for defense, but all their pleas were disregarded. It is doubtful, however, that the Russians could have withstood the invaders, even if they had united. The princes just did not have the military manpower or know-how. True, King Vaclav I of Bohemia did stop the Tatars in Czechoslovakia in 1241, but that was only after the invaders had overrun Russia, Poland, and Hungary and were greatly overextended.

In the division of Tatary after Genghis Khan's death in 1227, a grand-nephew, Batu Khan, one of the great warriors of all time, was given the vast territory lying between the Ural mountains and the

[26]

Dnieper. That mighty chieftain, with an army of 300,000 Tatars and Turks, annihilated the kingdom of the Bolgars (Bulgars) on the Volga as the first step toward seizing his inheritance. He entered Russian territory in 1237 and by 1241 had subjugated and laid waste almost all of Russia, Poland, and Hungary before withdrawing to a mobile field headquarters on the lower Volga to count his spoils.

Seemingly, nothing could stop Batu Khan except unfavorable terrain. Approaching the first Russian inhabited area, the small town of Ryazan, he ordered the delivery of a tenth of the population and its property. Ryazan resisted courageously, but was completely obliterated, its people put to the sword or enslaved. Next, Batu Khan headed directly for the seat of Russian power, Vladimir. It, too, resisted bravely, only to fall and have its cathedral and most of the reigning family within it burned to the ground. As the Tatars approached Vladimir, Yury II fled north in the hope of rallying new forces. Devastating everything in his route, Batu Khan pursued Yury to marshland north of the Volga and, on March 10, 1238, slaughtered the Russians almost to a man. The Tatars bypassed Novgorod that time because spring thaws made the roads impossible and turned south to wipe out the Polovtsy for good and all. After that, they eliminated the cities of Chernigov and Pereyaslavl. In 1239, Batu Khan returned to the Vladimir-Suzdal area and burned everything to the ground while the surviving populace fled to the woods to hide. Kiev's turn came in 1240. Travelers visiting Russia a half dozen years later reported that only two hundred of Kiev's houses remained, and that around one Russian city after another they found great piles of skulls and bones.

After the death of Yury II in battle, his brother, Yaroslav II (1238–46), assumed control of Vladimir, concentrating mainly on rallying the demoralized inhabitants of the principality. Batu Khan extended recognition to Yaroslav as grand prince, but ordered him to go to the court of the Grand Khan in Mongolia's Karakorum, where the Russian ruler was poisoned in 1246. Why Yaroslav was killed remains a mystery, particularly since he was not averse to the main task assigned him by the Tatars, collecting tribute from Russian domains.

Some relief from the gloom, despair, and defeat which had gripped the Russians with the Tatar invasion was furnished with the rise of a legendary figure in Russian history, Alexander, son of Yaroslav and Prince of Novgorod. In 1236, on the very eve of Tatar arrival at the

[27]

gates of Russia, the Pope had thought it expedient to launch a crusade against Russian Orthodoxy and had induced Sweden's Jarl Birger to captain the invading forces. With small, but effective, units Alexander surprised Birger on the river Neva, sank several of his ships, and defeated him decisively. Despite that victory, Novgorod's merchants, always engaged in disputes with their ruling princes, deposed Alexander, henceforward known as Alexander Nevsky. They reinstalled him with dispatch, however, a few years later when German (Teutonic) knights laid siege to Novgorod's subject city of Pskov, occupied Novgorod territory, and constructed fortifications blocking the merchant city's trade. Alexander destroyed the fort, relieved Pskov, and then invaded the German knights' territory to defeat them thoroughly on ice-bound Chudskoe Ozero (Lake Peipus) in 1242. Several years after that, Alexander similarly routed Lithuanian invaders attacking Torzhok, another subject town of Pskov.

In the year of his victory over the Germans, Alexander was summoned to the court of Batu Khan at Sarai on the lower Volga to make obeisance, as were all other Russian princes in their respective turns. His bearing was exceedingly noble and he was greatly admired by the Tatars. As a result he was given the unwelcome duty of being Tatar chief tax collector in Russia by being named by them as Grand Prince of Vladimir. In this fashion, for decade after decade, the grand princes of Russia became collaborators of the invaders, most of them unwillingly, but a few, unfortunately, most greedily.

Novgorod, which almost alone among Russian cities had escaped being overrun and devastated by Batu Khan's forces, was first visited by the Tatars in 1247, when Sarai sent tax collectors to gather tribute amassed under Alexander's direction. Unschooled in warfare, and therefore unacquainted with the might of the Tatars, the merchants threatened the lives of the tax collectors until Alexander convinced them that resistance was out of the question. Similar troubles besieged Alexander in the last year of his reign when a number of other towns not only refused to give tribute but drove out Sarai's tax collectors. Large Tatar forces were en route to correct that situation when Alexander made his fourth and last trip to the khan's capital to intercede successfully for his people. He died in 1263 on the return journey.

With the death of Alexander Nevsky, Russia, as an effective power and a state, for all practical purposes ceased to exist for the next two centuries, with the sole exception of Novgorod. Only that great and flourishing merchant city and the Orthodox Church kept Russia alive as a national entity during that long and dismal purgatory. In the central and eastern parts of the country, the general picture was one of princes succeeding princes as docile and obedient vassals of the all-powerful Tatars. In the west and south, territories and towns were nibbled away by fellow Slavs, the Poles, and by Lithuanians, Germans, and Swedes. Kiev, herself, fell under Polish dominion in 1386 and did not return to Russian rule until three hundred years later.

So terrible and overwhelming had been the devastation of the Tatar invasions that Russia's princes for a while forgot their traditional feuding. That allowed the succession to pass relatively peacefully to Alexander's brothers, Yaroslav III (1263–72) and Vasily of Kostroma (1272–76), Kostroma being a Volga settlement, then a secondary city, and then on to Alexander's sons, Dimitry I (1276–94) and Andrey III (1294–1304).

During that period of comparative calm, there were two developments which were to have significant effect on Russia and her history, although that might not have seemed so at the time. The first was the decline of Vladimir as the seat of power. To keep its vassals weak, the Tatars encouraged disputes between the Russian princes. They particularly abetted the rivalry of Vladimir's sister city, Tver. In fact, Yaroslav III had been Prince of Tver. The second and more important change was the emergence of Moscow as an important city, and that, too, had been the work of the Tatars. At first, this town on the Moskva, but near the greater rivers, had been a paltry place, left to younger sons; it had been the inheritance of Mikhail Khorobrit and Daniel, respectively, the youngest sons of Yaroslav II and Alexander Nevsky. But, as inhabitants of the more exposed cities to the east and south, and especially those along the upper Volga, had fled to it from Tatar attacks, it had grown by leaps and bounds. Moscow, of course, was not secure from Tatar raids, but it was more remote and somewhat more difficult for the Tatars to reach than most other cities.

3. EARLY MUSCOVY

As Moscow grew and Vladimir declined, inter-city rivalry between Tver and Moscow correspondingly increased. That competition reached a murderous peak during the reign of Grand Prince Mikhail of Tver (1304–19), the only son of Yaroslav III. Tver had been restless under Tatar rule and in 1319 Mikhail was summoned to Sarai. There he was cold-bloodedly murdered by his cousin, Yury, the son of Daniel of Moscow. Even the Tatars were appalled by the slaying, but nevertheless installed the killer as Grand Prince Yury III (1319–26). A few years later, Mikhail was revenged by a son, Dimitry (known as Big-Eyes), who killed Yury. Dimitry was murdered next, probably by an ally of Yury.

After that double slaying, the Tatars gave the satrapy of Russia to Dimitry's brother, Alexander, Prince of Tver, making him grand prince (1326–28).

The reign of Alexander II was short because the people of Tver butchered Chol-Khan, a cousin of the ruling Khan Uzbek, and his suite when the Tatars visited the city to collect tribute in 1327. Hearing of the fate of Chol-Khan and his followers, one of the least admirable figures in Russian history, Ivan of Moscow, the brother and successor of Yury, hurried to Sarai. He probably literally crawled before Khan Uzbek, who gave him a force of 50,000 Tatars with which he went to Tver and laid it waste. For his collaboration, Uzbek made the Moscow prince Grand Prince Ivan I (1328–40). That was the far from worthy way in which Moscow first became capital of Russia.

In addition to punishing Tver and collecting tribute from it for the Tatars, Ivan I also took upon himself the responsibility of collecting the annual taxes from the other Russian cities for Uzbek. For that he became known to his fellows as Ivan Kalita (Moneybag), since a good amount of the revenues stuck to his own fingers; and for that the Tatars made him and his successors grand princes in perpetuity.

When Ivan I arrived at the gates of Tver with troops of the Golden Horde (as the Sarai Tatars had then become known), the unfortunate Alexander fled to Pskov, and the Tatars gave men to his brother, Constantine, to search him out. While Pskov's mother city, Novgorod, and most of the princes of Russia tried to persuade Alexander to give himself up to Uzbek and so spare them possible vengeance, Ivan I stepped into the breach by inveigling the Metropolitan to excommunicate both Alexander and Pskov. Far from afraid of that, Pskov, long the most decent of Russian cities, offered to battle for Alexander, but he decided to flee farther west, to Lithuania, until the Tver uprising was forgotten.

Later, tragic Alexander, yet to be immortalized in Russian opera, returned to Pskov, to govern there in peace for ten years. In 1336, overcome by nostalgia for Tver, he sent a son to Sarai to intercede for him successfully. Alexander himself then journeyed to Uzbek, who returned Tver to his rule. Thereupon, Ivan I sped again to Sarai and persuaded the khan to change his mind; Alexander was recalled to Uzbek's headquarters and killed.

Despite his venality, Ivan Kalita did some good for Russia by establishing that the succession should pass to the eldest son of the rulers and not to brothers, a system which had caused much of the feuding which brought him to power. That principle was sustained for two generations after his death, giving Russia, despite Tatar overrule, a period of comparative peace during the reigns of Simeon (1340–53) and Ivan II (1353–59).

Dispute of succession was renewed, however, after the death of Ivan II. Contributing to that was the fact that the current generation of Russian nobles had no firsthand knowledge of Tatar power and was willing to challenge the Golden Horde. The primary factor, though, was the beginning of the disintegration of Tatary. Karakorum's ties with Sarai had become almost nonexistent; and the Golden Horde itself had become factionalized with khan succeeding khan by assassination. At Ivan's death, the Horde was in the midst of a three-way struggle for power, between two khans, Abdul and Murad, and the vizier, Mamai.

When Ivan died, his rightful heir, Dimitry, was only eleven years old. Abdul tried to take advantage of the heir's youth by installing another Dimitry, the Prince of Suzdal (1359–63), as grand prince.

But that was more a conflict between Tatars than a Russian feud for power. Ivan's Dimitry, who was supported by Murad, gained his inheritance with the support of the boyars (nobles) at the age of fifteen. Nor did Dimitry of Suzdal then dispute the accession of Grand Prince Dimitry of Moscow (1363–84).

The rightful Dimitry was a notable warrior prince and astute politician, who stood off the Lithuanians and repeatedly battled the Tatars and nevertheless managed to expand the dominion of Moscow almost tenfold during his reign. By his greatest battle, that against Mamai in 1378 in the fields of Kulikovo on the Don river, he gained the name of Dimitry Donskoy (of the Don) and thus joined the list of Russian heroes. The victory on the Don, although glorious, was not decisive. It was, however, the beginning of the end, although the

Tatar yoke was not finally lifted until a century later. In fact, during the reign of Vasily I (1384–1425), the son of Dimitry Donskoy, a much greater Tatar menace than the squabbling khans of Sarai, threatened Muscovy. Sweeping all before him, the great Mongol conqueror, Tamerlane, marched almost to the gates of Moscow in 1390, and then, much as Genghis Khan had done more than a century and a half earlier, suddenly withdrew south to India.

The death of Vasily I precipitated decades of bitter civil war in Muscovy before the rightful successor, Vasily II (1425–62), known as Temny (the Blinded), was able to establish himself. The trouble started over the same old bone of contention, the order of succession since, unlike his predecessors, who had outlived their younger brothers, Vasily I was survived by a brother, Prince Yury. On the death of Vasily I, a boyar whose daughter Vasily II had promised to marry had gone to the Horde and secured Vasily's nomination as grand prince. After that, not only did Vasily renege on the marriage arrangement, but his Lithuanian mother, who had provided him with a bride of higher rank, grossly insulted two sons of Prince Yury, Vasily Kosoy (Cross-Eye) and Dimitry Shemyaka, at the wedding festivities. Angered, Prince Yury traveled to Sarai in 1431 and was given the throne of his nephew in accordance with the old order of succession from brother to brother. The majority of the boyars, however, supported Vasily II, so Yury withdrew his claim. Nevertheless, Vasily Cross-Eye and Shemyaka, who had no legitimate rights, continued their struggle even after their father's death with Vasily Cross-Eye seizing the throne. At that point, Shemyaka abandoned his brother and helped reinstall Vasily II, who later put Vasily Cross-Eye out of the running for good by capturing and blinding him. Meanwhile, there had also been severe dissension in Sarai which resulted in the Horde's expelling Ulu Mehmet who then set up a separate Tatar state at Kazan in 1437. While leading troops against the Tatars in 1443, Vasily II was captured by Ulu Mehmet, who held the Russian prince for two years until payment of a large ransom. Returning to Moscow in 1445, Vasily was caught and blinded by Shemyaka and his men while giving thanks in church for delivery from the Tatars. Once again the boyars rallied to Vasily and drove out Shemyaka, who fled to Polish territory where he was poisoned by an underling of Vasily's.

Even though sightless, Vasily proved a strong ruler once the civil war had ended. He increased Moscow's territory on all borders, but principally to the south and west, to rule a state of some fifteen thousand square miles. Somewhat more importantly for the future of Russia, he had also persuaded the church to support the order of succession from father to son. And in the last years of his reign he made sure no civil war would follow his death by having his son, Ivan III, crowned as co-ruler.

The reign of Ivan III (1462–1505), called the Great by some historians, marked the beginning of the grandeur of Russia. Some of the distinction brought then to this land, which had long been a collection of weak and feuding city-states, can be attributed to the taking of Constantinople by the Turks in 1453. In 1472, Ivan married Sophia (born Zoë), the niece of the last emperor of Byzantium. With that marriage the aphorism was promulgated that with the fall of Constantinople Moscow had become the third Rome and that there would be no fourth Rome. Simultaneously, the Moscow Grand Prince assumed the title of Tsar (Caesar) to increase his prestige. Ivan matched his title and words with deeds. He brought Novgorod and its vast domains to the north and east under the control of Moscow; he pushed across the northern Urals into Siberia; he ended the long struggle with Tver by absorbing it, the same process he applied to lesser principalities in the Moscow area; he won victories over both Poland and Lithuania, gaining former Russian territory from each. Most importantly, in 1480 he refused tribute to Sarai, thus ending Russia's long vassaldom to Tatary and then went on to subjugate Kazan, defeat the Golden Horde and make the Crimean Tatars his ally. True, Tatary had been disintegrating for years, but it was Ivan III who gave it the death blow. On the less favorable side of the register, in his take-over of Novgorod, he introduced the custom, still common in Russia, of transporting political enemies, by sending fifty prominent Novgorod merchant families to Vladimir and moving 7,000 Novgorod petty nobles to the Moscow environs, transferring a similar number of Muscovite gentry to Novgorod.

Before his death, on the wish of Tsarina Sophia, Ivan III had their son, Vasily III (1505–33), crowned as his successor. More autocratic than his father, Vasily III was an empire-builder, too. He absorbed the remainder of Ryazan, the last remaining autonomous Russian principality, and he recovered the frontier city of Smolensk. At his death, his dominion stretched from Chernigov in the south, to the Gulf of Finland, to the White Sea and to the Urals.

When Vasily III died, his heir, Ivan IV (1533–84), later to become memorable as Ivan the Terrible, was only three years old. The infant's mother, Helen Glinsky, a Lithuanian princess of Russian origin, acted as regent. A poor ruler, Helen imprisoned her brothers-in-law, took as advisers her uncle, Mikhail Glinsky, and her lover, Prince Obolensky, and ended up sending her uncle to prison where he died. Additionally, she waged unsuccessful war with Lithuania while the Crimean Tatars, having taken control of Kazan, raided vast areas of Russia and seemed on the very verge of reestablishing Tatary.

4. IVAN THE TERRIBLE

In 1538, Helen suddenly died, probably of poison, and two powerful boyar families, the Shuiskys and the Belskys, battled for the regency, with power changing hands three times and a metropolitan being killed before the Shuiskys finally won out. Ivan IV, eight years old at the time that struggle commenced, was its chief victim. The boy was neglected and scorned by the regent, Andrey Shuisky, and the rest of the boyars. Left to himself, Ivan, withdrawn and introspective, read much, especially about the history of great rulers. His only diversion was cruelty to animals, tossing small animals to their deaths from Kremlin roofs. By the time he was sixteen, he asserted himself most dramatically. He had Shuisky seized by the kennel-keepers and torn apart by the dogs; demanded to be crowned tsar; and took as his bride Anastasia Romanov, attractive member of a lesser boyar family. From that moment on, the reign of Ivan the Terrible can be divided into two distinct parts, the good, and, dating from 1564, when he apparently went crazy, the bad.

The early and good period of the reign of Ivan IV was marked with signal successes, both internal and external. In 1547, when he had been tsar for barely a year, after Moscow had been ravaged by terrible fires, a mob, believing the catastrophe the work of witches and egged on by the boyars, killed the ruler's uncle, Yury, and were looking for Ivan himself. When the demonstrators came for him, Ivan dispersed them with his troops and later executed the boyars he believed responsible. His resentment and fear of the boyars, caused both by the Moscow riot and the way in which they had treated him during the regency, resulted in his establishment of councils of middle- and lower-class people.

The following decade was the era of Ivan's great military and political victories which consolidated and expanded Russia's dominion. In 1552, at the head of more than 100,000 men, he captured Kazan, held off the Crimean Tatars and defeated the forces of Sarai, thus completing the work of Ivan III. As the result of that battle, in 1556 he easily annexed Sarai's vast territory of Astrakhan and in the same year Cossacks of South Russia deserted the Polish-Lithuanian alliance and joined Muscovy.

After the Kazan victory, however, Ivan was beset with both physical and political troubles. In 1553, when very ill, he barely managed to get the boyars to swear allegiance to his infant son Dimitry. The opposition was led by his cousin, Prince Vladimir of Staritsa, who not only had his own aspirations to the throne, but also believed that yet another minor ruler would bring more internecine struggle for power. Five years later, in 1558, Ivan had more serious differences of policy, not only with the boyars, led by Prince Kurbsky, but also with the church. Both groups wanted him to round out his Kazan and Astrakhan successes with a crusade against the heathen Crimean Tatars rather than do inconclusive battle with the Poles and Swedes to the west. Ivan, however, appreciated that Russia lacked strength and resources for such an undertaking, so overrode his council and instead fought in the west. In his battles there, Ivan did score some initial advances, taking the old Russian city of Polotsk in 1563, and adding to Russian territory along the Gulf of Finland. In the next decade, though, he lost not only Polotsk, but also more than he had gained earlier in the western frontier campaigns.

Meanwhile, Ivan had also suffered a pair of bitter personal losses. His adored wife, Anastasia, had died—Ivan believed by poisoning—and their son, Dimitry, had not survived infancy. Ivan had always been cruel, as a youth throwing pets off roofs and tossing Shuisky to the dogs, and as a man delighting in the horrible Russian "sport" of setting bears on unarmed muzhiks. But after the deaths of his wife and son his psychosis took a decided turn for the worse.

The exact date when insanity gripped Ivan is impossible to determine, but the bad part of his reign began in December 1564 when he abandoned the Kremlin and his rule and literally disappeared. Early in 1565, he wrote from a monastery, blaming all troubles on the boyars and the church and claiming he was the friend and the protector of the people. In tears, the ignorant masses begged him to come back and "rule however he pleased" and that was just what Ivan did.

On his return, in woeful physical condition, the mad tsar embarked on a campaign of wholesale murder of his enemies, real or imagined. First he executed some boyars. Then he organized a private police force, the Oprichnina, gave it outright control of half his realm, primarily the north and center where the boyars still exercised some autonomy, and turned over rule of the remaining half of the tsardom to a Tatar prince who had become a Christian. Sworn to hold the commands of Ivan above those of God and other men, the Oprichniks so murdered uncounted thousands that a foreigner visiting Russia at the time said, "If Satan himself attempted to think of a plan for destroying mankind, he could have invented nothing more devilish." During the three years that the scourge was at its height, Ivan kept to his monastery, which had become Oprichnina headquarters, alternating between playing the pious monk and praying for his victims or joining his henchmen in feasting, drinking, and torturing prisoners.

Probably sated with the butchery, Ivan relaxed the terror for a year before having his old foe, Prince Vladimir of Staritsa, poisoned in 1569. It was in 1570, however, that he committed his most horrific deeds. In January of that year, at the head of 15,000 troops, including Oprichniks, he arrived at Novgorod to punish that great city because he suspected it of negotiating with Poland. Moscow's Metropolitan Philip had tried to intercede for Novgorod before Ivan left the capital and was strangled for his efforts. Once within the gates of the doomed city, Ivan had two archbishops killed and then idled and feasted there for five weeks enjoying the daily slaughtering of the populace of all classes and ages and of both sexes. After that "victory," Ivan returned to Moscow to stage public torture and execution of some one hundred men accused of treason. And later in that dark year of 1570, he turned on the Oprichnina itself and killed off several of its most notorious leaders.

The following year, 1571, was also a grim one for Muscovy. With the nation demoralized under the thralldom of its maniac leader, 120,000 Crimean Tatars swept north with ease to capture and burn Moscow, kill about 800,000 Russians in that campaign and carry off into captivity some 120,000 other subjects of Ivan. Just where the mad tsar was at that time has not been recorded, but there is no account of his having defended his capital or having fought the in-

[36]

vader. In 1582, a deadly return blow was delivered to Tatary. With no thanks to Ivan, but to the Cossack Yermak who invaded and seized large Tatar-held portions of western Siberia. Just before that, in 1581, Ivan murdered his own; in a frenzied fit he dealt a mortal blow with a metal-tipped stick to his eldest and favorite son, also named Ivan. Three years later death rid Russia of Ivan the Terrible himself, according to some accounts as the result of a stroke suffered while playing chess to win a sixth wife.

5. THE TIME OF TROUBLES

Russia was to pay dearly for the reign of Ivan IV. That image of misrule was to infect the whole nation, from principal boyars down to the lowliest slaves, and lead to virtual anarchy, or the "time of troubles" as that era of turmoil has been politely called by most historians.

Ivan the Terrible was succeeded by Feodor I (1584–98), the only surviving son from the union with Anastasia Romanov. Although Feodor was twenty-seven years old when his father died, a regency had to govern the land throughout his reign because the young man was imbecilic, a sad fate for the ruler who was to be the last of the House of Rurik. The first regent was his uncle, Nikita Romanov, who became ill and died a few months after taking office. Nikita's successor as regent was Boris Godunov, a prince partly Tatar in origin (as were the Romanovs as well), and, for his times, a good man, who was greatly maligned in the history written under the aegis of the subsequent Romanov dynasty. Feodor's short reign was undistinguished, except for the consecration of Moscow's Metropolitan Iov (Job) as patriarch, a development with which Feodor had nothing at all to do. That elevation of the church office was to give Orthodoxy invaluable authority in guiding the nation in the interregnum to come.

Long a henchman of Ivan IV, Godunov had used alliances with women to increase his influence: he married his daughter, Irina, to Feodor, and he himself married Maria Skuratov, daughter of the infamous Oprichnik chief. Needless to say, his regency was deeply resented by other princely families, especially the Shuiskys, Belskys, Mstislavskys, and Golitsyns, who not only gloried in the Rurik blood in their veins, but also wanted power for themselves. Godunov was attacked indirectly over the inability of Feodor to produce a male heir, but the greatest threat to his regency came in 1591 with the death of Tsarevich Dimitry, a legitimate claimant to the throne. Only nine years old at the time of his death, Prince Dimitry was the issue of Ivan the Terrible's marriage to his fifth and last wife, Maria Nagoi, a union the church had condemned. Dimitry was an epileptic. He had died accidentally from falling on a knife while in a fit, but Godunov was immediately and almost ever after accused of murdering him.

On Feodor's death, Boris Godunov first pretended he wanted the crown to go to Tsarina Irina and then stage-managed army and mob demands that he himself be acclaimed tsar (1598–1605). Next, to assure his power, he exiled rather than killed the rival boyars, a decidedly new departure. In 1601, he got rid of the threat from the Romanovs by making Nikita's brilliant son, Feodor, become the monk Philaret, and forcing Feodor's wife to enter a convent as the nun Martha. Feodor's only surviving son, Mikhail Romanov, was overlooked as being too young and unimportant.

Until then, Boris' reign had gone smoothly, but in 1601 and through 1604 Russia was ravaged by a frightful famine. Boris tried to meet the emergency by opening food depots, granting tax relief and cracking down on speculators. The end result, however, was that the peasants abandoned the farms for the free food of the cities, reserves were exhausted, the economy in ruin, and chaos rampant throughout the land. Everywhere rampaged great bands of looters and robbers, such as that of Khlopko Kosolap ("Slave Crooked-Paw") which killed one of Boris' generals in pitched battle before finally being eliminated.

In 1603, a much greater danger to Boris and Russia than famine and chaos emerged. Rumor that Tsarevich Dimitry was alive swept the nation, a rumor believed by princes and peasants alike. Mainly because of his extremely confident manner, as if to the purple born, there is a remote possibility that that pretender was really the son of Ivan IV. Generally, however, he is believed to have been the son of a minor Russian noble. He fled to Poland, safely out of reach of Boris' agents, where he made his claim to be Dimitry. The Poles, from King Sigismund on down, welcomed his pretension, since it not only gave them a hold on Muscovy, but also could be a device to reunite the Eastern and Western churches. For those two ends, Dimitry was affianced to Marina Mniszech—beautiful and ambitious daughter of a Polish nobleman—and converted to the Roman faith. The groundwork thus prepared, Dimitry entered Russia in October, 1604, at the head of a group of young Polish adventurers and Russian exiles.

Welcomed almost everywhere, Dimitry was soon joined by Cossacks and a host of malcontents. The leading boyars, including the unprincipled Prince Vasily Shuisky, rallied to Boris' support. By January 1605, despite valiant resistance, Dimitry's forces were shattered and the pretender had to flee south and take haven with the Cossacks.

A few months later, however, the unexpected intervened with the sudden death of Boris in April 1605. For some six weeks afterward, allegiance was sworn to Boris' son, Feodor II, a tragic figure then sixteen years old, whose good looks and early character augured well for Russia. Vasily Shuisky, the same man who had investigated Tsarevich Dimitry's death for Boris, ended Feodor's brief reign in June, 1605, by telling the mob that the pretender was legitimate. Feodor and his family were chased from the Kremlin to the Godunov home, which was later invaded by boyars and troops who strangled Boris Godunov's wife and clubbed his son to death. Prince Vasily Golitsyn forced Feodor to beg to be killed by grabbing the young tsar by the testicles while he was struggling with a trio of soldiers. At the same time that the Godunovs were eliminated, the Patriarch Job was deposed.

Within days, Dimitry (1605–06), called "the False," was summoned to Moscow, crowned, and married to Marina Mniszech. Pretender or not, Dimitry proved a capable and popular monarch. And to improve his claim, he brought Maria Nagoi from a convent and she recognized the young man as her long-lost son.

Worried by Dimitry's improving position, Vasily Shuisky told soldiers in the Moscow environs that they must save the tsar from the Poles who planned to kill him. Before dawn, in mid-May of 1606, Shuisky, other boyars, and the troops charged into the Kremlin. His guards surprised and overwhelmed, Dimitry was caught, seriously injured by a jump from his window into a courtyard. He asked his captors that he again be confronted by his mother, but that ubiquitous regicide Prince Golitsyn declared that Maria Nagoi had disowned Dimitry. Thereupon, Dimitry the False was summarily hacked to death. His naked, butchered body was suspended upside down outside the Kremlin walls by a cord attached to his testicles. Then, after Dimitry's remains had been thoroughly desecrated by passersby they were burned and the ashes shot from a cannon aimed toward Poland.

In short order, Prince Shuisky, claiming to be a descendant of Rurik, which he was, as were many other boyars as well, and a scion of Alexander Nevsky, which he was not, had himself crowned Tsar Vasily IV (1606–10). But the mob, the minor gentry, the peasants, even some of the less venal boyars could not stomach Vasily. To those, false or not, the slain Dimitry had been an idol and in their belief a true tsar, not an elevated boyar.

As a result, the country descended into abject chaos and new pretenders arose. Vasily had barely enthroned himself when Ivan Bolotnikov, a onetime Tatar prisoner and an ex-slave, organized wholesale class war, getting peasants to seize the property of the landowners and slaves to kill their masters and expropriate their womenfolk; and almost everywhere else in Russia, in the east and the deep south, and especially in the southwest, Cossacks, peasants, and slaves were in open rebellion against the boyars.

Bolotnikov's ally was a man who said he was Peter, son of Feodor I, whose only child was a daughter who died in infancy. Together, Bolotnikov and Peter ravaged the land to the gates of Moscow, where they were driven off by forces led by an able nephew of Vasily, Prince Skopin-Shuisky. Driven off, the rebels barricaded themselves in Tula, which was starved into surrender in 1608 by Vasily himself at the head of 100,000 men. The pretender Peter was caught and hanged and Bolotnikov was drowned.

Before the fall of Tula, the rebels had realized that the false Peter had little drawing power and had sent a message to the Poles asking for another Dimitry. Supported by Cossacks and another batch of Polish adventurers, a second false Dimitry emerged from Poland in the spring of 1608, defeated Vasily's forces on the Volkhov, and marched on the Russian capital to encamp at Tushino in Moscow's northwest environs. Known henceforth as the Tushinsky Vor ("Thief" or "Brigand"), the pretender was soon joined, not only by Tsarina Marina, who acknowledged him as none other than the first false Dimitry and later bore him a son, but also by Maria Nagoi, who likewise said he was the true Dimitry. Additionally, in capturing Rostov, the pretender's forces took Philaret (Feodor) Romanov and installed him as patriarch at Tushino.

The second Dimitry's star set in 1609, when King Sigismund of

Poland decided to capitalize on the Russian upheaval and march on Smolensk. At Tushino, disputes flared between Dimitry and his Polish allies and, dressed as a peasant, he fled by night south to Kaluga, where, a year after Marina had presented him with a son, he was murdered by his erstwhile supporters. Some of his adherents, however, swore allegiance to his son as "tsarevich."

After Dimitry fled Tushino, the siege of Moscow was lifted as his Polish units withdrew to the northwest. Vasily used that relief to hire 5,000 mercenaries from the Swedes. Led by Prince Skopin-Shuisky, the Swedes approached the Russian capital from the north, defeating the pretender's Poles en route and freeing Philaret Romanov from their control, to march into Moscow in March, 1610. Vasily feted his popular nephew at a banquet, where the younger Shuisky fell ill. He died two months later, probably of poison. With Vasily's military leader thus disposed of, the pretender's troops again threatened Moscow, so the capital citizenry of all free classes deposed Vasily in July, 1610, and forced him to become a monk.

With Muscovy without a ruler, and fearing a foreigner less than the mob and irregulars of the pretender, the boyars offered the throne to Wladyslaw, the son of Sigismund, and on the night of September 20, 1610, admitted Polish troops to Moscow. At first, the Polish occupiers comported themselves circumspectly and relieved the capital by driving off the forces of the pretender. By then, some of the boyars had become so abject that they supported Sigismund, who had decided that he and not his son should have Muscovy's throne. However, when the threat from the pretender was removed with his murder in December, 1610, Russian resistance to the occupiers, led by the church, gradually mounted.

Soon, Russian spirit rallied to such an extent that the Poles prohibited all Moscow citizens from bearing arms. In March, 1611, after a dispute with draymen, the Poles thinking the crowd looked ugly, even though unarmed, charged it with their German confederates. Before the fray was over 7,000 Muscovites had been cut down. Open rebellion broke out in the capital and in retaliation the Poles burned most of the city to the ground before retiring to the Kremlin and the inner town. By the end of that month, some 100,000 Russians were drawn up outside the capital, encircling it.

Torn by internal dissension and beset by troubles elsewhere in the land, that great host eventually dispersed without ever accomplish-

[41]

ing anything, except to hold the Polish garrison captive. Later that year, the Swedes took Novgorod and the Poles crushed the last resistance at Smolensk. In the Moscow area, the Poles in the Kremlin tricked the Cossacks in the Russian siege forces to defect, with the result that the Cossacks swore allegiance to yet another pretender who appeared in Pskov.

Despite that disarray and troubles, the church stood firm, principally in the person of Patriarch Hermogen, a true and heroic patriot, later starved to death by the Poles. In October 1611, an appeal from Hermogen calling on the Russian people to rise against the invaders reached Nizhny Novgorod (now Gorky). There, Kuzma Minin, a wholesale meat handler who was nearing bankruptcy because of the chaotic conditions plaguing Russia, responded by giving all his assets to the national cause and inspiring other men of property to do likewise. Soon, another liberating host was in formation led by Prince Dimitry Pozharsky, a rural boyar who had been wounded in earlier battle against the Poles. After the Swedes had been persuaded to remain neutral, that national militia, gathering forces along the way, arrived outside Moscow in August 1612, just in time to drive off a Polish column making another attempt to relieve the Kremlin garrison. Minin distinguished himself by leading an attack in that engagement. On October 22, Cossack units took the inner city by storm; and on November 22, the Poles in the Kremlin surrendered, having been reduced by a year and a half of siege to eating the bodies of their dead. And with that surrender, the captive boyars, among them the youth Mikhail Romanov, were freed.

6. EARLY ROMANOVS

Almost immediately, the young Romanov and his mother, the nun Martha, left for the safety of a monastery near Kostroma, some two hundred miles northeast of Moscow. Meanwhile, the liberators, after executing their Polish captives, summoned a Zemsky Sobor, composed of representatives of all classes except the serf slaves, to select a new tsar. There were several candidates, both national and foreign, with the Cossacks proposing the son of the second false Dimitry. Suddenly, the Cossacks changed their minds and seconded the nomination of one of the lesser nobles, Mikhail Romanov. Since that young man was the grand nephew of Ivan IV, thereby by marriage at least continuing the Rurikids, as well as the nephew and son of the popular

[42]

Nikita and Philaret Romanov, he had no difficulty in being unanimously elected by the assembly on February 21, 1613.

While Mikhail was awaiting word of that in Kostroma, Polish irregulars attempting to seize him captured a peasant, Ivan Susanin, who knew the young man's hiding place. According to legend, Susanin died under torture without telling where the young Romanov was. The nineteenth-century Russian composer, Mikhail Ivanovich Glinka, memorialized that event in his chief work, the opera *A Life for the Tsar*, so entitled by none other than Tsar Nicholas I, who wished his subjects would be as faithful as Susanin. The Communists have retitled the work *Ivan Susanin* and have rewritten the script so that the peasant gives his life not for the first Romanov but to shield Minin and Pozharsky. Safely arrived in Moscow, legend or no legend, Mikhail was crowned July 11, 1613, thus ending the time of troubles and starting a dynasty that was to collapse 300 years later in even greater troubles.

Mikhail (1613–45) was a colorless figurehead, frail in physique and, although not weak-minded, was certainly not much of an intellect. The real tsar was his father, Philaret (Feodor), who returned from Polish captivity in 1619 and ran Russia until he died in 1633. Mikhail made his father patriarch and also bestowed on him his own title, that of *gosudar* (sovereign). Before and after Philaret, boyar favorites managed affairs. It was in Mikhail's reign that the landowners, short of labor because of the time of troubles, began reducing the peasants to the status of chattels, from which they were not to emerge until 250 years later. Nor did the first Romanov distinguish himself militarily or diplomatically; he was at ineffective war with the Swedes until 1617; the troubles with the Cossacks in the south and southeast continued; Poles, helped by Cossacks, almost took Moscow again in 1618 (Poles captured in that attack were buried up to their necks and beheaded with scythes); a 50,000-man Russian army surrendered in 1632 in a vain attempt to retake Smolensk from the Poles; a relative handful of Cossacks took the Turkish Black Sea fortress of Azov in 1637, but Mikhail made them return it to the Turks for fear a campaign against Istanbul might prove too costly and bloody. Under Mikhail, however, there was a welcome letup in Russians being killed by Russians; the only slayings in that category were a few burned by Philaret as heretics. Mikhail died in tears after a fit.

Mikhail's heir, Alexis (1645–76) is known as "the Good Tsar" by

Slavophiles. The lucky autocrat might be a better title. His reign was marked by riots, serious religious dissent and major uprisings, but he managed to survive all unscathed and even increase Russian territory. As the result of a high salt tax and speculations of bureaucrats, waves of rioting broke out in Moscow in 1648 and extended to Novgorod and Pskov before being brought to a halt in 1650. During those upheavals, Alexis had to protect himself with mercenaries, uncounted numbers of Russians and foreigners were killed or tortured, and much Russian and foreign property was destroyed. In 1662, more rioting erupted after Alexis enriched his treasury by debasing the coinage; Alexis' life was saved then only by ruthless action of his guards in which some 7,000 rioters were killed and others were tortured, executed, or sent to Siberia.

The religious troubles started in 1652, when Alexis named the arrogant, peasant zealot Nikon patriarch. Anxious to be the leading patriarch of Orthodoxy, Nikon cleansed the liturgy and prayerbooks of Russianisms that had corrupted the original Byzantine rite. In the process, Nikon also ruled that Russia's faithful must cease crossing themselves with two fingers and spelling the name of the Saviour with a single iota and return to the original system of the three-fingered benediction and the use of the double iota in Jesus' name. Those two changes, particularly, caused a tremendous schism and the formation of the "Old Believers" (Raskolniki) who were to hound every succeeding Romanov as Antichrist and who survive until this day. Everywhere throughout the land Raskolniki were suppressed, many of them killing themselves rather than yield. In 1668, monks of the great Solovetsk monastery on the White Sea declared themselves and their garrison as Raskolniki and denied allegiance to Alexis. He sent troops against them and in 1676, the year of his death, the monastery was taken by storm and the leaders of the rebellion hanged.

Almost concurrent with the start of the monastery's resistance in the far north was the emergence in 1667, hundreds of miles away in the deep southeast, of the notorious bandit, pirate and rabble-rouser Stepan (Stenka) Razin. A Cossack of the Don and later a legendary hero to the Communists, Razin attracted hordes of rebellious, fugitive serfs and slaves, preached class warfare and organized a proletarian army and navy. He raided and seized cities and forts from the middle Volga to the Caspian and plundered the Persian Caspian seacoast until defeated at Simbirsk (Ulyanovsk) by an army sent against him by Alexis. Captured in flight by an ataman of the Don Cossacks, Razin was delivered to Moscow where, on June 6, 1671, he had his ribs pulled from his spine with red-hot pliers before being quartered alive. Even after the execution of Razin, disorders, killings of officials and landowners, and seizures of towns continued for several years and about one hundred thousand people lost their lives before order was reestablished.

Alexis' territorial acquisitions started in 1648 when Dnieper Cossacks revolted against their Polish masters and swore allegiance to Muscovy (the basis of Moscow's claim to the Ukraine ever since). In 1654, that precipitated the Thirteen Years' War, chiefly between Russia and Poland, but with Sweden also intervening and the Cossacks frequently switching sides when not busy killing some 200,000 Jews—the greatest anti-Semitic outrage prior to Hitler. Against the advice of his councilor, Afanasy Ordyn-Nashchokin, one of Russia's all-time great statesmen, who had urged the tsar to concentrate on access to the Baltic instead, Alexis persisted in what he regarded as a crusade against the Poles, despite many setbacks and the death of one-third of his subjects, mainly by plague. In 1664, however, Alexis won his gamble, chiefly because Poland disintegrated into anarchy, and at the Peace of Andrusovo he gained the Ukraine, got a two-year hold on Kiev (which Russia kept forever after in violation of the treaty), and regained Smolensk.

In the latter years of his reign, Alexis made a great contribution to Russia's future, albeit unwittingly. His confidant then was Artamon Matveyev, an extremely cultured man for those times in Russia. At Matveyev's house, Alexis, whose first wife had died in 1669, met and soon married Matveyev's ward, Natalia Naryshkin. As result of the union with Natalia, the daughter of a Scots royalist refugee from Cromwell, needed new blood was infused into the dynasty, as evidenced by the son of that marriage, who became Peter the Great.

By his two marriages, Alexis produced sixteen children, thirteen by his first wife, Maria Miloslavsky, and three by Natalia. Most of the sons of those unions, except for Natalia's Peter, either died prematurely or were physically or mentally ill. Several of Alexis' daughters, however, especially Maria's Sophia, were robust in both body and mind, a fact that resulted in yet another palace struggle for power. Additionally, the two marriages also produced feuding between the

Miloslavsky and Naryshkin families and their adherents.

In a deathbed attempt to prevent the troubles that were to come, Alexis named Maria's fourteen-year-old son, Feodor (1676–82), as his successor; his other surviving son by Maria, Ivan, was a half-wit and Natalia's Peter was only four. So sickly with a probable combination of scurvy and dropsy that he could hardly stand, Feodor was actually Feodor III but was titled Feodor II by the Romanovs as part of that family's studied obliteration of the Godunovs. Although frail of body, Feodor III had a good mind and his father had had him well-educated. He established Russia's first higher school, a church institution, but more importantly he Westernized his court and abolished *mestnichestvo*, the system by which the aristocracy ranked according to birth and ordered precedence based on service and merit. Feodor also had a run-in with the Old Believer opponent of his father, the monk Avvakum. That unrelenting cleric declared that Alexis had gone to hell because of his support of the ritual changes; for that, Avvakum was burned alive, going to the stake crossing himself with two fingers. Feodor III is also remembered for the Tsar Pushka (cannon), at the time the world's biggest artillery piece, which still graces the Kremlin grounds. Cast during the reign of Feodor I, the addlepated son of Ivan the Terrible, it was machined under the direction of Feodor III to handle a ball one meter in diameter. It has never been fired.

When Feodor died in April, 1682, his brothers and only potential successors were, almost as usual with the Romanovs, under-age. The simple-minded Ivan was sixteen years old and Peter ten, but the latter looked the age of his half-brother (at maturity, he was an almost unbelievable seven-foot giant). The boyars declined to name a successor so Patriarch Ioakim (Joachim) got a chance crowd in Red Square to acclaim Peter and therewith crowned the ten-year-old as tsar. Natalia assumed the regency, appointed her guardian Matveyev councilor, and the Naryshkin family, displaced by the Miloslavskys during Feodor's tenure, moved back into the Kremlin, but not for long.

Sophia, Peter's half-sister, as forceful and domineering as Peter himself was later to be, was not about to be sent to a convent, a favorite disposition of excess royal female baggage. With ambitions of her own, Sophia stirred up the *streltsy*. Three days after Peter had been crowned, those musketeers, cowards in the face of foreign enemies and heroes when fighting unarmed foes, stormed the Kremlin only to be bought off by the frightened Natalia. In mid-May 1682, told by the Miloslavskys that Ivan was being mistreated, the *streltsy* ruffians charged into the Kremlin again. Met by Natalia, with Ivan, Peter, and Matveyev at her side, the *streltsy* appeared placated by Ivan's assurance that he was all right. At that moment, however, the *streltsy* commander, Prince Mikhail Dolgoruky, arrived on the scene and cursed his men for their conduct. Enraged, the *streltsy* tossed Dolgoruky on their pikes and killed him, tore Matveyev from Peter's side and hacked him to death, and then charged into the palace for a three-day orgy of murder, killing every Naryshkin adherent they could find, including Peter's uncle, Ivan Naryshkin, and a German court doctor, who kept stuffed snakes and thereby was the poisoner of Feodor.

The Naryshkins eliminated or cowed in terror, Sophia took command. After granting amnesty to the *streltsy* for their blood-bath, she had herself named regent for Ivan and Peter as co-tsars, with Ivan being the senior. Some historians have been inclined to regard Sophia highly, since she improved the status of Russian women and considered freeing the serfs, while others regarded her as an ugly termagant who ruled Russia, and not too well, until Peter got old enough and strong enough to kick her out. To her credit, almost alone, is the fact that she did not use her power to murder Peter and Natalia. And she also gained control of the *streltsy* who were not only evermutinous, but also predominantly Old Believers. First, she outdebated them on religious matters after which they beheaded the monk who had been their losing spokesman. Next, she eliminated their new commander, Prince Ivan Khovansky, who had designs on the throne for himself, by aping Ivan the Terrible and abandoning Moscow. The boyars gave in and Khovansky was tricked into going to Sophia's residence in the countryside, where he was murdered at the gates. Leaderless, the *streltsy* gave her no more trouble. Sophia's seven-year regency was strongly influenced by two favorites, who also may have been her lovers, one a boyar, Prince Vasily Golitsyn, the other a commoner, Feodor Shaklovity. In her first international venture, Sophia gained for Russia, but did not fulfill her commitment. Poland ceded her Kiev and other territory gained by Alexis in the Thirteen Years' War in perpetuity for Russia's joining the Holy League of Austria, Poland, the Pope, and Venice and attacking the

Turks. To honor that agreement, Golitsyn led massive forces against the Crimean Khan, Turkey's ally, in 1687 and 1689. Both campaigns were abject failures. Sophia's second international move, made in 1689 just before she was overthrown, was little more than an acknowledgment of failure. She signed Russia's first treaty with the Chinese, by which she agreed to withdraw Russian settlers from territory they had occupied along the Amur River.

Throughout Sophia's regency (1682–89), Peter and Natalia were kept in virtual exile on a Romanov estate at Preobrazhenskoye (Transfiguration), a village in the western outskirts of Moscow. While Natalia sulked, Peter, left to his own devices, played soldier and sailed boats, activities which profoundly influenced the course of Russia after the young man had made himself emperor. His chief playmates were Alexander Menshikov, a commoner and the son of a civil servant, Prince Feodor Romodanovsky, and Prince Ivan Buturlin, who remained his confidants in later years, and who joined him in very realistic war games. Taking part in those mock battles were some three hundred youths, who eventually formed the cadres of the Preobrazhensky and Semenovsky Guards regiments, the elite of Russian forces throughout the rest of Romanov rule. When not playing soldier and sailor, Peter often ran almost wild in Moscow, preferring the quarter near Preobrazhenskoye that was reserved for the Germans. There he met two men, who did much to shape his character and interests, Franz Timmerman, a Dutch sailor who taught him geometry as applied to ballistics and building fortifications, and General Francois Lefort, a Swiss whose origins are unclear. In the German quarter, the young Peter also met Anna Mons, the daughter of a German wine merchant, his companion in frequent drinking bouts and in bed.

7. PETER THE GREAT

Early in 1689, to enhance her son's status, Natalia arranged Peter's marriage with Eudoxia Lopukhin, the pretty but boring daughter of a lesser boyar family. Peter went through with the ceremony but was soon back with his boats and "troops" and with Anna Mons, although he did have two sons by Eudoxia, Alexis and Alexander, the latter dying in infancy. No matter how little Peter cared about the marriage, it worried Sophia, far from ready to quit her rule. Golitsyn refused to support Sophia's machinations, but in August 1689 her minion Shaklovity spread the tale that Peter's men were coming to Moscow to kill Ivan, suggesting that that be thwarted by murdering Natalia but sparing Peter. Five *streltsy* were induced to carry out that plan, but two other *streltsy* sped ahead to Preobrazhenskoye and warned Peter. The young tsar, who had never forgotten the *streltsy* invasion of the Kremlin in 1682, fled in terror to a veritable fortress, Trinity Monastery. There he was joined by two companies of his Preobrazhensky comrades and some *streltsy* and later by the patriarch. In Moscow, Sophia tried to rally support, but failed. By early September, wavering *streltsy* units in the capital finally obeyed Peter's orders to report to him, forcing Shaklovity to accompany them. Under torture, Shaklovity named accomplices and within a week he and other *streltsy* conspirators were publicly executed, Golitsyn was exiled to the far north, not only for abetting Sophia but also for bungling the Crimean campaigns, while Sophia and her sister were interned in a convent. With that, the rule of Peter (1689–1725) was assured, although he let Natalia run the country until her death in 1694 and permitted Ivan to continue as co-tsar until his half-brother died in 1696.

Only seventeen years old by the time he crushed his opposition, Peter deferred accepting his duties until 1695 and spent the interim playing at soldier and sailor, visiting Archangel, Russia's only salt water port of that time, and frolicking with Anna Mons and other friends in the German quarter. He finally took over the reins in 1695 under Lefort's persuasion and formed a force composed of his one-time playmates of the villages of Preobrazhenskoye and Semenov-skoye and some Cossacks to attack Azov, but failed because he lacked the ships to block Crimean reinforcements and supplies. Thereupon he withdrew to build Russia's first navy of sorts and reappeared in 1696 at the Don estuary commanding his ships as Captain Petr Alek-seyevich to take Azov by amphibious assault and build fortresses to ensure Russia's hold on the area.

Lefort suggested that Peter cap that victory with a grand tour of Europe to gather know-how in shipbuilding and warfare as well as the techniques of industry and the professions. Peter welcomed the idea and decided to go incognito as Peter Mikhaylov, with Lefort leading the mission of some 250 specialists; the group left in March, 1697, slightly delayed by yet another *streltsy* plot, soon resolved after the *streltsy* commander confessed under torture thereby bringing execution for himself and several others named as involved.

The young monarch's first stop was at the Swedish-controlled port of Riga where his incognito attempt to inspect the fortifications was rebuffed. He then went on to Germany, Holland, and England, specializing in learning shipbuilding and naval tactics, but trying everything he encountered, from papermaking to dentistry. The host countries were impressed with the vigor of the tsar and his companions as well as somewhat annoyed with the Russians' heavy drinking and rough manners. One reason for the tour, gaining allies for Russia against the Turks, had no practical results, but the trip's secondary purpose, learning European techniques, was quite successful; more than one thousand European experts of several nationalities and ranging from a vice-admiral to a cook were brought to Russia to enter Peter's service. After arriving in Austria in July 1698, Peter had intended to go to Venice to enlist that republic's support against the Ottomans, but had to cancel plans for further travel because of news of trouble at home. The *streltsy* had once more risen against the tsar; accustomed to the comfortable life of their Moscow quarters, they resented having been put to work building the sea of Azov fortifications and thought their problems would be solved by putting Sophia back in power.

En route home to put matters right, Peter paused only for talks with the King of Poland, his satellite, before angrily and cruelly giving his country the greatest purge it was to experience until the time of Stalin. The *streltsy* mutiny had been quelled by his lieutenants using several thousand foreign troops well before Peter arrived back in Moscow, but the young tsar had had more than his fill of the *streltsy*. Vast numbers of them were rounded up and tortured into confession, much of it under Peter's personal direction. The tsar beheaded the first five condemned and compelled his aides to join in the killing; he swore at Prince Boris Golitsyn (who had put down the mutiny) for doing a bad job of dispatching his five, cheered Prince Romadanovsky for professional work, and had great praise for Menshikov for beheading fifteen. The tortures and executions became a great public spectacle, with masses of *streltsy* being taken in wagons day after day through Red Square and past their weeping families to posts to be knouted, to wheels to be broken, or to a small forest of scaffolds. How many *streltsy* were eliminated is debatable: conservative accounts said 799 were executed and another 222 exiled to the wilds of Siberia; other reports listed hundreds, even thousands more killed. Whatever the figure, the fact remained that Peter's purge eliminated all future threat from the *streltsy*, reducing it from a force of some 50,000 to an ineffective unit of several companies. At the same time Peter also disposed of his rebellious womenfolk for good by having his half-sisters Sophia and Martha shorn as nuns and sent to a distant convent as well as forcing his wife Eudoxia, who had supported the Raskolniki beliefs held by most of the *streltsy*, to take the veil. Concurrent with the *streltsy* purge, Peter started forcefully westernizing his nation, banning Russian customs he thought backward, a process which continued throughout his lifetime. The first steps in that campaign were shearing the beards of all Russian men except clerics and aged boyars, substituting European costumes for the long-sleeved and skirted Russian kaftans, putting his soldiers into European-style uniforms and moving the New Year from September 25 to January 1. All those innovations had been opposed by the patriarch with the result that when that dignitary died Peter named no replacement, thus putting the church under state control where it remained under the rest of the Romanovs.

In 1700, Peter opened his long but successful struggle to give Russia its Baltic "window to Europe." That campaign was a series of intermittent battles called the Great Northern War or the Twenty-One Years' War, primarily between Russia and Sweden, but with Poland and Turkey also participating and the Cossacks playing both sides. The chief antagonists were Charles XII of Sweden, just as rough and ready a character as Peter and a better soldier, and Peter, who proved the better administrator and organizer. In the initial attempt to seize Swedish-held territory on the Baltic, Peter was roundly defeated in 1700 at Narva on the Gulf of Finland. Leaving fortresses and garrisons along the Gulf of Finland and on the Neva river to protect his rear, Charles swept into Poland and easily overwhelmed Peter's ally, Augustus II, King of Poland and Elector of Saxony. Peter used Charles' preoccupation elsewhere to reorganize his troops, train them in sorties against the Swedish strongpoints and occupy much of what is now northwestern Russia, Estonia, Latvia, and Lithuania with nomadic tribesmen from the east, Kalmuks and Bashkirs, who ravaged the area. By 1702, Peter was strong enough to take the fortress of Noteborg (renamed Shlisselburg) at the eastern end of the Neva and expanded that victory in the spring of the following year by capturing Fort Nyenshantz at the mouth of the Neva. There, in 1703, he established a fort of his own, Kronstadt, and using forced labor started building his new capital, Petrograd (St. Petersburg), completed in 1718 at tremendous cost in money and lives.

Peter's exploits in the north were not all work and no play. At that time he met and was enamoured of a buxom and extremely good-natured Lithuanian servant girl, Martha (renamed Catherine after conversion from Lutheran to Orthodox belief) Skavronska, who had been passed on as spoils of war from a Swedish dragoon to a Russian soldier, sold nearly naked by the Russian to his general for one ruble and taken from that officer by Menshikov, who surrendered her to Peter. Despite that background, Catherine became not only Peter's constant companion in the field and in bed, but also the mother of his two daughters and subsequently his empress.

In 1704, while Charles was busy establishing a puppet in Poland, Peter took the towns of Koporye, Yama, and Dorpat in the Gulf of Finland area; captured the fortress of Narva; and defeated Swedish naval counterattacks at the mouth of the Neva. The following year, the Russians also took the more important towns of Vilna and Grodno to the south.

From 1705 to 1709, however, Peter's fortunes were not very bright. He was constantly distracted with serious internal troubles, four major revolts sparked by the Raskolniki, opponents of his reforms, *streltsy* remnants, Bashkirs and disaffected Cossacks of both the Don and the Dnieper. Before those uprisings were suppressed, there were mass killings and brutal reprisals by both rebel and government sides. And abroad, the Russians had been chased out of Grodno and a mixed force of Poles, Russians, and Saxons defeated by the Swedes at Poznan.

At the height of Russia's troubles at home, and with Poland in his pocket, Charles led a crack 33,000-man army across the Vistula in early 1708 to finish off Peter. By midsummer the Swedes had advanced easily to within 100 miles of Moscow and then halted to await a reinforcement and supply column of 18,000 men. That proved to be Charles' last success. The reinforcement column was cut off and decimated by the Russians in the autumn of 1708 and Charles decided to winter in the Ukraine before resuming battle the next year with assistance he expected from the vacillating Cossacks of the Dnieper.

[52]

In May, 1709, Peter's prospects improved when his forces ended internal resistance by storming and taking the Zaporozhe Sech of the (Dnieper) Cossacks. In contrast, the outlook for Charles was dim, since a severe winter had reduced his force to only some 20,000 effectives. Nevertheless, the Swede was confident of support—support which never came—from the Cossacks, Tatars, and possibly the Turks and clashed with Peter's 40,000 men near Poltava, southeast of Kiev, on June 27, 1709. The battle was won by the Russians in a matter of hours. Charles was wounded and fled to Turkey for asylum. During the remainder of that year, Peter won even more victories; he captured the great ports of Riga and Reval, took much of Finland and the fortress of Viborg and the town of Keksgolm; he also married Anna, the daughter of his half-brother Ivan, to the Duke of Kurland (Latvia), establishing her in its capital of Mitau (Yelgava) and thus bolstering that area against the Swedes.

Charles, however, was not to be finished off completely for another decade. In 1711, he persuaded the Turks to send an army of some 200,000 against the Russians. Neglectful of supplies, and wishfully thinking the subject Slavs of the Balkans would rise against the Turks in his support, Peter marched to the Prut River at the head of a scant 40,000 men. Except for a few Montenegrins, no Balkan Slavs rebelled and Peter was trapped in his entrenchments by the vizier's army, starvation his ultimate end unless he negotiated. Talks started and the Russian negotiators must have been exceedingly skillful; Peter and his army were allowed to withdraw after agreeing to surrender Azov, his first conquest. According to legend, however, Catherine was the heroine of those negotiations, surrendering her jewels to the vizier to soften the terms of the Turks. There may be some truth in that story for Peter married Catherine the following year and made her his tsarina in 1713 at a brilliant ceremony.

The Prut setback was Peter's last reverse. From that point on, his course was completely victorious on both land and sea and also diplomatically. In the last field, he was particularly well served by Prince Boris Kurakin, the husband of his sister Natalia, who is called the "Father of Russian Diplomacy" and who earned that distinction by keeping England from interfering while Russia reduced Sweden to the approximate size she is today.

Russian successes after the Prut debacle were brilliant, comparable only to those of Stalin and the Red Army in World War II. A mere chronological listing tells the story: 1711 Peter reestablished his ally Augustus II on the Polish throne; 1712–13 Poles and Russians under Menshikov drove the Swedes from Pomerania; 1713 Peter took Helsinki and Abo and defeated the Swedes at Tammerfors; 1714 the Russian fleet, with Peter aboard, defeated the Swedes at Hango-Udd and took Aland Island; 1715 Charles returned from Turkey to defend and lose the fortress of Stralsund; 1716 Charles lost Wismar and thereby Sweden's last hold on the south Baltic coast; 1719 with the Russian fleet controlling the Gulf of Bothnia, Russian troops landed near Stockholm, pillaged several towns and burned scores of villages; 1720–21 Russian troops again landed in Sweden.

In that decade of military victory, Peter also arranged a pair of alliances to gain allies in Europe; he married Catherine, the other daughter of his half-brother Ivan, to the Grand Duke of Mecklenburg, and married his own daughter by Catherine Skavronska, Anna (Catherine), to the Duke of Holstein. But, visiting France in the same period, Peter did not succeed in marrying his younger daughter by Catherine Skavronska, Elizabeth, to young King Louis XV.

In 1718, Charles was killed in Norway besieging a fortress in an effort to replace territory lost on the eastern and southern Baltic coasts with acquisitions in Scandinavia proper. With the loss of that able soldier-king, secret Russo-Swedish negotiations that had been under way ended abruptly, Stockholm resistance collapsed and the Swedes sued for peace. The end of the long war came August 30, 1721 at Nystad (Uusikaupunki, Finland). Under the treaty made there, Russia gained Livonia (northern Latvia and southern Estonia) —originally assured to Poland by Peter—Estonia, Ingermanland (the St. Petersburg area), the Karelian peninsula, and part of Finland. Peter had won Russia's Baltic "window to Europe," and considerably more. At a great celebration in the autumn of 1721, Bishop Theophan Prokopovich greeted the tsar as Peter the Great and in 1722 the title of Emperor of All the Russias was conferred upon him.

By then Russia had attained imperial proportions. In 1719, Russians sent to Peking were received courteously, not rebuffed as were Sophia's envoys. In 1721, in a campaign against Persia, Peter took the Christian principalities of Georgia and Armenia under his aegis. In 1723, two Russian frigates dropped anchor off Madagascar on a goodwill visit. And in 1725, just before his death, Peter had approved the

North Pacific voyages of Vitus Jonassen Bering, the Danish explorer who entered his naval service in 1704.

Although Russia was at war throughout Peter's reign, the major conflict was concluded with the Treaty of Nystad. Peter had carried on administrative, social, and economic reforms despite concentration on military campaigns, but once the war with the Swedes was over he had more time to devote to internal matters. First of all, of course, he gave Russia its first professional army, formed around a cadre of elite guard troops, and made his country a prime naval power. But he was also the founder of Russian industry, starting new factories himself or financing others to do so, building a canal from Lake Ladoga to the Volga and planning the Volga-Don canal, completed two and a half centuries later by the Communists. He was the great initiator in almost everything, ranging from modernizing the Russian alphabet and starting and editing Russia's first newspaper to abolishing the malfunctioning *prikazi* and establishing a new system of government ministries or colleges.

Others of Peter's autocratic reforms proved, however, to be less than blessings. Heading that list is the "Fiscals," originally a device to correct financial abuses, but ultimately an organization of government agents and informers that infected the entire country. For example, even under Peter, the head of the "Fiscals," one Aleksey Nesterov, an ex-slave, had executed a number of senior officials and hanged the governor of Siberia for defalcations before he, himself, was broken on the wheel for like offenses. Concurrently, Peter also introduced the poll tax, passports for internal travel and a massive new tax system which resulted in further nailing the serfs to the land. And in 1721, he issued a pair of ukases that endangered the very autocracy he wanted to reinforce: he abolished primogeniture for the throne and ruled that every emperor should name his successor; and he eliminated the patriarchate for good, substituting for it the state-controlled Holy Synod, thereby depriving the church of the stature and temporal authority that could have helped Russia in future times of trouble.

In the more personal field, Peter is inscribed upon the list of Russian rulers, from Ivan the Terrible to Stalin, who were ruthless to their kin and especially to their sons. Peter's luckless marriage to Eudoxia did little more than produce an heir, Alexis. With a man like Peter in control, to have been Eudoxia's son would have been enough of a handicap for that unfortunate tsarevich, but the youth was also as retiring and bookish as his father was domineering and little-lettered. Peter used Alexis in affairs of state by marrying him to Princess Charlotte of Blankenburg-Wolfenbuttel—important only because her sister was married to Holy Roman Emperor Charles VI (Charles II of Spain)—but otherwise called the tsarevich "useless" and a "very unfit successor." The conflict between father and son broke into the open in 1716, when Alexis abetted by courtiers and with Peter preoccupied with the war with Sweden fled to Vienna and asylum at the Austrian court. Alexis was spirited from the Austrian Alps to Naples but, operating in best cloak-and-danger fashion, Peter's agents found and returned him to Russia in the fall of 1717. At first, Peter pardoned the tsarevich, but "confessions" from the young man's confidants soon piled up against the young man. A civil commission found that the tsarevich and his supporters had planned mutiny and a reversal of all of Peter's reforms and in November, 1718, condemned Alexis to death. The day after the tsarevich's confinement in a St. Petersburg garrison guardhouse, he was declared to have died, reportedly after having been flogged by his father.

Again in 1724 Peter was involved in another fatal family squabble, although a less publicized one. Catherine, by then empress, had been accused of allowing William Mons, the brother of the Anna Mons of Peter's youthful days, certain unspecified familiarities. Mons was promptly beheaded. According to legend, Mons' head was pickled and put in a jar and that specimen was placed in Catherine's quarters as a reminder.

A year later, in January, 1725, weakened by a chill caused by rescuing some shipwrecked sailors, as well as failing from a long bout with syphilis, Peter died at the age of fifty-two. On his deathbed, he had attempted to provide for his succession according to his 1721 ukase, but all he managed to say was "Give all to . . . " before dying in the arms of his daughter Anna.

8. A NEW TIME OF TROUBLES

Due in part to Peter's changing the succession procedure, all that he had accomplished to bring Russia to the fore could have been lost by the weak and inconsequential rulers who followed him. Only the fact that Europe and Turkey were well preoccupied with their own affairs allowed Russia to escape molestation during that long, mean period of virtual nonrule that Russia experienced for more than three and one-half decades after the great tsar's death. The six who followed him on the throne survived only on the capital he had left them; not a one of them produced anything of his own. That tawdry half-dozen had two factors in common, each was almost equally inferior and each had gained the throne by palace revolution, a custom that was to continue into the beginning of the nineteenth century.

Palace plotting over the succession began even before Peter was dead. The princely families, such as the Dolgorukys and the Golitsyns, who had been downgraded by Peter's creation of a military and serving gentry that held high posts on the basis of merit rather than birth, hoped to install Alexis' son Peter, then ten years old. Peter the Great's body was not yet cold, however, before the new nobility, led by Menshikov, assembled the Preobrazhensky and Semenovsky Guards in the palace courtyard. Drums rolled, huzzas were yelled and Peter's widow, Catherine (1725–27), the onetime Lithuanian servant girl, was proclaimed ruler of All the Russias.

Catherine's brief reign was distinguished only by her extravagant waste of colossal sums on her personal pleasures, with no thought at all for the peasants from whom the revenues were wrung, and the assemblage of her Lithuanian relatives in the court. The real ruler was Menshikov, who controlled the six-man Supreme Secret Council and left foreign affairs to a Baltic German, Andrew Osterman, who had been responsible for the terms of the Peace of Nystad.

Before Catherine died, Menshikov persuaded her to name as her successor the youth who had been passed over before, Alexis' son, Peter II (1727–30). Initially, Menshikov ruled again, even moving Peter, just entering his teens, into the Menshikov palace and betrothing him to his daughter, Maria Menshikov. Within the year, however, the young Peter rebelled against Menshikov and sent his grandfather's advisor into exile in the Ukraine and later to Siberia where Menshikov eventually died in penury. Peter also transferred the court back to Moscow from St. Petersburg. With that, the Dolgorukys took over the regency and in November, 1729, Prince Alexis Dolgoruky betrothed his daughter Catherine to Peter. The nuptials were scheduled for January 30, 1730, but on that very day Peter died of smallpox. Legend has it that the desperate Alexis Dolguruky put his daughter Catherine into bed with the dying Peter in an unsuccessful effort to get her with child and secure a Dolgoruky claimant to the throne.

An almost immediate convocation of the nobles, new and old, followed Peter's death since all had assembled in Moscow for the intended wedding. With Menshikov gone, the old order, the Dolgorukys and the Golitsyns, were in control and nominated Anna of Kurland, the surviving daughter of Peter the Great's half-brother Ivan. The nomination was made with the proviso, however, that Anna accept the *Punkty*, a Russian-style Magna Carta under which all decisions of importance, even her possible remarriage, must be approved by the council of nobles.

Bored with her long rustication in provincial Mitau, Anna (1730–40) accepted the terms, which would have given Russia a constitutional monarchy of sorts, and hurried to Moscow. Almost immediately on arrival, she visited the Preobrazhensky guards, was named colonel of the regiment and joined the officers in drinks, a ritual initiated by Catherine I and followed by the successive female rulers of Russia to good avail. The troops thus behind her, Anna next arranged a banquet for the supreme council. In the midst of wining and dining, guard officers broke into the hall by Anna's prearrangement, declared the *Punkty* was supported only by the council, fell to their knees and begged her to assume autocratic power.

On cue, Anna theatrically tore up the *Punkty* and so ended one possibility of constitutional government, which Russia has never truly had under either tsars or commissars. Cowed by the display of the guards, the council was soon dissolved. The Dolgorukys and the Golitsyns were dispersed; their estates were confiscated, some were imprisoned, tortured, dismembered, otherwise executed or sent to Siberian exile at Berezov, the same place Menshikov ended his days.

Fearful of a possible change of heart by the Preobrazhensky and Semenovsky regiments, Anna instituted a third elite unit of her own, the Izmailovsky Guards, completely composed of Kurlanders (Baltic Germans) in whom she had more confidence. In governmental matters, she placed her trust in another Kurlander, a former groom and her onetime lover, Ernst Johann Biron. Imported from Mitau to be grand chamberlain, he changed his name (Buhren) to Biron, made himself a count of Russia and later, by means of bribery, elevated himself to Duke of Kurland.

With Biron running affairs of state, the empress soon won the name of "Anna the Bloody." Biron set up a secret chancellery to eliminate the remainder of the old noble families and to combat nationwide lower class unrest, caused by great famines, starvation, and pestilence. That repression, run by a vast network of spies and informers and backed by the Izmailovsky guards, became known as the "Bironovshchina." Before it ran its course, countless thousands were flogged, tortured, executed, or exiled. In one instance, some 20,000 were rounded up en masse for deportation to Siberia without even their names being recorded, let alone the offenses with which they were charged; 5,000 of those unfortunates were lost without trace en route to exile. Even Anna's cousin Elizabeth, the playgirl daughter of Peter the Great and Catherine Skavronska, fell afoul of the Bironovshchina; after informers advised that Elizabeth was having an affair with a sergeant of the Semonovsky Guards, Anna threatened to put Elizabeth into a convent, had the soldier's tongue torn out, and sent him to Siberia.

Anna the Bloody's most notorious cruelty occurred in 1739 when she was informed that the surviving scion of one of the old noble families, Prince Mikhail Alekseyevich Golitsyn, had wed a foreign woman of the Roman Catholic faith. Even though that woman had died, Anna made the prince marry an extremely ugly Kalmuk peasant, paraded the couple atop an elephant, accompanied by a retinue of freaks, and forced them naked into a bridal suite completely made of ice. And Anna was just as bloody with animals: priding herself on her marksmanship, she felled deer and other creatures in the imperial parks, or pot-shotted at birds loosed from cages within the palace.

The only accomplishments of her reign were the return of the capital to St. Petersburg and a brace of military victories won by two foreigners in her employ, Field Marshals Peter Lacy and Burkhard Christoph Munnich. During the War of the Polish Succession (1733–35), Lacy established a Russian puppet on the Polish throne and led Russian troops to the Rhine. In the war with Turkey (1735–39), Lacy and Munnich thrice invaded and devastated the Crimea and Munnich led the Russians to triumph at the battles of Hotin and Jassy. Munnich might have done better had not Russia's chief ally, Austria, concluded a separate peace. As it was, he gained a demilitarized Azov for the empress as well as some steppe territory south of Kiev.

Anna prepared for her succession by marrying her niece Anna, the daughter of Catherine of Mecklenburg, to yet another petty German prince, Anton Ulrich of Brunswick-Luneburg. A son, Ivan, was born of that marriage in August, 1740. Before her death three months later, Anna named the infant, Ivan VI (1740–41), her heir and appointed Biron regent.

Biron's rule did not last a month. Hardly was Anna dead than a guards colonel, mirroring rising Russian aversion to a foreign-controlled court, unsuccessfully attempted to throw out Biron. A few weeks later, however, Preobrazhensky Guards, led by Munnich their colonel, surprised and overcame Biron by night at the Summer Palace. First sentenced to be quartered, the former groom was eventually banished to Siberia and his vast, illegally gained property was confiscated. Later, though, he was allowed to return to Kurland.

Ivan's mother, historically known as Anna Leopoldovna, was made regent and Munnich was her right-hand man. A few months later, in March, 1741, that relationship collapsed. Munnich resigned, knowing that the regime of Anna, who spent all her time quarreling with her husband or closeted with her fellow Lesbian lady-in-waiting, would not last long. Osterman succeeded Munnich as virtual tsar, but his days were also numbered.

The end came on the night of November 25, 1741. Peter the Great's daughter Elizabeth (1741–62), her buxom figure laced into the uniform of the Preobrazhensky Guards and her blond tresses stuffed into a shako, led troops to the Winter Palace, awakened Anna from sleep with her lady friend and bundled both of them, plus Ivan, Anton, Munnich, and Osterman, off to Shlisselburg fortress. So ended that era of foreign control of Russia. Ivan remained a prisoner until he was killed more than a score of years later, but the others were later sent home or to the provinces.

Elizabeth has gone down in history as the "Good-hearted Empress," an apt title. She was good to her friends and allies and clement to her enemies, in fact, her reign was a welcome relief from internecine bloodshed and oppression. She promoted and rewarded her allies of the coup and made the Preobrazhensky regiment the imperial bodyguard for its part in the overthrow of Ivan's regents. She was unsuccessful in her effort to make abolition of the death penalty the law of the land, but she kept her pledge never to sign a death warrant against her soldiers and commuted every death sentence of others. That did not prevent her, however, from being capricious with one group of commutations: in January 1742, Munnich, Osterman and other foreigners of the old regime had been condemned to death and were just about to be executed when they were given amnesty. On the other hand, she almost immediately rehabilitated the victims of the foreigners, the Dolgorukys, Golitsyns, and other members of the old nobility.

Although Elizabeth had a mind of her own, she left much of the affairs of state, not to the old nobility, but to a group of comparative upstarts most of whom had been co-conspirators in the coup which brought her to power, and some of whom shared her bed. All played significant roles in developing Russia, although their political views and European ties varied. Her grand chancellor until the last years of her reign was Alexis Bestuzhev-Ryumin, a descendant of an English yeoman named Best who went to Russia in the fifteenth century. Pro-British, he was ousted in 1758 at the height of Elizabeth's conflict with Frederick the Great of Prussia, then an ally of Britain. Countering Bestuzhev-Ryumin was the vice chancellor Mikhail Vorontsov, who was pro-French. Internal matters were handled by two brothers, Alexander and Peter Shuvalov, with the first in charge of the police and the other chief of the war college and finances and later, under Elizabeth's successor, an outstanding diplomat.

An oversexed libertine, the voluptuous, and later fat, Elizabeth had an unending string of lovers. Her one true love followed the Semenovsky sergeant, Alexis Razumovsky, a half-Cossack Ukrainian peasant who had been sent to St. Petersburg as a choir boy and became the imperial lute player. Elizabeth thought enough of Razumovsky to marry him secretly in 1742 and make him a field marshal. A benign favorite, Razumovsky declared himself unfit for such high military honor and did not exploit his position, although his younger brother made the most of the family connection with the throne. Razumovsky was displaced, but not degraded, in 1749 by Ivan Shuvalov, the nephew of Alexander and Peter Shuvalov, who virtually pushed the younger man into the empress' bedchamber. Surprisingly, Ivan Shuvalov, like his predecessor, was unassuming and unambitious and used his position only for cultural pursuits for Elizabeth's advantage. It was he in 1755 who founded Moscow University, now named after Mikhail Lomonosov, the great poet, grammarian and physicist of that era. Although Lomonosov prepared many an ode for state occasions for Elizabeth, and Anna before her, his greatness was to be recognized only by later generations.

Elizabeth's reign began and ended with military victories. At the time of her coup, Russia was at war with Sweden, who hoped to capitalize on the troubles of Anna's succession by regaining territory lost to Peter the Great. The Preobrazhensky and other regiments left for the front almost immediately after Elizabeth had been installed and the Swedes were defeated decisively. By the Treaty of Abo in August, 1743, Sweden ceded yet another slice of southern Finland to Russia. In the next decade, Russia became involved in the Seven Years' War (1756–63), primarily a struggle between the Hohenzollern and the elder Bourbon-Hapsburg dynasties, with the Austrians and French fighting the British and Prussians and both sides wooing the Russians. Bestuzhev, of course, was rabidly pro-British, while Vorontsov and the Shuvalovs were pro-French. It was Elizabeth who tipped the scales and had Russia side with the Austrians and French, primarily because Frederick the Great of Prussia had made some nasty remarks about her love life and had threatened to help restore Ivan VI to the throne. From 1757 to 1759, Frederick and his Prussians suffered a quartet of unexpected and disastrous defeats—Gross-Jagersdorf, Konigsberg, Zorndorf and Kunersdorf—at the hands of the Russians, and in October, 1760, a raiding force of Cossacks and Kalmuks occupied his capital of Berlin for what must have been four frightful days for the inhabitants. On January 5, 1762, Russians led by Peter Rumyantsev captured the Prussian fortress of Kolberg and matters looked very dark for Frederick until the Russians suddenly disengaged and withdrew. It was the death of Elizabeth which had caused the Russians to retire and had saved Frederick from utter defeat.

Like Anna before her, Elizabeth, too, had arranged for her succession, in fact had done so within two months after seizing power. In February 1742 she had brought to St. Petersburg Karl Peter Ulrich (Peter III), the orphaned son of her sister Anna, Duchess of Holstein, and the grandson of Peter the Great. Almost feeble-minded—he played with toy soldiers as a grown man—vain and deceitful, that youth resembled his illustrious forebear in name only. Nevertheless, Elizabeth gave him the honor and loving care which he had not had at the Holstein court and, of course, chose his bride. The selection, made on the suggestion of Frederick the Great, who had not then

[62]

quarreled with Elizabeth, fell to Princess Sophia Augusta (Catherine) of Anhalt-Zerbst. Only fourteen when she went to Russia, Catherine was already well-read and fully developed in mind and body and able to cope with two handicaps, her father, who became a Prussian field marshal, and her mother, who was a political agent (spy) of Frederick the Great. Additionally, during the Seven Years' War, although Peter had been blatantly pro-Prussian, Catherine remained studiously pro-Russian, despite the hopes Frederick may have pinned on her.

In addition to his other shortcomings, Peter was impotent until operated upon, and after that, although he gained sexual power, he was sterile. Nevertheless, in the seventh year of that marriage—a period in which Elizabeth had badgered Catherine for not assuring the Romanov succession—a son, the Grand Duke Paul, was born to the young couple. In 1752, two years before that birth, Catherine had become enamored of Sergey Saltykov, a dashing but dissolute young courtier, and there is good reason to believe that Saltykov sired Paul, as Catherine herself suggested later in her *Memoirs*. There is also speculation that Paul may have been the son of Elizabeth and Ivan Shuvalov.

Her duty done with the production of Paul, Catherine, like Elizabeth, soon became involved with what was to be a long string of other lovers. There was no double-standard involved, however, since Peter took as mistress, Elizabeth, the daughter of Vorontsov. There was no issue from that alliance, but Catherine, who had several bastards, was pregnant with the son of Grigory Orlov, a handsome guards officer five years her junior and her third lover, when Elizabeth died.

9. CATHERINE THE GREAT

Peter III (1762) assumed power without incident. The guards, the nobles and the people in general, tired of years of female autocracy, were inclined to welcome a male ruler. The woefully incompetent Peter, however, was just not the man for the task. He started by recalling Biron, Munnich, and lesser Baltic Germans to court and visiting Ivan VI in Shlisselburg, not particularly bad moves themselves, but almost simultaneously his German background and inclinations spread in epidemic proportion. At heart the Lutheran he had been reared, he degraded the church. Next he enforced Prussian drill and uniforms on the troops and made his Holstein regiment the imperial bodyguards. Finally, his reign only months old, Peter committed the supreme error: in May 1762 he signed a treaty of alliance with Prussia and made plans for a summer campaign in which Russian and Prussian armies were to have delivered a knockout blow to Russia's ally, Austria.

During that reversal in Russian policy, Catherine had discreetly remained aloof, although she was well informed by her lover of the ground swell of opposition to Peter among the guards. The crisis came at six in the morning of July 9, 1762, when Catherine was awakened by Alexis Orlov, Grigory's brother, and was led out the rear entrance of her residence. A few miles outside St. Petersburg, the empress was joined by Grigory Orlov himself for a visit to the barracks of the Izmailovsky Guards. Within three hours of her awakening, Catherine gained the fervent allegiance of the Izmailovsky and Semenovsky regiments and was proclaimed autocrat in Kazan Cathedral. That done, with Grand Duke Paul at her side, she appeared on a balcony of the Winter Palace to receive the plaudits from the square below of some 14,000 enthusiastic troops, among whom were the third regiment, the Preobrazhensky Guards.

Catherine's first official act on the day of the coup was to order the Russian troops in Germany to cease operations. Then, dressed as her model Elizabeth had been in the uniform of the Preobrazhensky Guards, she galloped to Oranienbaum and told a panic-stricken Peter, who had made no effective effort to block the revolt, that his rule was over. A day later Peter abdicated and on July 11, escorted by Alexis Orlov and a squadron of hussars, he was sent to the country estate of Ropsha to await transfer to Shlisselburg. That transfer never came. On July 18, while banqueting, Catherine received a note from her lover's brother advising that Peter had been killed by his drunken guards. Some accounts say Catherine was unmoved by the news; others claim she cried and fainted. Whatever Catherine's emotional reaction to news of the assassination may have been, her pragmatic response was very definite. She issued a manifesto declaring her qualifications for and acceptance of the throne.

Thirty-three years old at the time of her coronation in October, 1762, Catherine was the woman Sophia Miloslavsky probably would have liked to have been. She was a born administrator and diplomat and had the versatile and brilliant mind of a master executive. In addition to possession of those talents, she was also attractive and although obviously greatly oversexed she must have had very strong personal and sexual appeal because all the men who served her as lovers or lieutenants, or both, were devoted to her far beyond the call of duty or self-service. Therefore, in the main, it was the unusual combination of her mind and body that made Russia a truly major power and entitled her to the appellation of Catherine the Great.

Her licentious love life makes fascinating reading. It would also be the envy of a professional prostitute because in matters that really counted that unique empress held the reins, not any of the men involved. That process started at her coronation, a brilliant affair of great pomp and ceremony. At its conclusion, she made Grigory and Alexis Orlov and their two brothers counts (their grandfather had been a *streltsy* sergeant, spared by Peter the Great because of his courageous stance before the executioners) and rewarded all others who had participated in her usurpation of power. A year later, in 1763, she put the handsome Polish aristocrat Stanislaus Poniatowski, who had preceded Grigory Orlov in her bedchamber, on the Polish throne. Her first lover, Saltykov, who had jilted her when her fortunes were insecure, got nothing.

Grigory Orlov reigned as favorite until 1771, when he was retired to estates given him by Catherine and replaced by Alexander Vasilchikov, a pretty court underling. Vasilchikov proved a relative passing fancy and was succeeded in 1774 by Grigory Potemkin, a onetime cavalry officer who had also been involved in the coup, an exceedingly able statesman and administrator, who became the empress' chief love and counselor. Catherine probably secretly married Potemkin because correspondence remains in which she addressed him as "dear husband" and called herself "your devoted wife." Later made a field marshal and Prince of Taurida, he directed foreign affairs and was responsible for Russia's expansion to the south and the founding of new cities there, some named after his patroness, such as Ekaterinburg, Ekaterinoslav and Ekaterinodar. He also has been burdened with the "Potemkin village," a veritable theatrical set instead of a real town that he erected for Catherine's grand tour of the newly won south. That foolishness aside, however, Potemkin actually did develop and settle the south, establish communications there and lay the groundwork for the great port of Odessa and the bastion of Sevastopol.

In 1776 Catherine and Potemkin mutually tired of each other as bed companions. Potemkin, though, was not pensioned off to an estate, but remained the empress' right-hand man of affairs. He also became her pimp, supplying almost all of some fifteen successive lovers. Only one of that lot is of interest, Ivan Rimsky-Korsakov, the forebear of the composer Nikolai Rimsky-Korsakov.

Russia's first educated ruler, Catherine built and enhanced palaces in St. Petersburg, improved the Kremlin, wrote plays, and patronized poet Gavriil Derzhavin and early journalists. She also had intense correspondence, not only with Potemkin, her generals and diplomats, but also with Frederick the Great, Gustavus III of Sweden, Joseph II of Austria, the German-born French writer Friedrich Grimm, Voltaire, and Diderot (who visited her in St. Petersburg in 1773). After the French Revolution, however, she banned circulation of Voltaire's works in Russia, imprisoned journalist Nikolay Novikov in Shlisselburg and exiled or took other repressive action against other Russian liberals. Early in her reign, she worked on an ambitious new law code, but never completed it. She also planned to improve the lot of the serfs, but ended up bestowing some 800,000 serfs on her favorites and considerably worsening their plight.

Since she had usurped power, Catherine was plagued throughout her reign with plots and pretenders, of whom many claimed to be Peter III or Ivan VI. The first serious attempt came in July 1764 when a group of young guards officers tried to rescue Ivan VI from Shlisselburg. Ivan's guards were under orders to kill him if there were danger of his being seized and when the plotters had broken into the fortress they found the deposed tsar already dead. The leader of that plot was executed and his co-conspirators were sent to penal labor in Siberian mines, as were most of the pretenders subsequently caught. In 1771, none other than the Grand Duke Paul himself and a group of nobles planned a coup to overthrow Catherine. Grigory Orlov, involved in the same year in restoring order in Moscow where some 100,000 had perished from plague, unearthed that plot; Paul confessed and was forgiven. There was also a lone female pretender, Princess Tarakanova, who claimed from Balkan asylum that she was the daughter of Elizabeth and Alexis Razumovsky. Alexis Orlov, commanding a ship of war in the Adriatic, lured her aboard at Ragusa (Dubrovnik) and took her to Russia where she was imprisoned and died in the Peter and Paul Fortress.

Those plots and pretensions, although a threat to Catherine's rule, were not as serious for Russia as the mass unrest of more ordinary folk that was a running, but imperially belittled, sore of her autocracy. At the very time that Peter was deposed, some 200,000 peasants were in open revolt throughout the land; those uprisings were quelled only by troops, often using artillery against the rebels, who were ill-armed or not armed at all. The greatest of those revolts, a mirror-image of that of Stenka Razin, broke out in May 1773 under the leadership of Yemelyan Pugachev, a Don Cossack, who claimed to be Peter III and set up a court of his own. A cruel but courageous and nearly unbeatable outlaw, Pugachev aroused thousands of malcontents, peasants, escaped serfs, Tatars, Cossacks, and other minorities, seized towns along the Volga, butchered and terrified landowners, hanged some 500 priests and officers and even threatened Moscow. He easily defeated regular troops sent against him and was finally run down only by a crack cavalry unit. He was brought to Moscow in an iron cage for public display. Although Catherine refused to have him tortured before trial, he was quartered in the old capital in January 1775. That spectacle was followed by mass executions of all involved in any way in the uprising. Surprisingly, despite those reprisals, from that moment the Don Cossacks became loyal and most faithful subjects of the Romanovs, remaining so until the March 1917 revolution.

Catherine's reign began with external as well as internal troubles. The Seven Years' War was still in progress, confused by Peter's switching allies. Catherine managed to play both sides off against each other and mediate the conflict to a conclusion in 1763. She used the prestige thus gained not only to put Poniatowski on the Polish throne but also to reestablish Biron in Kurland as her puppet. Her gift to Poniatowski meant little for him or the Poles, however, for in 1772 and again in 1792 and 1795 Russia joined Austria and Prussia in the infamous division of Poland and its complete elimination as a state, a process highly similar to the Hitler-Stalin division of that unfortunate country almost two centuries later. Her more glorious military victories and territorial aggrandizement came in two wars with Turkey, 1768–74 and 1787–92. In those conflicts, Peter Rumyantsev, the hero of Kolberg at the end of Elizabeth's reign, further distinguished himself; Potemkin proved himself as able a troop leader as statesman; a new star arose in Russia's military galaxy, Alexander Suvorov, probably his nation's greatest commander of all time; and Alexis Orlov brought honor to the Russian navy, refurbished and expanded under Catherine, with his victory at Chesme, which greatly impressed the other major powers. As the result of those two wars, Potemkin annexed the Crimea, Georgia was made a protectorate, and extensive territory was gained along the northern Black Sea coast, giving Catherine a "window to the south" to match Peter the Great's Baltic "window to Europe" won at the start of the century.

Catherine died somewhat unexpectedly of a stroke in November 1796 without realizing her great dream of completely defeating Turkey. So high had been her hopes for that, that she had named Paul's second son Constantine with the idea that he would someday be Prince of Constantinople. Nor did she seem aware that greater danger to Russia was already in the wings, Napoleon, winning his first victories in Italy. But whatever her failures, foibles and eccentricities, Catherine was the last great imperial autocrat of Russia. The six men who followed her on the throne were very pale shadows of autocrats indeed and were more like hereditary bureaucrats marking time until the end of the dynasty and the tsardom.

10. THE LAST PALACE REVOLUTION

The first, Paul (1796–1801), was an ugly, foolish, angry little man, bitter that his mother had kept him from the throne during the prime of his life. He was terribly suspicious of everybody, including his own family—there with reason— and his ego was vast. His brief reign was one contradiction after another: he restricted the rights of the gentry and reduced the forced labor requirement of the serfs; he imprisoned and exiled countless numbers on the flimsiest pretenses; and in his five-year rule he put down each of 278 peasant uprisings with troops; he banned European books and music and prohibited French garb, but respected Napoleon as a restorer of law and order. During his domination by Catherine, he had sublimated his ambitions by siring four sons and five daughters and by playing at soldier a la Peter the Great with 2,000 helpless lackeys at Gatchina, his country estate. However, unlike his illustrious predecessor, Paul did not have the dimmest conception of tactics, instead concentrated on decking out his "troops" in powdered wigs and Prussian uniforms, drilling them in Prussian fashion and brutally disciplining them for the most minor infractions. As tsar, he imposed the Gatchina methods and uniforms on the regular troops and gave the Gatchina unit precedence over the guards regiments. And for a trifling headquarters procedure not to his liking, he even dismissed Suvorov.

In 1798, when the revolutionary directorate in Paris threatened to restore Poland, he allied Russia with Britain and Austria against the French and had to ask Suvorov to return to service. At first all went well. In 1799 Russian warships took the Ionian islands from the French and Suvorov marched Russian and Austrian forces into Milan and Turin, driving the French out of northern Italy. Intent on driving to Paris, Suvorov, then seventy years old, next led the Russians over the Alps, in history's greatest mountain march, and took Zurich but had to withdraw in another storybook trek over the Alps because the Austrians failed to support him. Piqued at the Austrians because of their inaction and angered at the British because Russian units under their command had been defeated by the French in Holland, Paul withdrew from the alliance. Although promoted from field marshal to generalissimo because of his brilliance in Italy and the Alps, Suvorov was recalled to Russia in disgrace after Paul learned his commander had allowed his men to remove their parade ground wigs and garters. Insult was added to injury when Suvorov arrived back in St. Petersburg to be met, not by celebrations and parades of honor, but by Paul's valet. The old generalissimo died a few days later and Paul pointedly ignored the funeral.

In 1800 Paul switched his alliance from the British and Austrians to Napoleon. In September of that year he prepared for naval action in the Mediterranean against the British, who had 205 ships there to the Russians' 47 and dispatched a Cossack force to invade India in cooperation with the French. The naval engagement was stillborn and the Cossacks got no farther south than Orenburg. Paul's greatest error in switching to the French was internal in scope; he embargoed commerce with Britain thereby cutting off the gentry's supply of luxury items and halting Russian exports of hemp, timber, wheat, and flax.

By February, 1801, rumblings of discontent among the military, the gentry, and merchants about Paul's international and commercial policies had become so pronounced that martial law and a curfew were imposed in St. Petersburg and key intersections and gates of the capital were barricaded. That done, Paul next made his major mistake: he made a toadying Kurlander, Count Peter Ludwig von Pahlen, whom the emperor often had insulted and abused, governor-general of St. Petersburg with concurrent control of the guards, the foreign office, the police, the posts, and the ports and with surveillance over Grand Duke Alexander.

A traitor in the truest sense of the word, von Pahlen used his powers not to protect Paul but to connive with garrison officers who had secured Alexander's agreement that his father be deposed. The grand duke himself selected the date for the deed, March 12, 1801, when his battalion of the Semenovsky regiment was to stand guard at his father's Mikhailovsky palace. That night, a gang of officers, with von Pahlen not far behind, broke into the palace, found Paul hiding barefooted behind a screen and when he refused to abdicate, strangled him.

Paul's murder was a watershed of sorts in Russian history. It was the last time a Russian monarch fell in a palace revolution; from then on all serious threat to the tsar came from people who wanted not the throne but an end of autocracy. And it was Paul who contributed to eliminating one of the major sources of palace conflict: on the day of his coronation he decreed that succession to the throne should be on the basis of hereditary primogeniture in the male line. Otherwise, he did nothing for his country except marry the beautiful Maria Fedorovna (Princess Sophia Dorothea of Wurttemberg) and produce an attractive batch of sons and daughters thus improving the looks of successive Romanovs and giving Russia a handsome aggregation of grand dukes and grand duchesses to intermarry with foreign royalty and bolster the country's alliances.

11. THE MAGNIFICENT MYTH

The reign of Alexander I (1801–25) has been somewhat overplayed by historians and writers, particularly by the Russophiles or those of Russian origin. Primarily responsible for this are the facts that he was an extremely handsome and charming man and marched in Paris in triumph over Napoleon. A born leader, rather than a born tsar, would have more fully exploited those advantages for the good of his people. Alexander, however, was more the pretty boy of the crowned heads of the era who failed to do anything of importance with the good fortune that virtually fell into his lap.

Basically, he was two-faced; Napoleon called him the "Northern Sphinx" or likened him to a versatile French actor of the period; others regarded him as an enigma and a master diplomat. His youthful period as heir presumptive encouraged and strengthened those traits; he divided his time between the brilliant court of Catherine, where he was under the tutelage of the liberal Swiss scholar Frederic Cesar de La Harpe, and the Gatchina drill field of his martinet father and was able to comport himself unerringly in either milieu.

When Paul was murdered, Alexander was found in an apartment below, crying in the arms of his wife. Those may well have been crocodile tears, since Alexander recovered quickly when von Pahlen advised him "that's enough of playing the child." Although the exact role of Alexander in the assassination of his father has never been clear, it is extremely evident that he had approved the overthrow of Paul. Otherwise, he would have done more to the conspirators than exiling von Pahlen to Kurland, banishing others to their estates, and completely overlooking the complicity of the rest.

Immediately upon his accession, Alexander pleased the gentry and the guards by making peace with Britain and cancelling the Cossack expedition to India. On the other hand, he joined France in putting an end to squabbles among Germany's petty principalities, only subsequently to ally Russia with Britain, Prussia, Austria, Naples, and Sweden against Napoleon.

In the early years of his reign, he also dabbled in internal affairs. He abolished torture, but did not enforce his decree and then later instituted the brutal practice of punishing soldiers by making them run the gantlet. On the plus side, were only his modernization of government machinery by converting the colleges of Peter the Great into European-style ministries and his expansion of the university and secondary school systems. He toyed with establishing a representative form of government (duma), but never did more than create a council of state, in reality a collection of grand dukes. He also thought of improving the lot of the peasants—there were 32 million serfs during his reign—but did nothing.

His educational outlays were cut back and his liberal tendencies were halted with his entry onto the international scene. That came in 1805, when the French decided to come to grips with the Austrians and the Prussians. The first crucial battle came at Austerlitz where Napoleon overwhelmed the Austrians and the Russians— Alexander sat on the ground and cried at the defeat—mainly because the Prussians remained aloof from their commitment to the alliance. The Prussians' turn came next when Napoleon defeated them at Jena and Auerstadt, captured Berlin, and entered Warsaw. The Prussians

[71]

eliminated, the Corsican next moved against the Russians, driving them from the field at Eylau in February 1806 and defeating them at Friedland in June 1807.

At that point, Alexander decided to parley with Napoleon and met him on a raft in the Memel River at Tilsit. The result of that conference was that Alexander deserted his allies and joined Napoleon as both established division of the spoils, or respective spheres of influence. Russia's share was complete control of Swedish-held Finland, which was made a grand duchy, and the creation of a protectorate over that part of Poland that Napoleon had taken from the Prussians. In the course of that settlement, Alexander gave his Polish vassals a constitution of sorts and ended serfdom for the Baltic peoples under his dominion, rights he extended to none of his Russian subjects. The Tilsit about-face also gave Alexander the freedom of action to prosecute fully his 1806–11 war with a debilitated Turkey, a conflict which was concluded with Russia getting Bessarabia and Serbia being made autonomous. In 1809 Napoleon once more defeated the Austrians and again took Vienna. Alexander did not participate in that conflict, but as an ally he got Tarnopol in the Austrian sector of Poland.

Three years later, his attempt to subdue the British across the English Channel abandoned, and despite being well exhausted by his campaign in Spain, Napoleon determined on complete domination of the continent at least. In June, 1812, at the head of 600,000 troops, Napoleon crossed the Niemen River and entered Russia, bent on bringing Alexander to his knees. Up to that time, the side-changing tsar, who had had his clergy label Napoleon as the "Antichrist" prior to the 1805–07 defeats, had been far from popular with his subjects and troops because of his alliance with the French emperor. Once the situation was reversed, however, Russia rallied almost to a man to the standard of Alexander and to the defense of the nation. But more than loyalty and enthusiasm was needed to halt the superior French forces. Although the Russians scorched the earth and put up spirited resistance at Smolensk and the battle of Borodino (memorialized later by Leo Tolstoy), the French entered a Moscow in flames by autumn of 1812. Napoleon, who had considered and turned down the idea of driving on to St. Petersburg where Alexander was holed up, waited in Moscow for the tsar to sue for terms.

Aware, as was Napoleon, too, that the French were overextended and had thin to nonexistent lines of communication, Alexander refused to concede. (What the tsar's reaction would have been had the enemy's logistics been better, remains conjecture for Alexander's brave words of defiance were never put to the acid test.) Fortunately, for both opponents, the first winter snows made Napoleon decide to cut his losses and withdraw from Russia as best he could. The great French retreat that followed has been well delineated in song, saga, and oil, emphasizing that Napoleon left Russia at the end of 1812 with no more than 50,000 spent stragglers remaining of his once proud command. What has somewhat escaped that outpouring of chauvinism, however, are the facts that in the War of 1812 Russian troops won no battle at all and that the French were overcome by the same brutal climate, lack of communications, and hostile populace that defeated German sallies into Russia in the following century. Communist artists later depicted Russian peasant resistance to the French, but those versions are also somewhat suspect.

Whatever may have turned the tide in that storied war, Alexander certainly had little to do with it. Nevertheless, by January 1813 he had reassembled his troops and crossed the frontier with the avowed aim of joining Napoleon's foes in liberating Europe. After a series of initial reverses, Russia and her allies of the moment defeated Napoleon at Leipzig in October 1813; at the head of his guards and with his Cossacks putting on a colorful display, Alexander, on a horse once given him by Napoleon, entered Paris in triumph on March 31, 1814, and was hailed as a liberator. Less prominence has been given to the role played in that liberation by a French traitor, Prince Charles Maurice de Talleyrand, Napoleon's trusted advisor, who had long been corresponding secretly with the Russian tsar as "M. Henri."

His head turned by the acclaim he had been accorded in Paris and his subsequent reception at Vienna councils of the victors, international affairs became dominant with Alexander. He fancied himself as both a great military leader and statesman and for all intents and purposes dismissed the equally or more important problems at home with which he had trifled earlier in his reign. The more his ego puffed, the more autocratic he became with his neglected subjects.

Alexander's idea of his supreme venture in the international field was his 1815 brainstorm, the Holy Alliance. He conceived of it as a union of world leaders (with the Pope and the Sultan excluded, Britain and the U.S.A. remaining aloof and lesser rulers not invited) for peace. Actually, it was an extremely imperialistic and repressive

[73]

pact, designed to maintain the frontiers and status quo of the signatories against the growing tide of nationalism. (Exactly such a purpose is behind repeated Soviet efforts for an understanding between Warsaw Pact and NATO powers.)

For his own people, Alexander enacted two measures, both errors and both failures. In 1816 he decided the best way to garrison a large standing army was to establish military colonies whereby troops and peasants were established in new villages where tilling the soil and military drill went on hand-in-hand. To run that experiment, he called in the stern and often brutal Alexis Arakcheyev, once a drill sergeant at Paul's Gatchina establishment. The peasants were loath to quit their native villages and the soldiers cared little for farm work with the result that the colonies were in constant turmoil. In 1819, some 9,000 colony peasants rebelled and had to be flogged into submission. The other equally useless internal venture of the victorious tsar was to tie education on all levels, and especially in the universities, to religion even to the extent that the tenet was established that the Trinity was responsible for the triangle. The setback caused to learning by that innovation is hardly necessary to describe.

But the most serious developments in the internal field, matters which would shake Russia to its foundations and eliminate the Romanov autocracy a century later, came as an indirect result of Alexander's triumph in Paris. In the course of their march across Europe, thousands of Russians, especially educated young officers, had penetrated their country's iron curtain of those days and had seen constitutionalism, free trade and free peasants at work at firsthand. For all, the contrast they had glimpsed between the relative freedom of western Europe and the autocracy, serfdom, and general backwardness of Russia had been a tremendous shock. The situation was much the same as expressed in the popular song that followed World War I which asked, "How you gonna keep 'em down on the farm after they've seen Paree?"

As a result of their sudden new vistas, gatherings of Russia's young men, initially mainly junior officers, started informal discussion groups on their country's problems, upon their return home. They talked openly of putting an end to autocracy and serfdom and establishing constitutional and representative government. At that stage, Alexander, who knew some of the people involved, a few of whom he had talked with in a similar vein in his early days on the throne,

[74]

was sympathetic and was certainly not alarmed. In 1817, some discussion groups coalesced into the "Society of Salvation," a secret organization, although known to Alexander. Shortly, however, that group changed its name to the "Society of Welfare," which soon broke up into the "Northern Union" and the "Southern Union." There was little cohesion or unity of purpose among the members of those early societies but a militant leadership arose in time that advocated the assassination of Alexander (some actually made plans to kill him in 1826) as the only means of eliminating the autocracy. Names that became current in these activites were those of Paul Pestel and Alexander Yakubovish, guards officers, Conrad Ryleyev, a poet and former officer, and Peter Kakhovsky, all young men.

In 1820 Alexander's attitude toward the societies and their leading members changed drastically. That was caused by the mutiny of elements of his own Semenovsky Guards, protesting the harsh discipline of a commander. Alexander learned of the mutiny at an international conference at Troppau. Austria's Prince Klemens von Metternich, the chief statesman of the Holy Alliance, persuaded the tsar to renounce the few liberal ideas he had lest he be faced with worse than a regimental mutiny. Although his attitude hardened, it must be conceded that Alexander took no punitive action against mem-, bers of the secret societies believing that he, himself, had originally participated in and encouraged their "illusions." From 1820 on, however, Count Alexander Benckendorff, at that time chief of staff of the guards, was assigned to keep a watch on the societies, which were soon penetrated by police agents. And it was also in 1820 that Alexander found the writings of the young poet Alexander Pushkin too radical and banished him to Ekaterinoslav.

Partially due to the activities of Count Benckendorff, widespread and extremely seditious plans among guards officers were nipped in the bud in 1824. Again Alexander punished no one. By that time the tsar, who had frequently mentioned abdication, seemed weary of the throne, although then only forty-seven years old, and anxious to pass his duties on to others. Lacking male issue, he had already arranged his succession, having secured renunciation by Constantine, viceroy of Poland and the eldest of his three brothers, to his rights to the throne in 1822 because of a morganatic marriage. That was the stated reason for Constantine's action; actually Constantine wanted to have nothing to do with rule. That done, Alexander secretly

[75]

named his second eldest brother Nicholas as heir, but only hinted to Nicholas that he would be the next tsar; the younger man was never officially informed by Alexander of the arrangement.

In 1824 Alexander took two months to recover from being kicked in the leg by a horse. From that time on he appeared depressed and withdrawn, no longer traveling abroad for great power conferences or even being interested in such affairs. In 1825, he again mentioned his desire to retire and in the autumn of that year he joined the empress, then in ill health, for a vacation at well-isolated Taganrog on the Sea of Azov. There on December 18, 1825, Alexander was reported to have suddenly died of gastric fever. There has been a plethora of fanciful accounts about that death. Some held that he did not die until years later, that the Taganrog death was feigned and that he reappeared either as an ascetic in Siberia or a pilgrim in the Holy Land, that his tomb first contained a body other than his and later no body at all. But even if in death Alexander could continue to be an enigma, the fact of the matter is that his reign ended in 1825.

12. THE BEGINNING OF THE END

Nicholas I (1825–55) was one of the dullest and most despotic of Russian's tsars. A military zealot like his father, he was a very limited man and was called the "Gendarme of Europe" for his almost fanatic maintenance of autocracy and suppression of nationalism. His reign was most unfortunate for his country and subjects since he genuinely believed that the repressive measures and policies he enforced were in the best interests of the general welfare. Actually, however, he was an anachronism at least a century behind his times, who was convinced that he had been commissioned by God and that autocracy was the best form of government, especially for Russia.

Because of Alexander's secrecy and willfulness in arranging his succession, Nicholas' rule was beset with trouble from its very start. For several weeks after the elder brother's death, Constantine as viceroy in Warsaw and Nicholas in St. Petersburg staged the ridiculous spectacle of one proclaiming the other tsar. That silly interlude kindled the hopes of young guard officer firebrands of the Northern Union in the capital and the Southern Union in the Kiev area that the autocracy might be overthrown and constitutional and representative government established. On the very December day that Nicholas finally decided to proclaim himself tsar, several thousand guards, inflamed by Ryleyev, Kakhovsky and such officers as the Princes Sergey Trubetskoy, Eugene Obolensky, and Dimitry Shchepin-Rostovsky, Colonel Alexander Bulatov and two brothers, Alexander and Nikolay Bestuzhevs, mutinied in the heart of the capital, rallying to the cry of "Constantine and Constitution." (Many of the peasants in the rebel ranks believed that Constitution [Konstitutsia] was Constantine's wife.)

There were several useless parleys with the mutineers—in one of which St. Petersburg Governor-General Mikhail Miloradovich was shot and killed by Kakhovsky—before Nicholas arrived on the scene with loyal troops and artillery. The rebels were routed with grape shot; several score were killed and wounded. Somewhat concurrently with the mutiny in the capital, several thousand troops in the Kiev area, led by Colonel Paul Pestel, Sergey Muravyev-Apostol, and Mikhail Bestuzhev-Ryumin, also rose but were easily subdued, also with artillery. Nicholas supervised the investigation that followed, personally interviewing some of the ringleaders. Some 2,500 soldiers and civilians and about 600 officers were arrested. Nicholas reinstituted capital punishment, last used against Pugachev, and ordered the executions of Ryleyev, Kakhovsky, Pestel, Muravyev-Apostol, and Mikhail Bestuzhev-Ryumin. Thirty-one other principals were sentenced to hard labor for life in Siberia and an additional eighty-five were either exiled to Siberia for lesser terms or banished to provincial regiments. Those rebels who have come down in history as the Decembrists, have been called Russia's first revolutionists by some. Such a title is not correct since they neither had nor sought the support of the rank and file of the Russian nation. They were, however, both the first Russians to try to overthrow autocracy and the last threat to the dynasty by the guards.

As an organization, the Decembrists were never heard of again, but they were responsible for Nicholas' establishment of a police state in 1826. For that departure, he set up a new unit in the imperial chancery, the Third Section, and organized the Corps of Gendarmes. The Third Section was a civilian intelligence agency that controlled both its own networks of spies and *agents provocateurs* and the uniformed gendarmes. Count Alexander Benckendorff was named chief of both groups. Although the Third Section became "dreaded," it was a very weak forerunner indeed of the subsequent internal police organizations of Hitler and Stalin and his successors. In the capital and in a few other large cities, it was quite effective in hamstringing political thought and action, censoring books and publications and eliminating liberals from the educational field; in the provinces, however, it never really knew what was going on and certainly never exercised complete control. Best evidence of its incapability in the countryside were the more than 700 major uprisings of serfs that plagued Nicholas' reign, Nicholas' supervision of suppression of a military colony revolt for which 129 rebels were flogged to death, or the fact of forty-four serfs beaten to death, forty-two blinded, and thirteen otherwise mutilated on the estate of Prince Radziwill in one year.

Toward the end of his reign, perhaps because of the shoddy overall activity of the Third Section and the gendarmes, Nicholas declared, "I have no police, I dislike it." Nevertheless, in the large cities at least, he had the best organized and most oppressive police state of the era, and there his motto of "orthodoxy, autocracy, and nationality" was ruthlessly pursued.

Since the intellectuals and liberals gravitated to the cities, the scene of Russia's infant publishing and newspaper industries, and where they could meet and converse with their fellows, it was the intelligent people of Russia who took the brunt of Nicholas' reactionary policies. The choice for those unfortunates was extremely limited: either suppress their opinions and politics or face possible execution or exile or eliminate themselves from active participation by fleeing the country. One of the most notorious to take the latter route after long exile in Siberia was the aristocrat Mikhail Bakunin, the father of anarchism and one of the first Socialists. Feodor Dostoyevsky (and twenty others) was actually before a firing squad for being in a pro-Socialist group only to have a tsar's messenger commute the sentence to penal servitude at the last moment. Taras Shevchenko, the great Ukrainian nationalist, poet and painter, was exiled at hard labor. Mikhail Lermontov, the poet, was sent to the Caucasus for his reaction to the death of Alexander Pushkin in a one-sided duel. Alexander Herzen, the publicist, was exiled to Siberia and later left Russia for western Europe, as did Nikolay Gogol, the playwright, and Ivan Turgenev, the novelist. Peter Chaadayev, the writer and philosopher, was ordered declared insane by Nicholas himself for writing a diatribe about Russia's backwardness.

Nicholas was equally inept, bungling, and reactionary in foreign affairs whenever confronted with a major problem or adversary. Against a lesser foe, Persia, he did quite well in an 1826–28 war, acquiring territory along both sides of the Caspian and gaining Russian access to that sea. Fortune smiled on him again in an 1828–29 war with Turkey, by which further Slav autonomy in the Balkans was achieved and Greece won her independence, although Nicholas regarded the Greek liberators as rebels. In 1830, once more against an extremely weak adversary, Nicholas' forces mercilessly crushed a Polish uprising, eliminated Polish history from the books, enforced Russification and censorship, and did their utmost to wipe out Polish nationalism. And yet again, in 1849 Nicholas obliterated a weaker opponent, sending 150,000 troops to Hungary to quell Lajos Kossuth's bid for liberation from the Hapsburg's dual monarchy.

Earlier, in 1833, Nicholas had concluded a new Holy Alliance with Austria and Prussia in hopes of bolstering autocracy and checking the nationalism sweeping Europe. That alliance, however, did Russia no good whatsoever when she went down to defeat before major foes in the 1854–56 Crimean War, a conflict and outcome that could have been avoided if Russia had had an abler leader. Austria and Prussia remained aloof from the Crimean debacle while numerically much stronger but poorly armed and equipped Russian forces—despite Nicholas' posture as a military man—proved no match for the better equipped and better supplied troops of the British, French, and Turks, and even the Sardinians.

No doubt dispirited but as autocractic as ever, Nicholas died of a cold in early 1855 before the fall of the great bastion of Sevastopol had brought Russia to final defeat. His thirty-year reign had been a disaster for Russia internally and externally. On the one hand, by his repressive measures he had sowed all the seeds for the eventual dissolution of the dynasty. On the other hand, the combination of his complete lack of diplomacy and pigheaded insistence on colorful but greatly outmoded parade ground drill instead of newer equipment and techniques for his armed forces eliminated Russia as a great power and an influence in world affairs, a position she was not to reattain for almost another century.

13. TERROR

Nicholas had done his best to make his eldest son and successor, Alexander II (1855–81), as much a military man as he had aspired to be himself. Alexander's military training had started at the age of six, but that had been leavened somewhat by the influence of the heir's tutor, the poet Vasily Zhukovsky, a friend of Pushkin. Nevertheless, Zhukovsky's best efforts did not prevent his charge from becoming another parade ground tsar, in the best tradition of Paul and all the other autocrats who came after him.

Partially as the result of his mixed educational background, Alexander was a very conservative ruler, although essentially humane, an autocrat, benevolent at least in the first part of his reign, and Russia's last real tsar. The chief features of his rule were emancipation of the serfs and other reforms, all long overdue and most of them poorly executed, vast territorial expansion to the east and south, and the rise of a small but fanatic cult of revolutionaries, terrorists, and assassins committed to the overthrow of the autocracy.

His first task upon succession was settlement of the Crimean imbroglio. Not only deserted but threatened by his Holy Alliance partner Austria, he gained peace by reluctantly giving up part of Bessarabia and the Turkish bastion of Kars as well as surrendering rights to maintain warships and fortresses on the Black Sea. Foreign affairs thus in hand, he then attempted to put his internal house in order.

It had taken the humiliation of the Crimean War, not qualms of conscience or a sudden social awareness, to bring it home to the autocracy that Russia, despite her numbers, was in no position to compete with Europe militarily, economically, or in any other fashion, so long as her way of life was backward and based on serfdom and feudalism.

The process of liberating the serfs was painful, with landowners and other reactionaries opposing it at every step. After six years of arguments, however, the ukase of emancipation was finally issued on March 5, 1861. Better than America's subsequent emancipation of her Negro slaves, it gave rights of land ownership to the twenty million serfs, but was critically received by both serfs and landowners, since it was a poor compromise that satisfied neither. In the first year of emancipation, there were some 500 peasant risings; in one disturbance, at Bezdna, students demonstrated in sympathy when fifty peasants were killed, another 300 wounded, and their leader executed as a result of dissatisfaction with the ukase.

At the start of his reign, Alexander was also benign in other respects: Nicholas' restrictions on travel abroad were lifted, censorship and student controls were modified, Dostoyevsky was allowed back from Siberian exile, and there was a general amnesty for all surviving Decembrists. In 1863, he decreed educational and court reforms; by the first, some of Nicholas' controls were relaxed, but never fully, and greater opportunity for schooling was given the rank and file; by the second, trial by jury and tenure of judges were partially established, but branding and flogging were retained. In the period 1861–65, Alexander also applied his advisors to reforms in the armed services, but there, too, because of opposition from old-time military chiefs, little was accomplished except for the establishment of universal military service.

An appreciation of the stopgap approach of Alexander to the basic problems of Russia was obtained in 1862, when thirteen nobles of Tver, no doubt carried away by the emancipation of the preceding year, dared to propose a limitation of the autocracy. That brash lot was thrown forthwith into the Peter and Paul fortress. After being declared lunatics all, they were later released with loss of civil rights. Alexander's real attitude to subject foreigners was just as backward and severe. Initially he had indicated support for Polish nationalist aspirations. In 1863–64, however, when the Poles tried to make fact out of that hope, he not only cruelly suppressed their insurrection, but even eliminated Poland as a name and called that area under his control the "Ten Provinces of the Vistula."

The last of Alexander's reforms was the institution of the "Zemstvos," a modified form of local self-government, in 1864. At first those groups were welcomed enthusiastically with many qualified men seeking local office, but when it became apparent that scope of the Zemstvos encompassed only local tax collection and education, interest speedily waned. The Zemstvos were not even the prototypes of representative government, nor were they meant to be more than a sop to keep the politically interested out of serious affairs. Concurrently, a move to reestablish some type of town and city government died stillborn. Additionally, local self-government in any form under Alexander was extended only to the Russian-populated provinces, never to the areas peopled by non-Russian subjects.

Alexander's great territorial acquisitions were pure happenstance. Not only did he have nothing to do with gaining them, but it was an almost embarrassing fact that Russia waxed greater without Alex-

[81]

ander even being consulted. Blocked by the Crimean debacle from further meaningful activity in Europe, his generals and captains turned south and east. For a while they considered a penetration of India, but a subdued roar from the British diverted them to easier prey. Therefore, more or less to keep themselves occupied, Russia's imperialists of that era took territory east of the Amur River from a debilitated China in 1857–60, completed annexation of the relatively primitive Caucasus in 1859 and by 1865 had completed seizure of such famed but moribund cities as Bukhara, Samarkand, and Tashkent and incorporated adjoining areas of Central Asia into the Russian empire. The Russian navy also registered a new departure in this era with fleets making formal visits to New York and San Francisco at the height of the American Civil War in 1863. Four years later Alexander sold Alaska to the U.S.A. for a pittance. He attempted unsuccessfully to capitalize on that bargain in 1871–72 when he dispatched his third son, the Grand Duke Alexis, on a grand but meaningless tour of the U.S.

The only serious venture into foreign affairs of the "Tsar Liberator," as his lackeys called him after the emancipation, came when he acceded to Pan-Slav pressure to intervene in Balkan struggles for independence and thus got Russia involved in yet another war with Turkey, that of 1877–78. Alexander had been able to prepare for that conflict by taking advantage of Europe's preoccupation with the 1870–71 Franco-Prussian War to abrogate part of the Crimean War treaty and return warships to the Black Sea and rebuild fortresses there. Although Russian troops fought almost to the threshold of Constantinople, European opposition, primarily that of Britain, blocked the victory that Alexander might have attained, and essentially, the result was a diplomatic defeat for Russia. Territorially, Alexander gained southern Bessarabia and Turkish-held Ardahan, Batum, and Kars. Politically, however, he had to agree to Bulgaria, liberated by Russian troops, being divorced from his sphere of influence and to the provinces of Bosnia and Herzegovina going under Austrian control.

In the 1860s, while Alexander was busy with reforms and acceptance of territory proffered by his generals, Russia was experiencing the emergence of an intelligentsia, primarily radical in political outlook. That intelligentsia was a decidedly new departure, being composed of people, all young, drawn from a cross section of the nation, an all-union combination of noblemen, technicians, workers, ex-serfs, and sons of serfs. The first to blossom were the Nihilists of Dimitry Pisarev, the Socialists of Nikolay Chernyshevsky, and the so-called Russian Revolutionary Committee, led by the psychotic Sergey Nechayev, sanctified by latter-day revolutionists. At the start, those groups were little more than collections of dreamers, idealists, and idle chatterers and might have amounted to nought had they been in a more enlightened milieu. However, since they were in autocratic and despotic Russia, they soon ran afoul of the ubiquitous Third Section. For talk and scheming that would have been laughed off or dismissed in civilized Europe, those youngsters were treated as most dangerous criminals, raided, rounded up, tried, imprisoned, or sent into exile. The result was that the more dedicated, the cleverer, soon either fled to Europe, usually Switzerland, or went underground in Russia. Although pitifully small and badly splintered, those groups of youngsters literally went to war on autocracy.

At the outset, the battle was sporadic. The first blow struck was lone and erratic: in April, 1866, while Alexander was entering his carriage in St. Petersburg, he was shot at and missed by Dimitry Karakozov, an unbalanced youth who was speedily hanged. The police used the attempt as an excuse to round up other young radicals even though it was known that Karakozov was a lone operator and had no organization behind him. A year later, in Paris, a Polish woman tried unsuccessfully to shoot down Alexander while he was riding in a procession with Napoleon III. Obvious nationalism, not opposition to autocracy, was the motive of that attempt.

In 1871, the mentally disturbed Nechayev was imprisoned for life in the Peter and Paul Fortress—where he subsequently died of malnutrition—for the cold-blooded murder of Ivan Ivanov, a wavering disciple. Because of the collusion of his guards, Nechayev was able to keep the spark of revolt alive by letters from the prison. In 1874, partially inspired by Nechayev, the Populist (Narodnik) movement got under way with students and intellectuals going to the provinces, trying to educate the peasants politically and make them aware of the injustices being done them. The movement failed because the peasants were interested only in land, not in politics, but that did not prevent mass arrests and exile of the activists, often on direct orders of Alexander. By that time, the tsar's early liberalism had switched to rigid conservatism, mainly as a result of the premature death of his eldest and favorite son Nicholas in 1865, and the Karakozov attempt of the following year.

The Narodnik movement virtually destroyed both by peasant disinterest and police activity, the youthful opponents of the regime regrouped into the *Land and Freedom* (Zemlya I Volya) society. In 1876, members of that organization, influenced by Georgi Plekhanov, then a Socialist but later Russia's first Marxist, and led by Alexis Bogolyubov and others, demonstrated, in the main peacefully, in front of St. Petersburg's Kazan Cathedral. Police broke up the gathering and imprisoned its leaders. Some two years later, on the grounds that Bogolyubov had been flogged in prison, Vera Zasulich, Russia's first female revolutionary terrorist to take to the streets, shot and seriously wounded General Fedor Trepov, the capital's police chief. At the trial, the jury acquitted the young woman, to the indignation of Alexander and his police. Zasulich escaped efforts to rearrest her on other charges by fleeing abroad to Switzerland, but as the result of her acquittal the tsar re-formed military tribunals to try political cases.

Although unsuccessful, the Zasulich attempt marked the beginning of a three-year period of terrorism throughout Russia. Later in 1873, Sergey Kravchinsky, a former artillery officer with the revolutionary pseudonym of Stepnyak, used a sword in broad daylight in St. Petersburg to murder General Nikolay Mezentsov, chief of the Third Section, and then escaped abroad to write of his exploits. In February 1879, the governor-general of Kharkov, Prince Dimitry Kropotkin, a cousin of the notorious anarchist Prince Peter Kropotkin, was assassinated while leaving a theater by Grigory Goldenberg, a young Ukrainian Jew, who escaped but was arrested later and turned into a police agent. In March 1879, the new (and last) chief of the Third Section, General Alexander Drenteln, was wounded in St. Petersburg by the handsome, young, and hot-blooded aristocratic dandy Leon Mirsky, who also became a Third Section informer after imprisonment; and in April, 1879, Alexander was barely missed by five shots fired at him outside the Winter Palace by Alexander Solovyev, another young revolutionary whom Nechayev claimed as one of his adherents, and who was captured and executed.

At a general meeting in mid-1879, the *Land and Freedom* society split into two factions, a moderate one, led by Plekhanov and called the *Black Partition* (because it pursued the peasants of the black earth) and which soon disintegrated, and a radical wing of assassins and revolutionaries. Those extremists took the name of *People's Will* (Narodnaya Volya). They were led by Sophia Perovskaya, a young noblewoman and the daughter of a dismissed governor-general of St. Petersburg, and her lover, Andrey Zhelyabov, a Ukrainian of peasant origin, who claimed to be a metal worker, although there is no record of his having practiced that or any other trade, except that of a revolutionary.

In September, 1879, in the first of the many manifestos and communiqués it was to issue, *People's Will*'s executive committee condemned Alexander Romanov to death. Zhelyabov and others set out almost immediately to carry out the threat by mining the tracks of the railroad train by which Alexander was scheduled to return from a visit to the Crimea. In three attempts they succeeded only in blowing up the tsar's baggage train. After those failures (for which two conspirators were caught and executed in 1880), the committee succeeded in infiltrating a daring young peasant, Stepan Khalturin, into the Winter Palace as an ikon refinisher. For several months, completely undetected, Khalturin brought dynamite in small quantities into the palace for what was truly an infernal machine that he set up beneath the imperial dining room. On the evening of February 5, 1880, he set the charge and left the building, escaping eventually to Rumania. The device went off as scheduled but Alexander was unscathed due to the half-hour delay in the arrival of a guest, Prince Alexander of Battenberg. The unintended victims were ten Finnish guards killed, another thirty-three wounded and twenty-three civilians injured. St. Petersburg was put under a virtual state of siege, but Khalturin was not apprehended and executed until March 1882, when he returned to Russia and together with Nikolay Zhelvakov, another member of *People's Will*, killed Military Prosecutor General Strelnikov on a street in Odessa.

Finally alarmed by the Winter Palace attempt, if not by earlier actions of the terrorists, Alexander gave what was tantamount to dictatorial powers to an Armenian petty noble, Count Mikhail Loris-Melikov, who had a distinguished record as a civil administrator and as an able general in the Turkish war. Within days of taking office, Loris-Melikov was shot at—but missed—by Ippolit Mledecki, a converted Ukrainian Jew. Caught, Mledecki was tried and hanged forty-eight hours later as the new security boss took severe measures lest another outrage endanger the constitution he hoped to persuade Alexander to approve.

Later, establishing what he called a "dictatorship of the heart," Loris-Melikov abolished the Third Section (on paper, at least) and put all police powers in the hands of Count Vyacheslav Plehve, chief of the *gendarmerie*. Political prisoners were given amnesty in batches, censorship was relaxed, powers which Alexander had whittled away were restored to the Zemstvos. There were no terrorist attacks throughout the remainder of 1880, giving Loris-Melikov new hope that the tide had turned to the extent he could get Alexander's approval of a constitution.

The inactivity of the terrorists proved, however, to be little more than the lull before the storm. In actual fact, the executive committee of the *People's Will* had used the period of relaxation to gird its loins and had kept its hand expert in the use of explosives by mining several streets and bridges in St. Petersburg over which Alexander might pass.

In January, 1881, however, the final entrapment of a former Third Section clerk, who had long been supplying the *People's Will* with names of police agents and other security information, forced the terrorists to push almost frantically toward their ultimate goal. Roundups of terrorists followed the police clerk's apprehension. And among those arrested was Zhelyabov, who hinted to police that a major attempt against Alexander was in preparation.

The day after Sophia Perovskaya's lover's arrest, March 12, Alexander was advised of Zhelyabov's revelation. On March 13, a Sunday, after signing preliminary drafts of Loris-Melikov's constitutional reform, Alexander reviewed a guards formation and then called at the residence of his cousin, the Grand Duchess Catherine.

Meanwhile, four members of the *People's Will*, Ivan Yemelyanov, a 19-year-old student, Nikolay Rysakov, a mining student, Ignaty Grinevitsky, a graduate student and Polish aristocrat, and Timofey Mikhaylov, a metal worker, had been armed with bombs and posted on the streets along which Alexander might have passed. The bombs, stored in the apartment of Gesya Helfman, a Ukrainian Jewess, had been made by Nikolay Kibalchich, the brilliant son of a priest and a former engineering student who might have been one of Russia's great scientists had he not chosen the role of revolutionary. Although there was hardly a denizen of St. Petersburg who could not recognize

Alexander and his entourage by sight, for some reason never explained Sophia Perovskaya was posted at a strategic elevation with a white handkerchief to signal to the bomb throwers as the tsar approached.

Aware (as the result of Zhelyabov's arrest) of the mined streets and bridges, Alexander altered his route home from the grand duchess' to the Winter Palace and was driven along the Catherine Canal which the police had reported as safe. The terrorists, however, were acquainted with the change, doubtless from Perovskaya who maintained good connections in the court despite her politics. Yemelyanov did not throw his bomb as the imperial entourage passed, planning to hem it in, in case the tsar reversed his course. At the signal from Perovskaya, the second bomber, Rysakov, tossed his device, enveloping the cavalcade in smoke and flame. Several members of the Cossack escort took the brunt of the blast, and Alexander, who apparently had escaped unharmed, got out of his carriage to see to the wounded. At that moment, Grinevitsky threw his bomb. Alexander, his legs almost severed from his body, was mortally wounded, as was Grinevitsky. Alexander demanded he be taken home to the palace, where he died shortly after arrival in the arms of his morganatic wife, Princess Catherine (Dolgoruky) Yuryevsky.

The reign of Alexander III (1881–94), the second son of the "tsar liberator," was a period in which Russia virtually stood still, making no progress whatsoever in any field except her economy. A brute of a man, called "the bull" by many, Alexander III could bend a horseshoe in his hands and stood six feet three inches, the tallest tsar since Peter the Great. His thinking and every action were molded and directed by his former tutor, Constantine Pobedonostsev, a reactionary, archconservative, with a fanatic belief in autocracy, regarded by Loris-Melikov as a relic of the sixteenth century, who functioned as the tsar's "gray eminence."

Shortly after his father's assassination, Alexander III moved permanently to Gatchina, where surrounded by four special guard units he was almost a prisoner. Almost as could have been expected, his father's proposed constitution was completely disregarded and Loris-Melikov was dismissed. Suppression was the order of the day and the chief characteristic of a dismal reign.

Plehve was assigned to the assassins' case. Rysakov confessed and in April, 1881, he, Zhelyabov, Perovskaya, Kibalchich, and Mikhaylov were hanged before a great crowd in St. Petersburg, the last public executions to be staged in the capital. Because she was pregnant, the death sentence against Helfman was commuted to life in prison, where she died within the year, a madwoman.

The year 1881 was also the date of promulgation of a special edict, in effect martial law, by which entire districts were made subject to arbitrary search, seizure, arrest, and imprisonment without trial and the Third Section was reestablished, but under the new name of Okhrana. Both the special law and the Okhrana were to last until the overthrow of the autocracy. In the first years of Alexander's reign, isolated acts of terrorism continued but the effect of the special law and the powers of the Okhrana became overwhelming by 1884 when some 400 suspected revolutionaries were rounded up and the *People's Will* thereby eliminated as an effective organization. Despite the disappearance of *People's Will* from the scene, in 1887 the Okhrana claimed to have discovered a plot to assassinate the tsar. Among those arrested were Alexander Ulyanov, the elder brother of Lenin, and Joseph Pilsudski, the future dictator of Poland. Ulyanov and four others were executed; Pilsudski was among those exiled to Siberia. An attempted plot was rumored in 1888, when a train carrying Alexander and his family derailed and wrecked at Borki. There were no fatalities or injuries in the royal car, but twenty-one other people were killed. Subsequently, the young railroad official Sergey Witte, who was later to become tsar of Russia's economy, determined that the accident had been caused by excessive speed.

Early in Alexander's thirteen-year term of misrule, new and repressive measures were enacted against education and the press and a wave of anti-Semitism swept the country, the latter not discouraged by either the tsar or Pobedonostsev. Secondary schooling was forbidden to the lower classes, autonomy was taken from the universities, student clubs were banned, further Russification was enforced in Poland, the Baltic provinces, Finland, and Central Asia, liberal newspapers were closed down and the importation of all modern Western books was prohibited with the sole exception of Marx' *Das Kapital*, probably because that text was too abstruse for the censors. The anti-Semitism, partially induced by the role of Helfman in Alexander II's assassination, was marked by 215 pogroms in the first year of Alexander III's reign and the emigration of almost one million Jews from Russian territories in 1882. The educational controls provoked student revolts, unrest which continued into the reign of Alexander's successor. The major university risings under Alexander were those of 1882 in Kazan and St. Petersburg and of 1887 in Moscow, Odessa, Kharkov, and Kazan, which resulted in hundreds of students being banned from the universities or exiled to Siberia.

With Alexander as no more than a bystander and with Witte at the helm, Russia entered the industrial age in the final decades of the nineteenth century. New factories, steel, cotton, flax and other textile processing plants opened in every major city. The manufacture of vodka was made a state monopoly and continues as such to the present. Worked originally by exiled forced labor, the gold mines and the other vast natural resources of Siberia were further developed by Witte, primarily by linking Vladivostok with the West with the Trans-Siberian railroad, which that financial genius started in 1891. A byproduct of that expansion of production and trade was the development of a proletariat as peasants moved to the cities for work in the factories. Alexander refused to regard those new workers as any more than peasants temporarily removed to the cities, but Plekhanov and his followers appreciated their potential political impact and introduced Marxism to the factory hands. A severe blow to the expansion of the economy was dealt by the disastrous drought of 1891. Since the government had been exporting grain, there were no reserves with the result that the country underwent a great famine, followed by a cholera epidemic, in 1891–93. Although many foreign nations, including the U.S.A., gave aid to the victims, the real heroes of the calamity were the Zemstvos, which became the best relief organization and thus gave the peasants some appreciation of the faults of autocracy.

About the only good thing that can be said about Alexander III is that he kept his country out of war, but even that has to be tempered by the understanding that Alexander was fortunate rather than wise. In 1882 Russia was again isolated from Western Europe when Austria, Germany, and Italy formed their Triple Alliance. As after the Crimean War, Russia again turned to petty imperialism, the conquest of primitive neighbors, driving to the Afghanistan border by taking the Merv Oasis in 1884, and crushing the tribesmen of the Pamir Mountains in 1891. In 1886, Alexander tried to make a super-puppet out of his cousin, Prince Alexander of Battenberg, the ruler of Bulgaria, with the result that Battenberg was ousted and a pro-Austrian ruler installed in his place in Sofia. Left with no ally in Europe except tiny Montenegro because of his Bulgarian intervention, Alexander finally had to turn for friendship to none other than France, the cockpit of revolution and liberalism, as well as a source of loans and matériel of war.

A baffled but unrepentant anachronism, Alexander died of nephritis in November 1894, leaving an awakening volcano for his heir, the last and weakest tsar of all.

14. GÖTTERDÄMMERUNG RUSSIAN-STYLE

Nothing much good can be said about Nicholas II (1894–1917) except that he was not an evil man. It is also true that too much has been said about him: had he lived in an earlier era, when diaries were not fashionable, letters were not preserved en masse, memoirs were not compulsive, photography and current journalism yet unborn, a more balanced and proportioned view of the man might have been obtained.

Last tsar of the Russians, he was indeed a little man, not only in stature, but also in character and intelligence. He was sometimes called the "Little Colonel." Actually, the "Little Lance Corporal" would have been more appropriate. He could run nothing; everything he tried to handle went awry; he knew nothing about people and he learned nothing by experience. Fate could not have picked a more unqualified man to rule the empire, especially at the time of his reign. In vulgar terms, he literally did not know which end was up.

Granted he was kind and well-mannered, but let the plaudits end there. Otherwise, he was a cross on the back of his country, a disaster for Russia and a real plague for the rest of the Romanovs, all of whom seemed men of parts as compared to him. Perhaps it was because the dynasty had been too long inbred. Instead of ruling, he was indecisive and weak-willed, and merely played at being tsar.

As if that were not enough on the minus side, he married yet another petty German princess, whose chief claims to distinction were that she was a granddaughter of Britain's Victoria and carried hemophilia in her veins. Renamed Alexandra Fedorovna for Orthodox proprieties, at first she was reluctant in conversion to the Russian faith and then became a fanatic. An extremely narrow-minded, bigoted and really ignorant woman, she dominated Nicholas until his very death. It was Alexandra Fedorovna who wore the pants in that period of misrule.

Nicholas' reign started most inauspiciously. As part of his coronation festivities, food, drink, and trinkets were distributed to the lower classes at Khodynka field outside Moscow. Poorly handled, the crowd of some three hundred thousand panicked and before calm had been restored several hundred had been trampled or crushed to death. Nevertheless, that night, with the Kremlin festooned with lights, the new tsar was insensitive enough to carry on with the evening's reception as scheduled. From that time on, he was known by his opponents among the people as "Bloody Nicholas." Certainly, that cognomen was an exaggeration for such a wan character as Nicholas. However, it is a fact that whether he willed it or not more people were killed, imprisoned and exiled during his reign, and as a result of his reign, than in any comparative period in Russian history, with the sole exception of the Communist era.

Despite Khodynka, in the beginning of Nicholas' reign there were many who hoped that he would be an enlightened monarch who would bring constitutional and representative government to his nation. But he speedily showed himself an antediluvian believer in autocracy and his divine rights, a misconception supported to the hilt by the tsarina. Blunt indication of that was given in early 1895 when Fedor Rodichev of the Tver Zemstvo somewhat naïvely supplicated him to give the people greater participation in the nation's affairs. Not only was Rodichev turned down cold, but for his effrontery he was banned from St. Petersburg.

Nicholas' reaction to that simple plea of Rodichev was received as a direct challenge by the tiny corps of terrorists living abroad. Ever since the assassination of Alexander II, that group had been decimated and made relatively inactive by the Okhrana. Given a new spur by the Rodichev incident, survivors of the Narodniks and the *People's Will* reorganized in 1895 and formed the Socialist Revolutionary Party, later more familiarly known as the SRs. That was the first Russian political party, and the one that did the most and sacrificed the most members to overthrow the autocracy. It appealed primarily to the peasants—with varying success—and to the intelligentsia. The second Russian party, the Social Democratic Workmen's Party, or SDs, was not organized until 1898. It concentrated on the

[91]

proletariat. At a meeting in London in 1903, the SDs split into the Bolsheviks (majority), who sought immediate revolution and dictatorship of the proletariat under the aegis of Lenin, and the Mensheviks (minority), who favored a more gradual course toward Marxism under the leadership of Plekhanov and with the early support of Leon Trotsky. Russia's other two parties of note, the Constitutional Democrats, known as Kadets, and the Octobrists, both moderate, liberal groups, were not formed until 1906.

In their formative years, the political parties posed no special threat to the autocracy. What did plague it in that period was continuing unrest among the students, workers, and peasants. The students sparked the troubles. In 1896, they went on rampage in Moscow and after being suppressed by Cossacks had 400 of their fellows imprisoned, another 150 exiled to the provinces and Siberia and scores of others expelled from the university. In 1899, Cossacks used whips against them when they rose in St. Petersburg, but the troubles spread to Moscow to be put down only after numbers of rebellious students were forcibly enlisted in the army; and in 1900, a gathering of hundreds of Kiev students was surrounded by Cossacks, with the result that 500 were arrested, out of which 183 were put into the army and the rest expelled, but nevertheless student rebellions followed in Moscow, Kharkov, and St. Petersburg. The student unrest reached a high water mark in 1901 with the assassination of Professor Nikolay Bogolepov, the reactionary minister of education, by a university expellee Peter Karpovich, one of the most redoubtable of the SR terrorists.

The early workers' protests were marked by strikes, particularly in 1896–97. For almost a decade after that, however, strikes were limited in effectiveness, due to the ingenuity of a most unusual Okhrana chief, Sergey Zubatov, and the naïvete of the workers. With the connivance of Moscow's governor-general, the tsar's uncle, the Grand Duke Sergey, Zubatov established Okhrana-controlled unions in which police agents saw to it that most of the worker's demands were met. Peasant unrest at the turn of the century was widespread, with the most serious trouble occurring in 1902 in Poltava province where they burned and looted farms, and murdered landowners before troops were sent in and thousands were arrested.

In that same period, almost as a footnote to history, and decidedly not as the mythology it later became, political activity was begun by a pair of men who subsequently had a most telling effect on Russian and world events. In 1895, Lenin was arrested in St. Petersburg, while spreading Marxist propaganda among workers, and was given three years of rather comfortable exile in Siberia before leaving for Switzerland and seventeen years of unimpeded plotting and planning. And in 1902, Joseph Vissarionovich Dzhugashvili (Stalin) was arrested in Georgia for indoctrinating oil field workers with SD tenets. Exiled to Siberia for that, Stalin escaped (the first of his six escapes from tsarist authorities) and had his first meeting with Lenin at an SD gathering at Tammerfors, Finland, in 1906. And that is the sum total of what those two men did to overthrow the autocracy, if one overlooks a little plain thieving by Stalin.

The real threat to the autocracy at that time was posed by the SRs and its terrorist group, known as the Battle Organization. Terror had always been the handmaiden of the Narodniks, the *People's Will* and their successor, the SR, but it was not until 1902 that the Battle Organization was formed with the specific mission of assassinating all supporters of the autocracy, up to and including the tsar. The chief figure in that group was an able and still quite mysterious Jew named Yevno Azev (Aseff), who had voluntarily joined the Okhrana as an agent in 1893, but nevertheless managed to run the Battle Organization until 1908, when he was exposed by the loose tongue of a deposed, high-ranking Okhrana officer. Despite his double-dealing, Azev had been so effective that after his exposure the Battle Organization fell apart, partially due to the loss of his direction, but also because the SR had surfaced from an underground group into a legitimate party. In its heyday, the Battle Organization had hundreds of fanatic, self-sacrificing young people on its rolls (many of whom Azev delivered to the Okhrana), but those who played a major part were Bogolepov's assassin Karpovich, Grigory Gershuni, Igor Sazonov, Ivan Kalyayev and Boris Savinkov.

The Battle Organization's first major act was the assassination of Dimitry Sipyagin, the interior minister, in 1902. Gershuni masterminded that deed and the actual killing was done by Stepan Balmashev who was subsequently hanged. In 1903, General Nikolay Bogdanovich, the governor-general of Ufa, was murdered for having ordered troops to fire on strikers. In 1904, the new minister of the interior, Plehve (a constant consultant of Azev's and the man who had also run the police for Nicholas' father and grandfather), was killed by a bomb thrown by Sazonov (who later committed suicide in Siberian internment). And in 1905, the Grand Duke Sergey was similarly killed by Kalyayev outside Moscow's Kremlin. Azev's last operation, the assassination of the tsar himself, in 1908 aboard a warship, was not successful only because the sailor assigned to do the killing changed his mind at the last moment. (Azev died of natural causes in Berlin in 1918; Karpovich was a member of the provisional government that followed Nicholas' abdication; and Savinkov, lured back to Russia after the Bolshevik take-over, died in OGPU hands in Moscow in 1925.)

Nicholas seemed completely unaware of the long-range effect on autocracy of the rise of political parties, even though underground. Thinking his antiquated system would go on forever, if only his bureaucracy would properly acquit itself of its duties, he toyed instead with the concept of empire, when not in the bosom of his family, the only vocation he was really cut out for. In 1903, thinking to get a tighter hold on Finland, despite solemn agreements for its virtual autonomy, he launched a program of Russification of the grand duchy. To carry out the program, he named the severe General Nikolay Bobrikov as governor-general of Finland. The Finns proved too tough, however, and in 1904 the Russification program went by the boards after Bobrikov was assassinated by a Finnish student. And it was in 1903 that Nicholas' Okhrana published the infamous fabrication the *Protocols of the Learned Elders of Zion*, according to which Jews went in for the ritual killing of Christians. The result of that was pogroms, the worst being the Kishinev massacre in which hundreds of Jews were killed or wounded. Since Nicholas himself was almost openly anti-Semitic, the police either encouraged or did nothing to stop those atrocities.

Distraction from disorders at home was offered in early 1904 with the outbreak of war with Japan. Japan was annoyed with Russian encroachments in the Far East and particularly with her tardy withdrawal of troops sent into Manchuria for the Boxer Rebellion of 1900. Nicholas grabbed at that conflict (the Russo-Japanese War, 1904–05) with the hopes of a speedy victory to brighten his image and on the advice of some ministers, including Plehve, not yet bombed to death, who was reported as saying a "small, victorious war" was the proper recipe to solve internal troubles. Initially the nation backed Nicholas enthusiastically, mainly because Japan had attacked without formal declaration of war, but that support was soon lost when the conflict proved to be far from victorious, although fairly speedy and small. In fact, the war was a catastrophe for Russian arms—a series of disastrous defeats on land and at sea.

All that was gained from those engagements was the establishment of Japan as a first-class power. But they also showed up the bankruptcy of the Russian regime and the tsar's utter incompetence as an administrator, plus the basic military unfitness of that last parade ground soldier-ruler of Russia. Of course, Nicholas himself had little appreciation of that: his attention then was riveted on the birth in the war's last month of an heir, the Tsarevich Alexis. The boy was most welcome since Nicholas' other four children were all girls, but the joy over his arrival was short-lived. Within six weeks after Alexis' birth he was found to be afflicted with hemophilia. That discovery made the tsarina even more erratic and psychopathic and, in the opinion of eminent historians, distracted Nicholas from the business of ruling.

Nicholas' distraction with Alexis did nothing to allay his nation's dissatisfaction with the war in particular and life in general. Even before peace had been made, the country was racked with disorder and discontent, practically from border to border. Plehve's assassination was one sign of the unrest. Another and far more serious indication of trouble was the increasing organization of workers and strikes for better pay and working conditions and shorter hours in St. Petersburg and the other large cities.

That unrest came to a head in St. Petersburg on Sunday, January 9 (22), 1905, ever after known as "Bloody Sunday." Thousands of workers had been on strike. The Okhrana thought everything was under control. Using the system originated by Zubatov, they had an agent of theirs, Father Georgy Gapon, a somewhat deranged priest, leading the workers. The plan was to petition the tsar at the Winter Palace, although none apparently knew that Nicholas had abandoned that residence for good earlier in the month after a gun in the Peter-Paul fortress had lobbed a shell into the building during a religious ceremony. Nevertheless, at the appointed hour, the workers marched by the thousands, carrying ikons and singing religious and patriotic songs. Somewhere along the way, Father Gapon lost control and the capital government authorities lost their nerve. Efforts to dispel the marchers and keep them from the Winter Palace failed; they were fired on by troops. According to conservative historians, "many" were killed.

With that, Russia's first revolution got under way. Strikes broke out virtually everywhere and peasant risings swept the country. The Grand Duke Sergey was assassinated. The crew of the battleship "Potemkin" rebelled and terrorized the Black Sea until forced into internment in Rumania by lack of supplies. The naval bases at Kronstadt and Sevastopol mutinied. By late summer almost the entire nation had degenerated to a state of anarchy. Leon Trotsky, then still a Menshevik, was running the St. Petersburg Soviet of workers and practically the capital. By October, there was a general strike, all communications were severed and Nicholas was isolated at his country residence. Russia was paralyzed, but the leaders of the revolt, socialists, liberals, and Trotsky, did not know how to exploit the situation.

That lack of unity, leadership, and direction was all that saved Nicholas. Of course, he could have called out the troops, but since the rank and file of his army came from the "lower classes," there was a very good possibility that the soldiers would have joined the people.

The tsar's only alternative, and the way out which he took, was to surrender some of his ill-used power. He first turned to nobles, but they wanted no part of the responsibility. So, he turned to Witte, whom he did not like, despite the fact that he had saved Russia from what might have been a humiliating settlement of the war with Japan. He made Witte chairman of the council of ministers, or in effect, premier. Then, with Witte prodding him, he issued what is known as the October Manifesto in which absolutism was brought to an end, a Duma (parliament) was permitted and civil rights were granted. The manifesto was a step toward constitutional government, but it should be noted that no real, written constitution was ever granted by Nicholas. That lack, as well as Nicholas' constant whittling away at the authority granted the people in the manifesto, more than anything else lay behind his downfall. He just had no understanding whatsoever of the era in which he lived and tried to rule.

Since Nicholas seemed always to be doing the wrong thing at the worst possible time, it is somewhat poetically apt that within a fortnight after issuing the manifesto he met Grigory Rasputin, the real wrecker of the Romanov dynasty. A quack, a scrofulous and nefarious

[96]

"monk," Rasputin possessed the extreme cunning of a peasant, a class with which Nicholas had neglected to become acquainted. Therefore, Rasputin had no difficulty worming his way into Nicholas' confidence and particularly that of the unbalanced tsarina. Apparently, he had some hypnotic powers which he used to alleviate the tsarevich Alexis' hemophilia and thereby secure his hold on the naïve imperial couple. Rasputin's control was of fairy-tale proportions, but it was also peculiarly Russian.

Almost as could be expected, Witte, distrusted by the tsar and despised by the reactionaries, did not last more than a few months, being replaced by a colorless nonentity more subservient to the tsar. And even that noboby (Ivan Goremykin) failed in short order: the first Duma met in May 1906 and even though the SRs and other leftists were not in its membership since they had boycotted the elections, Nicholas could not stand that castrated legislative body's ineffective chattering about democracy in action. Accordingly, the tsar promoted his tough and able interior minister, Peter Arkadyevich Stolypin, to the premiership. In July, 1906, Stolypin prorogued (the better term is locked out) the Duma and called new elections for which the candidates were more carefully screened by an arbitrary ruling of the "government." The second Duma met in February, 1907, but since the tsar was inherently antagonistic to the barest traces of representative government he dissolved that one in June, 1907, on the excuse the SD's were trying to spread propaganda among the troops. On the day of dissolution, Nicholas issued yet another law that further restricted Duma membership with the result that the third Duma, which met in November, 1907, was a very pale form of democracy indeed. Nevertheless that Duma lived out its five-year term and under Stolypin's direction effected some major educational and agrarian reforms—the latter greatly feared by the Bolsheviks who later made nought of them. (The fourth Duma which assembled in 1912 and lasted until the eve of the tsar's overthrow in March 1917 was little more than a debating forum.)

Despite the obvious reforms of the third Duma, while Stolypin was interior minister and in the early days of his premiership, a wave of great unrest continued throughout the nation in the wake of the aborted October, 1905, revolution. Political assassination had become almost the order of the day. Convervative reports hold that in the period 1906–07 alone more than four thousand people, mainly

[97]

government officials, were murdered by terrorists of all categories. Stolypin brought that to an end, but in a very severe manner: he established scores of courts-martial with summary powers and almost seven hundred persons were executed and hundreds more imprisoned and exiled in a mere eight months of that bloody era.

Stolypin himself was a target for the terrorists. In 1906, his home was dynamited. The premier escaped that attempt, but more than a score of others were killed and many were injured, including a son and a daughter of Stolypin's, who were maimed for life. But, once such disorders had been quelled, a period of comparative calm followed and lasted for almost four years, although student and worker discontent was increasing. Russia's history might have been different had it not been for the premature death in 1911 of Stolypin, the penultimate major political assassination of the tsardom. While all security precautions were concentrated on Nicholas (evidently in the belief that ministers were expendable), Stolypin was shot down in a Kiev theater by one Dimitry (Mordecai) Bagrov, an unbalanced young Jewish lawyer, who had been working for both the Okhrana and the anarchists.

To succeed the comparatively able Stolypin, the tsar named yet another ineffective nonentity as premier. In 1912, partially as a result of having no one at the helm, workers at the Lena gold fields in Siberia went on strike, halting production. Troops were brought in to suppress the strike and more than two hundred workers were killed in what was known as the Lena Gold Fields Massacre. Other workers throughout the country struck in sympathy and soon Russia was undergoing another round of general strikes. By 1913, the proletariat more and more assumed the proportions of the backbone of revolution. Lenin, secure abroad, making another of his frequent mistakes of judgment, deemed the moment had come for the nation to rise against the autocracy.

Outside distraction, however, soon forestalled an uprising and gave Nicholas another reprieve. The Balkan Wars of 1912–13 had aroused the Russian nation's old Pan-Slavism once again, despite the treatment given the Polish Slavs under their dominion and the fact that Russia's onetime puppet, Bulgaria, had been the overall loser in that conflict.

Russia thereby was ripe for Germany's declaration of war in August, 1914, and her entry into World War I. At first, all went well.

Patriotism was rampant and Nicholas was greeted with enthusiasm by the populace for the first time in his life, and the last. All were for the tsar and the war except the Bolsheviks, who wanted defeats and peace for the road to world revolution.

However, early victories over the Austrians in Galicia and the Carpathians soon were turned into massive defeats at the hands of the Germans who were far better equipped and generaled. By August, 1915, Russian losses had soared to three million men killed, wounded, or captured and mountains of matériel. The Russian soldier was not responsible; he had been remarkably heroic and self-sacrificing. The real culprit had been on the home front. The ministers behind the soldiers were the normal proportion of good, weak, and evil men, but all of them were really no more than functionaries. Not a one of them was a real man of stature. And the same weakness applied to the men of the Duma. As a result, transport, supply, the delivery of weapons and shells to the front, were woefully bad in the extreme. All the evils of an autocracy in the hands of a man like Nicholas had finally become apparent.

Utterly incapable of doing anything about the mess, the tsar resorted to heroic grandstanding. In September, 1915, he dismissed his cousin, the Grand Duke Nicholas, who as supreme commander of Russian troops had done fairly well considering the handicaps he had. Nicholas, the parade ground soldier of another era, made himself commander-in-chief. He blithely went to the front, where he could do nothing worthwhile, leaving the horrible muddle at home to none other than the rattlebrained tsarina.

Once more Russia followed the best traditions of a bad fairy tale. The tsarina did not call in the neighbors to help: not being on speaking terms with them or any of her family, she turned to Rasputin. That wily character was a natural choice for her, for, in fact, he had been controlling all the premiers and most of the ministers ever since Stolypin had gone to his reward.

From that time on, defeat followed defeat at the front and disintegration began at home as the people started to appreciate the debacle they were facing. Unity between farm and factory was finally established when it dawned on the peasants that they were supplying the cannon-fodder for the ever-losing army. It was the same reaction given the defeats of the Russo-Japanese war, but multiplied many-fold. In October, 1916, there was a sign of the beginning of the end:

[99]

soldiers in the capital, renamed Petrograd as part of the war effort, joined strikers.

Venom was also building up against Rasputin, the best of the scape-goats, both in court circles, including members of the imperial family about to abandon the sinking ship, and among the general populace. That feeling was echoed in early December, 1916, in a Duma speech denouncing Rasputin. And in late December, 1916, the frenzy against the interloper reached a peak with the murder of Rasputin at the hands of relatives of the tsar and a right-wing member of the Duma.

As if their stars were hitched to that profligate monk, the end of the Romanovs followed his murder by mere months. In early March, 1917, no bread in the shops because of faulty distribution was enough to loose a tidal wave of looting, strikes, student protests, and troop mutinies throughout the nation. Eight days of total anarchy followed. By mid-March, 1917, a provisional government was attempting to rule and Nicholas had abdicated.

Almost immediately, the Petrograd Soviet started wrangling with the Provisional Government in a struggle for power. And within a month of the new government's establishment, Lenin, Grigory Zino-viev, Lev Kamenev, Karl Radek, Anatoly Lunacharsky, et al., de-scended on Petrograd like vultures having been sent home by the Germans in a sealed train. Trotsky came in from New York a little later. Stalin was already in the capital, but few knew about it or cared until he started to write Russian history.

In mid-July, 1917, Lenin and company organized an antiwar riot in Petrograd, but it was quickly quelled by Alexander Kerensky, an SR, who had taken over control of the provisional government. Trotsky was arrested and Lenin had to hide near the Finnish border. After that there was a move to quash the Bolsheviks and the soviet once and for all but a squabble for power between Kerensky and military leaders aborted that attempt. As a result, Kerensky lost sup-port and had to free the arrested Bolsheviks. By October, Trotsky had thoroughly propagandized the troops in the capital area. And on November 7, 1917 (Red October 25th according to the old calendar), the troops supported the Bolsheviks in a fairly bloodless rising and shelled the Winter Palace and the Admiralty. Ministers of the provi-sional government were made prisoners and Lenin took power.

In the light of what happened to Russia with the Bolshevik take-over, the fate of Nicholas and his family is little more than a dastardly footnote. In the summer of 1917, Kerensky sent the imperial family to Tobolsk in Siberia. After the Bolsheviks seized power, they planned a public trial for Nicholas, with Trotsky as prosecutor, and moved the imperial family to Ekaterinburg (Sverdlovsk), farther west in Siberia. However, in the summer of 1918, former Czechoslovak prisoners fighting with White Russian forces in the civil war then sweeping Russia, were about to overrun Ekaterinburg. Fearing his captives would be freed, Lenin agreed to their execution without trial. In the early hours of July 17, 1918, Nicholas, his wife, and five children, plus the family doctor, three servants, and a dog were murdered in the cellar of the house in which they had been kept prisoner. Attempts were made to destroy the bodies with fire and chemicals. What remained was thrown into an abandoned and water-filled mine a few miles away.

CHAPTER II

Tsarist Bodyguards

1. PRINCELY GUARDS

Since Russia's prehistoric Slavs were in the main a peaceful people, their rulers probably had no need for bodyguards. But, as they prospered and the more primitive people surrounding them began raiding their settlements, they sought help from the more warlike Vikings or "Varangers" who visited their area, seeking trade there and to the south.

The Varangers raided, traveled and traded in quasi-military groups, or companies. Each company, whose size was indeterminate, had a leader. The leader was a man of outstanding physical prowess, a man proficient in the weapons, ship-lore and horsemanship of his times, who could guide his company to victory in raids and protect its booty from the attacks of others when in the more peaceful pursuit of trade.

Usually, if the leader failed or fell, there was no replacement within the company. That meant that members of the company were either absorbed by other groups, or taken prisoners and perhaps later sold as slaves. To prevent that, stronger members of the company sailed, rode, and fought beside the leader and, in effect, became his bodyguards, although they had no such title. Trusted companions were, perhaps, the closest words to describe them. They were the elite of the company, though, of course, none of them, individually, could best the leader.

Rurik, the Varanger, the first ruler of historic Russia, apparently had such a group of trusted companions when he took over control of Novgorod toward the end of the ninth century. And he must have used them to quash an attempt by discontented Slavs and another Varanger, one Vadim, to overthrow him. Whatever was done with Vadim was not recorded, but he was never mentioned again in chronicle or fable. It seems as if he was disposed of forthwith by Rurik's trusted companions since it is known that a few decades later —or in the tenth century—Byzantine rulers started using Varangers as bodyguards and continued to do so until the Turks conquered Constantinople in 1453.

Therefore, it can be presumed that Oleg, Rurik's immediate successor, retook Kiev from Varanger usurpers with the help of his bodyguards. And it can also be presumed that it was the bodyguards who killed off the usurpers once they had been lured aboard Oleg's ship. Oleg's bodyguards must have been quite capable because despite his raids, battles and widespread travel he died a relatively natural death—from snakebite.

That was far from the case of the next Grand Prince of Kiev, the tenth century Igor, the son of Rurik. Reports of Igor's death at the hands of primitive tribesmen make the first reference to bodyguards of Russian rulers as such. It is recorded that Igor tried to collect tribute twice in a row from the Drevlyane; bodyguards accompanied him on both collections. But on the second and fatal trip he had brought along a smaller number of bodyguards and they were overwhelmed.

In the succeeding reign of Igor's wife, the regent Olga, very definite reference is made to the *druzhina*, or the princely bodyguard. It was the *druzhina* that rallied to Olga, not only to maintain her in power, but also to help her avenge herself on the Drevlyane for Igor's death.

And under Svyatoslav I, Igor's son, another and somewhat confusing term was given the *druzhina*—that of *Rus*. That is a degeneration of *Ros*, the Slavic name for the Varangers. But by the time of Svyatoslav, when the Varanger strain had been adulterated as the result of attrition and intermarriage with Slavs, *Rus* really was the nobility, Varangers, Slavs, even some Poles, Lithuanians, Hungarians, and knights-errant from the steppes, who supported the rule of the Kiev grand prince. Actually, the *Rus* appears to have been a collection of liege lords, sworn to uphold and protect the ruler, rather than bodyguards in the true sense. At the same time, Svyatoslav's

[103]

druzhina became more his personal army than his bodyguard.

That muddling of nomenclature and jobs by Svyatoslav probably cost him his life; and it also seems to have abetted struggles for power among his successors for years to come. If Svyatoslav had had real bodyguards of the old Varanger style, chances are they would have rescued him from ambush by Pecheneg nomads. And if he had not debased the bodyguards from a motley band of adventurers to outlaws, Yaropolk I, his rightful successor, might have reigned in peace instead of being murdered in fratricidal conflict.

The decline of the ruler's bodyguard was contemporary with—if, indeed not the cause of—the start of more than half a millennium of a Russian twilight, of anarchy by princelings and boyars, and of terrible subjugation by the Tatar invaders. Instead of bodyguards, the petty princes and rare ruler of stature of that grim period had little more than *ratniki*, warriors degenerated to soldiers, who looted and butchered defenseless townsmen and were usually cowards when faced by real foes.

2. STRELTSY AND OPRICHNIKI

Both these organizations were the brain-children of Ivan the Terrible (1553–84).

The mad tsar—and truly insane from about 1565 until his death—was the first Russian ruler since the heyday of Kiev to appreciate the need of formally organized bodyguards. That was partially the result of the harassment given him by the boyars before he mounted the throne and a desire to be protected from them when ruling. And it also may have been caused somewhat by the disintegration of Tatar control which had long determined up to that time who the Russian puppet ruler should be.

The *streltsy* were an innovation of the earlier, the saner, part of Ivan's reign. They were not as bad as the Oprichniki, but neither were they very much better.

The first *streltsy* group was about 1,000 strong. Basically, it was infantry, originally expert archers—elite troops in those times —and later musketeers. But some of them also bore such weapons as pikes, halberds, and swords. When first put together they were a Moscow outfit, whose main function was to guard the Kremlin and its chief occupant. During their 130-odd years of operation, they had various commanders and unit officers, but at the start, Ivan the Terrible was their real and only commander.

Although their garb was varied, as was that of all soldiers of that era, they were to some extent the first uniformed bodyguards of a Russian ruler. Comparatively, the bodyguards of the Rurik-Kiev period could only be distinguished from other members of a ruler's equipage by their stalwart physiques and handiness with weapons.

In the time of Ivan the Terrible, the *streltsy* were present at most of their ruler's outrages—including the sack of Novgorod—but in general they were not initiators of those horrors and cruelties. Those duties were left to the capable hands of the Oprichniki.

The creation of the really mad Ivan, the Oprichniki lasted only seven years (1565–72) but such a scourge were they to Russia and so horrible were their deeds that the organization will never be forgotten by man—civilized or uncivilized. Stalin thought highly of the Oprichniki and only criticized them and their master for not wiping out more boyars and priests.

Unlike the *streltsy*, the Oprichniki had a very distinctive uniform. They were Horse Guards, completely clothed in black, including a cowl. Their mounts, reins, and harness were black and on their saddles they carried the twin embroidered device of a broom and a dog's head. That insignia defined the Oprichniki's mission, to sweep out and sniff out the *kramolniki* (seditious persons), or one and all who displeased Ivan and anyone unfortunate enough to fall into the hands of his underlings.

A carefully selected corps, the Oprichniks were about 6,000 strong, but some accounts say there were ten thousand of them. They were a motley array, drawn from unscrupulous scions of princely and boyar families, foreign adventurers, felons and itinerant, half-demented monks. Ivan was their leader, confessor and chief torturer. Among the scum from whom he drew his lieutenants were Alexis Basmanov, Malyuta ("Babe") Skuratov-Belsky and Prince Afanasy Vyazemsky. Ivan himself wrote that one Ivan Peresvetov gave him the idea of the Oprichnina but there is no record of that worthy having played any role in the organization's activities.

At the height of their power, the Oprichniki possessed half the realm and a good part of Moscow—ceded them by Ivan—and controlled the rest of the country. Their stronghold was at Aleksandrovskaya Sloboda, a monastery that was really a fortress with a moat, walls, and dungeons about seventy miles northeast of Moscow. And they also had a palace headquarters in their sector of Moscow.

There is no wonder that Stalin admired Ivan the Terrible and his Oprichniki. He probably also envied them, and to a lesser extent, Lenin's Cheka. To get rid of his enemies—imagined as well as real —Stalin had to make a pose of legality, follow "laws" and hold "trials."

No niceties like that troubled Ivan IV and his band of cutthroats. The Oprichniki had orders to be extremely cruel. They had the unquestioned privilege of killing, robbing, beating up, torturing, raping, looting, and setting fire to the property of any and all they labeled as enemies of the tsar. They could also seize and extort money at will, the monks and their monasteries being the chief sources of that income. Additionally, they had the right to denounce completely innocent people. Much like their successors, the Tsarist Okhrana and the Soviet Communist NKVD and KGB, they had spies and *provocateurs* and frequently resorted to framing their victims or planting forged documents on them. To the Russians of that time, the earlier Tatar incursions must have seemed like the good, old days, for the bestialities of the Oprichniki were not the outrages committed by foreigners, but the work of Russian against Russian.

As a result, whenever the Oprichniki swept into cities or towns, cautious citizens deserted the streets, while those caught abroad spared no effort to denounce family members, friends, or neighbors in hopes of saving their own miserable skins. It was a truly horrible period, but examination of it gives a better understanding of many Russians of today.

The chief criminal, Ivan, lived with his underlings, either at the Aleksandrovskaya Sloboda "monastery" or at their Moscow headquarters. The wretch divided his time torturing and executing prisoners, watching with mock disapproval the rape of seized women, often from boyars' families, carousing with the Oprichniki who wore monks' costumes at the "monastery," or fasting and praying for his victims.

Despite his religious pretenses, Ivan the Terrible was a true Antichrist to the church. It was that body of Russia's elite on which he wreaked his worst, having his Oprichniki kill off churchmen wholesale, including metropolitans and archbishops. His chief foe was Metropolitan Philip of Moscow, an outspoken opponent of the Oprichniki and a good and apparently uncowable man. In 1569, Philip went so far as to rebuke Ivan and refuse him his blessing in public at the Uspensky cathedral. For that, the Oprichniki rigged "evidence" and a "trial" for the prelate—those legalities a sop for the Muscovites who dearly loved the metropolitan. That done, a gang headed by Basmanov invaded the cathedral, seized Philip at the altar, ripped off his robes and stuffed him into a monk's habit. The Oprichniki bundled him off for torture and death. Some accounts say he was murdered by strangling at a monastery in Tver; others hold he was hanged by a hook in the cellars of the Aleksandrovskaya Sloboda "monastery"; but all versions agree that Malyuta Skuratov, the bloodiest of the Oprichniki, was the killer.

Comparatively, Ivan was less vicious toward the nobility of Russia proper, if one discounts, of course, his rapes of their womenfolk and his pillaging and stealing of their lands. Nevertheless, some nobles of note did fall afoul of Ivan and fatally. Chief among them was Prince Vladimir of Staritsa, who had been uncautious enough to assert some right to the throne for himself in Ivan's troublous times of 1553. The tsar applied considerable patience to eliminating this enemy, after steadily divesting Prince Vladimir of his supporters. Finally, in 1569, the Oprichniki seized the prince, took him to their "monastery," and killed him. Most accounts say they used poison to dispatch that victim.

The year 1569 not only marked the slayings of Metropolitan Philip and Prince Vladimir but also the peak of Ivan's blood-thirst. For it was in that year that he determined to destroy the great merchant city of Novgorod and murder its citizenry en masse.

In size, the force Ivan led on Novgorod was not much: some 15,000 in all, *ratniki* and *streltsy*, led by Oprichniki. But in deeds of horror, it far outmatched the Tatar hosts that once swept the land. Ivan's rabble set out for their objective in December of 1569, but did not reach it until January of the next year.

The delay was caused by tarrying along the way: thieving, torturing and murdering at the town of Klin beyond Moscow; killing untold thousands at Tver (now Kalinin), butchering any and all travelers unfortunate enough to be on the road, and looting and devastating all monasteries on or near the route.

Once arrived at Novgorod, a cordon was thrown around the city —some accounts say a wooden wall was built around it, but the purpose was the same—to keep the doomed inhabitants from fleeing.

In keeping with tradition, Novgorod's Archbishop Pimen met Ivan on the bridge over the Volkhov River which divides the city. Equally typically, the tsar blasphemously rejected the cleric's blessing and called him foul names, but did permit him to conduct rites in the cathedral and hold a banquet. Once the wining and dining had started, Ivan screamed, a signal for the Oprichniki to plunder the cathedral and the bishop's palace and start their orgy of torture and murder.

That went on for five weeks. The usual torture was roasting the victims alive, but there were many refinements as well. And the tsar and his son Ivan assisted in those ceremonies. Husbands and wives were made to watch each other tortured; mothers had to watch their babies maimed, axed or disemboweled before they themselves were burned or otherwise put to death. A favorite method of killing wholesale was to lash the victims together, live, dying, and dead, and throw them into the Volkhov near the bridge, whose shelter kept ice from forming. Eager Oprichniki patroled the banks, or cruised that part of the river in small boats, slaughtering all who showed signs of life.

According to conservative accounts, more than sixty thousand people of Novgorod were put to death in that horrible fashion. Finally tiring of the slaughter there, Ivan and his henchmen burned, dumped, or otherwise destroyed all the city's food reserves, leaving the remnants of the population to face death by starvation, or from plague and disease then sweeping the land. There is still a Novgorod on the map, but Great Novgorod, as it had been known, never recovered from that onslaught of the mad tsar and his Oprichniki.

Before returning to Moscow, Ivan had the idea of giving Novgorod's sister city of Pskov the same treatment, but was talked out of it by Pskov's able prelate.

Back in Moscow, however, the madman and his underlings found new victims for their mania. The excuse for laying Novgorod waste had been reports it planned treating with one of the current enemies, Lithuania. The excuse for another horrible scene, the public torture and killing of more than a hundred people in the capital in mid-1570, was that they had been involved in the Novgorod plan. But for good measure, those unfortunates were also accused of treating with the Crimean Tatars, Poland, and Turkey. Chief among the victims were Prince Ivan Viskovaty, who held a post equivalent to foreign minister, and Nikita Funikov-Kurtsev, treasurer of the realm.

But Ivan also used the occasion to dispose of the cook who had poisoned Prince Vladimir of Staritsa the year before, probably to seal his lips for good.

For the great day, an open area of Moscow was equipped with a huge kettle of boiling water and eighteen gibbets. At the appointed hour, the Oprichniki rounded up unwilling and terrified citizens to furnish an audience. Ivan, armed to the teeth, and more than a thousand of his mounted cohorts thundered up. And the condemned, most of them crippled by earlier torture, were led by.

The tsar had Viskovaty hung upside down. Malyuta Skuratov started the killing by cutting off an ear of the prince; other Oprichniki then sliced him to pieces like a cut of meat. The fate of Funikov was to be thrown into the kettle of boiling water. Then the tsar and the Oprichniki entered the fray en masse, hacking and spearing their victims to death with sabers, axes and pikes. When it was all over, Ivan celebrated by going to Viskovaty's house where he raped the widow while his son, the heir presumptive to the tsardom of All the Russias, did likewise to the eldest daughter.

That public orgy of slaughter was the beginning of the end of the Oprichniki. In a fit of madness later in that bloody year of 1570, Ivan turned on his chief killers. He ordered Alexis Basmanov killed by his own son, Fedor (Theodore) Basmanov, and then had the son killed. Ivan was more subtle with Prince Vyazemsky; he called him to the palace for a friendly conference, while "loyal" Oprichniki were at the prince's house murdering his supporters and servants. Vyazemsky was allowed to go home and stumble over the bodies before he was seized and thrown into a dungeon, never to be seen again.

Some authorities say that the real cause of Ivan's turning on his Oprichniki was remorse over the killing of Metropolitan Philip and the reaction to that murder by the people of Moscow, who loved the prelate. However, that explanation seems a little farfetched, considering the seas of blood of churchmen on Ivan's hands and the tsar's complete disregard of any of his subjects, including his own son. With Novgorod on the record, one needs little imagination to appreciate how Ivan would handle the mutterings of a few Muscovites, if he were really concerned about unrest. So, that reasoning smells like the usual Russian apologia for bloody Russia.

But, whatever the explanation, the fact remains that the killings of the Basmanovs and the elimination of Vyazemsky were followed

[109]

with a great purge of the Oprichniki in the best Russian tradition. And it was done in the usual manner, denunciation, false or otherwise. Only Malyuta Skuratov, an exceedingly wily fellow, escaped, but he was later killed in battle for Livonia.

For a while, even with the purge, Oprichniki ranks were refilled with willing others taking the place of the denouncees. But most historians believe that by about 1572 the Oprichnina cased to exist as an operating and mass organization. There is no record of Ivan ever formally dissolving it, however. Thus it seems highly probable that some Oprichniki were still extant at least as late as 1577 when Ivan attacked the Livonian city of Wenden (now Cesis, in northern Latvia). After some of Wenden's citizens blew themselves up in the local castle rather than fall into the hands of Ivan and his rogues, all the rest of the city's people were butchered in true Oprichniki style. But, seven years later, after Ivan the Terrible's death in a final fit, the Oprichniki were never heard of again, except in legends and horror stories.

Explanations of the Oprichnina are many and varied. Most authorities agree that the purpose of the organization was to guarantee the tsar's personal security—or to serve as his bodyguards. True, they butchered his enemies, as well as those who were not his enemies, unmercifully. True, their ruler did not meet death at the hands of a rival. But somewhat studiously lacking in all the reasoning about Ivan and the Oprichniki—especially that done by Russian historians—is an examination of why some Russian noble, churchman, simple muzhik, or disaffected Oprichnik did not put an end to that beast in tsar's robes. Horrible as they were, the Oprichniki were not as ubiquitous, as all-powerful, as later Communist bodyguards who have been developed into superb, almost invincible shields for their rulers. But that was certainly not the case with such a scruffy lot as the Oprichniki. That nobody killed off Ivan the Terrible was due either to luck, or most likely to the Russian character as expressed by Dostoyevsky in his *Grand Inquisitor*. The Inquisitor's statement that the Russian people found the burden of freedom too onerous is probably the best explanation of not only Ivan and the Oprichniki, but also of all subsequent Russian rulers and their bodyguards—good, bad or indifferent.

The end of the Oprichniki marked the passage from history for some time of an elite type of Russian bodyguards that were confidants and lieutenants of the ruler. With the death of Ivan the function of protecting the ruler returned—more by default than plan—to the *streltsy*, formed by Ivan in his less mad days to guard him from the boyars. From their start as a group about one thousand strong, the *streltsy* eventually expanded into twenty-three regiments. Although the strength of those regiments is not known, they probably numbered about one thousand each.

In the last years of the sixteenth century and in the first half decade of the seventeenth, or during the end of the reign of Ivan's feeble-minded son and that of the usurper, Boris Godunov, the *streltsy* suffered another, but briefer eclipse. Tsar Boris, probably because he was once an Oprichnik himself, plus the fact of his foreign origin, had little confidence in the *streltsy* to keep him on the throne. Boris thought it wiser to rely on foreigners rather than Russians for his protection. So, he imported a group of (Baltic) Germans to serve as his bodyguards. Little—except the existence—is known of that organization. But it is recorded that denunciations, tortures, killings, and subjugation of boyars and churchmen continued under Boris. Therefore, it is reasonable to assume that his German bodyguards were efficient, even though less storied and infamous than the Oprichniki. And one of its chiefs, a cousin of Boris Godunov, seems to have scored a success of sorts for those days by learning the correct identity of one of the early pretenders to the throne.

In the interregnum, or the "time of troubles" (1605–13) that followed the death of Boris, the German bodyguards were disbanded. Nor did the *streltsy* serve any particular function in that unhappy period beyond being among the participants in the elevation or elimination of the various pretenders and would-be usurpers. In such a time of anarchy, of course, the concept of protecting the leader was somewhat exotic.

When order returned in 1613 with the boyars' election of the first Romanov, Mikhail (Michael), the *streltsy* went back to their usual jobs of guarding the Kremlin gates and inner chambers. The real security of the tsar, however, seems to have been turned over to a Boyars' Council, or the leaders of the nobles who had selected the young Romanov. In a way, Mikhail did not need very much protection. First, he was weak and inoffensive and his father really did the ruling. Secondly, the boyars were so tired of the time of troubles and so anxious for the stability of legitimacy that they were not interested

[111]

in challenging the tsar. But the establishment of the Boyars' Council was an interesting development. It showed that Russia was maturing, could no longer get along with a mere gang of husky roustabouts to protect the leader, but also needed a more advanced and administrative type of organization to guarantee the security of the regime as well.

The Boyars' Council was of great service in the upheavals that marked the reign of the next tsar, Alexis. It was the Boyars' Council that investigated the 1670–71 Cossack uprising of Stenka Razin and had that rebel executed by quartering in Moscow. Alexis himself also instituted a Secret Office, the forerunner of the imperial political police organizations. However, under Alexis the Secret Office concentrated more on details about the tsar's falcon and was dissolved with that monarch's death.

The *streltsy* played their part too under Alexis. There are accounts of that tsar leaving the palace with prominent boyars standing on the sides of his carriage which was surrounded by a bodyguard of some hundred foot soldiers who beat off the curious with their pike staffs. Some accounts make direct mention of the *streltsy*, calling them the bodyguard of Alexis and telling of their wearing brightly colored uniforms with some carrying gilded pistols and others with cudgels to beat off the crowds. But there was also an indication that Alexis was not too satisfied with the effectiveness of the *streltsy*. After he had barely escaped manhandling by an angry crowd in the early part of his reign, he recruited foreign musketeers to bolster the *streltsy*. But, no matter whether they were foreigners or Russian *streltsy*, Alexis kept his bodyguards busy indeed, protecting him from or controlling the unruly mobs common in Moscow in those days.

The high-water mark—and the resultant disbanding—of the *streltsy* came after Alexis' death with the struggle for power between the young Peter the Great and his half-sister, Sophia. In fact, in that brief period it was the *streltsy* who determined the leader rather than serving as his bodyguards.

In 1682, after the ten-year-old Peter had been proclaimed tsar in preference to his elder, feeble-minded brother, Ivan, Sophia was beside herself. She incited the streltsy—by some accounts then about 50,000 strong—to march on the Kremlin, where Peter was installed with his mother, Natalia. By persuasion, and much payment of money, Natalia managed to get the *streltsy* to leave, but they soon returned, again egged on by Sophia. That time, Natalia, surrounded by Peter, his half-brother, members of her family, and advisors, met them on the steps of the palace, the so-called Red Staircase. Natalia had just about persuaded the guards—many of them drunk—to leave for a second time, when their commander, Prince Mikhail Dolgoruky, arrived and cursed them for their behavior. For that he was tossed on *streltsy* pikes and butchered as the rest of the *streltsy* mob stormed into the palace, cut down Natalia's supporters, and exiled her and Peter to the Preobrazhenskoye suburb.

Made regent, Sophia (1682–89) at first granted amnesty to the *streltsy* for the outrages at the palace. But she soon brought them under control, first killing off their new commander, Prince Ivan Khovansky, who was deluded by the idea that having been tsar-maker he could be tsar himself. Next, she issued a decree making it impossible for the *streltsy*, or anybody else, to run rampant in the Kremlin again, at least during her regency. The order described in detail who was to be permitted to enter the palace, through which entrances, and designated the stairs and passages to be used for different sections of the palace. No entry at all was allowed to the environs of the imperial family quarters, not even to boyars. Barriers were built around the imperial quarters and offices and, in the language of those times, all were warned ". . . never to enter or bring anybody with themselves, no matter what kind of business there is . . ." And advice was given ". . . to boyars, to high-ranking officials, to people close (to the imperial family) not to bring anybody with themselves or permit anybody from the ordinary people to pass behind the barriers. And for this reason in those places the Streltsy Prikaz (office) has established guard (watches) and must give strict orders to the watchmen about it. Passages from the Palace to the Troitskoye Podvor'ye will be kept closed and no one will be permitted to pass through those doors and passages without an imperial order. Strict orders about this are to be given to boyars' children, firemen and watchmen who passed through those places . . ." It was also forbidden to enter any part of the palace with arms. This included those who, according to the customs of that time, bore arms at all times. Foreign ambassadors and their suites were also required to remove arms on entering reception rooms.

That early "iron curtain" decree and other measures of Sophia sufficed to keep the *streltsy* fairly well under control until the end

[113]

of the regency. In 1689, however, one of the regent's underlings, Shaklovity, induced a few *streltsy* to go to Preobrazhenskoye and murder Natalia. Other *streltsy* betrayed the plot to Peter, who took up a defensive position in a nearby monastery, supported mainly by boyhood friends. Soon, though, most of the *streltsy* rallied to Peter's support. Finally in real control, Peter had Shaklovity and his conspirators among the *streltsy* executed and exiled Sophia to a convent. But their belated support for Peter did the *streltsy* no good. His memory still fresh about their killing spree in the Kremlin when he was only ten years old, the young tsar not only disdained them as bodyguards, but, with certainly enough reason, also had no confidence in them at all and soon sent them as virtual labor troops to build fortifications in the south. Missing their former soft quarters, the *streltsy* mutinied in 1698, forcing Peter to cut short his European tour. Although the uprising had been quelled well before his return to Moscow by his lieutenants, his erstwhile boyhood friends, the tsar had had enough of the *streltsy.* Under his personal direction, great numbers of them were tortured and forced to confess. Most of the *streltsy* officers and noncoms were then executed publicly in Moscow, again under Peter's personal direction, and the *streltsy* as a bodyguard organization ceased to exist.

Long after that, the name *streltsy* continued in the Russian language—after all, they were musketeers—but Peter ended their function as bodyguards of the ruler forever.

3. PREOBRAZHENSKY AND SEMENOVSKY GUARDS

The Preobrazhensky and Semenovsky Guards regiments, the elite troops of Russia until the fall of the House of Romanov, were first formed from the cadres of boyhood companions with whom Peter played his realistic war games at Preobrazhenskoye while under the thrall of Sophia.

In effect, those youngsters evolved into just as true and trusted bodyguards for Peter as were those of the early Rurikids. There was never any question of their giving their lives for Peter and otherwise protecting the ruler to the utmost.

It was those young men who rallied to Peter's defense when he fled to the monastery from Sophia's *streltsy* group. Later, after having been organized into regular regiments, they were the ones who fought at his side in the young tsar's first victories in the field. And it was also they, helped by foreign mercenaries, who put down the *streltsy* uprising during Peter's absence in western Europe.

From very early on—perhaps because Peter was their "commander" in his youthful mock battles—the Preobrazhensky men took a bit of precedence over the Semenovsky companions. For that reason, and also probably because their personal relationships with the tsar were closer, the Preobrazhensky men became better known, especially such leaders as Prince Fedor Romodanovsky and Prince Ivan Buturlin, as well as Alexander Menshikov, who later became a very capable general. That, however, did not mean that the Semenovsky group took second place in Peter's esteem as guards. Nevertheless, it was a fact that during Peter's reign the leadership of the Preobrazhensky Guards ran both regiments.

That was effected by the institution of the Preobrazhensky Prikaz (Office) in 1697. The organization—run by Prince Romodanovsky, and after his death by his son, Prince Ivan—was first set up to be an administrative group for the guards. But it was speedily given other tasks, including controlling the newly-developing tobacco trade, and especially that of serving as a political police directorate. In its police work, the Prikaz was assisted by another innovation of Peter's, the "Fiscals," a vast network of government agents, originally intended to oversee tax collections and prevent financial abuses, but who specialized more in encouraging informing and denouncing en masse.

The Preobrazhensky Prikaz was refreshingly small considering its tasks, consisting only of Prince Romodanovsky, a pair of chief clerks and about a half-dozen assistants. The contacts with the "Fiscals" and other courier work, as well as arrests, were handled by officers and noncoms of the Preobrazhensky and Semenovsky Guards, acting under orders of the Prince and sometimes those of Peter, himself. In that way the tsar's real and potential enemies were arrested, imprisoned, exiled, executed, and otherwise disposed of. And it was in that way the Preobrazhensky Prikaz handled the regime's security during Peter's absence abroad and once Peter had returned home dealt with the roundup, interrogation, and disposition of the *streltsy* mutineers. Under the Prikaz, protecting the ruler was a very simple matter, indeed—despite the vastness of Russia, even in those times —perhaps mainly because the ruler himself was a very simple and direct man.

Besides the Preobrazhensky Prikaz and the "Fiscals," in the latter part of his reign Peter instituted a third high security organization, the Secret Chancellery, formed to adjuge the tsar's son, Alexis, and help remove the stigma from the sovereign for the eventual death of his presumed heir. Its job done, the Secret Chancellery was closed down in 1726, shortly after Peter the Great's death. And the Preobrazhensky Prikaz lasted only a few years longer, ceasing to exist after its chief, Prince Ivan Romodanovsky, retired in 1729.

The closing of the Prikaz marked the end of the Preobrazhensky and Semenovsky Guards exercising police control in the realm. But their role as chief bodyguards of the ruler—plus their activities as tsar-makers and deposers—continued for another century. The two units suffered a brief eclipse under Tsarina Anna (1730–40) who formed the Izmailovsky regiment, completely composed of Baltic Germans, as her bodyguards. But with Anna's death, the Preobrazhensky and Semenovsky Guards came back into their own.

It was Preobrazhensky and Semenovsky huzzas that installed Peter's widow, Catherine I, on the throne and kept her there until her death two years later. It was General Menshikov—of Preobrazhensky origin—who persuaded Catherine to name Peter II (1727–30) as her successor. And it was the Preobrazhensky regiment that Anna used—or misused—to violate the agreement she made with the Council of Boyars. As she dumped the Preobrazhensky Guards in favor of her Izmailovsky stalwarts, she also in effect reconstituted the Preobrazhensky Prikaz under another name, that of the Chancellery for Secret Investigations, run by General Andrey Ushakov, who had been a member of Peter the Great's former Secret Chancellery. The actual function of Anna's chancellery, however, was more like that of the Preobrazhensky Prikaz, a sort of controlled Oprichnina. It had spies all over the nation; it arrested and exiled important boyars and their families in countless numbers; and it also improved upon the more traditional Russian torture devices by importing from Western Europe such refinements as the "Peking water-drops," the "Nuremberg maiden," and the "Spanish boots."

After Anna's death, the Preobrazhensky Guards twice interfered with the succession. First, they overthrew Anna's former lover whom she had named as regent. Next they put Peter the Great's daughter, Elizabeth (1741–62), the virtual darling of the regiment, on the throne. Although Elizabeth adored the Preobrazhensky regiment, she was also cautious enough to continue the secret chancellery, with General Ushakov, for a while, at least, as its head. The general worked hard to keep himself in Elizabeth's good graces, especially in the Natalia Lopukhina affair.

That attractive woman first drew Elizabeth's attention, and ire, for appearing at a ball in a costume identical with that of the empress. For that, Elizabeth publicly cut Madame Lopukhina's dress to shreds, removing a good part of the unwise woman's locks in the process. Chances are that Elizabeth would have speedily forgiven and forgotten Lopukhina had not General Ushakov seen the incident as an opportunity to ingratiate himself. That worthy settled Lopukhina's fate and ended her future court encounters by charging her with implication in a plot to overthrow Elizabeth. Lopukhina, her husband and son, were condemned to death on the wheel. Elizabeth, however, sworn to keep death sentences from marring her reign, graciously commuted the sentences to exile in Siberia, but only after Ushakov's three victims had been knouted and had had their tongues slit.

Not long after that judgment was carried out, Ushakov was retired and his place taken as head of the secret chancellery by Alexander Shuvalov, the uncle of one of Elizabeth's lovers. Because of Elizabeth's aversion to death sentences, Shuvalov's activity as her chief policeman was not too bloody. His appointment was really more interesting in that it marked the beginning of an almost continual line of Shuvalovs in political police work as well as in his choice of assistant, the quite fearsome Stepan Sheshkovsky, who would distinguish himself in a subsequent reign.

Soon after Elizabeth's death, the imperial bodyguards once again determined the ruler. They deposed Peter III and made his wife, Catherine the Great (1762–96), the ruler. Although Catherine first used the Izmailovsky and Semenovsky Guards to usurp power, she got herself acclaimed by the Preobrazhensky regiment as well. Her turning first to the Izmailovsky Guards was a matter of convenience, not politics; their barracks was closer to her residence. And by then, the one-time Baltic German outfit had long been thoroughly Russianized. Finally, before galloping off to break the news to her ousted husband, Catherine had carefully aped the coup technique of Elizabeth by first donning a Preobrazhensky uniform. And it was the old Russian-style Preobrazhensky uniform she wore, not the Prussian-style imposed by Peter III, one of the many reasons for his overthrow.

During his brief reign—in keeping with a Russian tradition all too familiar—Peter III had formed the Secret Bureau before publicly announcing the dissolution of the Chancellery for Secret Investigations. Additionally, Peter decreed that instead of reporting directly to him, the renamed political police organization should be controlled by the Senate. To keep the record clear—that Senate had not a shadow of resemblance to those of ancient Rome or modern republics; it was a group of flunkies, probably best called a cabinet, dreamed up by Peter the Great to take the details of the regime's administrative operations from his shoulders. The reason for Peter III's subordination of his political police to his cabinet is obscure; it may have been that he loathed having someone like Sheshkovsky— who had risen by then to be head of the political police—reporting to him in person. But, whatever the reason for the change, it seems a fact that the resulting additional paper work and confusion so preoccupied his political police that they failed to unearth the plans for Catherine's coup. And oddly, the same kind of meddling with the political police structure was contemporary with the assassination of a far-better tsar more than a century later.

Once firmly in power, Catherine the German proved as two-faced about the political police as any truly Russian ruler. She, too, announced that the Chancellery for Secret Investigations had been dissolved. And she, too, kept it secret that the chancellery's place had been taken by the Secret Bureau. She also retained Sheshkovsky and made the slight alteration that he was to report to the chief of the Senate, called the procurator-general, rather than to the entire Senate organization.

Early in her reign, Catherine's only remaining legal rival, the unfortunate Ivan IV, was killed off by his guards at Shlisselburg during an unsuccessful attempt by a group of irresponsible guards officers to liberate him. Knowing nothing of it, Sheshkovsky did nothing to scotch that attempt but he did play the major role in the interrogations, leading to the execution of the conspirators. Sheshkovsky's particular forte was interrogation, almost always ex post facto and therefore his political police work was based more on mistreatment and terrorization of his victims than on astute use of spies and penetration of potential rebel ranks. Posing as a pious man—as Ivan the Terrible did before him—he had his interrogation chambers decorated with ikons and would chant prayers to drown out the cries of his victims under his whip—or better, that especially Russian-beloved instrument, the knout. Holding himself a gentleman, he gave those personal attentions only to the upper classes, leaving the workouts on lesser unfortunates to his underlings.

As with the Shlisselburg conspirators, Sheshkovsky, despite his calling himself the watchdog of Catherine, knew nothing in advance of two other noteworthy attempts to unseat his empress, the Tarakanova and Pugachev cases. Of that pair, the attempt of the so-called Princess Tarakanova, a pretendress among the many male pretenders of those days, was more comic than serious, although it was handled as if it had been a real threat to the throne. After the "princess" had been kidnapped in Dalmatia by Alexis Orlov in the best latter-day KGB fashion, she was delivered to Sheshkovsky before being sent to the dungeons of the Peter-Paul fortress for the rest of her days. Likewise was the great Cossack rebel Pugachev apprehended not by the political police but by army units and that only after his comrades had betrayed him. Pugachev, too, was delivered to the political police for interrogation before execution. But that interrogation must have been disappointing to Sheshkovsky because Catherine had given direct orders that the rebel leader was not to be tortured. However, there is no doubt that Sheshkovsky put his ikons, prayers, and other devices to good use while interrogating lesser figures rounded up with Pugachev.

Nor did Sheshkovsky's watchdog's nose sniff out the half-baked plot of Catherine's only legitimate progeny, the Grand Duke Paul, to overthrow his mother. That was done by the other Orlov brother, Grigory—another of her paladins, most of them guards officers and in effect her actual bodyguards. And of course Sheshkovsky never got the opportunity to interrogate the weird Grand Duke Paul.

Like his predecessor, General Ushakov, Catherine's chief political policeman was a great hand at working over women who aroused his empress' displeasure. He was once instructed to kidnap an army general's wife, with whom Catherine was provoked, from a ball, give her a good whipping at the Secret Bureau, and then return her with all courtesies to the party.

By the early 1790s, Sheshkovsky's prowess as an interrogator was so well known that "too liberal" writers, especially Alexander Radishchev and Nikolay Novikov, deemed it wiser to confess all rather than be tortured before the first was sent to Siberia and the latter to Shlisselburg fortress.

It was in those closing years of the eighteenth century that Sheshkovsky was busiest. The French Revolution and the guillotining of Louis XVI and Marie Antoinette had frightened the daylights out of Catherine with the result that she gave her chief political policeman virtual carte blanche to haul in and interrogate all writers he pleased, in fact almost anyone rash enough to express liberal thoughts out loud. Fortunately, however, for his victims, Sheshkovsky's days of greatest glory were interrupted by his death in 1794. But, his last work did give indication of the change in direction of threat to the ruler—from the people rather than the hierarchs.

However, those early rumblings were to take some time to really develop. Tsar Paul (1796-1801), succeeding Catherine without incident, kept the Secret Bureau running, retaining Sheshkovsky's successor, Alexander Makarov. Although Makarov was almost a normal person as compared to the psychotic Sheshkovsky, he was well-occupied with sending hundred of persons to prison, exiling many others and stamping out scores upon scores of peasant risings. But like Sheshkovsky with Peter III, he failed in his ultimate objective, protecting the ruler.

Much of the blame for that can be layed on Paul himself. That foolish tsar switched his bodyguards, giving the Gatchina group with whom he played soldier during his long stretch as heir-presumptive precedence over the far more redoubtable Preobrazhensky, Semenovsky and Izmailovsky Guards. Furthermore, he also treated the veteran units in the same Prussian manner he used on the Gatchina group. And, as if that were not enough, he finally gave the Kurlander, Count von Pahlen, the governor-generalship of St. Petersburg as well as control of the guards and police. Having thus abused and insulted his bodyguards and police, as well as delivering every aspect of his overall security into the hands of an ambitious, toadying foreigner, it was small wonder that Makarov was unable to prevent Paul's assassination.

Alexander I's (1801–25) role in deposing his father is indisputable, although it does not seem likely he was agreeable to his being killed. Alexander selected the time, the night when his battalion of the Semenovsky Guards was to stand guard at his father's palace. To that degree, the bodyguards once more determined the ruler, eliminating his opposition in the course, even though the motley group of drunkards that murdered Paul could hardly be described as elite guards, or anybody's bodyguards as such. But, the only significance of that sordid event from the standpoint of tsars' bodyguards was that it marked the last time the guards made and supported a revolt from within the palace. From that date, all opposition to Russia's imperial rulers came from without the palace. That change made the guards regiments just as anachronistic as the autocracy and reduced them to little more than ceremonial outfits and elite troops.

Alexander I was as haphazard and unpredictable with internal problems as with military and diplomatic affairs. So it was small wonder that his personal security arrangements became very loose indeed. Shortly after his accession, he went through the formality of abolishing the Secret Bureau for good and releasing most of its hundreds of prisoners. Political police work, however, was far from abolished. To carry that out, this very deceitful tsar established a multiplicity of organizations that frequently were in conflict with one another. First, the task was given to St. Petersburg's military governor-general, who cooperated with the interior ministry. Soon, however, since Alexander was prone to form committees to handle problems he wished to avoid, a committee responsible for political security took over control of the governor-general's operations. In effect, that group, known as the Committee of January 13, 1807, became the successor to the Secret Bureau and was continued until a few years after Alexander's death. Next, in the period 1811–19, the security picture was further confused with the establishment of a police ministry, with that ministry being subordinate to the committee. And finally, within the police ministry there was a Special Chancellery, specializing in political matters. The Special Chancellery scored only one notable achievement—and a very doubtful one at that—by arresting and eliminating Mikhail Speransky in 1812, before the police ministry was abolished in 1819 when the chancellery and security matters were returned to the interior ministry. Alexander had given Speransky, a brilliant statesman, the two formidable assignments of formulating a new law code and a constitution.

But, while Speransky labored, the unpredictable Alexander's ardor for reform cooled under the influence of a new, and more lasting favorite, the brutal and extremely reactionary General Count Aleksey Arakcheyev, the same man who had once been Paul's drill-sergeant at Gatchina. From that time on, as the right-hand man of the tsar for internal affairs, Arakcheyev was really Russia's top security boss under Alexander. It was only as a result of mismanagement and a need for window-dressing by that would-be "liberal" tsar that the committee, the interior ministry and the Special Chancellery continued to handle security matters as well. But lest that trio err, Arakcheyev maintained his own private force of spies and informers. Actually, therefore, despite the confusion in security nomenclature and assignment purposefully established by the tsar, Arakcheyev was a kind of Malyuta Skuratov of that era.

So, the final confusion perpetrated by Alexander—that of his succession—and the ill-fated Decembrist revolt of 1825 to which it gave rise, should have been expected. A quarter century of poses, pretenses, false promises and a muddled security situation reaped reward in a people, rather than a hierarchy, finally becoming aware of the intrinsic rottenness of autocracy. And by the time of the Decembrist revolt, even the twilight of the Guards as protectors of the ruler had long passed. There were guards units of a sort that took part in that uprising on one side or the other, but by then the term "guards" had become generic in Russia and had lost its original, specific meaning. Or, in other words, even the guards were beginning to see the light.

4. THE CORPS OF GENDARMES AND THE THIRD SECTION

With the accession of Nicholas I (1825–55), the whole concept of bodyguards of the ruler and political police was modernized. From that time on, protection of the Russian leader became a professional matter, with the guards regiments and the various chancelleries and bureaus being relieved of such duties. Of course, guards units of various types continued to cluster around the ruler until the end of the tsardom, but their tasks were more decorative than practical.

Shocked by the Decembrist attempt, Nicholas deigned to interrogate many of the conspirators personally. Although his ancestor, Peter the Great, took a similar role with the *streltsy*, Nicholas' questioning was not brutal, but foreshadowed techniques current today. He professed to show such sympathy with and understanding of some of the plotters that they fully confessed. Although there is no intimation that Nicholas used this approach cynically, it should be made clear his sympathy did not extend to sparing the lives of the chief Decembrists.

Hovering in the background during the aftermath of that attempt on the throne was the suave and gentlemanly General Count Alexander Benckendorff, who had been the guards chief of staff under Alexander I and had some appreciation of the unrest among the younger officers and the nascent group of intellectuals. But it is strange, indeed, that such a mild man was the progenitor of the police state. His successors, not only in Russia, but in other parts of the world as well, have been of a very different stripe.

The idea, however, was completely Benckendorff's. His original recommendation was to reestablish the police ministry and set up a *gendarmerie* inspectorate, the latter to be evolved from the army gendarmes who functioned as military police under Alexander I. Nicholas agreed in principle with the Benckendorff plan, but wanted to have the investigative function completely under his control and not that of a ministry. Therefore, he first appointed Benckendorff Chief of the Corps of Gendarmes and then in July, 1826, established the investigative branch, or what he called the Third Section of the Imperial Chancellery. At the same time he made Benckendorff's post dual by appointing him head of the Third Section as well.

Although it was subordinate to the Third Section and its successors, the Corps of Gendarmes became a permanent institution that lasted throughout the later Romanov era. Somewhat like the guards regiments under the Preobrazhensky Prikaz, it was the arresting arm of the secret police. And since originally they were also intended to protect the people from exploitation by administrators, bureaucrats, and faulty legal work, the gendarmes were given uniforms that were purposefully showy, light blue with white accoutrements and white gloves. Equally typical of the "do-good" simulation was the banner of one gendarme group, the Moscow regiment, a white flag bearing the legend *Le Bien-etre General en Russie.*

Army gendarmes formed the original cadre of the new corps, but Benckendorff tried hard to attract superior young army officers and educated young nobles with military aspirations to its ranks. Initially, due to the idealistic tone with which the organization was launched as well as to its distinctive uniforms, he had some success in recruiting better types. Soon, however, the "right" type of recruit came to shy away from being a policeman. The result was that the corps, for all its snappy uniforms and pretty flags, had to rely largely on second-raters in the army for the bulk of its manpower. In the last decades of the nineteenth century it was renamed the Special Corps of Gendarmes, but that did nothing to change its basic make-up and functions until its dissolution with the Bolshevik take-over.

By the end of Nicholas I's reign, the Corps of Gendarmes had expanded into regional regiments with a total strength of some eight to nine thousand men. During its ninety years of existence, however, the corps grew much larger and its functions increased. It gained mounted units, used as antiriot troops in the cities and as posses in the country. As Russia entered the industrial era, some units were permanently assigned as railroad and port guards. And under the special antisubversive edicts of the last Romanovs the corps gained the power—especially in outlying areas—of summary arrest, trial, and exile of political suspects. Nevertheless, despite its powers and all-pervasiveness the corps was not worth much when the chips were down. In the final periods of real trouble and uprisings it was the Cossacks who served as the last bulwark of the autocracy, not the prettily uniformed Corps of Gendarmes.

The corps' original parent body, the Third Section, although comparatively insignificant in size, had and carried out a sense of mission —that of protecting the ruler—and thereby, for its time, was quite formidable. Like the gendarmes, it had its "do-good" façade; according to a somewhat apocryphal account, when Benckendorff sought instructions for the newly formed Third Section, Nicholas gave him a white handkerchief and said, "Here are your orders, take this and wipe away the tears of my people." But those benign poses of Nicholas and Benckendorff were mere façades, for the Third Section inherited without a qualm the interrogation and torture devices of its predecessors and refined them. It likewise continued the almost timeless Russian censorship of mail and literature and improved upon it. It also had its spies, agents, and informers to complement the information gathered by lesser gentry of that ilk working for the gendarmes. Nor were those spies limited to internal work: from the time of the 1830–31 Polish uprising they were increasingly posted abroad, at first infiltrating and informing on Polish independence groups and then broadening the field to include traveling Russians and anyone else thought to be a threat to the tsar. And the Third Section also improved on that old Russian institution, surveillance, not only of local subjects, but also of visiting foreigners to the extent that an American diplomat informed President Andrew Jackson that most of his St. Petersburg staff of domestics were secret police agents. Ironically, the Third Section—and its successors—frequently were objects of surveillance themselves. Jealous rivals, the lesser police of the interior ministry, local police departments, and the personal bodyguard of the last tsar, always distrusted the higher police and spied on and tailed them whenever possible. Of course, that led to conflicts and security mismanagement that eventually were as disastrous to the last Romanovs as they were to Paul who first caused such interservice rivalry.

Under Nicholas I, the Third Section was lucky. That ruler died in bed of natural causes. In his reign, assassination of the ruler or overthrow of the autocracy was virtually unthought of. Whatever unrest there was either came from foreign sources—the Poles and the Crimean War, from easily quelled peasant risings, or from the thin, thin veneer of upper-class intellectuals, who in later days would have been classed as nothing more serious than parlor pinks.

Despite the nature of its work, in its formative days the Third Section was run almost as if it were a gentlemen's club. Benckendorff enlisted a fellow Baltic German, Maxim von Vock, the civilian head of the interior ministry's political police, as his second-in-command of the Third Section. And he initially made General Leonty Dubbelt —also of foreign origin—chief of staff of the gendarmes. Von Vock died in 1831—perhaps the Polish uprising had been too much for him—but the polished and astute Dubbelt (really the brains of the Third Section under Nicholas I) continued as second-in-command of both the gendarmes and the Third Section until he was retired at his own request in 1856.

Benckendorff himself died in 1844, without his brain-child ever being put to a real test. Nevertheless, as far as he deemed it gentlemanly to do so, he busied himself with study of reports from the Third Section's growing numbers of informers and spies. And his special penchant was harassing the intellectuals. As did many a security chief after him, the good count truly believed he could make the intellectuals see the error of their ways and bring them around to supporting the regime. He devoted personal attention to Alexander Pushkin, not only to his writings and attitudes, but also to that unfortunate poet's marriage, death, and funeral. Benckendorff also

[125]

had the opportunity to devote similar attentions to such other intellectuals as Alexander Herzen, Mikhail Lermontov, and Peter Chaadayev, with the last being declared insane, a political police tactic still in vogue in Mother Russia. After Benckendorff joined his maker, Dubbelt kept up the good work, hounding Vissarion Belinsky, the critic, to his death and treating Fedor Dostoyevsky to his notorious last-second reprieve from execution. For the record only, it should be noted that Count Alexis Orlov succeeded Benckendorff as top cop and served until his voluntary retirement in 1856, but it should also be pointed out that Orlov was a lazy political appointee who left the real work to Dubbelt.

It is also of interest to note that during the Benckendorff-Dubbelt period no intellectual, since all were fellow members of the gentry, was made to pay the supreme penalty, death. To be sure, many were imprisoned or exiled to Siberia, the Caucasus, or their country estates. Others moved or fled abroad, a privilege now long-denied to dissidents to the dictatorship of the proletariat. But, lest the Benckendorff-Dubbelt hands falsely appear too clean, it should not be forgotten that peasants and such lesser subjects got the full treatment of torture and death for protesting their lot. Those were the unpeople of that day. But, although they were virtually faceless, their numbers uncounted and most of their fates unknown, they amounted to almost nothing as compared to the legions that met far worse under Stalin, and even his successors. Therefore, and to keep things in perspective, the Third Section, even though known as "dreaded" in its time, would be preferred beyond all doubt to the KGB by present citizens of Russia.

Shortly after Alexander II (1855–81) mounted the throne, the twin post as chief of the gendarmes and the Third Section was offered to and refused by Dubbelt, who was ready for retirement. More or less as the result of a lack of takers, the job was given to Prince Vasily A. Dolgorukov, a former minister of war, but really not much more than a well-meaning and noble functionary. But Dolgorukov's appointee as his second-in-command of the Third Section, Count Peter Shuvalov, was of an entirely different stripe, a hard-boiled activist who not only did his best to reorganize the gendarmes, but also was, for those times, the closest thing Russia had to a real political policeman. Unfortunately, however, and particularly for Alexander himself, Shuvalov's toughness was limited by Alexander's flabbiness and vacillation.

[126]

Bent on reform when he became tsar, Alexander got off to an initial easy start. The bothersome intellectuals of Nicholas' time had become aged-in-grade and had more or less shot their bolt so far as real challenge to the autocracy was concerned. But, with the advent of the 1860s, and somewhat fanned by the Polish uprising of 1863, a new threat was developing from an emerging group, somewhat misnamed the intelligentsia. It was misnamed because it was a mishmash of youth, nobles, workers, and peasants, whose general claim to intellect was not much more than some schooling and the ability to read, write, and do sums. Curiously, those youngsters first surfaced as nineteenth century hippies, complete with long and freakish hairdos, colored eyeglasses, blankets instead of capes and coats, hostility to their elders and thereby to the "establishment" of their times, advocacy of women's liberation, atheism, communal living, and a general intolerance for the ideas of others. At first, those young people puzzled or amused the world into which they had thrust themselves, but as antagonism mounted against them, they were given the collective name of Nihilists, a term used for them by Ivan Turgenev in one of his novels. And as with the latterday hippies and their successors, many of them gravitated toward revolution and destruction of the existing order as the ultimate means of grasping their would-be utopias. It is also interesting to note that as with the latter-day hippies, those young Russians of the 1860s and a decade later while wishing to end the obvious evils of their era usually offered not better systems in their places, but forms which would have been even more repressive and unbearable. Of course, however, it must be appreciated that they were not intellectuals, but intelligentsia.

Although their numbers were triflingly small, those young radicals spread and split across the face of Russia almost cancerously. From Nihilists they metamorphosed into Narodniks, into Anarchists and into the *Land and Freedom* and the *People's Will* groups. Their heroes were equally varied, ranging from such true intellectuals as Alexander Herzen, Dmitry Pisarev, Nikolay Chernyshevsky, and Mikhail Bakhunin to the crackpot Sergey Nechayev.

In almost every conceivable way, the Third Section under Dolgorukov made a true mess of handling the situation. Frightened by the Polish uprising and peasant unrest, instead of paternalistically allowing the youthful cults to run out what would have been natural courses, it cracked down on them with a heavy and awkward hand.

[127]

First, it arrested and exiled the young radicals almost wholesale. That truly decimated the young people's ranks, but at the same time it converted fads into ideologies and youthful enthusiasts into martyrs. Next, because political prisoners were then regarded as a cut above the garden variety of inmate, many of those jailed were allowed to send out letters, pamphlets, indeed entire books to fan the flames of dissidence and revolt. Finally—and this was a continuing gross error of omission throughout Alexander II's reign—the Third Section made no special new efforts to safeguard the person and environs of the ruler, even though it was well advised by infiltrated spies, double-agents and informers of almost every plan being hatched by the revolutionaries. So, from hindsight, it was mainly the romantic, slipshod operations of the radicals that prevented the tsar's being done in earlier, not the work of the Third Section.

A tightening-up of sorts followed the Dmitry Karakozov attempt against the tsar in 1866. Since the Third Section was well aware of plots to kill Alexander, Karakozov's proximity to the ruler in the Summer Garden seems almost unbelievable, but that was a looser, laxer era. Nevertheless, that attempt accomplished one thing—the resignation of Dolgorukov in shame.

The successor was Peter Shuvalov, promoted to chief of both the Third Section and the gendarmes. Exploiting the flurry caused by the Karakozov attempt, Shuvalov persuaded the tsar to retire the easy-going and ineffective governor-general of St. Petersburg and replace him with General Fedor F. Trepov as prefect of the capital, but actually its security police boss. Whatever their negative characteristics—Shuvalov became known as Peter IV—both were able and tough men, determined to protect the leader and make the capital safe for him. They were the best security chiefs available in Russia at that time.

Proof of Shuvalov's efficiency lay in the very fact that in the eight years he ran the Third Section and the gendarmes not a single terrorist attempt was made against Alexander II or anyone else of note. The revolutionaries were not out of business; they were as active as ever in plotting and planning. But, that was as far as matters went, due to Shuvalov's capabilities.

One of Shuvalov's strong points was examining and checking on anybody, no matter how innocent-appearing, who had any contact with the tsar. That included even the tsar's lady-love and her family, some of whom were involved in shady business dealings. For that, obviously more interested in his amour than his security, Alexander gave Shuvalov the gate in 1874 by making him ambassador to London.

Whether he had a subconscious death wish or was a fool unconcerned about his own safety is a moot point, but the facts are that Alexander named a series of three lightweights to succeed Shuvalov. The first was a General Alexander Potapov, known as a "birdbrain" even in those days, whose appointment gladdened the hearts of the security rivals in the interior ministry and must also have been received with pleasure by the revolutionaries. Potapov was so bad he had hardly warmed his office chair before being replaced by a General Nikolay V. Mezentsov, whose chief claim to fame was as a "good-time Charlie."

Meanwhile, the radicals made the most of the deterioration of the Third Section. At that moment in history, their specialty was trying to arouse unrest among the peasants, who could not have cared less. Many of the young people were arrested. There were many trials, some of them mass affairs. But control was so lax that most were released to return to more revolutionary work, completely unchastened. As a result, and as should have been expected, matters came to such a pass that in January, 1878, the young terrorist Vera Zasulich shot and wounded General Trepov so seriously he had to retire. That, abetted by Zasulich's acquittal and subsequent escape abroad, let loose a veritable wave of terror, with tsarist officials being attacked and killed throughout the length and breadth of the empire. Then in August, 1878, a subpeak was reached when the relatively harmless Mezentsov was knifed and killed by Sergey Stepnyak-Kravchinsky, who likewise escaped abroad to write his memoirs.

The appointment of another ineffective, General Alexander R. Drenteln, as Third Section chief, brought no change. The terror continued. In February, 1879, the governor of Kharkov was gunned down. A little more than a month later, Leon Mirsky, the would-be Polish patriot, shot at and missed Drenteln on the capital streets. And in April, 1878, Alexander Solovyev shot at and likewise missed none other than Alexander himself, while the tsar was strolling in the grounds of the Winter Palace.

That attempt again jolted Alexander from his security lethargy. But he did not recall Shuvalov or seek a Third Section boss of similar

[129]

caliber. Instead, with the addiction to the military to which all the latter Romanovs were so prone, he turned the job over to the army. He divided his realm into northern, central, and southern parts with three top generals as overall security bosses in each. And he retained Drenteln as Third Section chief, despite the fact he had just about quartered his authority.

Big and bloody crackdowns on terrorists, terrorist suspects, and many completely innocent people followed, especially in the south, thereby supplying more fuel to revolutionary flames. In Kharkov, the central sector, Count Loris-Melikov tried a mixture of severity and the velvet glove with mixed success. In the north, the general in command was hamstrung, since he had to share authority with Drenteln, but take the ultimate responsibility.

Nothing daunted, the *People's Will*—by then the main arm of the terrorists—devoted the remainder of 1879 to unsuccessful attempts to blow up the tsar in his train and to publicly publishing his death sentence.

Meanwhile, by a routine piece of luck, Third Section underlings found plans for the Winter Palace in terrorist hands. With that, Drenteln, who at least had some sense, wanted to tighten security at the palace. But guards all over the place would have interfered with Alexander's love-life. That came first, so he turned down the security chief's plea.

The upshot of that piece of blatant stupidity on the part of Alexander came soon. With hardly any difficulty at all, *People's Will* got Stepan Khalturin and his dynamite into the Winter Palace. The dynamite exploded on the evening of February 5, 1880, with Khalturin standing outside to watch before getting away for future terror. The tsar escaped by pure luck. A late guest delayed the dinner for which the explosion had been timed.

Although by then well frightened, Alexander again refused to take even the most rudimentary security steps. His sole reaction was to appoint a commission to study the problem. And he named Mikhail Loris-Melikov to head the group, solely because that ambitious Armenian had taken a softer approach while running security at Kharkov.

With almost unseemly speed, Loris-Melikov made rubber stamps of the rest of the commission and established what he called a "dictatorship of the heart." To secure his dictatorship, he got rid of Drenteln forthwith, made Count Vyacheslav Plehve top gendarme and a General Petr Cherevin head of the Third Section. Of the latter two, Plehve had security police ability, certainly more so than his chief.

That paper-shuffling and the near supreme powers given Loris-Melikov did little or nothing to stop the terrorists. Hardly in office, the dictator was shot on February 20, 1880, in the unsuccessful attempt by the Ukrainian, Ippolit Mledecki. Seemingly, at least, Mledecki's almost summary execution took the wind out of the terrorist sails. Therefore, throughout the rest of 1880, Loris-Melikov proceeded with a program of relaxation and reform, which he hoped would lead to a constitution. And in August 1880, in a move designed to assuage the radicals, he decreed a paper shuffle abolishing the Third Section and creating a new Department of State Police subordinate to the interior ministry, making himself chief of that ministry. Nevertheless, throughout that period of apparent respite, the regime continued to be harsh toward captured terrorists, executing one pair and sending others to Siberian exile, with half-shaven heads and in chains.

For its part, the *People's Will* did not swallow the regime's pose of comparative moderation, as events soon proved. In late January, 1881, a fluke—the arrest of a minor but well-informed police official who had joined *People's Will*—precipitated the arrest of other terrorists and the possible complete collapse of their organization. Therefore, on March 13, 1881, with their ringleader already in police hands and talking, the rest of the terrorists carried out their death sentence against Alexander II.

Count Shuvalov, Alexander's only real security chief, had died of natural causes some two years before the assassination. One can nearly envision his having rolled over in his grave in disgust. But the blame cannot be foisted off on his successor, Loris-Melikov. Nor is any credit due the terrorists, despite the false halos given them by subsequent revolutionaries and Communists. Each and every one of those young people was a rank amateur. The true responsibility for Alexander's death rests right with the tsar himself. It was he who gave amour precedence over security. It was he who named one incapable man after another as his chief of security. And it was he who crippled his protection by allowing interservice rivalry and permitting security to enter the wilds of administrative mess. The only wonder is that Alexander was not killed earlier.

5. THE OKHRANA—FORMATIVE YEARS (1881–1900)

When Alexander III (1881–94) succeeded his assassinated brother, he moved the court, bag and baggage, to Gatchina in the country. There, a virtual prisoner from terror, he surrounded himself with foot soldiers, cavalry, and plainclothes policemen. And he remained at Gatchina throughout his reign except for carefully guarded trips to other imperial residences.

The move from St. Petersburg to Gatchina was made on the insistence of Alexander III's former tutor, the arch-reactionary jurist Konstantin Pobedonostsev who in many ways was the predecessor of Stalin's viceroy, the infamous Alexander Poskrebyshev of some fifty years later. Although by title merely procurator of the Holy Synod, Pobedonostsev actually ruled not only as co-tsar in all important foreign and domestic affairs, but also controlled the autocracy's security for about a quarter century. And, despite his sweeping powers, that "gray eminence" as some called him also stressed the small details of security. Because of that emphasis on previously overlooked details, the last two Romanov tsars at least escaped assassination while on the throne.

One of Pobedonostsev's first steps was to force the resignation of the pretty well disgraced Loris-Melikov in April, 1881. In the Armenian's place as acting police boss of the realm was installed Count Nikolay P. Ignatyev, a professional diplomat, as minister of the interior. From the Ignatyev appointment on, tsarist Russia fell into line with European tradition with the interior minister becoming the nation's top political security chief.

Although he held office for barely more than a year, Ignatyev—doubtlessly at Pobedonostsev's prodding—reorganized the entire security structure. He freed the gendarmes from control of the various governors-general. Some two months later, he obtained a ukase for a state of emergency under which the gendarmes and the governors-general could make summary arrests, ban public and private meetings and otherwise maintain law and order arbitrarily. That ukase, in one form or another, remained in effect throughout the rest of the tsardom.

Seemingly almost as an afterthought, Ignatyev next established special political police units in St. Petersburg, Moscow, and Warsaw. At first those units were called *okhrannyye otdeleniya*, or protective sections. Gradually, they were expanded into the Administration for

Protection of State Institutions and Public Security, soon shortened to Okhrana, meaning literally protection or guard. And as the organization expanded, Okhrana offices were established in virtually every city and town of importance. On paper, the Okhrana was a special part of the Police Department, while that department was subordinate to the interior ministry. In fact, however, the Okhrana exercised almost supreme power over the tsar's subjects, not only because it was a secret organization, but also because it had such rights as entry without warrant, deportation to Siberia without trial, surveillance of anyone, and in important cases the right to impose the death penalty administratively, or without trial. By the time of its extinction with the abdication of Nicholas II, the Okhrana had become a law unto itself.

Under Ignatyev were two figures who were to play a dominant role in security and Okhrana affairs for the next quarter century. The first was Count Vyacheslav Plehve, who served as Director of the Police Department from 1881–84, as Deputy Minister of Interior (and actual boss of the ministry) from 1884–92, and as Minister of the Interior from 1902 until his assassination by the SRs' Sazonov in 1904. The other was Peter N. Durnovo, the abler of the two, although extremely severe and reactionary, who served as Director of the Police Department from 1884 until the latter days of Alexander III's reign, when he irked the tsar by using his police powers to check up on his mistress, but eventually became Minister of the Interior under Witte in 1906.

Ignatyev's short tenure ended when he sympathized with the idea of *zemsky sobor*, or national assembly. Pobedonostsev, who wanted nothing that smacked of constitutionalism, replaced him with a reactionary former education minister, Count Dmitry Tolstoy. That worthy lasted as Interior Minister until 1889, when he was replaced by a real slow-wit, known as "calf-head" by many, Ivan N. Durnovo (no relation to Peter). Durnovo was succeeded by another incompetent statesman, Ivan Goremykin, in 1895. Goremykin held the interior post for four years, by default became Prime Minister under Nicholas II and ended by being killed by the Bolsheviks, certainly as lightweight a victim as his tsar.

Actually, however, those goings and comings in the interior ministry in the last two decades of the nineteenth century should be regarded as no more than matters of record. Okhrana and security work continued and waxed in that period in spite of those figure-heads, due primarily to Plehve and Peter Durnovo—the real chiefs of the secret police.

Too much credit, however, should not be given Plehve, Durnovo and other early Okhrana functionaries. They were more dabblers than experts. The plain facts are that they faced little to no real challenge. For all serious intents and purposes, the executions of the assassins of Alexander II in the spring of 1881 broke the back of the *People's Will* and terror tactics against the autocracy practically ceased. A main cause of that was the cowardly confession to Plehve of one of the assassins, that latter-day "hero," Rysakov. He implicated every fellow conspirator whose name he could recall. Most of his colleagues either went to prison and Siberian exile or became Okhrana agents. One of the few exceptions was that odd hatchet woman, Vera Figner, who survived to plot—but never take an active part in —SR terror and lasted long enough to observe the niceties of Chekist and Stalinist terror from the sidelines. In March, 1882, she inveigled Khalturin, the Winter Palace bombardier, into assassinating a particularly brutal Odessa gendarme chief. Almost needless to say, Khalturin paid with his life for the deed, while Miss Figner eventually escaped abroad. By 1884, however, hundreds of terrorists and suspected terrorists had been rounded up and imprisoned or exiled by the Okhrana and effective revolutionary action had been brought to a halt. Nevertheless, toward the end of that decade, there were some sporadic incidents, notably the alleged 1887 attempt against the tsar by Lenin's elder brother and his co-conspirators and the likewise alleged attempt against Alexander III's train in 1888. Since the train affair was later patently exposed as a pure accident, there is also reason to doubt the romantic claim of Alexander Ulyanov and his fellows that they were successors of *People's Will* terrorists. That case smells of at least some excessive zeal and fabrication by the Okhrana, especially since Pilsudski, doubly suspect as a Pole as well as a revolutionary, was given only Siberian exile. But the execution of the elder Ulyanov, routine as it may have been at the time, was to prove costly indeed for latter-day members of the Okhrana.

Also costly was the involvement of the early and subsequent Okhrana in pogroms and other anti-Semitic measures—usually indirectly through its gendarme arm—which caused a backlash by giving many an otherwise harmless Jewish youth good cause to join the terrorists. For example, much of the responsibility for the 1881 Kiev pogrom can be placed at the door of the feckless Drenteln, who was governor-general of the Ukrainian capital at that time. The fact that the Third Section meanwhile had been replaced by the Okhrana meant nothing at all to the revolutionaries. That change did not alter Drentlen's spots as a security chief.

In the early 1880s, shortly after the establishment of the Okhrana, there was a somewhat typical example of an attempted symbiosis between a disillusioned revolutionary and the security police, a mutual approach which would become quite common after the turn of the century. At the time it happened, however, it was quite singular and remained so for many a year, no doubt as the result of its unfortunate outcome. Grigory Sudeykin, an ambitious St. Petersburg Okhrana officer, posed as secretly sympathetic to revolutionary aims and thereby struck up what he thought was a working relationship with one Sergey Degayev, a former member of the *People's Will* who had turned police informer. Part of Sudeykin's lure was the promise that if the collaboration proved successful Degayev would one day join him in running Russia. Initially, Degayev swallowed the hook and turned in his terrorist colleagues. But, on a mission to Switzerland to hoodwink Leo Tikhomirov, an expatriate terrorist, into returning to Russia, Degayev had second thoughts and confessed everything to Tikhomirov. The stronger character, Tikhomirov reenlisted Degayev in terrorism, but with the proviso that he kill off Sudeykin on his return to Russia. Degayev agreed and murdered Sudeykin a few months later with the aid of two colleagues before fleeing to the U.S., where years later he died a natural death under an assumed name.

Despite its ultimate collapse, the basic organization of the Okhrana was practicable and one which has since been polished to near perfection by other security organizations, especially the KGB. Its three prime groups were called the External Agency, the Internal Agency, and the Foreign Agency. And early in the twentieth century what was called a Central Agency was also in operation. All of the titles, except that of the Foreign Agency, were somewhat misnomers. The External Agency was the most ordinary group, consisting of spies and informers, usually disguised, who performed routine surveillance of suspects and possible suspects. The Internal Agency also was made

[135]

up of spies and informers, but it specialized in revolutionary and suspected revolutionary organizations and thus was under much deeper cover. The Foreign Agency was a combination of External and Internal agents operating abroad, mainly in those areas where Russian revolutionaries and dissidents congregated, such as France, Switzerland, and Britain. The Central Agency was a very deep cover operation, handling double-agents, revolutionaries who also worked for the Okhrana or police agents who had infiltrated revolutionary groups. Every effort was made—not always successfully—to keep the various agencies strictly compartmentalized. That not only protected the agents from exposure but also gave the Okhrana checks on its operatives since agents unwittingly frequently reported on other agents. And in the later and more sophisticated Okhrana days, unnecessary exposure of agents was also lessened by the use of pseudonyms and the establishment of safe houses, practices followed ever since by even the most rudimentary intelligence organizations. But, despite all that admirable organizational structure, the Okhrana never could rid itself of its most glaring tsarist defect, unpredictable fluctuations in the chain of command. Sometimes, it was actually run by the interior minister himself. At other times that chore was taken on by the director of the police department. And on still other occasions, the primary work would be done by the chief of one of the agencies, with the police director and the interior minister seemingly indifferent unless some debacle occurred, which was often the case.

The External Agency, although comparatively commonplace, was really quite redoubtable and has probably not been matched by the Communists since their many restrictions on normal life make their choice of such operatives limited and obvious to all but the most naïve visiting foreigner. Jews and Poles, of course, were excluded, but in its ranks were agents who posed as cab drivers, concierges, doorkeepers, waiters, peddlers, railroad men, soldiers, and even officers. Since their main task was surveillance, they specialized in memorizing photographs and likenesses of political suspects and thereby frequently got onto unsuspecting revolutionaries when they surfaced from hiding or abroad. Prosaic and routine as was much of the work of External Agency agents, there was an element of risk: through carelessness or mere chance, some were recognized and killed by terrorists. Being the real workhorse of security, the External

Agency not only tailed and arrested suspects, it also spotted clandestine meeting places, printing presses, and explosives factories.

In spite of its name, the Internal Agency was much more mobile than the External Agency and frequently operated abroad. The Internal agents were a cut above their External colleagues, usually drawn from army noncommissioned ranks, and ranged from workers, students, prostitutes, professional men, party leaders, and, in the latter days of the tsardom, even to representatives of the Duma. And Internal pseudonyms were more carefully evolved and more frequently changed. The better name for the Internal agents would have been collaborators, who were attracted to the Okhrana by disillusionment with revolutionary aims, an interest in secret police work, feuds within the revolutionary movements, or plain greed for money. There were even those who worked with the Okhrana—as Stalin was suspected of having done—as a means of advancing themselves and eliminating rivals within their movements. But, no matter what the motivation, all were given money and had to sign receipts for it, no matter how trifling, as a means of tying them to the Okhrana. Since the Internal Agency's chief task was to bore within the movements of the SRs, SDs, Anarchists and other subversive groups, its agents were abroad watching emigrés as frequently as they were home at secret meetings of suspect organizations. Needless to say, the Internal agents' work abroad served as a check on the Foreign Agency, but it also increased the costs and the paperwork.

Unfortunately, since almost all Okhrana records were destroyed, seized, or simply disappeared with the fall of the tsardom and the subsequent take-over of the Bolsheviks, very little is known about the Central Agency. It appears, however, that it was a very small and elite branch of the Internal Agency, handling not run-of-the-mill revolutionary collaborators, but top-level activists among antiregime organizations. The veteran Moscow Okhrana chief Zubatov, himself a revolutionary as a youth, is credited with the establishment of the Central Agency. Its most renowned co-workers were Father Gapon of 1905 "Bloody Sunday" fame and the notorious Evno Azev and Roman Malinovsky. It stands to reason that there were others besides that trio, but the elimination of records leaves that only a supposition. Ironically, despite the little that is known about it, the Central Agency brought down the most opprobrium upon the Okhrana, to the extent that even some of the security chiefs who survived the revolution professed to loathe Zubatov's brainchild. The reason for the Central Agency's ignominy was its basic technique: it knowingly operated with and financed revolutionary and terrorist leaders, acting on the principle that if the criminals were given enough rope they would hang themselves. And although too frequently that was not the case, the Central Agency also believed that by being in the driver's seat it could thwart outrages, eventually causing the terrorists enough failures to convince them to halt their operations. It was such work by the Central Agency that gave the whole Okhrana the somewhat unjust repute of *provocateurs*.

Comparatively, the Foreign Agency was a refreshing even though relatively ineffective outfit. That branch was organized in Paris in 1883 by Peter Rachkovsky and remained in operation until 1917. Unlike the other Okhrana agencies, its activities are quite well known because its records were preserved and were given to a U.S. university. But in general, except for some anecdotes highly similar to spy fiction, the Foreign Agency's record is not very impressive and would be of scant value to latter-day students of security and intelligence. In the main, although he kept a sharp eye on emigré terrorists, Rachkovsky was not an expert police officer. His chief delight was coups, one of them an out-and-out provocation in which he financed a revolutionary attempt against Alexander III before delivering all of the conspirators, except his agent who had started it all, to French authorities. But shortly after the turn of the century, Rachkovsky got more criticism than praise when he probed too deeply into the activities of a French "healer" who had wormed his way into the tsar's confidence. And in hindsight, Rachkovsky's most astute move was to refuse to have anything to do with Azev and let Zubatov take over control of that conscienceless double-agent. Nevertheless, so far as is known, despite its panoply of external and internal agents and much money, the Foreign Agency never caught one major terrorist, never thwarted one principal plot. And when terrorism went out of style after Azev was uncovered and the SRs strove for legality, Foreign Agency operations became almost meaningless except for a rather inconsequential flurry of activity with the Germans caused by World War I. However, ineffective and almost playboy as it was, a certain amount of infamy is attached to the Foreign Agency: there appears good reason to believe that its principal chief, Rachkovsky, had much to do with the Okhrana fabrication of the *Protocols of the*

Learned Elders of Zion, that awful canard still purveyed by anti-Semites.

From a strictly pragmatic point of view, the Okhrana, even though bumbling in many respects, had a good record in the nineteenth century. Despite student unrest, an emerging proletariat, troubles with the peasants, and terrorists to crackpots at home and abroad, Alexander III went to his rest unaided by assassins and the ruler's family and ministers suffered no assaults. Nicholas II (1894–1917) and his relatives and functionaries likewise lived in comparative peace in the first years of the last tsar's reign, despite similar troubles and the horrible "massacre" at Khodynka field, whose hundreds upon hundreds of "martyrs" would have been well exploited by opponents in a later era.

6. THE OKHRANA—TERROR (1900–10)

The first decade of the twentieth century was most dangerous for Nicholas II, his family, and his officials. Terrorism, on a scale that the world experienced neither before nor since, was rampant. Comparatively, the earlier wave of terror that culminated with the assassination of Alexander II, was almost nothing. In that period at the start of the century, Russia's ruler's life was constantly in danger, one after another of his high officers fell victim to assassins while lesser functionaries were murdered by the hundreds.

Fortunately for Nicholas at least, the Okhrana functioned quite well in that era of great risk. Although it did not succeed in saving many of his top officials, including Okhrana members, it did manage to protect the ruler throughout by means of a grim and unwilling collaboration of sorts between security police and fanatic revolutionaries. Before and long after the downfall of the tsardom, the Okhrana was attacked by a veritable plethora of personalities, both great and small, for its methods in handling the terrorists. Nevertheless, it is extremely doubtful that any other group or persons, past or present, could have come up with a better solution to the problems faced by the Okhrana at that time. And given the handicaps under which those security men worked, the only wonder is why some of them, at least, did not throw up their hands in disgust and quit.

In that dark decade, three men stood out as superior Okhrana officers, even though their efforts were not well appreciated by many, including the tsar. That trio was Zubatov, Rachkovsky, and

Colonel (later General) Alexander Gerasimov, who, as chief of the Central Agency from 1905 until he retired in 1909, was a most capable security officer and the last real boss of the Okhrana. There were also two minor and much less effective figures, Leonid A. Ratayev, chief of the Foreign Agency until dismissed in 1905, and (Gendarme) Colonel Alexander Spiridovitch, Palace Commandant from 1906 until the eve of World War I. And finally, almost as a counterfoil of a kind, an unusually weak man and poor police officer, who played a dark and negative role, Aleksey Lopukhin, served as Director of Police from 1902 until forced to resign in 1904. The name Lopukhin should be a synonym for infamy in security annals.

In that heyday of terror, interior ministers, of course, did at least nominally control Okhrana operations. But only two of them were effective, Plehve who served from 1902 until assassinated in 1904, and Stolypin who functioned both as prime minister and interior minister from 1906 until he, too, was killed by a terrorist. The easygoing Prince Svyatopolk-Mirsky succeeded Plehve only to resign in disgrace after "Bloody Sunday" of January, 1905. The ineffective Alexander Bulygin next filled the post until replaced by Peter Durnovo in October, 1905. And Durnovo served only until April, 1906, when Stolypin took over but retained Durnovo as his deputy in the interior ministry.

The first victim of the new wave of terror was the reactionary education minister, Professor Bogolepov, assassinated in 1901 by ex-student Karpovich. Although Karpovich was an SR, and later a member of its chief terrorist group, the killing of Bogolepov was not so much an attack on the autocracy as a reaction to repressive measures taken against university students.

But the real SR campaign against the tsar and the autocracy followed very swiftly. In January, 1902, the SR central committee authorized the creation of the Battle Organization, a terrorist group organized and directed by Gershuni, son of a Moscow millionaire and a fanatic and often-imprisoned activist who got his start with survivors of the *People's Will* in the eighties. At first, the Battle Organization was enjoined from attacks on Nicholas—lest the apolitical peasantry the party mistakenly pursued take affront at action against the "Little Father"—and concentrated on killing off any and all government officials regarded as cruel and repressive and devoted particular effort to the elimination of top police and regime administrators.

Later, however, as Nicholas combined half-hearted liberalism with more repression, the tsar was given the top position on the list of those marked for death.

Meanwhile, though, the SR and even its newly formed Battle Organization were badly riddled with informers, in the main onetime revolutionaries who had been caught and decided to work for the Okhrana for money, but also by a type of entrepreneur who was able to work both sides of the street at a profit in the conflict between the Okhrana and the terrorists. How much that latter genre was the direct responsibility of the Okhrana or was merely a case of the Okhrana making the most of a natural development, remains a moot point. Nevertheless, on the one hand it is interesting to speculate on what might have been the future of the autocracy if the security had been successful in that deadly game. And on the other hand it is just as interesting to wonder what the fate of the SR and Russia might have been if the revolutionaries had won the struggle. However, as matters worked out, the conflict was an exhausting standoff for both sides that resulted in the nonparticipatory SDs, or Bolsheviks, moving in to seize the spoils like veritable jackals.

Both the Okhrana and the SR were plagued by many entrepreneur informers, actually double-agents, but somewhat misnamed then and forever after by revolutionaries and leftists in general as *provocateurs*. The outstanding figure then, and probably for all time, among that sorry lot was Azev, the Jew, who had the code name of "Raskin" with the Okhrana and the pseudonym of "Valentin" among the SRs.

Physically, Azev was just as unprepossessing as he was morally, but there is no doubt that he was extremely adroit mentally. As a youthful jack-of-all-trades, he fled Rostov-on-Don when local police took an interest in his connections with city leftists, the modish although not necessarily ideological milieu for young people of that era. He had a lifetime propensity for easy money, or other people's money, and he ran true to form when departing by absconding with some eight hundred rubles of his firm's butter sales receipts. He surfaced in Karlsruhe, Germany, where he entered a technical school. Within a year, or by 1893, he volunteered to work for the Okhrana—and thereby somewhat eased his financial plight—by reporting on the Russian emigrés among his classmates. His record at Rostov-on-Don was known, of course, and that induced the Okhrana to take on Azev as one of their thousands of petty informers, at a fee of fifty rubles a month. His schooling was completed in 1899—he qualified as an electrical engineer—and his services as an informer had improved to the extent his monthly fee had been raised to one hundred rubles, plus bonuses and vacation allowances.

During that six-year novitiate, Azev had worked, nominally at least, under the direction of Rachkovsky's Foreign Agency. However, it appears that when he finished that training and his schooling Rachkovsky—for reasons unclear—wanted nothing to do with him.

Accordingly, he was sent back to Russia and put to work in Moscow under Zubatov, who although at that time was still deep in police-controlled union activity was also starting the framework of what became the Central Agency. As one of Zubatov's men in the latter section, Azev was given the assignment of boring into Moscow revolutionary groups, but soon concentrated on the SRs, the most active organization.

By 1900, Azev had penetrated the SRs so well that his monthly fee was increased to 150 rubles. By 1901, Zubatov had enough confidence in Azev to send him abroad with the task of penetrating SR emigrés and especially the party's Central Committee. Within short order he bored deeply within the SR structure abroad to the extent that he gained the trust of Gershuni, then busy with the nascent Battle Organization and planning the assassination of either Sipyagin, the Interior Minister, or Pobedonostsev.

Azev, however, had not told the Okhrana of the assassination plans. Instead, he persuaded Zubatov not to molest Gershuni when the latter reentered Russia early in 1902. As a result, Sipyagin was murdered by Balmashev, working under Gershuni's direction, in April, 1902. At the time of that assassination, Azev covered himself by working in Berlin as an apprentice-engineer for the General Electric Company.

Summoned to St. Petersburg in July 1902, Azev was taken to task about the Sipyagin assassination but managed to circumvent the investigation. His usual and effective dodges in such cases were several: either finger lesser terrorists or those who might suspect him or endanger his position, cloak the real perpetrators with fictitious names, or claim that he could not reveal all and that too much action against the terrorists would imperil his position. Somewhat to the discredit of the Okhrana, it swallowed all those excuses throughout its dealings with Azev. Actually, however, it also had no choice: Azev was so singular as a deep-cover police agent that he had no replacement.

The upshot of the Sipyagin affair was that Azev salved the Okhrana by betraying lesser SRs and Plehve, Sipyagin's successor, entered the case personally and ordered Azev to join the Battle Organization as a means of preventing future slipups.

Azev's compliance with Plehve's orders was almost too simple, but fact is often stranger than fiction in such matters. Without any special effort on his part, he was made a member of the Battle Organization in the autumn of 1902 and by March, 1903, Gershuni, sensing his time was short, named Azev his successor as leader of the terrorists. Events then followed in quick succession. Gershuni directed the next major assassination, that of General Bogdanovich, the Governor-General of Ufa, in May, 1903. Soon after, Gershuni, who had a price of fifty thousand rubles on his head, was arrested and shortly after sent, for what the Okhrana hoped would be the rest of his life, to a Siberian prison. Azev, who may have gotten at least some of the Gershuni reward, quickly scampered abroad and at a June, 1903, meeting of the SR in Geneva was made head of the Battle Organization. If that choice seems unusual or foolish, it should be pointed out that Azev was an able administrator and judge of people and did not have the hot head and romanticism of the average terrorist.

In the period 1902–03, there had also been turbulence in the top Okhrana echelons. Lopukhin, who had long had indirect connection with the Okhrana through the justice ministry, was made police director in 1902 by Plehve, a very poor selection as later developments proved, since Lopukhin was a wishy-washy character at best and certainly not of security caliber. In the same year, Rachkovsky, who apparently had gained no prudence after his earlier arousal of the ire of Alexander III by reporting on the goings-on in France of the morganatic widow of Alexander II, was eased out of the Foreign Agency for telling the facts about the French fakir Philippe, with whom Nicholas II was enthralled. And in 1903, Zubatov, Azev's original trainer and controller, was dismissed after one of his police-controlled labor groups went on the rampage in southern Russia. Finally, about that same time Leonid Ratayev, a bonvivant, useless dilettante, was "promoted" out of St. Petersburg Okhrana headquarters to be head of the Foreign Agency, and more importantly, as such, Azev's control. That shakeup reflected the weakness of a security organization that was subject to the whims of an incapable ruler and his nonsecurity-minded advisors. The changes and the ensuing muddle were of great benefit to the terrorists and the regime was to pay bitterly for them.

In the meantime, Tsarist Russia enjoyed the luxury of another pogrom, the horrible affair at Kishinev in April, 1903. Plehve was held responsible—with good reason—for Kishinev, and much of Russia and the outside world was disgusted and outraged. As an immediate result, the coffers of the Battle Organization speedily were swelled with donations and masses of volunteers sought enrollment in terrorist ranks. But, as was to prove more telling, that massacre also had its effect on the newly appointed head of the Battle Organization, Azev, the Jew. The SR had long been contemplating the assassination of Plehve, but it was Azev's reaction to Kishinev that put the murder organization into full swing.

There was more than one false start, most of them exploited by Azev to inundate Ratayev with lies or otherwise throw him off the track by betraying rival terrorists, all of which did Ratayev's reputation no good at St. Petersburg headquarters. But at last in July, 1904, Sazonov, directed by Boris Savinkov, Azev's second-in-command, threw the bomb that obliterated Plehve. Azev, in Warsaw masterminding the assassination, immediately scuttled to Vienna to cover himself by wiring Ratayev of his "indignation." Rather shockingly— although somewhat understandably considering Lopukhin was nominally at the helm—there was no real investigation of Plehve's assassination. The Okhrana seemed to be just as glad as the SR that he was dead.

Actually, however, more serious matters than assassination and terrorism intervened. Seeking glory abroad that he could not find at home, Nicholas had gotten Russia involved in the disastrous 1904–05 war with Japan. Battle after battle lost and defeat piled upon defeat culminated in the January, 1905, "Bloody Sunday" workers' march on the Winter Palace. In the main that was a grievous mistake of the Okhrana and one that should have been expected under the direction of Lopukhin. Zubatov's successor had grossly misjudged the character of the unprincipled Father Gapon and the priest's ability to control the workers. Later, the SR and the Battle Organization almost made a similar error with Gapon before they caught him trying to work for the Okhrana and killed him off.

Despite the onrush of events caused by the Japanese war and "Bloody Sunday," the Battle Organization was not idle. Donations poured in again after the Plehve assassination. The Battle Organization's chief plan was to kill the tsar's uncle, the Grand Duke Sergey, Governor-General of Moscow. At the same time, a splinter SR terror group led by one Mark Schweitzer—and there were many of those splinter terror groups during the brief lifetime of the Battle Organization—had a more ambitious and less carefully conceived plan to blow up ranking nobles, government ministers, and the capital's governor-general during a March 1905 memorial service in the Peter and Paul Cathedral for the assassinated Alexander II.

But—as Azev doubtless foresaw—only the assassination of the Grand Duke Sergey succeeded, when young Kalayev threw his bomb in February, 1905, in accordance with the plans prepared by Azev and Savinkov from abroad.

There is also good reason to believe that Azev well appreciated the repercussions the assassination of the tsar's uncle would cause in the Okhrana. In fact, the security shakeup that followed the murder of Sipyagin was almost nothing as compared to the changes made as result of the killing of a relation so close to the ruler. Within moments of learning of the Grand Duke's death in Moscow, the Governor-General of St. Petersburg dashed into Lopukhin's office, uttered the single word, "murderer" and then stalked out. Lopukhin had no option but to resign forthwith. Although that misfit as a police director was finished apparently once and for all, he nevertheless managed to flicker across history's pages a couple of years later in the scurrilous role of a tool for the SR. Somewhat ironically, Rachkovsky, whose dismissal papers had been prepared by Lopukhin on Plehve's orders in 1902, succeeded Lopukhin as top chief of the Okhrana. One of Rachkovsky's first moves was to fire Ratayev and take control of Azev, although that was not a profitable relationship for either. And Rachkovsky's reemergence was brief. He was finally dismissed for good in June 1906, to some degree as result of Azev's intransigeance. Nevertheless, in that short time he was a target for SR assassination himself because of his attempt to take Gapon under his control, a fact Azev disclosed to Rachkovsky only after Gapon had been murdered.

Earlier, on the very eve of Rachkovsky's struggle to regain power, Gerasimov, the most astute of all Okhrana bosses, emerged from the lower echelons to become St. Petersburg Okhrana chief in February

1905. And in fact, Gerasimov was the man who really ran the Okhrana for the next four years, and especially from the time Stolypin became interior minister in April 1906 and prime minister as well in July of that year. The relationship between Gerasimov and Stolypin was most intimate and continued so until Gerasimov's retirement, at his own wish, in 1909. In that period, and later as well, the police department directors and most other ranking Okhrana chiefs were comparative nonentities from a security standpoint.

Gerasimov had been in office less than a month when Schweitzer blew himself up with the explosives he had been preparing for the Peter and Paul Cathedral outrage, scheduled for three days later. Gerasimov had little trouble rounding up the remainder of those terrorists. They had been betrayed by an SR police agent who was killed off later by Battle Organization representatives.

After Schweitzer's group had been eliminated, and thinking the dust had settled from the Grand Duke Sergey's assassination, Azev and Savinkov returned to Russia. Having barely arrived in St. Petersburg, Azev, disguised as the cabdriver "Philipovsky" (like the Okhrana, the terrorists used disguises, safe houses, and other security techniques), was arrested in April 1905 while staking out an attempt to assassinate Durnovo. Furious at being picked up by External agents—and frightened as well—Azev was taken to Okhrana headquarters. Earlier, in the process of settling into his new job, Gerasimov had questioned Rachkovsky about the existence of Azev under any of his aliases, but Rachkovsky had denied any knowledge of the Okhrana's top agent. First placing Azev in a cell, despite all his protestations, Gerasimov arranged a confrontation between Rachkovsky and Azev. At first Azev was recalcitrant—Rachkovsky had earlier blocked several of Azev's attempts to communicate with him —but after Rachkovsky agreed to pay him five thousand rubles, Azev became communicative. From that time on, Gerasimov became Azev's control although Rachkovsky sat in on some of the sessions until his dismissal in 1906.

With his take-over of Azev, Gerasimov also established new Okhrana policy toward police agents high in revolutionary groups. Up to that time, the system as established by Zubatov had been to round up entire revolutionary groups once the police agents had penetrated and identified the top echelons. But Gerasimov recognized that revolution had become a mass movement, that hosts of new members stood ready to take the place of those arrested, and that such arrests might either reveal the agents to the revolutionaries, or at least put them out of action. Gerasimov's technique, therefore, was to refrain from arresting revolutionary top echelons in which he had agents, but simultaneously use his agents to control and curb revolutionary activities. One of Gerasimov's control devices was the use of otherwise incompetent External agents, called "branders" by the Okhrana. Once he learned from Azev, or other agents, that an assassination plot was underway, he assigned the "branders" who trailed and watched the terrorists so clumsily and obviously they could not help but learn they were under police observation and thus—frequently on Azev's advice—gave up the attempt.

Gerasimov's initial work with Azev, however, was not very profitable for the Okhrana. Although Azev characteristically betrayed minor plots and terrorists, especially those who were any challenge to him within the SR, he at first gave no information about major terrorist activities. At least some of the reason for that apparent low level of cooperation was that once again major events were overshadowing individual terrorist acts, making them less important and in a certain way unnecessary. Sparked by "Bloody Sunday," a brushfire of political—albeit revolutionary—awakening raced the length and breadth of Russia throughout 1905. Cossacks and troops—by that time the gendarmes had degenerated to little more than ornately uniformed bailiffs—were putting down peasant uprisings, naval mutinies, and strikes almost everywhere. The climax and virtual loss of control by the regime came with a general strike and the establishment of the Soviet of Workers' Deputies, let by Trotsky, in October 1905. That finally jolted Nicholas into issuing his manifesto of October 17, whereby he halfheartedly permitted a Duma, or national assembly, and limited civil rights.

In that crisis of revolution, Gerasimov showed a much greater concept of his role as bodyguard of the ruler and was far more than a mere spy-master. He arranged conferences between capital authorities and troop commanders and thus spared St. Petersburg the bloodily quelled workers' uprising that struck Moscow in December 1905. And he had the foresight and courage—even though Durnovo and other senior officials recommended against it—to break up the Soviet in December, 1905, and take Trotsky and the rest of its members into custody. But only the capital—since Gerasimov was not only new to his post but also could not be everywhere—was spared upheaval in the last month of the 1905 Revolution. The outbreak in Moscow had its counterparts in Kharkov, the Don Basin, the Baltic, the Caucasus, and Siberia. And all were crushed mercilessly.

In the meantime, the Tsar's manifesto had provoked a crisis of sorts within the SR. In the main, the Central Committee believed the manifesto had made terrorism passé and wanted the party to become legal and participate in Duma elections. Savinkov, though, opposed abandoning terrorism and saw it as the only way of overthrowing the autocracy. Azev remained somewhat aloof from the dispute—perhaps already tiring of his dangerous double game (he had recently survived an attack by Rachkovsky Okhrana toughs, an attack that was more on purpose than accidental). For a brief period, therefore, the Battle Organization was in effect dissolved. But the brutal repressions of the December, 1905, uprisings also resulted in the SRs and other revolutionaries being driven underground again. As a result, the Central Committee was forced to take terrorism out of mothballs and at a meeting in Finland in January, 1906, decided to regroup the Battle Organization.

Soon after that, Gerasimov, his larger scale duties in the capital ended successfully, resumed active collaboration with Azev. Azev for his part was pleased to resume work with a security officer of Gerasimov's caliber. Under the provisions of the newly instituted Okhrana policy, Azev was able to get by with betrayals of such minor objectives as explosives factories, illegal printing presses, and naïve or inept terrorists, keeping the SR Central Committee and the Battle Organization intact for serious and worthwhile handling by himself and Gerasimov alone. On paper, at least, that was a most ideal arrangement for both agent and controller.

Shortly before the first Duma met—after several delays—in May, 1906, there was another brief hiatus for the Battle Organization when the SR Central Committee deemed it should foreswear terror for the occasion. Azev used the interlude to send Savinkov to Sevastopol, ostensibly to keep Savinkov on his terrorist toes by assassinating an admiral who had brutally put down a 1905 naval mutiny. Actually, Azev's purpose was to get Savinkov far south of the capital for betrayal to the Okhrana. As things turned out, however, the admiral was somewhat prematurely killed by local terrorists. Savinkov arrived on the scene just in time to be caught, lodged in the local lockup, liberated in a commando-like operation by other Battle Organization members, and escape abroad to Rumania. In that same early period of recollaboration with Gerasimov, Azev had done better than with the admiral and had managed to thwart several other SR terrorist attempts. Under his aegis as Battle Organization chief, a plot to kill Durnovo failed, as did attempts against Moscow's Governor-General and other authorities of that rank, all without arousing SR suspicions. Otherwise, however, the Battle Organization was as good as inactive throughout the rest of 1906.

There is no doubt that the Gerasimov-Azev collaboration was responsible, in part at least, for that inactivity, but the prime reason was the advent of Stolypin, that era's only strong man, as prime minister in July 1906. Of course, he was soon marked for death by the Battle Organization, but he was to outlive that organization for several years. And as some authorities pointed out, from that time on the situation was reversed and it was really a matter of Stolypin, Gerasimov, and Azev campaigning against the Battle Organization. On the other hand, however, even though Gerasimov and Azev eliminated top-level terrorist acts, it is a fact that in the years 1905–07 hundreds of lesser functionaries of the regime were murdered. But, in 1906–07, that was countered by field courts-martial that sentenced at least a thousand terrorists to death, with most of them being shot or hanged within twenty-four hours of conviction. And in the period 1907–09 military courts took over action against terrorists, sentencing at least five thousand to death and sending many more thousands to prison or into exile.

One of the chief problems of both Gerasimov and Azev was recurring clusters of inexperienced but very fanatic SR terrorists who scorned the careful tactics of the semiprofessional Battle Organization and struck independently. A prime example was that of the so-called "Maximalists," a tiny splinter faction, that made a shambles of Stolypin's country villa in August, 1906, killed themselves, maimed Stolypin's two children for life, but failed to even injure the prime minister. Azev was extremely annoyed by that ill-conceived attempt, both for his self-esteem as chief of the Battle Organization and because of its possible bad effect on his collaboration with Gerasimov. He took the unusual step of asking the SR Central Committee to denounce and deny the Maximalist attempt and oddly enough the committee complied.

By the autumn of 1906, the action of the field courts-martial, the Gerasimov-Azev collaboration, and Gerasimov's use of his "branders" had effectively curbed most terrorist activity and the morale of the Battle Organization and even of some of the fanatic splinter terror groups was at a very low level. That problem was the main subject of an SR central committee meeting held in Finland in October, 1906. Azev and Savinkov stressed that Okhrana preventive tactics had become too sophisticated and that the Battle Organization needed new methods, new techniques—possibly mines that had been used effectively in western European terror. But the meeting was rancorous and there was no agreement. For all intents and purposes, Azev and Savinkov withdrew from the Battle Organization, and three splinter groups took over terror operations.

The splinter groups struck in January, 1907. Their prime victim was the St. Petersburg commandant, Vladimir von der Launitz, who, as Governor-General of Tambov in 1905, had brutally suppressed a peasant rising. Three other ranking government officers were also killed in the same month, but the SR terrorists' chief target, Stolypin, escaped unharmed. That was due to Gerasimov. A police agent—not Azev—had warned him of a plot to kill both von der Launitz and Stolypin during a government ceremony. Gerasimov advised both men to stay away. Only Stolypin took the advice. Von der Launitz, who disliked Gerasimov, disregarded it. The terrorists responsible for the killings were rounded up almost immediately, again betrayed by Azev. But they were executed under their pseudonyms lest Azev's role be revealed.

Perhaps to be on the safe side during those betrayals, Azev was vacationing in Italy in January 1907. He also made a side trip to Germany where he met a man who had drawn up plans for a flying machine. With that he got the idea that an airplane might be just the device needed to assassinate the tsar. That remained an idea only, but Azev must have been entranced by the flying machine because a copy of the plan was found among his papers after his death.

During that vacation, Gerasimov had become concerned that he was out of touch with his chief informant about terrorist plots and plans. And Azev was also interested in party developments, so he returned to Russia in time to take part in another SR Central Committee meeting in Finland in February, 1907. The chief business at that session was honoring Gershuni, who had just completed the odyssey of an escape from Siberia, via Japan and the United States, and while in the United States had been given many donations for the revolutionary cause. But the meeting was also devoted to a general discussion of Battle Organization assassinations of the tsar, Stolypin, and the Grand Duke Nicholas, in that order. From the time of Stolypin's virtual suppression of the first Duma in 1906, Nicholas had taken the top position on Battle Organization death lists since the SR had come to appreciate the tsar's actual participation in—if not management of—the affairs of the autocracy. Because of the constant fractioning of SR terror, due in part to fanatic hotheads, but also because of able individuals' discontent with Battle Organization foot-dragging intentionally caused by Azev without their knowledge, there were several plots to assassinate Nicholas. But, since Azev was in ultimate control, none of them stood a chance, unless he so decided.

A good example of that type of frustration occurred in March, 1907. Spiridovitch, the Palace Commandant, had learned of an SR plot to assassinate Nicholas from a Cossack guard, who had hoped to enrich himself by playing both ends against the middle. Spiridovitch, who made much of the case in his subsequent memoirs, was in a veritable tizzy, but he really had no cause for worry. Azev had informed Gerasimov of the plot well in advance. As a result, the twenty-eight terrorists involved were allowed to thoroughly incriminate themselves before being rounded up en masse in April, 1907.

At that point, Stolypin decided to exploit the case for political advantage. The SR had some thirty members in the current Duma and exposure of the SR terrorists could not fail but compromise the party. Accordingly, a big trial was staged of the SR terrorists caught red-handed in what became known as the "Conspiracy against the Tsar." Gerasimov emerged as the hero of the case, was praised as the man who had saved the tsar and was promoted to general. Indirectly, those plaudits were also of much benefit to Azev, since Gerasimov thereby valued him more and guarded him more closely from exposure. Azev had also come to the personal attention of Stolypin. The two never met face-to-face, but Gerasimov, at Stolypin's insistence, often sought Azev's political opinions and analyses, which were always astute and might have been the spy's actual métier in happier times.

While the "Conspiracy against the Tsar" was at its height, Azev wisely absented himself for a rest in the Crimea, where he actually occupied himself betraying local Battle Organization members to the Okhrana. Betraying SR terrorists who were not under his actual command and control had become for him much more than a job for the Okhrana. It had become an addiction.

By mid-1907, the SR central committee decided that an all-out effort must be made to kill the tsar. In the interim since the "Conspiracy against the Tsar," splinter groups, especially "Karl's Detachment," run by the able and fearless SR terrorist Karl Prauberg, had carried out a number of assassinations of reactionary but lesser officials. But the committee decided the time had come for concentration on the main objective and therefore ordered the splinter groups to cease their minor actions and put themselves under Azev's control. At the same time it authorized Azev and Gershuni to go abroad again to revamp the Battle Organization and its techniques. Savinkov, who normally would have joined the two in that venture, disagreed with their proposed techniques and stayed aloof. Although Azev left Russia in July 1907, as planned, he soon returned and more or less marked time for the remainder of the year. The fact was he was beginning to tire of his double game and although he had escaped many a denunciation by both fellow terrorists and other police agents, he perhaps sensed the odds were getting critical. That belief is bolstered by the knowledge that in the latter part of 1907 he spoke to Gerasimov—but without success—about retirement as an unknown, faceless engineer somewhere in the hinterlands of Russia.

On the day after Christmas 1907, however, Azev's interest in his work, and especially the funds he garnered from both the Okhrana and the Battle Organization, was unexpectedly renewed. In a St. Petersburg cafe, he met Madame N___, a cabaret singer of German origin, otherwise known as "La Bella Hedy de Hero." Although Madame N___ had had an active past, replete with grand dukes and lesser gentry, and Azev had a wife, an SR adherent, and children, it was a case of love at first sight. They remained together for the next ten years, or until Azev's death. Madame N___ had expensive tastes, as did her new lover, and in order to gratify them, Azev had to continue working.

The die thus cast, early in 1908, Azev informed Gerasimov about all the splinter groups, including "Karl's Detachment." The betrayal amounted to annihilation. All of the lesser SR terrorists were rounded up and speedily executed, imprisoned, or exiled. The particularly dastardly part of the denunciations was that Azev had not told Gerasimov that the splinter groups had been put under his control.

At the same time, a completely unforeseen development increased Azev's risk of exposure to the SR. Other Okhrana agents contributed to that by scoring a fluke of sorts that also contravened Gerasimov's policy toward high-level terrorists. Acting on a denunciation, External agents accidentally arrested Karpovich, who earlier had escaped from prison and, as a result of Gershuni's illness and Savinkov's intransigeance, had been made Azev's second-in-command. Fully aware that it could compromise Azev, Gerasimov arranged Karpovich's "escape" in typical Okhrana fashion, but only with difficulty. The guard "transferring" Karpovich through the capital in a cab "carelessly" left the young terrorist to his own devices not once, but twice, before the young man decided it was not a trap and "escaped."

Because of that and the denunciations of the splinter groups, Azev thought it prudent to absent himself again. He went abroad in March, 1908, taking Madame N____ with him, and it is believed he also visited Paris where Gershuni was dying. It is also possible he planned not to return and to abandon both the Okhrana and the Battle Organization. While he was away, however, SR terrorists carried out a daring robbery of a Turkestan bank. Some one hundred thousand rubles from that seizure were earmarked for the Battle Organization. Since a good part of such sums always ended up in Azev's pocket, he had no alternative but to return to St. Petersburg for Easter, 1908, bringing Madame N____ back with him.

Once back, he was extremely active, no doubt enthused by the refurbishment of the Battle Organization treasury. But he did have much real work: arranging the transfer of the loot from Chardzhou, conferring with fellow SR Central Committee members, and most important of all, planning the Battle Organization's assassination of Nicholas when the tsar traveled to the port of Reval to meet the King of England. And of course, he also had to give Gerasimov all details he thought necessary about the attempt on the tsar.

The Reval plot showed more than any other attempt how highly placed were Azev's sources of information as well as how irreplaceable Azev was for Gerasimov's task of protecting the ruler. Attempting to mislead the Battle Organization, the Okhrana made many changes in the tsar's rail route and schedule to Reval and in Nicholas' possible stopping places. In the course of their frequent conversations, Gerasimov was very uneasy to learn from Azev that the Battle Organization was aware of every alteration. And once, Gerasimov's unease became shock when Azev advised him of a change that the Okhrana chief learned of only on the following day through "strictly confidential" channels. Gerasimov pressed Azev for the name of his informant, but Azev refused, saying revelation would compromise him and endanger his job of preventing the attempt. Extremely worried, Gerasimov then reported the matter to Stolypin. At first, Stolypin refused to believe the matter was more than a pure happenstance and demanded complementary verification. After being supplied with that by Gerasimov, he then decided to drop the whole matter, since exposure of such a highly placed informant would not only provoke scandal, but also would endanger Azev. The name of that traitor in high places, possibly within the imperial family itself, has never become known; but, neither was the Reval attempt successful.

However, despite his having arranged Nicholas' escape at Reval, Azev's conscience apparently got the better of him, particularly since he was well-supplied with funds from the Turkestan robbery. He decided to quit both the Okhrana and the Battle Organization. After all, he was past forty and had been doing his dirty and dangerous work for fifteen years. But he also felt that he should do one last, memorable feat for the Battle Organization and really end the autocracy by assassinating Nicholas.

So, in June, 1908, he left Russia with the idea of never returning, after making arrangements for Madame N___ to join him later. His first stop was Paris, but his ultimate destination was Scotland. On the ways in Glasgow was the cruiser "Rurik," being built for the tsar's navy to replace some of the ships lost in the Russo-Japanese war. Members of the Battle Organization were at the shipyard, as were less dangerous representatives of both the SR and SD parties, the latter attempting to spread propaganda among the cadre crew that was to take the "Rurik" to a tsarist port.

When Azev arrived in Glasgow, the Battle Organization was considering two plans: either to get a member of the crew to kill the tsar when he inspected the ship; or to smuggle a Battle Organization terrorist aboard to do the job. But no agreeable crew member had been found, so a hiding place was located for a Battle Organization stowaway. At that point, Azev went aboard under a pseudonym, so loose was the security. He inspected the proposed hiding place, found it too small for a terrorist to be confined in for the possible several weeks before the tsar made his inspection, and rejected the plan. In short order, two friends of Savinkov and Karpovich were found among the crew and they volunteered to assassinate Nicholas.

The "Rurik," with the two assassins aboard, departed Glasgow for Russia in mid-August, 1908, and Azev, as a Central Committee member, went to London for an SR meeting.

Meanwhile, however, and totally unbeknown to Azev, suspicions of his being an Okhrana agent, or a *provocateur,* had reached a new danger point. Vladimir Burtsev, an SR chronicler of sorts, whose real forte was exposing *provocateurs,* had long believed that the continuing Okhrana capture of Battle Organization terrorists was caused by a traitor very high in the party and probably in the Battle Organization itself. And Burtsev was convinced, even though he lacked hard proof, that Azev was the traitor.

Burtsev was particularly alarmed that Azev had attended the London conference and so wrote an old party friend, denouncing Azev. His letter eventually reached the SR Central Committee and many members of that organization wanted to put Burtsev on trial for libeling Azev. Savinkov and others, however, opposed the very idea of a trial, holding that it would be a slur against the Battle Organization. Shortly after that, Savinkov, who believed that Burtsev was honorable, even though ignorant, told the writer in full about Azev's roles in the Battle Organization and even let him know about the "Rurik" attempt, hopefully due to be carried out within a short time.

Those disclosures put Burtsev in a very difficult position indeed, but then luck came his way. On a Cologne-Berlin train, he ran into none other than the disgruntled Lopukhin. Burtsev had long known that a very important police agent had the cover name of "Raskin" and he was convinced that "Raskin" and Azev were one and the same. The former police director repeatedly denied any knowledge of a "Raskin," but then, within a distressingly short time from the Okhrana's standpoint, admitted, "I have seen the engineer, Evno Azev, several times."

That was all Burtsev needed. Almost immediately after his talk with Lopukhin, he advised the SR that he was going to make his accusation against Azev public in the emigré publication he issued. With that, the Central Committee had no choice but to "pacify," or try, Burtsev. So, in October, 1908, a so-called court of honor, including such veteran party members as Vera Figner, met in Savinkov's Paris apartment.

For almost a month—while Azev put on an act of being care and conscience-free by gallivanting abroad, first with his wife and children and then with Madame N____—Burtsev's allegations dragged on, without making any impression. Finally, at his wits' end, and although he had promised Lopukhin he would not, he told the court of the former police director's statement. His revelation was a veritable bombshell. The court no longer questioned Burtsev's claim. But first the party decided to send a representative to St. Petersburg to get the accusation directly from Lopukhin himself. To the SR delegate, Lopukhin not only repeated his statement to Burtsev, but told all he knew about Azev's Okhrana activities. He even volunteered to go to London to give all the facts to SR Central Committee members.

By that time, November 1908, the no longer so carefree Azev had been tipped off by a member of the court, possibly by Savinkov. He, too, made a trip—hurried and secret—to St. Petersburg. He went immediately to Gerasimov. Next both Gerasimov and Azev futilely tried to get Lopukhin to repudiate his accusation. (Later, Lopukhin was duly tried and sent into Siberian exile before eventual pardon, but that in no way repaired the damage he had done the Okhrana.)

Ironically, despite such convincing proof, many party stalwarts and Battle Organization members threatened reprisals if action was taken against Azev. Faced with that, and fearing a possibly party split, the Central Committee took no immediate action beyond asking Azev to counter Lopukhin's claim. Azev must have been badly rattled, for surprisingly his alibi was full of obvious holes and smacked very much of having been prepared by the Okhrana.

That ended the SR Central Committee's indecisiveness and on January 5, 1909, after deciding that Azev should be executed quietly in the environs of Paris—to avoid complications with French authorities—it sent a delegation to his Paris apartment. The plan was to invite Azev to a delegate's home on the following day and eventually take him to a villa outside Paris and kill him. When the group arrived, Azev had no final card to play. What might have saved him, his intended master coup, the assassination of Nicholas, had failed miserably. When the tsar went aboard the "Rurik" off Kronstadt, the two sailors met him face-to-face, but did not shoot. Why remains forever a mystery: some accounts say the intended assassins lost their nerve at the last moment; others hold they feared killing the tsar might have wrecked a planned (but never carried out) take-over of Kronstadt by the cruiser's crew; or it may simply have been that Nicholas charmed them out of it. Lacking that ace, Azev played much upon his past exploits and denied all connection with the police, but promised to go the next day to the delegate's Paris home. Instead, once the group had left, he told some final lies to his wife, packed his bags and in the wee hours of January 6, 1909, dropped from sight so far as the SR and the Okhrana were concerned.

Actually, however, using one of his many false identities, he rendezvoused with Madame N____ in Germany and went with her on a grand Cook's tour of the Mediterranean before settling down with her in Berlin as the affluent stockbroker Alexander Neumayer. But his fortunes crashed with the outbreak of World War I since he had speculated heavily in Russian securities. Shortly after he made a try at operating a corset shop with Madame N____, the Germans arrested and imprisoned him as an enemy alien. He was released with the Russo-German armistice of 1917. In poor health, he died in a Berlin hospital in April, 1918. His only mourner was Madame N____, but at least SR and German Communist activists who hunted him for years never gunned him down.

For all intents and purposes, the exposure of Azev wrote finis to the Battle Organization and SR terror. (Bogrov's assassination of Stolypin in 1911 was an isolated incident, certainly not the work of professional terrorists, and even may have been done with the connivance of Tsarist reactionaries.) Savinkov (who was to know only failure and death as a chief of terror organizations) tried to get the Battle Organization going again. But he was plagued with traitors—minor ones, no Azevs—and lack of drive and ability, so never succeeded.

Not entirely coincidentally, Gerasimov, the Okhrana's one and only great chief, retired the same year that Azev disappeared. He, too, had worked under a strain nearly as great as Azev's. And he also probably fully understood that with Azev gone the palmy days of SR terror were over. Stolypin likewise must have appreciated Azev's complex role, for when Azev was exposed the regime first referred to him as a "governmental advisor," a description which even though later withdrawn was essentially correct.

When Gerasimov quit, he gave his other agents, the lesser Azevs, the choice of also retiring or continuing with his successor. As a singular mark of Gerasimov's ability is the fact that the majority of those agents retired along with him and the names of none of them ever became known.

7. THE OKHRANA—DEGENERATION AND COLLAPSE (1910–17)

With the resignation of Gerasimov and the subsequent assassination of Stolypin, Russia's imperial security service raced down an increasingly sharp incline toward eventual disintegration. Many were to blame for the horrible muddle that followed. And the inane Nicholas and his unbelievably foolish Alexandra were not the least of those responsible.

The hard facts of the matter are that Tsarist Russia really had no government, other than in name only, after the death of Stolypin. One nincompoop favorite of Nicholas, Alexandra, or even Rasputin after another so incompetently filled cabinet posts or other top positions that to a man from another planet it might have seemed they had been purposefully selected to speed the autocracy to its fall. To be sure, there were some able and responsible men, but they were exceptions, frustrated and lost in the rush toward extinction.

Just as worthless and ineffective as the prime ministers who followed Stolypin were the types chosen to fill that reactionary but strong man's second post, that of interior minister. All of those who failed to fill that top police post in tsardom's last years were so nondescript that a mere alphabetical listing suffices, viz: Aleksey Khvostov, Alexander Makarov, Nikolay Maklakov, Alexander Protopopov (the last), Prince Nikolay Shcherbatov, and Boris Stuermer. Nor were those interior ministers' seconds-in-command, the directors of the police department, appreciably better. Among those were Stepan Beletsky, a toady to Rasputin, Kovalensky, E. Vuitsh, M. Trusevich, and a rogue, one Yevgeny Klimovich, and Aleksey Vasilyev, the last, who distinguished himself more by writing about the Okhrana and refusing to work for the Bolshevik security than as a police director. Closest to being bright spots on that sorry security roster—and only because all the others were so much worse—were a pair of deputy interior ministers, General Pavel Kurlov, and General Vladimir Dzhunkovsky. But, Kurlov was a pogrom prone anti-Semite, while Dzhunkovksy was so much more a do-gooder than a policeman that he wrecked the Okhrana's only good penetration of the Bolsheviks.

At a more important level, and just as sorry an example of ineptitude, was Gerasimov's successor, Colonel Sergey Karpov. That worthy arranged the "escape" from prison of terrorist Alexander Petrov, believing he had recruited him for the Okhrana. Instead, Petrov blew the Okhrana chief to smithereens with explosives planted in one of Karpov's obviously poorly managed safe houses. To be sure, Petrov was caught and almost summarily executed, but that did not bring Karpov back into operation. And in the same era of increasing carelessness and slipshod work, Radom, a chief of gendarmes, was murdered almost as a matter of routine.

Somewhat earlier, and almost contemporarily with the rise and flourishing of Gerasimov, Spiridovitch had been given the task of supplying an actual bodyguard for Nicholas (a purely physical rather than an intelligence entity) and carried out that function until his retirement in 1916. Unfortunately for Nicholas, Spiridovitch was more a courtier than a bodyguard in mentality. That characteristic was certainly brought out in his subsequent memoirs in which he tells more about the family life and comings and goings of Nicholas than about real security work for the tsar, which after all was not his métier, but the Okhrana's.

Nevertheless, Spiridovitch would have his readers believe that it was he and his organization alone that saved Nicholas from terrorist attack and assassination during the ten years he commanded the palace guards. But he did organize and take overall command of the imperial bodyguards, consisting of a somewhat motley conglomeration of gendarmes, Cossacks, units from the various guard regiments, and railroad troops that were incorporated into an outfit called the personal infantry regiment of the tsar, or more formally "his majesty's imperial combined infantry regiment." That regiment guarded palace buildings and grounds and elements of it accompanied the tsar on all his travels. It was also supported by other units from time to time. For instance, whenever the imperial train traveled the twenty-six miles south from St. Petersburg to Tsarskoye-Selo, a favorite residence of the latter Romanovs, guards would be stationed

[159]

every one hundred paces of the parallel but completely separate track.

Spiridovitch can also be credited with an innovation—or importation—in the routine of guarding the ruler, a practice followed for later Communist successors. He introduced to Russia the use of police dogs—Dobermans, German shepherds, or large terriers—to accompany guards on their rounds of the ruler's establishment. But that novelty and the organization of the imperial regiment were all that Spiridovitch contributed to the task of protecting the ruler and they finally proved far from being enough. If he had been a man and officer of different caliber—he was a gendarme by origin and liked to wear the gaudy uniform of the calvary—he might have imbued his officers and men with an esprit de corps. But that he did not accomplish, probably did not even think of doing. As a result, when the chips were down and Nicholas was forced into abdication, his vaunted imperial regiment proved to be no Swiss Guards. Rather, almost to a man, it was a sniveling outfit that either fled or became turncoats against the ruler. It certainly did not guard him in his hour of supreme need.

But, and despite all that, Spiridovitch fancied himself as the real guarantor of the tsar's security, even though his security abilities and especially his knowledge of the outer world, the revolutionaries' world, were limited. Far from helping the Okhrana, in the very small way he might, he was consistently jealous of it and always critical of it. True, he unearthed the half-baked plot against the tsar in 1907, but it was the Gerasimov-Azev combination that really blocked that. He was also very busy later that year guarding the tsar from the Reval plotters. But again, it was Gerasimov and Azev who aborted that attempt. And so far as the "Rurik" plot of 1908 went, Spiridovitch had not the slightest clue about that; and neither, in all fairness, did Gerasimov.

About a year after Gerasimov's retirement, the Okhrana developed an agent whose specialty was revolutionary politics, rather than revolutionary terror. That agent was Roman Malinovsky, a burglar who was co-opted in prison by Beletsky in 1910 for the usual starting fee of fifty rubles a month. Because Malinovsky was an SD of the Bolshevik wing, and thus connected with Lenin, his role as a double-agent has been exaggerated. Erroneously, almost mythically, he has been compared to Azev by Communists and those who have accepted Communist views. Actually, however, despite all Azev's drawbacks, he stood head and shoulders above Malinovsky in courage, intelligence, organizational ability, knowledge of his fellow men, and even in ethics. Azev was a double-agent, a person who played a dangerous game skillfully and with dangerous adversaries. Malinovsky was a common criminal converted into a police stool pigeon, who never worked against the Okhrana, as did Azev, and who betrayed a much more callow group, the SDs, even though they avenged themselves by killing him, but only after they had attained power.

It would have been interesting to have seen how Gerasimov, if he had continued in Okhrana service, would have controlled Malinovsky. Not only did Gerasimov have experience with handling the much more redoubtable double-agent, Azev, but also he had shown political astuteness and courage in recognizing Trotsky's 1905 St. Petersburg Soviet for what it was and crushing it before it got out of hand as later political developments did with his successors.

As things turned out, however, the Okhrana chiefs who followed him not only mismanaged Malinovsky, but also showed not a whit of political sense. They were smart and clever in a way, but so smart and clever and pleased with themselves that they failed to cooperate with the democratic and liberal groups of their time and failed to evaluate properly Lenin's organization as the real threat it eventually proved to be. They were fools enough to be convinced that the Marxists and Bolsheviks were little more than wild-haired economic talkers and dreamers.

Under such direction and circumstances, Malinovsky was assigned to penetrate SD and St. Petersburg labor ranks. He did both jobs quite well, because he had a certain charisma and like Gapon was an able mob-rouser, even though poorly educated. Using the Zubatov ploy—which by then should have been pretty well discredited—to penetrate labor showed the decline of genius and originality within the Okhrana, but in the main the working men of those times were still grossly politically naïve. As a result, Malinovsky was able to exploit his position as a labor union secretary to enter the 1912 elections for the fourth (and last) Duma as an SD (Bolshevik) candidate from a Moscow constituency. Why he ran from Moscow rather than St. Petersburg is not clear, except for the fact that it seemed the Okhrana had the elections under better control in the old capital.

Also it appears the Okhrana felt it was simpler to hide Malinovsky's arrest and prison record in Moscow and it is known that the police eased things considerably for their agent by imprisoning or intimidating his rivals for the Duma seat.

Once elected, Malinovsky speedily took control of the SD thirteen-man Duma group despite the fact the Mensheviks had seven deputies as compared to the six Bolsheviks. Part of the reason for that minority rule of the majority may have been Malinovsky's skillful play-off of the two factions against each other, although his professed allegiance was to the Bolsheviks. An able orator, he made many a Duma-stirring speech. However, almost all of that oratory, supposedly prepared under the aegis of Lenin, had been well edited by Beletsky.

Seemingly a man of parts, Malinovsky had time for more than Duma duties. In 1912, he also became Treasurer of the Bolsheviks' new paper, *Pravda*. Lenin thought he inspired and guided the editorial policy of that publication. Actually, however, *Pravda* was much more an Okhrana paper than one run by Lenin from abroad. Not only was Malinovsky giving the police all and sundry details about it, but also its editor, Miron Chernomazov, was an Okhrana agent as well. For obvious reasons, therefore, Lenin became disenchanted with *Pravda*'s party line and sent Yakov Sverdlov and Stalin (the latter also alleged to be at least a onetime, part-time Okhrana agent) to St. Petersburg to put matters in order. Malinovsky handled that pair with ease. He reported his problem to the Okhrana and in due course Sverdlov and Stalin were shipped off to Siberia to await the March, 1917, revolution and the downfall of the autocracy.

Surprisingly, the apprehension of Sverdlov and Stalin did nothing to arouse Lenin's suspicions of Malinovsky. Despite many reports that Malinovsky worked for the Okhrana—his ease of frequent travel from and to Russia alone should have been reason for some doubt—Lenin persisted in regarding the Okhrana's current star double-agent as a sort of working man's rough diamond. (Latter-day glorifications of Lenin as one who saw all and knew all are prone to hold that the Bolshevik leader was fully aware of Malinovsky's role and regarded a double-agent of that proportion as just as valuable, if not more, to the Bolsheviks as he was to the Okhrana. However, that seems to be little more than just another Lenin myth.)

Indeed, pragmatically it is more correct to believe that things might have continued swimmingly for Malinovsky for some time had it not been for Burtsev, the same man who earlier brought Azev to book with the SRs. Always busy looking for traitors high in revolutionary ranks, Burtsev had had his eye on Malinovsky for some time. In time, as he had done with the SRs, he broached his suspicions to the Bolshevik hierarchs and tendered proof of a sort. That resulted in the same sort of party trial as the SRs had staged with Azev, but with marked difference—Malinovsky was acquitted and allowed to continue his good work for the Okhrana.

The Okhrana, however, was not so sure of Malinovsky as were Lenin and his group. And that he was so suspect to the Bolsheviks as to be put on trial was more than enough for police with the Azev case on its records. Accordingly, in May, 1914, Dzhunkovsky interceded and ordered Malinovsky to resign from the Duma and in effect ended his work for the Okhrana. (However, Dzhunkovksy's move was not caused by premonition or smart police perception, but quite the contrary. Distinctly out of character as a security police officer, Dzhunkovsky slammed the book on his double-agent not because he judged him a bad risk, but because he was averse, in principle, to the Okhrana's soiling its hands with the use of agents of penetration.) Nevertheless, the end result was the same, Malinovsky and the Okhrana parted company. But, unlike Azev, Malinovsky did not die peacefully in bed of natural causes. Out of work, for all intents and purposes, Malinovsky wandered abroad, where he should have stayed. Instead, in 1918, with the Bolsheviks in power, he returned to Russia to face another and final trial. Unbeknown to him, when revolutionaries invaded Okhrana headquarters in March, 1917, probably more on purpose than accidentally, the Malinovsky file had not been destroyed. As a result, Burtsev's allegations were finally shown to be true and Malinovsky was shot in short order, with Lenin refusing to intercede.

In a way, the Malinovsky case was the last high-water mark for the Okhrana. From that time on, everything went downhill, faster and faster. The advent of World War I, of course, played its part in reducing police concentration on political activity and also, for a time at least, made the operations of revolutionaries and other political groups more passive. For a time, the concentration of both supporters and opponents of the regime was diverted to the war. And at that juncture, instead of politics, the Okhrana got involved in a conflict with the military about who should control espionage and internal subversion. Almost as could have been expected, the police lost that dispute. But the military opposition to having police agents in its ranks was aided and abetted by Dzhunkovsky who held that such practice would impugn the honor of the armed forces. In that way, Dzhunkovsky, more than anyone else in Okhrana ranks, sped the downfall of the autocracy. If the police had been up-to-date about the growing disaffection in the armed forces and the revolutionaries' penetration of their ranks, the fall of the House of Romanov might have been delayed a little, at the least.

As things turned out, the maladroit Dzhunkovsky got his comeuppance about a year later, but in a manner that did the regime no good at all. He stuck his nose into the only affair of note handled by the Okhrana in those final days—and certainly not handled well—the Rasputin matter. That rotten monk was just as much loathed by the Okhrana as by the so-called respectable people of that era and that bias doubtless contributed somewhat to Dzhunkovsky's ineptness. In the summer of 1915 he made the tactical mistake of leaking to the press a report of Rasputin's indecent exposure and other obscene actions in a Moscow gypsy café. That was an open-and-shut case, despite Rasputin's lofty connections, a matter for the regular police, not the Okhrana. Of course, Dzhunkovsky should have been aware of it, but his knowledge should have been circulated through lower echelons. As it was, however, he aroused Alexandra's ire and was fired on her direct orders.

Nor did the Okhrana distinguish itself in the windup of the Rasputin affair—the monk's assassination in December, 1916. Aleksey Vasilyev, the last Tsarist director of the police department, investigated that ugly matter, but about all he really did was to keep the imperial family's skirts clean.

Perhaps Vasilyev deemed it useless to do any more. He may have felt in his bones that everything was coming apart at the seams, with the armed forces defeated everywhere in the field and with rottenness and inefficiency at an unbearable height behind the lines.

When the (February) March, 1917, revolution broke out, as Petrograd troops mutinied and joined locked-out and striking workers and street mobs, Vasilyev found a ready-made excuse for not going to his office. His discretion was wise because one of the first objectives of the revolutionaries was Okhrana headquarters. The Okhrana officers within the building were able to destroy some files before the mob arrived but the majority of the records—valuable to both historians and Russian political groups—was subsequently burned or otherwise destroyed by the invading revolutionaries. However, as the Malinovsky case established, some highly classified records were preserved, either by turncoat Okhrana officers or by revolutionaries who had joined the invaders of Okhrana headquarters for that very purpose. It is more than likely that those "lifted" records were later destroyed by the Bolsheviks and their successors, primarily so that many connections—possibly including Stalin's—with the Okhrana should never become known.

Once he had learned the fate of his headquarters, Vasilyev went into hiding at the homes of friends for several days. In that brief interim, lesser Okhrana officials and police officers were not so fortunate: some gave their lives defending crumbling Tsarist strongpoints; others were apprehended and executed; but most just disappeared from sight, the uniformed personnel donning mufti, while members of plainclothes units went into hiding. In time, a few, including Vasilyev, escaped abroad. So ended the Okhrana.

Within a few days after the revolution, Vasilyev, many other top Okhrana chiefs, and prominent members of the Tsarist government were arrested and "tried" by the Provisional Government's "Extraordinary Investigating Commission." That body learned nothing from the Okhrana officers beyond the fact that there was a plethora of confusion in the Tsarist political police command structure, a matter that was quite well known to all concerned. Released after the "trial," some of the Tsarist officials thought it best to try to find a new life abroad. Most, however, stayed on in Russia and many of those later were shot by the Bolshevik Okhrana, the Cheka.

Even though the gendarmes and the Okhrana had disintegrated in the early hours of the revolution, one of the first steps of the Provisional Government was to make a formality of disbanding both organizations. The gendarmes were replaced by a motley kind of militia that had many released common criminals in its ranks and elected its officers. Security matters more or less fell to a Colonel B. Nikitin, chief of the counter-espionage section of the Petrograd military district. Nikitin's prime job was apprehending German spies that had almost flooded Petrograd and the rest of Russia, but most of the persons he arrested were soon released from prison by mobs.

[165]

Therefore, by the time the Bolsheviks seized power in (October) November, 1917, there was no longer even a modicum of political police control that could have helped or shielded the Provisional Government.

Nikitin's organization hardly falls in the same category, but both his outfit and the Okhrana signally failed in their basic mission of protecting the ruler. So far as the Okhrana and the purpose of this study are concerned, absolutely nothing is accomplished by putting part of the blame—even though justifiable—on the imperial family, the form of government and Russian society of those times. For goodness knows, there was nothing particularly admirable about the succeeding Communist leaders, their form of government and the Russian society thus created. But, despite such similar and perhaps heavier handicaps, it is a fact that so far, at least, the Communist forms of the Okhrana have managed to protect the leaders.

Part Two

COMMUNIST EXPERIMENTS
AND INNOVATIONS

CHAPTER III

Communist Bloody Russia

1. COMMUNIST TAKE-OVER (1918–28)

In the millennium and more in which Russia had been ruled by princes and tsars, the ruling class advanced from fighting among its own for power to guaranteeing the power of an autocrat against threats from the people emerging from a long night of ignorance and political backwardness. And in all those thousand and more benighted years, no matter who was the ruler, it was always the people who paid the price, either as slaves and serfs or as "liberated" peasants and exploited industrial workers.

During the death throes of the autocracy, millions of words and thousands of promises had been expended on the plight of the Russian people by the country's thin veneer of intelligentsia. The SRs espoused the cause of the peasants—the overwhelming mass of Russians of those times. The SDs, especially the Bolshevik faction, concentrated on the workers and completely disregarded the peasants, primarily because those tillers of the soil had not been deemed important by Marx and his theories.

Therefore, when the autocracy finally fell, many Russians and a number of other decent people in the world hoped that a new era had dawned for that great and vastly rich country. Its future could have been almost unlimited, not just so far as Marxist material wealth was concerned, but also to include vast cultural and philosophical advances. There was no reason then to believe that as much could not be gained from the Russian awakening as had been gained earlier from the American and French revolutions.

However, thanks to the Bolsheviks' seizure of power, and the character of their leaders, especially Lenin, that was not to be. True, for a while most thought anything would be better than the autocracy. But, sadly for Russia and especially the Russian people, long after those opinions proved erroneous, partially because of wishful thinking, or the expediencies of international politics, or just plain ignorance, apologies were made and continue to be made for the Communist autocracy and imperialism that succeeded Tsarist autocracy and imperialism.

Mainly because it is recent-to-current history, many experts and some not so expert have devoted much thought and literally billions of words to the Communist leadership of Russia, its allegations, successes, and failures. Actually, though, the bulk of that examination and reporting is of not much more importance from a truly historical standpoint than were the views and opinions of some long forgotten minor boyar, noble, or foreign emissary about the peccadillos of a bygone prince or tsar. And since Russia's Communist autocracy is so much more in the minority and so much more oppressive than that of the princes and tsars, the purpose of this study is to examine how it maintains itself in power. Great though their numbers be, the Russian people do not apply in such an examination any more than they really did in the days before the Communists. In other words, it is still the people who are exploited and pay the price.

When the Communists seized power in the so-called glorious October revolution (November 7, 1917) almost any well-organized small group such as they were could have done the same. And given the pair of rabble-rousing demagogues such as they had—Lenin and Trotsky—it was that much easier. The Provisional Government and the thin framework of democratic parties had never gotten going. The army had long since collapsed as an effective fighting force, the Germans were pushing in the west and everywhere else mobs beefed up by deserting soldiers had taken over the cities and the peasants were seizing the land wholesale. It was anarchy such as the most rabid anarchists had never dared envision. Therefore, despite the contrived art work of the "storming" of the Winter Palace, it was a relatively simple matter for Lenin and his little gang to move in. Nor should it be forgotten that using the usual Communist prevarication, that later became so nauseatingly common to the entire world, the Lenin group was promising "democracy" and was supporting industrial strikes. And although it had no interest in, and in fact no control of, the peasants, it was encouraging their rampages in the countryside, but only for the reason that the peasants made up the rank and file of the army in which the Communists were abetting wholesale desertion and mutiny, as well as fraternization with the enemy, to assure their take-over of power.

Once in the saddle, the Communists secured themselves in Petrograd's Smolny Institute, a former Tsarist girls' school, surrounded by a motley array of military deserters, mainly sailors and Latvian soldiers, as guards. Meanwhile, butchery of helpless opponents—real and potential—went on apace, with gun-toting revolutionaries, real and pseudo, shooting down all who looked like *bourgeoisie* in the cities and with peasants continuing their slaughter of landowners and clerics in the countryside. The total thus killed was immense, but the exact number was never reckoned, never will be.

At the same time, unfortunately for Russia and the masses it represented, the SR organization disintegrated in factional fights, splitting into right and left wings. The latter, a decided minority, at first supported the Communists and was countenanced by them until no longer needed by Lenin. The first Communist government was a fifteen-man Council of Commissars (Ministers)—all Communists—with Vladimir I. Ulyanov (Lenin) as Chairman. Other prominent members were the former Menshevik Leon Trotsky, Foreign Affairs; Aleksey Rykov, Internal Affairs; Joseph Stalin, Nationalities; and Anatoly Lunacharsky, Education. To assure SR support, Lenin initially endorsed their program of land seizure by the peasants, and then named some SRs as commissars, but not for long. That playing up to the SRs was mere expediency.

After being in power scarcely a month, Lenin started muzzling the opposition. His first target was the press, with rightist and conservative organs being eliminated first, while leftist publications that did not push the Communist line were killed off more slowly, but just as definitely. His next step was to order the arrest and trial—before revolutionary military tribunals—of leaders of conservative and liberal groups in the Duma.

To keep himself in power, Lenin used the same device as the tsars and princes before him, a corps of secret police. Created December 20, 1917, it was called the Extraordinary Commission for Combating Counterrevolution and Sabotage, but soon became known by its abbreviated form, the Cheka. Like Ivan the Terrible's Oprichnina, it had unlimited powers and was a truly horrible organization that conducted the "Red Terror" of 1917–22, during which countless hundreds of thousands (some authorities estimate 1,750,000 persons of all classes) of Russians and subject peoples were killed offhand, tortured, imprisoned, and enslaved. The Cheka was the forerunner and example for the GPU, OGPU, NKVD, NKGB, MGB, MVD, and KGB. And it was another child of the warped mind of Lenin, who mouthed polemics about peoples but cared not a whit for persons. Lenin not only countenanced the wave of terror but instigated and demanded it, despite subsequent Communist mythology that attempts to portray him as a humanitarian. When Maxim Gorky and others less bloody remonstrated about the terror, Lenin countered with such sophisms as "omelets cannot be made without breaking eggs." Therefore, the protests of latter-day Communists about Stalin's excesses are just so much balderdash: the "holy" Lenin set the example. And perhaps if he had retained his capacities and lived longer, that part-Kalmyk might have outdone his Georgian successor as a bloodletter.

Actually, Lenin sinks lower than Stalin, when comparison is made between his role in the "Red Terror" and that of Stalin in his push for power. Unlike Stalin, Lenin lacked the guts to mix into terror personally. He delegated the dirty job of organizing and running the Cheka to a willing and fanatic Pole, Felix Dzerzhinsky, the son of a wealthy landowner, who up to that moment had been marking time as mere Commandant of Bolshevik headquarters at the Smolny Institute. Subsequently converted into a minor saint in the Russian Communist pantheon, Dzerzhinsky showed no qualms about wholesale slaughter: after all, the victims were only foreigners to him. Nevertheless, on taking over his assignment, he retreated to dialectics and expounded this thesis in justification of his impending brutishness: "Do not think I am on the lookout for forms of revolutionary justice. We have no need of justice now. Now we need a battle to the death."

In mid-January, 1918, when that Polish paladin had been on the job for less than a month, an attempt was allegedly made on the life of the boss-man he was supposed to protect. Various accounts—all somewhat suspect—describe how Lenin was shot at then, and missed, while being driven through the streets of Petrograd. As the stories go, one Fritz Platten, an itinerant Swiss Communist carpetbagging in Russia who was another occupant of the car, shielded Lenin's body with his own and thus saved the Communist leader from assassins' bullets. It is true that Platten was slightly injured by flying glass from the smashed windshield. And it is also true that the chaffeur drove away from the area at breakneck speed. At that point, however, fact seems to give way to fiction. The more likely explanation of the incident appears to be that the Lenin vehicle had inadvertently entered an area where a common armed robbery or a shoot-out between "revolutionists" was in progress and a stray shot smashed the car's windshield. Otherwise, it is incomprehensible that even Stalin would have dared to eliminate such a "hero" as Platten in the purges of the thirties. Whatever the explanation of the incident, no one was caught or even directly charged with the alleged attempt. But it did spur on Dzerzhinsky to more summary executions of unfortunate opponents, "enemies of the people" and such, who, of course, had nothing to do with the shot supposedly fired at Lenin's car.

Genuine or not, that attempt did nothing to slow Lenin's drive for power, as was shown at the first—and last—meeting of the Constituent Assembly two days later. Elected only the previous November, that body had an overwhelming SR majority, but that daunted Lenin not at all. He packed the Petrograd hall with Kronstadt sailors, Red troops and Chekists and even had machine guns and artillery drawn up outside. With that show of force, the Bolsheviks ended the threat of democratic government to communism once and for all and the assembly was closed even more easily than Nicholas II once shut down the Duma. Despite those tactics, from that time on in Russia, communism has been "legal" and attempts to form any other kind of government have been "illegal." And, of course, all in the name of the "people."

And in case there were any doubts about how "illegal" the Constituent Assembly had been, on January 19, 1918, the day after that body had been put out of existance, Bolshevik sailors stormed into Petrograd hospital and murdered two conservative (Kadet Party) leaders, Professor Fedor Kokoshkin and Dr. Andrey Shingarev. Other sailors went on a rampage in the south a month later, when units of the Black Sea "fleet" massacred the *bourgeoisie* of Sevastopol.

While struggling for internal control of his Russian base for the

[173]

worldwide Communist take-over, Lenin also had his hands full with foreign affairs, especially with the windup of World War I, then in its last stages. Kaiser Wilhelm's government, which had allowed Lenin passage across Germany in 1917 to stir up chaos in Russia, wanted Russia out of the war so it could concentrate on deteriorating conditions on its western front. For his own grandiose plans, Lenin was even more desirous that Russia get out of the war, no matter what the cost. Soon after seizing power, he gave Trotsky, his Foreign Affairs and War Commissar, the task of negotiating with the Germans. The negotiations were difficult and lasted for several months. But in the end, on March 3, 1918, the Communists signed the infamous Brest-Litovsk treaty with the Germans. Under its terms, Russia agreed to withdraw from Finland and what later became the Baltic republics, evacuate the Ukraine, return all occupied territory to Turkey and demobilize its army. Just before signatures were affixed to that document, the Germans had put final pressure on the Communists by advancing toward Petrograd and clashing with units of the newly constituted Red Army. It was fear of that advance—nothing else—that caused the transfer of Russia's capital from Petrograd back to Moscow, a safer distance from the German lines.

Later in March, 1918, the SRs, who opposed the Brest-Litovsk treaty, withdrew from the government, which from that time until the present has been composed of Communists only. Some SRs remained in the Cheka, but in much the same fashion as they had bored within the Tsarist Okhrana, but even that non-Communist representation did not last long. What had happened was that the Communists felt strong enough to no longer need the SRs, while the SRs, for their part, finally realized the perversion the Communists were perpetrating and so reverted to the same tactics used—more successfully—against the tsars, open and underground opposition.

Concurrent with the emergence of that political opposition to the Communists came military opposition that developed into a civil war in which Russian bloodily battled Russian and his allies, rather than the German enemy, from 1918 to 1921. Russia's World War I allies, primarily Britain and France, and to a lesser extent the United States and Italy, were extremely averse to having their forces harder pressed in the west by Russian withdrawal from the war. As a result, Britain, France, and the United States, plus an organization of former Czechoslovak prisoners of war and the Japanese, first tried to bolster the Kerensky regime and then went into direct opposition to the Communists—but with never more than insignificant token forces of their own. Instead they mistakenly relied on funding and supplying poorly organized and ineffective remnants of Tsarist forces holding out against the Communists in the north, west, south, and east and in all of Siberia. Communist "historians" have greatly exaggerated that allied and Tsarist opposition and called it a war on six fronts. But even though there were many cruel and merciless individual actions, it was never a war as such. Britain and France were not so much interested in fighting an enemy as in protecting and exploiting commercial interests. Japan's only concern was in trying to grab Far Eastern territory while Russia was in trouble. And the United States effort was only to keep the Japanese from doing that and securing the Trans-Siberian railroad and its auxiliaries. Even though their attempts never amounted to anything, history has accorded a small niche to such Russian leaders of the civil conflict's anti-Communist forces—or White Guards as the Communists call them—as Generals Nikolay Yudenich, Anton Denikin, Yevgeny Miller, Aleksey Dutov, Nestor ("Batko") Makhno, Admiral Alexander Kolchak, and Baron Peter Wrangel. Two of those Tsarist leaders, Miller and Wrangel, survived that struggle to become the equally ineffective rallying points of Russian emigrés in Western Europe for the next two decades.

Another pair of anti-Communist—and former Russian—leaders of that era, Finland's Marshal Carl Mannerheim and Poland's Marshal Joseph Pilsudski (who had plotted against Alexander III with Lenin's brother), were successful in their struggles with Lenin's forces. Mannerheim was at least a minor military genius, while Pilsudski was assisted by France's brilliant General Maxime Weygand, and both were fighting for liberation of their countries from centuries of Russian domination. Both also secured some revenge for that domination by grabbing sizable chunks of Russian territory (annexations that both countries lost again, and more, in World War II).

Even though it was one of the so-called "six" fronts, the Finnish struggle was more or less dismissed by the Communists, probably because Finland had long had autonomous status. But in their conflict with the Poles, the Communists, despite all their mouthings about self-determination and international brotherhood, were just as chauvinist as the Tsarist regimes.

[175]

As war commissar and thereby chief commander of that 1918-20 struggle on the Polish front, Trotsky had wanted to halt the Russian advance at the ethnic frontier between the two countries. And the Pole surfaced in Dzerzhinsky who supported Trotsky's view. But they were overruled by Lenin, bent on the conquest of Poland as a step in his drive to make the world Communist. Stalin, that man of no principle, of course pandered to Lenin, even though he was supposed to care for the national minorities that had been subjugated by the tsars.

Acting under the Lenin order, the Red Army's Mikhail Tukhachevsky drove to the outskirts of Warsaw. But Tukhachevsky's forces had pretty well spent themselves. Cossack Semen Budenny's fine cavalry unit—with Stalin attached to its coattails—was supposed to go to the support of Red Army troops at Warsaw's gates. Instead, Budenny pushed toward Lvov, apparently influenced by Stalin's desire to garner military laurels with the capture of that ancient city. As a result, Pilsudski, with Weygand's counsel, was able to regroup and rout both Tukhachevsky and Budenny. By the 1921 Treaty of Riga that formalized that Russian defeat, Poland gained, not only sizable chunks of White Russia and the Ukraine, but also a frontier that denied Russia direct contact with Lithuania.

Nevertheless, despite the Finnish and Polish setbacks, and despite Lenin's interference and Stalin's military incompetence, Trotsky, a brilliant organizer, had formed a most formidable force of the Red Army in the 1918–21 period. Servile Communist historians, naturally, have completely denied Trotsky his due. Instead, they have exaggerated the roles of such survivors as Semen Budenny and Kliment Voroshilov; given much false credit for nothing to Stalin; and made it appear as if lowly loyal workers and inspired simple peasants bore the bulk of the responsibility for the Red Army's success. And the picture has been further muddied by many a romanticized to purely fictionalized account of White Russian prowess.

The facts are vastly different. The 1918–21 interventions of Britain, France, and Japan were purely selfish; that of the United States at best can be described as naïve and weak-kneed. And besides, approve of it or not, the foreigners supported Russians most of whom not only wanted restoration of the autocracy and all its iniquities, but also were often just as guilty as the Reds of unspeakable atrocities. Despite all the chaos then rampant, an overwhelming number of

[176]

former faithful military men of the tsar saw the light. Trotsky's Red Army was not made out of whole cloth overnight because of a speech by Lenin. It was the former officers and noncoms of the tsar—Tukhachevsky was only one of thousands upon thousands—disgusted by the foreigners and their Russian collaborators, who rallied to Trotsky's ranks and gave them the cadres and the know-how to defeat the adversary. In sum, Lenin, despite his internationalist pose, was saved by Trotsky's nationalist forces, whose drive sprang from patriotism, not communism. That misnamed civil war was just as much a Great War of the Fatherland as that fought in World War II by the Red Army subject to Stalin.

Somewhat concurrent with the full-scale outbreak of the civil war in spring 1918, the home front experienced a final—and speedily crushed—offensive by the SRs and other opponents of the Communists. And, of course, the Cheka was as busy as ever rounding up and executing everyone who did not look like a worker or a peasant, plus many that did. For two days in April, 1918, those virtual outcasts, the Anarchists, engaged in a mass shoot-out from their Moscow headquarters before finally being subdued forever by the Cheka and Red Latvian troops.

SR action against the Communists, organized by Boris Savinkov, Azev's trainee who was once admired by a youthful Winston Churchill, did not get under way until several weeks later. Then in late June, 1918, Moisey M. Goldstein, better known by the name V. Volodarsky, the press and agitprop commissar, was killed on the streets of Petrograd by an SR terrorist.

All-out SR operations started in July, 1918. Their first and hardest blow was struck July 6 when SR members of the Cheka killed Kaiser Wilhelm's ambassador to the Lenin government, Count Wilhelm Mirbach. That murder was committed in the erroneous belief the Germans would be so outraged by Lenin's secret police killing their envoy that they would revoke the Brest-Litovsk treaty and force Russia back into the war. Lenin's government hastened to assure the Germans the murder was the work of outlaws, while Dzerzhinsky went to Mirbach's residence in an effort to gain control of the SR Cheka men. At the same time other SRs seized Cheka headquarters and Moscow's post and telegraph office, cutting off all communications out of the capital and for a while it looked as if the Communists had lost control of the city. However, although Dzerzhinsky was captured and held briefly by Mirbach's killers, he soon regained command. SR representatives, including Maria Aleksandrovna Spiridonova, a veteran revolutionist and leader of the Moscow uprising, were arrested while attending a Soviet Congress. The telegraph office and Cheka headquarters were wrested from SR control and SRs were driven from other strongpoints, sometimes with point-blank artillery fire. SR Chekists were summarily executed. Spiridonova and other SRs were sent to Siberian prisons.

That ended the SR attempt to take over Moscow—and it also ended SR membership in the Cheka, which became all-Communist from that time on. To the east and north of the capital, however, the situation was not so sanguine for the Communists. Savinkov was leading SR uprisings in twenty-three Upper Volga cities and towns, all scheduled to coincide with Spiridonova's Moscow attempt. Some accounts say the French had promised him the help of foreign troops from the Allied base in the Archangel area. But no such help ever arrived and it is extremely doubtful the French ever made such a promise. Outnumbered, the SRs soon lost one town after another to the Communists, with Yaroslavl holding out the longest, until July 23. Hundreds of captured SRs were slain on the spot by the Chekists, but Savinkov escaped abroad as he had so frequently done in Tsarist days. Lenin reacted to the SR attempts by personally ordering increased Red Terror in the Middle and Upper Volga and Urals regions. Well-to-do farmers and suspected White Guardists were the chief victims while peasants were required to surrender hostages to guarantee the delivery of grain to the cities. The Communists murdered Nicholas II and his family at Ekaterinburg (Sverdlovsk) in the same period, but those killings were not reaction to the SR attempts. They were committed because Ekaterinburg was in danger of falling to the Czecho-slovaks.

All mass attempts of the SRs to seize power from the Communists ended at Yaroslavl. But isolated SR terrorist action—individual acts and pale shadows of the Azev operations—continued for some time. On July 30, an SR terrorist killed the German commander of the Ukraine, an indication to the Germans they were highly unwelcome to many Russians, even though they had sent another ambassador to Moscow to replace Mirbach. And on the morning of August 30, 1918, another SR terrorist murdered Moisey Uritsky, the bloody-handed chief of the Petrograd Cheka.

Dzerzhinsky dashed immediately to Petrograd to supervise investigation of the Uritsky killing, only to learn as his train arrived that an attempt had been made to assassinate Lenin earlier that day. That would-be killer was Fanya (or Dora) Kaplan, an SR revolutionary who was nearly blind as the result of eleven years spent in a Tsarist prison for a Kiev outrage. The Communists have claimed she was operating under Savinkov's direction, but there is absolutely no truth in such allegations. She was a lone operator, determined to kill Lenin because he had destroyed the Constituent Assembly. And she might have succeeded, had her sight been better. Also, if she had really used dumdum and poisoned bullets in her revolver, as the Communists claimed, Lenin would never have survived her shots.

Kaplan had been waiting for Lenin outside a Moscow factory, where he had been making a speech. As he was about to get into his car, she fired at him three times before being overpowered. One shot went through his neck and penetrated a lung. Another hit his left shoulder. The third made a harmless hole in his overcoat. Lenin was rushed to his Kremlin apartments where he underwent emergency treatment and operation and eventually recovered. Although Communist mythology has detailed ad nauseam the hours after the wounded Lenin arrived at the Kremlin, his life was never really in danger. One of the two bullets that struck him was not removed from his body until after his death almost six years later.

Kaplan was also rushed to the Kremlin immediately after the shooting. She, however, was taken to no plush apartment but to cellars under the quarters of Yakov Sverdlov, first Soviet President, who became acting head of government after Lenin was incapacitated. Dzerzhinsky sped back to Moscow to handle Kaplan's interrogation, whose techniques are better left to imagination. But the assassin's travail did not last long. Condemned to death, she was shot September 3 in the back of the skull—a system long since common with Chekists and their successors. Her executioner was one Pavel Malkov, the first Communist commandant of Kremlin bodyguards.

The combination of the murder of Uritsky and the attempt on Lenin gave Dzerzhinsky, the Cheka, and other bloody-minded Communists what they had long been wanting—the excuse for wholesale elimination of all opponents, real or imagined. Sverdlov, who meddled much in police affairs, used the very evening of the attempt against Lenin to issue a proclamation telling the "working classes" that Red Terror should be used against the "counterrevolutionaries." Many sycophants telegraphed support to Sverdlov. Stalin's message said his "military soviet of the North Caucasus" would organize "open and systematic mass terror against the *bourgeoisie* and its agents." And on September 2, the Communist regime made Red Terror "legal." It stated: "The workers and peasants will answer the White Terror of the enemies of the workers' and peasants' power with mass Red Terror against the *bourgeoisie* and their agents." At the same time the nation was declared under arms, or in a state of siege, thereby legalizing the unlimited powers of arrest, torture, execution, imprisonment, and exile the Cheka already had been using.

By a too strange coincidence, it just so happened that on the very day of the Uritsky and Lenin incidents Bruce Lockhart, the British consul-general in Moscow, was arrested and taken to the Cheka Lubyanka headquarters. In fact, Kaplan, who been taken first to the Lubyanka before intensive interrogation at the Kremlin, passed by Lockhart in the corridors of the police stronghold. Picked up after news of the Uritsky assassination had been received, Lockhart was charged, along with an old colleague, Sidney Reilly, with trying to bribe the Latvian unit guarding the Kremlin. The charges against the two British subjects were crude fabrications but they were needed by the Communists to complete their pretence of being surrounded by foes, both native and foreign, so as to "legalize" the Red Terror. Nevertheless, there is also very considerable evidence that Lockhart (who died peacefully at home in 1971) and Reilly (who was murdered by the Communists in 1925) were very unusual "diplomats." Actually both could probably best be described as cloak-and-dagger romanticists, if not would-be kingmakers. The British countered Lockhart's arrest by holding Maxim Litvinov, then Soviet ambassador to Britain. Both were released some two months later. But British-Soviet relations had been ruined for some time to come, especially since the Soviets had invaded the British embassy in Petrograd and shot the British naval attaché. The French were also harassed by the Cheka in that period but their troubles were not as serious as those of the British.

Unfortunately for the mass of Russians, the Lockhart affair somewhat obscured the horror of the Red Terror since foreign concern was concentrated on the far less important and rather unnecessary Soviet-British diplomatic imbroglio. Overlooked to a considerable extent, therefore, was the wholesale Cheka slaughter of innocents. Eliminated were not just the *"bourgeoisie* and their agents"—although all in that category bore the brunt—but also almost all the clergy of all confessions, workers who had believed Lenin's professions of socialism and demanded their rights, peasants who did not want to surrender their new independence and ownership of land, plus practically everyone individual Chekists suspected, disliked, or had a grudge against. It was a return to the times of Ivan the Terrible, but with many more people as victims.

Powerless against the Red Terror, the great majority of the SRs and other opponents of the Soviet regime either bowed their heads in submission or fled abroad. Some of those who fled—including Savinkov—tried to organize networks of agents within and without Russia, much the same as other revolutionaries had done in Tsarist days, but all those efforts amounted to little more than entrapment of the revolutionaries themselves. The Cheka and its successors penetrated the nets even more easily and thoroughly than the Okhrana had done before them. It is easy after all these years to criticize Savinkov and his fellows as ill-prepared and foolhardy. Somebody had to learn the first time—although those lessons are mostly disregarded by later generations. Savinkov and other early revolutionists against the Communists just happened to be the first. Those who followed them have not done as well, nor even made the attempt.

As a result of the SRs being forced offstage, terror became a one-way street for the Communists alone. From then on, incidents caused by opponents were sparse in number and relatively trivial in effect. In late 1919, a bomb killed twelve Communists, including Moscow Party Secretary Vladimir Zagorsky, and injured fifty-five others at a Moscow Communist party meeting that Lenin had been supposed to, but did not, attend. The Cheka blamed that outrage on Anarchists and White Guardists—much as Communists later blamed all and everything on "reactionaries" and "imperialists"—but it could just as well have been the work of disaffected Communists. As the result of that bombing, the Cheka went on a rampage of searches, seizures, arrests, shoot-outs, and executions during the remainder of autumn, 1919. The Cheka named names of plotters caught, but since those names were unknown to all but the Cheka, the bomb attack still remains a mystery. For Communist records, however, the crime was "solved."

Despite that, the Cheka did manage to kill off a few well-known real life people in 1919. Among those were two respected politicians, Nikolay Shchepkin, a conservative, and Alexander Astrov, a liberal. Both were dispatched at Cheka Moscow headquarters. The year 1919 also saw the Lenin pose of not being well-guarded further bolstered. Angelica Balabanoff, the veteran revolutionist and troublemaker, whose last appearance on the public scene was participation in the post-World War II split-up of the Italian Socialist party, spread this yarn about the "unprotected" Lenin: on his way by car, with an armed guard aboard, to visit his sick wife, Nadezhda Krupskaya, at a hospital in the Moscow outskirts, he was halted and robbed by bandits. Lenin tried to identify himself, but all his two accosters wanted was his money. However, they let him keep the bottle of milk he was taking to Krupskaya. What the Balabanoff story and the accounts of the Kaplan attempt glossed over was the fact that Lenin's guards were no good when confronted with determined people of any type.

Even though all organized opposition had long ceased, the Cheka continued the Red Terror for several years more, until the civil war came to a complete end with the surrender of the Far Eastern maritime provinces in 1922. The combination of terror and war had earlier reduced Russia's economy to ruins. Baffled and frustrated, the peasants were producing only enough for their own survival and refused to deliver to the cities. Some city people who could get the transport and avoid the Cheka black-marketed comparative luxuries to the peasants in exchange for food. And even if enough food had been produced for all, transport was in such a woeful state it could not have delivered it. Almost all the Communist-run cooperative farms were failures because the ideologists knew nothing about agriculture. The result of that mess—plus a very poor crop year in 1921—was a great and terrible famine that swept Russia in 1921–22. Foreigners rushed in to help—the Americans under the direction of Herbert Hoover—but deliveries from abroad fell far short of demand and millions literally starved to death. Other millions—and particularly the children who were running loose like gangs of pack rats—managed somehow to survive but diet deficiencies experienced then hampered them the rest of their lives. Additionally, the foreign do-

[182]

gooders were often harassed by the Cheka, which regarded all of them as spies.

In August 1920, before the famine had reached crisis proportions, peasants in the Tambov area, southeast of Moscow, had had enough of Cheka interference. Led by one Antonov, a guerrilla, they revolted. There were other peasant risings aplenty, of course, but the Tambov revolt was the most serious for the Communists. To suppress it—bloodily as usual—they used militarized Cheka units, helped by Red Army forces under Tukhachevsky.

Lenin cared nothing about the fate of the Tambov peasants, but he may have been frightened by the approach of nationwide famine. Whatever the reason, in March 1921 he gave up trying to force communism down the throats of the mass of Russians, for a while, at least. At the tenth party congress of that date, he confounded the ideologists, present and future, by decreeing, in much the same authoritarian way as the tsars before him, a New Economic Policy, or NEP as it has come to be called. Purely and simply, NEP, which lasted for several years after Lenin's death, was an economic retreat. It not only gave freedom to the peasants, such as they experienced neither before or since, but it also granted virtually free enterprise to the rest of the economy, from industry to the smallest shop. Under the seven years of NEP, Russia almost bloomed, recovering from war, civil war, famine, and Communist mismanagement.

Lenin was not so kind, however, to his fellow Communists at that Party congress. In another important decree—one which has remained in force until this day—he forbade individual Party members to criticize the Party leadership, meaning Lenin and his successors. That decree not only made the party moribund by gagging all opposition within the party, but it also made the party monolithic. It legalized dictatorship, not of the proletariat, but of one man, and laid the groundwork for the eventual so-called "cult of personality." It was the Cheka and its successors that enforced that decree with the result that the revolution not only consumed its own children for a time—as most revolutions have done—but forever, or so long as what is called Leninism lasts.

Most likely not coincidentally, as the party faithful gathered in Moscow for that tenth congress, the Kronstadt sailors, once ardent supporters of the Bolsheviks, did more than mutiny, as they had under Nicholas and Kerensky. They openly revolted against Communist rule. Several months before that, in nearby Petrograd, workers and peasants alike had been protesting the harsh regime of Grigory Zinoviev, the local Communist boss. They made such proclamations as: "Workers and peasants need freedom. They don't want to live by Bolshevik decrees. They want to control their own destiny."

Once called "the pride and the glory of the Bolshevik revolution," the Kronstadt sailors finally reacted to the growing discontent in the former capital. Joined by soldiers and workers, a force of about 16,-000 rallied in the fortress March 1, 1921. A revolutionary committee was elected. It demanded—as was so often demanded in vain in the Soviet Union and later Communist states—freedom of speech, press, and labor organization, secret balloting, no more political commissars in the armed forces, no more forcible grain collections from the peasants, and the right for the peasants to sell their goods on the open market.

The decree banning criticism in his pocket, Lenin struck hard at the Kronstadt dissidents. He dispatched some 60,000 Red Army and Cheka units against them, under the leadership of Trotsky and Tukhachevsky, the Tsarist renegade of Tambov fame.

As they went into battle, the sailors declared: "Here is raised the banner of rebellion against the three-year-old tyranny and oppression of Communist autocracy which has put in the shade the three hundred-year-old despotism of monarchy." Despite those brave words and hundreds upon hundreds of struggles to the death, Kronstadt courage alone could not match Communist numbers. The fortress fell on March 17, with thousands of sailors and workers lying dead on its streets. Most of those who survived were summarily executed by the Cheka, but a few hundred managed to escape to Finland, where they told the story to an unheeding and unsympathetic world. South of the fortress, on the mainland at Petrodvorets, one of the former summer palaces of the tsars, some Red Army units rose in support of Kronstadt. But the soldiers' revolt was also speedily and bloodily quelled.

A few weeks prior to Kronstadt, on February 11, 1921, Stalin had seized on Lenin's concentration with the forthcoming party congress to settle scores with his native Georgia. That tiny Caucasus state had become independent in 1918 and was ruled by a Democratic-Socialist government, run by Stalin's first teacher. Some three years later, and acting without prior approval of the Politburo, Stalin sent his flunky, Grigory Ordzhonikidze, and Red Army forces to crush little Georgia's relatively harmless regime. He already had three fifth columnists of a sort within Georgia, Sergey Kirov, Anastas Mikoyan, and Lavrenty Beria, so the struggle was soon over, with Tiflis, the capital, surrendering on February 25, 1921. Resistance continued in the mountains and remote hamlets for some time, but Stalin eventually stopped that by installing a stooge Communist government with further help from Ordzhonikidze and his three other toadies. That ruthless action against Stalin's fellow Georgians eventually came to Lenin's attention and Dzerzhinsky was sent to investigate. By that time, Dzerzhinsky was already in Stalin's pocket and the investigation was a whitewash. But, although ill, Lenin fully understood what Stalin had done, to the extent that he left a testament declaring that Stalin should be removed as party leader. Despite all the subsequent Communist hoopla about respect for Lenin and Lenin's infallibility, that testament was conveniently shelved at the appropriate time.

Unfortunately for millions of Russians, Lenin had not learned the facts about Stalin's character until after Stalin was made General Secretary of the party—his power position from that time on—in April, 1922. And then, in May 1922, Lenin suffered the first of three strokes that were to incapacitate him and eventually lead to his death.

The party's worry about Lenin and fear of Stalin's machinations were briefly assuaged a month later. Divertissement was furnished in June 1922 with the first of many show trials staged by the Soviet Union and its puppet states. That prototype, however, had one glaring difference—none of the defendants confessed. The Soviet secret police had not yet attained such finesse. The defendants were twelve SRs with a long record of imprisonment, even the death sentence, under the tsars. At first, foreign defense lawyers, including Theodore Liebknecht, brother of the murdered German Communist leader, were permitted, but the presiding judge, Georgy (Yuriy) Pyatakov, soon sent them packing. Of course, the twelve SRs were found guilty. Under the Soviet system of "justice," no one is brought to trial unless the authorities have determined he is guilty. The trial is only window-dressing and an opportunity to air a little propaganda. Pyatakov sentenced the entire dozen to death, but higher authorities ruled they should be held in camps and prisons as hostages to be executed in event of another rebellion. The sentences were finally carried out against the unfortunate twelve during the Stalin purges of the late thirties. By crude Communist poetic justice of a sort, their judge, Pyatakov, also met death during the same purges.

In March, 1923, Lenin had a third stroke which incapacitated him for good, He spent most of the remaining months of his life in the expropriated villa of a wealthy businessman at Gorki (not named after Maxim Gorky, but meaning low hills), a health resort outside Moscow. To keep up with party and government affairs, he either used the telephone, sent his wife as a messenger of sorts to Moscow, or had his underlings come to him at Gorki.

Nevertheless, despite his efforts to keep the reins in hand, it was quite apparent that Lenin was losing control. Most of the Party hierarchs reacted with worry and sympathy as their leader's situation worsened, but Stalin, with his peasant astuteness, sensed that Lenin was dying. Instead of being downcast, he started capitalizing on the situation. In fact, he started preparing for Lenin's death. He organized a triumvirate with Lev Kamenev and Grigory Zinoviev to oppose Trotsky whom he correctly regarded as Lenin's logical successor. He, of course, had Dzerzhinsky in tow, as well as Ordzhonikidze, Kirov, Mikoyan, Beria, and other flunkies. And in 1923, Stalin also tested his power against another party hierarch, by using the Cheka's successor, the GPU, to arrest his opponent. Stalin's victim was a Tatar Communist leader, Mirza Sultan Galiyev, who sought some autonomy for his people—the same mistake the Georgians had made earlier. That was the first time the secret police had been used against a Party hierarch: a practice that was to become monotonously repetitive after Stalin had attained complete power. Initially, many in the Central Committee were shocked at that action. But the majority finally approved Stalin's move, and thereby also approved, albeit unwittingly, their own eventual extinction via the same route. Later in 1923, Dzerzhinsky was given authority to require that Party members give all information about dissidence within their ranks to the GPU. (In February 1922, Lenin had dissolved the Cheka and replaced it with the GPU—or State Political Administration—and in November, 1923, the secret police name was again altered, that time to OGPU, the additional "O" standing for United.) The ultimate result of those 1923 maneuvers by Stalin and his cohort, Dzerzhinsky, was that the basis for the Stalin police state had been well established months before Lenin's death.

Therefore, except for tears, both real and crocodile, the struggle for power among the successors had been pretty well settled by the time Lenin finally died at Gorki in January, 1924. There are endless accounts of Lenin's last hours, none of them reliable. Only two people, Krupskaya and Trotsky, could have given credible versions, but Krupskaya was in Moscow on a mission for her husband in the critical hours. She was also too naïve about secret police machinations and too emotional about her husband's failing condition to do so, and Trotsky was miles from Moscow at the time of death. There was an autopsy, to be sure, but the doctors performing it, as well as those attending Lenin at his end, were all selected and controlled by Dzerzhinsky's OGPU, and even those doctors were dead or had disappeared within a few years. Most of the OGPU guards and servants at Lenin's Gorki villa also dropped from sight in short order. The only hard facts remaining are that Lenin's death occurred more suddenly than most expected, even though he had long been ill, and the autopsy reported that he died of arteriosclerosis. Confusion exists about the actual time of death; rumors linger about Stalin having OGPU guards or doctors exchange Lenin's medicine for poison; while Kerensky—who certainly had no firsthand knowledge—declared in New York City in a last statement about Lenin's death in 1970 that he died when syphilis, from which he had long suffered, finally invaded his brain. Trotsky, however, insisted up until the time of his own death that Lenin had been poisoned by Stalin, and there is no denying the fact that that accuser was murdered by an agent of Stalin. Such allegations, suspicions, claims, and counterclaims probably will long continue, but none will completely untangle the elements of mystery surrounding Lenin's death.

With Lenin out of the way, Stalin concentrated on his struggle with Trotsky, who, after the dead leader, was the only man with enough personal magnetism to challenge the Georgian's drive for absolute power. Trotsky was admired by the Red Army and much of the youth, but by character he was more a permanent revolutionary and was averse to seeking power for himself. That characteristic more than simplified matters for Stalin.

Trotsky had been ill in the Caucasus at the time of Lenin's final battle for life. And, due to an "error" by Stalin, he did not even arrive in Moscow in time for the funeral. By that, Stalin won the opening round. As chief mourner at the rites, some of the aura traditionally accorded dead leaders by the Russians was given the apparent successor. Although fully aware of that, Stalin trod very warily at first. He posed as a member of the Politburo's "collective leadership," but at the same time was leader of the triumvirate arrayed against Trotsky. In the latter role he whittled all of Trotsky's supporters away from positions of influence, particularly those in the Ukraine, sending most on assignments abroad.

That done, Stalin was well prepared for a crucial meeting of the central committee in May, 1924. The prime matter before that gathering was the reading of Lenin's "testament," calling for the removal of Stalin as party General Secretary. In addition to the "testament," the committee was also mindful of Lenin's later attack on Stalin in the January 25, 1923 *Pravda* in which he blasted as ineffective and woefully mismanaged the Commissariat of Workers' and Peasants' inspection run by Stalin. The Georgian had used that seemingly harmlessly named organization to gain entry into and eventual control of almost every activity in the country, an initial step in his march to power.

On the appointed day, the "testament" was read. Stalin did not bat an eye, nor did Trotsky, who still had the Red Army and the young people behind him, make a move. Instead, Stalin's first stooge, Zinoviev, declared to the committee that although every order of Lenin would be fulfilled, there were no grounds to Lenin's fears about Stalin with whom everyone could get along. Stalin's second stooge, Kamenev, seconded that by calling on the committee to retain Stalin as General Secretary. The only protest of note was made by Krupskaya. All the rest of the committee got on the Stalin bandwagon.

Later, thinking he had Trotsky on the run, Zinoviev—beyond all doubt under Stalin's instructions—belabored Trotsky with a denunciation of his past criticism and a demand that he cease all future criticism and admit his errors. Trotsky did not start fighting back until the autumn of 1924 and by then it was too late for more than polemics. He issued a pamphlet calling for a return of democracy to the party and suggesting indirectly that the attitudes of Zinoviev and Kamenev—if followed—would have brought the Bolshevik revolution to the same disaster as that met by the German Communists in 1923.

Although the exchange between Trotsky and Zinoviev did not help Trotsky very much, it did diminish the stature of the two stooges. And that, too, was to prove helpful to Stalin. Meanwhile, the image of Zinoviev, head of the Comintern, had already been marred by the so-called "Zinoviev letter," a fraudulent attempt to show the Communists were about to seize power in Britain during the 1924 general elections.

Therefore, in late 1924 Stalin entered the fray himself. First, he advocated "socialism in one country"—in Russia—the antithesis of Trotsky's (and, of course, Lenin's) push for international communism, of world revolution. Next, he directly attacked Trotsky's proposal to collectivize Russia's twenty-five million farms, said it would bring "civil war to the country" and claimed Trotsky was "too fond of terror"—that from the Georgian who was later to unleash a reign of terror unmatched in world chronicles against not only Russia's peasants but also all her people.

Stalin's sally against Trotsky's collectivization proposal served to stack the seven-man Politburo against his enemy. Three members in particular of that organization, Premier Aleksey Rykov, ideologist Nikolay Bukharin, and trade union boss Mikhail Tomsky, wanted NEP to continue and expand. The other members were Stalin himself, Trotsky, Zinoviev, and Kamenev. Stalin long had had the latter pair well in hand, therefore, it was no surprise to anyone, including the victim himself, when the Politburo ousted Trotsky as War Commissar in January 1925 and assigned him to trifling economic tasks.

During those critical years of 1924–25, a sideshow of sorts distracted some attention from the massive political struggle then going on. Boris Savinkov, evidently deluded into believing that Stalin's OGPU was no more effective than had been the Okhrana in the "good old days" of the tsars, got himself smuggled back into Russia by the "Trust," a hopeless organization of emigrés and anti-Communists that had long been penetrated wholesale by the OGPU. As a result, Savinkov was caught in August, 1924, within hours of his arrival. At his trial, although he confessed all and called communism the way of the future, he was sentenced to be shot. Someone—perhaps Dzerzhinsky—had that sentence commuted to ten years in prison. For the following few months, Savinkov was held in comparatively plush quarters in the Lubyanka, where he was treated as sort of a chained, tame bear by Dzerzhinsky and even occasionally allowed auto tours through the streets of Moscow, under guard, of course. But, in 1925 the luckless veteran SR terrorist, who had long outlived his era, was suddenly dead. How he died is not known. Some accounts say he jumped from a window of the Lubyanka, but that appears more fictional than factual. The only hard truth was that one of Stalin's most active opponents had been eliminated and the age of SR terror brought to a close, for all intents and purposes.

While that little skit was being played out in the wings, Stalin continued his machinations toward power. Early in 1925, he dropped Zinoviev and Kamenev, who had served their purpose and were no longer useful to him, and picked up Rykov, Bukharin, and Tomsky instead. Ironically those five men were still deceived by the idea that they had something to do with the affairs of Russia. They could not see the woods of Stalin's power drive for the trees of their petty party dialectics and Stalin let them continue in their self-deception. In Communist jargon, Zinoviev and Kamenev became known as "leftists" and as such became allied with their former enemy Trotsky and his international and agrarian policies, while Rykov, Bukharin, and Tomsky joined Stalin in the "rightist" roles of supporting "socialism in one country" and NEP.

Stalin filled the vacancy in the War Commissar post with Mikhail Frunze, a senior officer of the Red Army during the civil war. But Frunze speedily made the grave mistake of not only being sympathetic to the ideas of his old chief, espoused by Zinoviev and Kamenev, but also of opposing OGPU meddling with the armed forces. As a result, his tenure was short indeed. He died in November, 1925, under an OGPU surgeon's knife. Frunze suffered from stomach ulcers but his doctors recommended against an operation, holding his heart would not withstand it. Stalin got an OGPU surgeon and his "consultants" to countermand Frunze's doctors and the operation took place under their direction. At this date, it is hard to prove murder, but there are grounds, at least, for a civil case of malpractice instigated by Stalin.

Frunze had hardly been buried when his successor, Kliment Voroshilov, was installed in December, 1925. From Stalin's standpoint, that was a much better selection for the war post. It was Voroshilov who had allowed "military expert" Stalin to make a mess of things at Tsaritsyn (Stalingrad) during the civil war; a mess from which Trotsky extricated both with Stalin hurrying to the scene to take the "glory." Besides, Voroshilov was also a tiny man in physical stature, being even more diminutive than his boss, Stalin.

With the War Commissar post finally in good hands—and that was very important since it meant control of the Red Army, Stalin proceeded to pack the Politburo. In December, 1925, he increased the membership of that body to ten, installing three sycophants, Voroshilov, Vyacheslav Molotov, his slow-witted crony from Tsarist days at *Pravda*, and Mikhail Kalinin, a colorless, gutless figurehead. The addition of that trio meant that Stalin no longer had to depend on the support of those three who occasionally had ideas of their own, Rykov, Bukharin, and Tomsky.

Thus armed with supporters—and their supporters—Stalin had little difficulty in overwhelming the opposition by a more than four-to-one vote at the Fourteenth Party Congress in December 1925. The usual Communist polemics aside, that gathering saw the last struggle of Zinoviev and Kamenev. Trotsky did not even count. Long disheartened, he remained aloof—in retrospect, a foolish act. Equally ineffective was the mass of Communists at that congress. Some even presaged the days of revolting adulation to come by shouting "long live Stalin" when the Georgian won. The importance of that congress was that it marked Stalin's last difficult moment. From that time on, he ran the party and Russia, with no true accounting to either. Although none recognized it then, the age of Stalin had really begun.

Capitalizing on his congress victory, Stalin sent Sergey Kirov, his stooge of Georgia take-over days, to Leningrad in early 1926 to wrest party control of the old capital from Zinoviev, a relatively simple affair. Despite that, the opposition's delusions continued and Zinoviev and Kamenev organized a *troika* of their own with Trotsky, believing that speeches by Zinoviev and Trotsky from the same platform could still turn the tide. Old Krupskaya was not so misled, however; she said that if Lenin himself should reappear, he would be arrested by Stalin.

Nevertheless, as a forerunner of a July 1926 Central Committee meeting, the opposition trio and its supporters held meetings in some woods outside Moscow—in true, old Bolshevik fashion. They toyed with—but no more than that—the idea of staging a *coup d'état* and seizing control from Stalin. At the committee meeting, the *troika* group claimed the leadership was supporting the *kulaks* against the poor peasants and leading the country back toward capitalism with its NEP policies.

Stalin easily sneered down the opposition complaints. But, im-

[191]

mediately after the meeting, he took the precaution of kicking Zinoviev off the Politburo and giving Kamenev's Foreign Trade post to his Armenian crony Anastas Mikoyan, whose greatest eventual contribution to the Russian masses was the introduction of the American ice cream cone. At the same time, he relieved a high military officer who had supported the *troika* from his command and kicked him off the Central Committee. Worried, Trotsky and his group recanted, but then tried to promote their ideas at workers' meetings. That was a foolhardy step. The OGPU was at all those gatherings working for Stalin. The initial reaction was the arrest and deportation of lesser figures of the opposition, tactics Stalin later was to use en masse. But the ultimate result was a crackdown in October, 1926, by the Central Committee and the Central Control Commission of the party, both by then well under Stalin's thumb. Trotsky was removed from the Politburo. Kamenev lost his candidate membership in that organization and Zinoviev was fired from his job as head of the Comintern.

At the height of the midsummer squabble of 1926, formalities in the form of obsequies briefly intervened and allowed a semblance of unity around a bier. Dzerzhinsky died suddenly in July. His death was perfectly normal. There was nothing suspicious about it, for the very good reason that that leader of the Red Terror, hated by millions, had always taken more careful steps to protect himself. There is a Communist account of an unidentified woman having taken a shot at him in Kharkov, but even Dzerzhinsky regarded that assailant as deranged and not politically inspired.

In a way, the death of the originator of the Cheka and the OGPU was of benefit to Stalin in his power struggle. It is true that Dzerzhinsky had pandered to Stalin, even during Lenin's lifetime, but it is also true that the secret police boss was a Lenin appointee. Thereby he had been able to maintain some integrity and was not a complete Stalin stooge. His death, therefore, was welcomed by the Georgian, enabling him to place another scion of a wealthy Polish family, Vyacheslav Menzhinsky, at the nominal helm of the OGPU. Actually, however, Stalin's position was even more improved. Well before Dzerzhinsky's death, Stalin had been using the services of an ambitious OGPU underling, Genrikh Yagoda, a Polish Jew and a onetime pharmacist with a lifelong penchant for poisons. Although Yagoda became only the OGPU second-in-command with Menzhinsky's elevation, it was Yagoda who really ran the police organization for the next decade. Menzhinsky, despite years of assistance to Dzerzhinsky, was just not of Communist secret police caliber and let Yagoda do the real dirty work. Additionally, Menzhinsky's wife was a close friend of Lenin's wife Krupskaya.

Another distraction to the waning power struggle was supplied in 1927 by concern about foreign affairs. Relations with Britain had gone from bad to worse, due to trouble with a Soviet representative in London, ending with severance of diplomatic relations and the dissolution of an Anglo-Soviet trade group. Additionally, China's Chiang Kai-shek bit the Stalin hand that fed him and turned against the Chinese Communists. Those and other foreign developments advanced the constant Russian Communist bogey of foreign intervention to a mania.

Unhappily for Trotsky—and perhaps his fellow Russians—he awoke from a period of relative dormancy to misjudge both the foreign situation and party reaction. Snorting around like an old warhorse eager for the fray, he thought his hour had finally come. Asininely, he hinted that he be given dictatorial powers to run the country and met the emergency—an emergency that never existed.

Promptly, Trotsky—and Zinoviev for good measure—were expelled from the Central Committee. Despite that, the *troika* and other members of the opposition still thought they had a chance. On November 7, 1927, the tenth anniversary of the "glorious" October revolution, they tried to stage street demonstrations in Moscow and Leningrad, demonstrations that were quickly quelled by the OGPU.

The smashing of the Moscow and Leningrad street protests marked the actual end of Trotsky and his followers. Stalin was careful to formalize matters before a full party gathering, the Fifteenth Congress of December, 1927. At that session, after Kamenev's speech in support of the principle of opposition had been dutifully booed down, Stalin rose and declared "an end must be put to this game." At that, the congress demanded Stalin's opponents recant or be expelled from the party.

Seventy-five delegates—including Trotsky—had the principle and guts to refuse and were tossed out of the party forthwith. Zinoviev, Kamenev and some others with less character and courage agreed to eat their words, but even that did not guarantee their party membership. The decision about expelling them was left to the General Secretariat—or Stalin—who eventually was to make that cringing pair a bloody example to all others daring to challenge him.

At the start of 1928, Stalin took even more severe measures against his erstwhile opponents. He exiled more than thirty of them to the more benighted places of the Soviet Union, under OGPU guard, of course. Later, as events proved, none survived his lust for power. Trotsky was sent to Alma-Ata and then deported to Turkey in 1929. For the next eight years, he lived in Turkey, France, and Norway, before being expelled from the last country on Stalin's complaint in 1937. He then went to Mexico where he stayed until axe-murdered by one of Stalin's NKVD agents in 1940. The other expellees from the party in 1927 did not live that long. They, along with millions of other Russians and many foreigners, met their deaths during Stalin's purges of the late nineteen thirties.

2. RUSSIA UNDER STALIN (1928–41)

With Trotsky out of the way and silenced so far as Russia was concerned, Stalin was well-embarked on his dual course, gaining absolute power for himself and making Russia one of the world's truly great powers. Actually in his somewhat Asiatic mind, the two aims were not only parallel, they were identical. His conceit was such that he could never be satisfied with being ruler of a second-rate power. In that drive he used no magic formula, but merely capitalized on the age-old Russian chauvinistic urge to be a dominant nation. Nor were his instruments unusual, being simply elements of cruelty, ruthlessness, and absolute control to which Russians historically are so well inured. As a Georgian, his concern was naturally limited, if it existed at all, for the Russians who had to pay the terrible price for their concept of glory. Before his death a few unheeded voices objected to that course and cost, but once he was entombed a veritable cacophony rose to criticize him. In retrospect and in all honesty it must be admitted that it is most probable that had the Devil incarnate appeared instead to lead the Russians along that road to "greatness," they would have followed just as willingly and dutifully. Nevertheless, even though that may somewhat explain what has come to be called Stalinism, it in no way justifies such a horrible and bloody course.

Ironically, at the same time Stalin booted out his opponents of the "left," he cynically espoused—or appropriated—their policies that he had earlier so severely criticized, when it had been expedient to do so. And by belatedly finding merit in the Trotsky program of forced agricultural collectivization and industrial expansion, he at the same time ran counter to his erstwhile supporters of the "right," Rykov, Bukharin, Tomsky, et al., whom he was to obliterate as effectively as he had the "leftists."

When Trotsky had advocated such a program, Stalin sneered that it would cause civil war, but when Stalin developed it, he waged a one-man war in the Soviet Union against not only the Russians but also all his other subject peoples such as had not been known since the days of the Tatars and Mongols.

To accomplish "his" newly found program, which dumped NEP, Stalin decreed collectivization of the farms and the first of the many five-year plans for industrial expansion. At the same time—during the tenth anniversary rites—he threw out several sops, including lower taxes and old age pensions for peasants and Red Army men, and equal status for all men. The latter may sound fine on paper, but it really was a measure to force women into labor ranks, a condition from which they have not yet been "liberated" by Communist rule. In the Soviet Union, women—wives and mature married daughters —must work, not for their egos, but to keep the wolf from the family door. Husbands and fathers do not earn enough on their own to provide more than the most minimal income. The women's work is often most menial, including cleaning the streets of Moscow and other cities and towns.

The industrial program that got under way in the late twenties soon brought results, even though there was a mania for heavy or capital industry only, a mania which still afflicts the country. New manufacturing cities and towns were founded, many of them in the Urals and previously undeveloped Siberia. Since the starts were made from relatively nothing, production of iron, steel, oil, coal, and electricity doubled, trebled, and more, while transport and related industry similarly expanded. However, since the far-flung Soviet Union enjoys the greatest accumulation of natural resources of any nation in the world—and with a relatively modest population to live off it—it remains doubtful that such expansion could not have been accomplished by any other type of regime. After all, the start was made from scratch after a decade and a half of war, civil war, and gross political interference and mismanagement. And it must never be forgotten that that expansion was not done to improve the lot of

[195]

Russia's millions—they were its forced labor gang—but primarily to gird the Red Army, first for self-defense and ultimately for world domination, once so piously decried by Stalin.

During the nascent years of that new "utopia," a small group of foreign engineers and technicians, European and American—the UAW's late Walter Reuther was among them—literally swarmed to help. (The fact that jobs were scarce in the Western world, then in major economic difficulty, may have contributed to that influx.) Many of those foreigners became disillusioned in time with the "noble experiment," recognizing it for what it was. After all, they were workers themselves, whereas Stalin had never been known to dirty his hands with any real work—and a few were made scapegoats for early Soviet failures.

A glaring example of the dangers of working for Stalin's industry came all to early, in May 1928, when the influx of foreign experts had barely started. That occasion was the first of Stalin's many show trials of fifty-two engineers from the Donbass coal basin, where production had not immediately zoomed—through no fault of the defendants— as planned. That sad lot was crudely framed by the OGPU and accused of "sabotage." That case also gave the outer world its first view of that loathsome Stalin tool, Andrey Vyshinsky, who was to forge on to become the Soviets' chief prosecutor—or persecutor—and later Foreign Minister and United Nations representative. So much did the case stink to high heaven as a cover-up for Stalin's planning flunkies' failures that Menzhinsky tried to intervene. He wanted the OGPU framers themselves tried for sabotage for lowering the morale —and the production—of the rest of the Donbass workers by the false accusations. But, since Stalin's real purpose was an assault on middle-class technicians who had cooperated with the Communists since the Bolshevik take-over, Menzhinsky was speedily slapped down. Not only were five of the unfortunates executed, but also their trial marked the first use of relatives to denounce the accused, a practice that later was to become all too disgustingly common. The son of the chief defendant was so "revolted" by his father's "crimes" —and so controlled by the OGPU—that he even changed his name.

During the first five-year plan, there were also three other "legal" preludes of what was soon to come for untold masses of Russians. The first, held in the last two months of 1930, involved eight members of a nonexistent "industrial" party, led by a Professor Leonid Ramzin, an engineer. That group was falsely accused of industrial sabotage and plotting for foreign intervention. Five of them got death sentences, later commuted, and all were incarcerated in prisons or camps. The most interesting feature of their "trial" was the half million innocents—or workers—who dutifully marched beneath the courtroom windows screaming "death to the wreckers." Next, in March, 1931, fourteen Mensheviks were framed with charges of plotting with an emigré member of their party, who had reentered Russia for the purpose, to return capitalism to the country. The defense established that the emigré leader had been in fact in Belgium at the time of the "plot," but that did not prevent the accused from being sent to prisons and camps from which they never emerged.

The principal "trial" of that quartet of "sabotage" frauds was held in April, 1933. It involved British and Russian engineers employed by the British firm of Metro-Vickers, which was doing work for the Soviets. The OGPU forced the defendants, including six British subjects, to sign "confessions." Later in court some of the British engineers denied their "confessions," but all the defendants were given prison sentences, with the Russians, of course, getting the longer terms. The British defendants were eventually expelled from the country or released from prison, but their arrest and trial resulted in a temporary breach of relations with Britain.

In the same period, there was also a startling instance of Stalin using the OGPU to warn possible foes of the dangers of trafficking with his political enemies. In 1929, acting on Stalin's order, the OGPU apprehended and executed summarily one of its own, the old veteran Chekist Yakov Blyumkin, the very same agent who as an SR rebel had taken part in the 1918 murder of Count Mirbach, the German ambassador. Blyumkin's "crime" was that his devious operations had led him to make contact with Trotsky in Turkey—apparently on direct orders from Stalin and the OGPU. Whether Blyumkin did something wrong, or was merely expendable as a bloody example is not known, but his summary execution did serve one purpose, if only for a time. Since he had long been a faithful convert to the party as well as an OGPU, more important Communist flunkies under Stalin's aegis were frightened enough to express their disapproval, lest they, too, die in similar traps. As a result, when one Mikhail Ryutin, a very small fry indeed with the party, had the guts to demand Stalin be fired as a General Secretary in 1932, he escaped with no more than loss of party membership and exile. But, it also should be pointed out that Ryutin was never heard of again.

In reality, however, those "sabotage" and "plotting" farces, and the Blyumkin and Ryutin affairs, were little more than backdrops, or screens, for Stalin's elimination of possible rivals of the moment and preparations against potential opponents of the future.

In that period, much of Stalin's attention was devoted to the Communist form of politicking—getting rid of his rivals—which in Stalin's case meant dumping his erstwhile supporters of the "right," Rykov Bukharin and Tomsky, and hacking away at the remnants of Trotsky's "left." In the course of that, he again packed the Politburo, increasing its membership to nine by adding to it Valerian Kuybyshev, a Red Army leader in the civil war and a long-time flunky in the general secretariat and Yan Rudzutak, a Latvian and the Communist-type of trade unionist. As candidate members of the Politburo, he also installed Kirov and Mikoyan, the Jewish Lazar Kaganovich, another general secretariat stooge who had helped him Stalinize the Ukraine, and Andrey Andreyev, a Soviet type of farm "expert." The latter three, super stooges with enormous powers of survival, lasted in one capacity or another throughout Stalin's reign, no mean feat.

For a time after Stalin's announcement of the five-year plan and its agricultural collectivization and industrial expansion, Rykov, Bukharin, and Tomsky were politically naïve enough to believe that meant Stalin had endorsed their policies. They also made the mistake of believing that those two thorough Stalin stooges, Kalinin and Voroshilov, would support them and thus give them a majority on the Politburo.

They were soon enlightened but then compounded their error by reconciliations with their two old opponents, the outcasts Kamenev and Zinoviev. With fine political acumen, Stalin added to their confusion in 1929 by naming Bukharin as leader of his opposition, that time of the "right." Earlier he had even further muddied the waters by a halfway rehabilitation of Zinoviev—allowing him to return from exile along with such other "leftists" as Karl Radek, one of Stalin's chief propagandists as long as the Georgian needed him, and old-time Leninists Georgy Pyatakov, Ivan Smilga, and Grigory Sokolnikov. The net effect was that Stalin had all his potential opponents in one handy basket, to dispose of at his convenience. For a while, the losers continued to wriggle within the basket, protesting the harsh (ruthless and cruel would be better words) aspects of the five-year plan. For that, in 1929, Bukharin was booted out of the Politburo and Tomsky and Rykov were fired from their jobs (with Rykov's post of Chairman of the Council of Peoples' Commissars—or Prime Minister—going to Molotov in 1930). That unfortunate and miserable trio tried to talk themselves back into Stalin's good graces, but failed. They were exiled to await their victor's eventual bloody pleasure. Other opponents of Stalin, who were able to, decamped abroad, a smaller wave of "pink" emigrés to join the earlier exodus of "Whites" in the West and in the Middle East, with a considerable number going just across the frontier to Iran. Thus Stalin had eliminated all possible rivals on the horizon at that time.

That lack of opposition allowed him to crush the peasants and establish the slave labor system that was to become an integral part of Soviet life. Although they were faceless, so to speak, in their millions, the peasants, too, represented opposition to Stalin and his complete domination of every living soul in Russia. As long as they were not collectivized—the more euphemistic term is "socialized"—they exercised a certain, albeit limited, form of independence. Therefore, in the Georgian's lights, they either had to be brought to heel or eliminated. One should skip his mouthings about the "benefits" of collectivization, how it would improve production—something that is yet to happen—how it would better the life of the peasants and the economy of the nation. All those words of Stalin and his satraps are just so much window dressing for an unparalleled drive for power, with absolutely no regard for what might happen to production or the economy as a result. Less primitive—or more Westernized— Slavic dictatorships have had similar problems with the basic independence of their peasants. The Polish peasants are still to be completely subjected. And the Yugoslav peasant, particularly the hardy Montenegrins, have forced the regime to compromise and not go the full route to "socialization."

Despite the terrible inhumanity it involved, Stalin's technique in attaining collectivization is admirable as an example to other autocrats faced with similar problems. Capitalizing on man's everpresent conflict with his fellow man, he divided the peasants into three groups—the *kulaks*, or the ablest and most well-to-do, the middle class, and the poor. That was pure and simple rabble-rousing on the meanest and most cynical level. In short order, the envy of the middle-class peasants was stirred against the *kulaks*, while the jealousy of the poor was aroused against both. The immediate result was a regime-countenanced civil war among the peasants in which the genuine *kulaks* were speedily despoiled of their lands, instruments, and beasts. The two lower classes were aided and abetted by the OGPU and sometimes the Red Army, with the eventual result that the *kulaks* were shot offhand, sent to slave labor camps, exiled to the bad-lands of the north and Siberia, or reduced to wandering across the face of Russia.

That elimination of the genuine *kulaks*, however, had not accomplished the subjugation of the peasants, or "collectivization." In fact, it made the witless survivors just that much more cocky and independent—but not for long. In late December, 1929, just as those fools were beginning to enjoy their spoils, Stalin, the archperverter of words and terms, decreed the liquidation of "all *kulaks*." From that point on, just who was a *kulak* was adjudged by the chance denunciation of an enemy within the village, by family or political connection, or by arbitrary action of the OGPU or the Red Army. Any peasant, even the poorest, could thus be determined to be a *kulak*. It was a pretty picture of greed, old jealousies, hatreds, and injustices being exploited to the hilt for the greater glory of "collectivization."

When it was far too late, many thousands upon thousands of peasants, regardless of which of the two lower categories into which they fell, realized the trap into which their acquisitiveness had sucked them. Whole villages rallied and tried to defend themselves, but those unfortunates, armed with sticks and farm tools at best, were no match for the machine guns and artillery of the OGPU and Red Army units sent against them. When resistance had been wiped out, the OGPU, party *apparatchiks*, party members among workers in the cities moved into the devastated villages, set up vaunted machine tractor stations to serve large agricultural areas, using the surviving peasants as the lowest form of peon or coolie labor. Thus did Stalin eliminate peasant independence and "collectivize" the farms in a few short, terrible years. The whole job was finished by 1933.

The cost in Russian souls was monumentally terrible, but of course that did not concern Stalin in the least. So wholesale were the slaughter and losses he caused the farming communities that no exact figures are known or ever will be. The best guess is that during the 1928–33 "war against the peasantry" more than ten million were thrown out of the villages. About one-third died as a result of action by the OGPU and the Red Army or by execution, one-third were sent to slave labor camps, and the final one-third trickled off to the bad-lands. During their resistance, the peasants killed off some fifty per-cent of their farm animals rather than see them fall into enemy hands. Also, as a direct result of that war against collectivization, another five and one-half million peasants—more than half of them Ukrainians—died in the horrible famine of 1932–33. There were many instances of cannibalism, frequently with parents eating chil-dren. Nevertheless, and despite such horror, Stalin exported one and three-quarter million tons of grain in that year of famine to pay for his industrial program.

In part, the elimination of the peasant opposition also supplied Stalin with the slave labor force with which he and his successors have been able to expand the economy at home and dump cheap goods on foreign markets at politically opportune times. In 1930, with the flow of peasants to slave labor camps ever swelling, Stalin set up the OGPU-run GULAG (Main Administration of Camps) to run those barbaric establishments. Prior to the influx of the peasants by the millions, the populations of those institutions had run in the tens of thousands only, consisting mainly of strictly political oppo-nents. Of course, in both the early camps and the GULAG installa-tions, there were also common criminals—murderers, rapists, thieves. Those nonpoliticals served as trusties and slave drivers—and still do—of other prisoners assigned to such massive earth-moving projects as canals, dams, railroads, and highways and in such dread areas as the Vorkuta coal mines in the far north and the Dalstroy gold fields of the arctic northeast. Firsthand and eyewitness tales—most soon forgotten—have been told of how the common criminal trusties murdered, tortured, and raped politicos in the camps and how other politicos died by the hundreds of thousands of malnutrition, disease, and cold or from being confined for days on end in unheated, unwa-tered, unrationed boxcars and ships.

Since it is common in the more civilized West for labor organiza-tions to complain from time to time about work being taken from them by prison labor, one might wonder why the so-called more enlightened "trade unionists" of the Soviet Union did not voice objections to the slave labor camps. The reason for that compliance was simple: in the same year Stalin set up GULAG, he fettered the workers by reintroducing the internal passport to hold them at their jobs and keep them from seeking better ones elsewhere. Thus, although they escaped the great earth-moving jobs and the mines of the north, where it is difficult to recruit regular labor, the workers retrogressed to a worse position than under the tsars, while the peasants were forced back into the worst kind of serfdom. At the same time, Stalin began developing his bureaucrats or managers—the new class described by Milovan Djilas—to run his slave empire. It is meaningless to speak of such lesser restrictions as no right to strike and piece labor or of such "benefits" as a decline in illiteracy, better education for the masses, and permission for some peasants to own bits of land and a few animals, when one considers the broad picture of the life Stalin decreed for the masses of Russia. Under that concept the masses had no freedom of movement or choice of work whatsoever. They stayed put in the fields or the factories, unless moved elsewhere, usually en masse, by some decree from on high. The only people to escape such control—and that to a limited degree only—to be allowed higher education, some choice of profession or occupation, and occasional travel abroad (under supervision), were members of the new class—the dictator's minions—and their children. And all, whether masses or new class, were under overall control of the secret police of the Communist autocracy.

For quite some time, foreigners heard little that was truthful about the collectivization program or anything at all about the famine and the horrors of the slave labor camps. Partially, that was due to Stalin's iron control of travel, all sources of information and dissemination of real news—as opposed to propaganda. Lack of foreign information about the facts of the power technique of the Georgian was also caused by naïveté to willful distortion, and often on the part of foreigners themselves. Although the word combination "fellow-traveler" was first made by Trotsky, the term was not yet then in international parlance. Many visitors to Russia in the early thirties fitted that term, some innocently, others intentionally. For example, George Bernard Shaw, who found so much to criticize in his own open society, visited a slave labor camp and praised it as a model institution reeducating wayward Russians. He did not know it, of course, but the OGPU, taking a line from Potemkin's eighteenth century village for

Catherine the Great, had removed watch-towers and barbed wire, stocked the mess hall with goodies instead of swill and filled the yard with happy "prisoners" well in advance of his visit. What Shaw reported with acclaim had been nothing more than a guided tour of the worst sort.

Busy as it thus was at home in that era of initial repression on a mass scale, the OGPU was far from being laggardly abroad. For it was in 1930 that it first had notable success in eliminating regime opponents having residence or refuge in foreign countries—a terror tactic that later became all too common until the host countries started taking proper protective measures. Earlier, of course, Soviet secret police had wiped out some of its international agents who had run afoul of Stalin or his underlings. Its expertise thus developed with practice on such small fry, the OGPU then kidnapped Lieutenant General Pavel Kutepov, the leader of Russian emigré resistance forces. So accomplished and confident had the OGPU agents become that the deed was carried out on the streets of Paris in broad daylight. The French police never made any arrests or found Kutepov. The facts, unearthed later, too late, were: the kidnapping was the work of two veteran Chekists posing as "diplomats," Lev Helfand and Vladimir Volovich—who later advanced to being one of Stalin's lesser goons; Kutepov had been chloroformed, stuffed into a car and rushed to a Soviet freighter waiting off the French Atlantic coast. To cover the OGPU, the Soviet press claimed Kutepov had decamped to South America with emigré funds—a usual tactic—but it is believed because of the effect of the ether on the general's known weak heart that he was dead before he was smuggled aboard the freighter.

Although the OGPU had hoodwinked the gullible Shaw, Nadezhda Alliluyeva, Stalin's second wife and the mother of two of his three children, was not so naïve about the horrors being perpetrated by her husband, even though she remained generally aloof from government and party affairs. Daughter of a veteran but lesser Communist (Sergey, who hid Lenin out in his Petrograd apartment in 1917), she eventually had enough of Stalin's attacks on his fellow Bolsheviks, his terror against the peasants and the unnecessary famine. One evening in November, 1932, at a gathering of Stalin and his cronies, she spoke her mind about her husband's actions. When Stalin flew off the handle and showered his wife with abuse, she left for their Kremlin apartment. The next morning she was dead. Officially, Alliluyeva was a suicide, but there are many reports and suggestions Stalin throttled his wife in a rage. That may well have been the case. The Georgian never showed any particular affection for close family members, except for his mother and his daughter, Svetlana. The only child by his first marriage, another son, he allowed to be killed in German captivity during World War II, even though arrangements for an exchange had been suggested and could have been completed.

Whatever the cause, Stalin reacted completely uncharacteristically to Nadezhda's death, an indication there may have been more on his conscience than the final quarrel. First, he buried her in a Moscow church cemetery and had quite an attractive monument placed at the grave. Next he made his one and only offer to resign as party leader, but that offer was probably stage-managed in advance because his stooge Molotov leapt into the breach and demanded he continue. Then in early 1933, he abruptly turned off the terror against the peasants (though none of the millions were released from the slave labor camps) and helped famine victims by releasing Red Army grain stores and making large grain purchases from the United States. There is considerable doubt his third step was caused chiefly by reaction to Nadezhda's death; at the time it was taken, Adolf Hitler had come to power in Germany and Stalin was probably more worried about possible eventual need of peasants for Red Army cannon-fodder than concerned about the plight he had caused them. Additionally, he had to butter up the peasants to get the farm economy going again and avoid more expenditures for foreign grain purchases. But for all the softsoap given the peasants then by Stalin, and his successors in the future, Russian agricultural production never again attained the yield percentages of 1916. The reason was not hard to come by: in wiping out the *kulaks* and eliminating much of the "middle-class" peasantry, Stalin had so reduced the farming community to the lazy, the shiftless, and the incompetent that it will take generations—if ever—to breed a new crop of competent, hard-working Russian farmers.

Of the three steps Stalin took in possible reaction to Nadezhda's death, only his theatrical offer to resign was to cause him any real trouble. Some of his not yet completely subdued fellow hierarchs thought they could exploit that gesture. What they thought was their chance came at the Seventeenth Party Congress in 1934. First, they maneuvered a demotion of Stalin to "Secretary" of the party rather than the more grandiloquent "General Secretary." Next, they moved Kirov onto the Central Committee Secretariat to take a position there equivalent in power and prestige to that of Stalin and his two flunkies, Kaganovich and Zhdanov. Then they tried—but failed —to make Kirov rather than Stalin the party leader.

As Leningrad party boss, Kirov had cleared up the mess made by the vindictive Zinoviev. In doing that, he had restored the confidence and morale of the party rank and file in the nation's second capital. Additionally, he was forty-eight as compared to Stalin's fifty-five, and he was good-looking as compared to the pockmarked, runtish Stalin with the semicrippled left arm. Although unassuming, he also had a certain unforgettable charisma. Naturally, therefore, as a result of both his talents and his personality, he was looked upon by many as Stalin's most probable successor and was the real hero of the Seventeenth Congress. People, even many non-Communists, really liked him. But his unwitting admirers at the congress went too far. They gave him just as much applause—if not more—as was accorded Stalin.

In the same period, changes occurred in the secret police which made it an even stronger instrument of Stalin. In May, 1934, the OGPU chief, Menzhinsky, died. There were some reports—later made "fact" by Stalin's minions—that he had been poisoned. Although Menzhinsky's death may have been hurried a bit, those reports seem dubious, since he had long been in very poor health. Then in July, 1934, the OGPU was "abolished." In its place came a much more powerful organization, the NKVD (People's Commissariat for Internal Affairs), which comprised not only the political police, but the regular police, firemen, and other services as well. The artful Yagoda, who had succeeded Menzhinsky as head of the OGPU, was made Chief of the NKVD at its start. In that same year, which later was to prove so critical for the Soviet Union and its party, Stalin also made two other changes, which at the time, passed relatively unnoticed. He named the vicious little dwarf Nikolay Yezhov to the powerful Orgburo (the Organization Bureau) that controlled all party members. And he established the so-called Special Branch of the party's Central Committee. In reality, that Special Branch was no concern of the Central Committee. It was purely and simply Stalin's personal police organization—or bodyguards—that oversaw the political police that ran the rest of the nation for the dictator. At the head of the Special Branch, Stalin put his most obedient virtual alter ego, and somewhat mysterious Aleksandr Nikolayevich Poskrebyshev, who also served as chief of the Georgian's personal secretariat.

Thus, by 1934, as some contemporary historians of the Soviet scene have pointed out, Stalin already had positioned his chief dramatis personae. Those who would not only secure his position as dictator but also at the same time would make him the terror of the Soviet Union and much of the world: Poskrebyshev, his chief bodyguard and man-of-all-work, Andrey Vyshinsky, his tame prosecutor, and Yagoda and Yezhov, a brace of ruthless, unscrupulous, and expendable secret police chiefs.

After the 1934 congress, there was some give-and-take between Stalin and Kirov about the latter surrendering his Leningrad post and going to Moscow. But that move never came to pass. On December 1, 1934, Kirov was murdered in the halls of the Smolny Institute, the local party headquarters. The background of that killing was somewhat explored years later by Nikita Khrushchev. However, since Khrushchev's main intent had been to denigrate Stalin, whose faithful henchman he had once been, that overly-celebrated "exposé" served more to cover Khrushchev's crimes against the Russians than to explain the Kirov slaying.

Well before Khrushchev's declaration, it had been pretty well established by less biased sources that the prime mover behind the Kirov murder was Stalin. It was most obvious that the Georgian was extremely jealous of Kirov's popularity and had every reason to fear him as a very serious rival. Additionally, the timing of Stalin's reorganization of the secret police and creation of his own private goon-squad cannot be disregarded.

Although the motive is therefore obvious, the method will always be somewhat moot, for the simple reason that Stalin sped to Leningrad to take personal charge of the investigation of the murder and seal the lips of all immediately concerned with instant execution or incarceration to await later, but certain, elimination. Of course, hundreds of other completely innocent persons also were summarily executed while thousands were sent to camps never to return, but that action was needed to bolster the "discovery" of a "plot" by that fine little investigative team of Stalin, Poskrebyshev, and Yagoda. The fabrication of that "plot" was needed to "involve" Zinoviev and Kamenev, who were later given ten- and five-year terms, respectively, at hard labor. And the "plot" also gave a "legal" basis for Stalin's so-called "Law of December 1, 1934"—promulgated before Kirov's body was cold—which allowed the political police to round up, "interrogate," and execute all of Stalin's possible enemies at the dictator's pleasure. That infamous "law" was not removed from the books until 1957 and Khrushchev only took that action after he had safely, albeit less bloodily, removed his rivals.

As with most assassins of important men, the instrument of Kirov's murder was a nonentity. One Leonid Nikolayev, he was likewise somewhat mentally unbalanced and thereby a very pliable tool. He was labeled a "Trotskyite," of course, although there is no indication his political development even advanced beyond the mouthing of catch phrases.

But it is a waste of time to examine that unfortunate young man too closely. Any other misfit would have just as well served the purposes of the NKVD, acting under the direction of Yagoda, who in turn was under the orders of Stalin and the supervision of Poskrebyshev. Nikolayev committed the murder. He confessed. He was executed. Period. What Stalin's personal "investigation" carefully did not unearth were these facts: twice before the murder, Nikolayev had entered the Smolny with a revolver, a weapon returned to him by the NKVD, and the same weapon Nikolayev used when he entered the third and fatal time; at the time of the killing, Kirov's bodyguard was nowhere in the vicinity.

Therefore, there remains no doubt that Kirov's killing was engineered by the NKVD. And anyone who believes that Stalin had no knowledge of such action by the NKVD may be as mentally troubled as was Nikolayev. Finally: no one, absolutely no one, could have entered a Communist headquarters with a weapon, even in those times, without NKVD connivance; and no Communist hierarch, especially of Kirov's stature, would have been without his NKVD guard at all times, unless the NKVD had arranged it. Wisely, Stalin's "investigation" never disclosed Nikolayev's multiple armed entries. But so carefully was the murder engineered that he was able to make a pose of asking why Kirov's guard had been absent. "Unfortunately," however, the NKVD worthy who could have supplied that answer was killed in a vehicular "accident" while en route to Stalin's inquiry chambers. For more than two decades, Russians, especially Communists, had to swallow the Stalin fabrication of the Kirov murder. Unfortunately, for too long many non-Russians and non-Communists—and some in high places—have also swallowed it and without any compulsion.

With Kirov out of the way, Stalin's road to absolute power was wide open. His problem of overcoming real opponents was over. From then on all he had to do was wipe out the last vestiges of the old Lenin group, keep any possible newcomers beneath the horizon, and liquidate his minions from time to time as bloody examples to keep others in line. In retrospect, this account of Stalin's surge to power and maintenance of dictatorship may seem oversimplified. But, for him, it was relatively easy, he was the lone hawk in a yard full of chickens. While they—including Trotsky—clucked about the fine points of Marxism-Leninism, scuttled to international gatherings for parleys with other "thinkers," or dreamt of a Communist utopia. Meanwhile, Stalin was busy taking over and expanding the secret police and installing his flunkies in subordinate control positions throughout the nation. And he did it all behind the shield of "socialism in one country." Far too late, better but less ruthless men realized his program actually was socialism for one man in one country, and more countries later when opportune. In the course, he rose to be a demigod —and still is to some benighted souls. Millions mourned when he was no more, but so had many a Russian cried when Ivan the Terrible died.

Marxism had been a foreign import, but Stalin purged it of its inherent Western weaknesses and converted it into an instrument for dictatorial power and something completely Russian.

For a time after disposing of Kirov and provisionally eliminating Zinoviev and Kamenev in the latter couple's closed-door trial of January 1935, Stalin again seemed to be marking time. But, actually he was preparing the groundwork for subsequent mass action against his "opposition."

During the month of the Zinoviev-Kamenev "trial," allegedly natural causes—heart trouble—suddenly and conveniently permanently disposed of one of Stalin's less staunch admirers, Politburo member Valerian Kuybyshev, who also ran the State Planning Commission. And in February 1935, the Georgian made four important shifts of his minions in preparation for the bloody action soon to follow: Vyshinsky was advanced to Chief Prosecutor, Yezhov was given Kirov's place on the secretariat while Zhdanov was made

Leningrad party boss, and so far unnoteworthy but eager Nikita Khrushchev was promoted to Moscow party boss. Next, in April, 1935, Stalin partially "legalized" what was to come by decreeing that all penalties, including the death sentence, should be applicable to all the unfortunates under his control down to children of the age of twelve. The following two months he closed down the Society of Old Bolsheviks and the Society of Former Political Prisoners and Exiles and had Yezhov seize the records of both for future distorted use. The only other notable activity in that otherwise "quiet" year came in July when Kamenev was again tried behind closed doors and sentenced to an additional ten years in a slave labor camp.

As things turned out, however, Kamenev's increased hardship lasted little more than a year. In August 1936, all preparations—forced confessions, fabricated testimony and documents—had been completed for the first of the many subsequent Communist "legal" theatrical productions. For six summer days, a frightened Russia and then-baffled world watched as zombie-like Zinoviev, Kamenev, and fourteen lesser "Trotskyites" were trotted out by Vyshinsky before a military court of the so-called Supreme Court of the U.S.S.R. Well-conditioned by prior NKVD "interrogation," that sorry lot "confessed" arranging Kirov's murder and planning to kill Stalin, Kaganovich, Voroshilov, Zhdanov, and other Politburo members they were told to name. Members of the foreign press and "spectators" watched the degrading spectacle with many of the first group accepting those "confessions." Only later—and long after the principals had been executed—did those newspapermen learn that they had been duped and had been just as much a part of the Stalin production as were the "spectators"—NKVD officers all.

As an immediate aftermath of Stalin's first show trial—which has come to be known as the "trial of the sixteen"—action was taken against lesser associates of the defendants still within party ranks. Stalin ordered some five thousand of those miserable creatures, previously condemned to exile or forced labor camps, to be shot forthwith. Yagoda and Yezhov prepared and disposed of that list, all, of course, without benefit of trial. And Tomsky evidently read the handwriting on the wall. He committed suicide, or so the Stalin records say. Also dead in that first year of Stalin's great bloodbath was Gorky. How that writer really died is anyone's guess. First, he was reported to have died of natural causes. But later, Stalin found it convenient to accuse the NKVD of poisoning him. The facts appear to be that Stalin sped Gorky's death by denying him a more favorable climate in his later and ailing years. Long disillusioned by the Georgian's techniques, the writer had wanted to go to Italy for health reasons. But Stalin, fearing he might tell all once abroad, refused him a passport.

The greatest immediate consequence of the "trial of the sixteen," however, was the beginning of the end of Stalin's current chief butcher, Yagoda. After all, he was one of the few survivors to know the facts of the Kirov murder. Accordingly, in September 1936 Yagoda was reduced to commissar in charge of postal services. In making the demotion while vacationing at one of his Caucasus retreats, Stalin growled that the NKVD was four years behind the times in ferreting out "opponents" of party and state. That growl was a reference to Yagoda's failure to kill Ryutin in 1932 when that courageous man called for Stalin's ouster.

Apparatchik Yezhov was given Yagoda's post as head of the NKVD. For some time, Stalin had been grooming the vicious dwarf for the major bloodletting that still lay ahead, an era that has become known as the "Yezhovshchina" and that far outshone the "Oprichnina" of Ivan the Terrible. Naturally, Yezhov brought a clean broom to his new job. All Yagoda adherents and supernumeraries were killed off immediately, while some terrified NKVD brutes helped Yezhov's executioners by killing themselves. An equally terrified Russia watched that dog-eat-dog horror as a good riddance, but that was a mistake. The successors and the survivors within the NKVD became even more brutal, hoping thereby to spare themselves the fate of Yagoda's henchmen. As a result, they butchered fellow Russians by the millions.

In a way, the "trial of the sixteen" was not a complete performance, but merely a first act to be followed by others. Kamenev had supplied the continuity by involving other old Bolsheviks—with script furnished by the NKVD—before he went to meet his maker. Therefore, the second act, or the "trial of the seventeen," was staged from January 23 to 30, 1937. The director was again Stalin, the producer was Yezhov, the cuer was Vyshinsky, and the setting was the same, the Supreme Court's Military Tribunal, a group of foreign newsmen and a claque of NKVD "spectators." Different only were the protagonists, chief among them Pyatakov, Deputy Commissar of

Heavy Industry and Ordzhonikidze's protégé, and Radek, the propagandist who had duped so many in the West. The script—again prepared by the NKVD—had the same stale "Trotskyite" overtones, but with the variation that the accused "confessed" such mass sabotage as wrecking mines, industry, and transport plus the high treason of plotting to surrender parts of Russia to Germany and Japan. Pyatakov and most of his co-defendants were found guilty and shot. Radek, like Kamenev before him, supplied the NKVD with continuity for a subsequent act by involving other old Bolsheviks. For that, he and some others were given only terms in slave labor camps. But Radek was never heard of again. Some reports say he was shot in 1941.

The immediate effect of that "trial" was the death of Ordzhonikidze, the chief of heavy industry and a man who had maintained some independence despite Stalin. The cause of his death, like so many that occurred under Stalin, is again moot. Officially, Ordzhonikdze, up to that moment a stalwart and healthy man, succumbed to a heart attack, but there are reports he died of gunshot wounds and it is highly probable he was killed by some NKVD exterminator. However, there are other accounts saying that he killed himself, or as the Soviets put it ". . . he walked out from life."

Since the mills of a demigod must grind even more slowly than those of a true god, Stalin's purge production seemed to halt briefly again after the "trial of the seventeen." But that was more for a change of set than for the convenience of players and audience. Hint of future action—on a much broader scale—was not long in forthcoming.

In April, 1937, Yagoda was given his final demotion. He was arrested. Only years later was it learned that Rykov and Bukharin had been arrested as well. Those two arrests were made several weeks earlier, following Stalin's last showdown with the Central Committee, which he soon purged into the cowardly obeisance that was to last the rest of his life.

After that trio of arrests, there seemed to be yet another halt in the purge. Actually, though, it was continuing, but it had changed course temporarily, to garner a new group, or class, of victims. An indication of that—an indication that was appreciated only much later—was given in mid-May 1937 when the post of Political Commissar for the Armed Forces, which had been abolished in 1925, was reactivated. Initially, the job went to Yan Gamarnik, a tough old Bolshevik who had been in charge of the political administration of the armed forces since 1929. Days later, however, on June 1, 1937, Gamarnik committed suicide. At that time, the reason for his killing himself was a mystery, but it is now known that he chose suicide rather than follow Stalin's orders for virtual genocide of the nation's officer corps.

However, even in those days, what was going on was made blindingly clear to all by a horrible entr'acte staged July 11 and 12, 1937. That production was staged privately, but at its conclusion, its gist was furnished to a shocked Russia and an amazed outer world. Eight high-ranking officers, Stalin let it be known, had been found guilty of treason and had been executed immediately thereafter.

The chief "defendant" at the officers' "trial" was Marshal Tukhachevsky, who had previously been suddenly demoted from being Deputy Commissar of Defense and simultaneously relieved from the assignment of representing the Soviet Union at the coronation of Britain's King George VI. The other victims included General Iona Yakir, commander of the Ukraine—whose family, like those of thousands of other similarly found officers, was sent to a labor camp and whose son was to rise in opposition to Stalin's successors years later —the commander of White Russia, the military attaché to Britain, the director of the military academy, the chief of antiaircraft, the deputy chief of cavalry, and the chief of personnel. Originally, Budyenny was to have been the ninth victim, but he managed to butter up Stalin and Vorshilov and thus became a member of the "court" that wiped out the bulk of the officer corps rather than one of the defendants.

The action against Tukhachevsky was long overdue. Not only had he been right and Stalin wrong way back in 1920 when the Red Army failed to capture Warsaw, but he had also become immensely popular among the rank and file of the armed forces. Thus he posed an everpresent threat to the unprepossessing Stalin and reduced Voroshilov, the titular Commissar of Defense, to nothing more than the incompetent figurehead he actually was. But, of course, those were not the charges made at the "trial." Tukhachevsky and his co-victims were "found guilty" of decidedly other charges, namely: conspiring with the German high command. The "evidence" for that, or the frame-up, according to some historians, had been most obligingly provided by none other than the Nazi intelligence, only too happy to assist Stalin in weakening his armed forces. What the historians did not mention was that the "evidence" was more likely originally provided to the Nazis by Stalin. The particularly iniquitous part about the charges against the Tukhachevsky group was the fact that at the very time they were made, none other than Stalin himself was busy wheeling and dealing with the Nazis. In other words, he executed the completely innocent for traffic he himself was committing with impunity. Initially, the Georgian acted through an intermediary in his dealing with the Germans. Several months before Tukhachevsky was arrested, Stalin had sent David Kandelaki, a fellow Georgian and a stooge from his secretariat (or elite bodyguard) to Berlin with the cover of commercial attaché. It was Kandelaki who prepared the groundwork for the cynical and unprincipled Stalin-Hitler pact of August, 1939. As with so many others who did Stalin's dirty work, Kandelaki fell from favor after he had started the ball rolling and died in a northern slave labor camp in 1938.

Under the guidance of Lev Mekhlis, Gamarnik's successor and another graduate of Stalin's secretariat, the bloodletting of the Red Army officers corps continued apace well into 1938. It extended even into the Far East, where Russian troops were engaged in serious frontier skirmishes with the Japanese occupiers of Manchuria, resulting in the entrapment and execution of the chief of Soviet forces there, the colorful Marshal Vasily Blyukher. Only one senior officer in that area escaped, Gen. Genrikh Lyushkov, chief of the NKVD frontier region. He defected to the Japanese. The information he supplied Tokyo was subsequently relayed back to Moscow by Richard Sorge, the Soviet's posthumously honored super-spy. Lyushkov's escape was Mekhlis' only serious miss. By the time he finished, some 35,000 officers of the Soviet armed forces had been killed off and untold more thousands sent to slave labor camps, from which only a very exceptional few ever returned. And the slaughter of the officers specialized on the senior ranks, with about ninety percent of the generals and some eighty percent of the colonels being killed off. As a result, practically nothing was left of the Soviet high command on the eve of World War II. Therefore, in addition to the millions he killed deliberately, Stalin was also guilty of the deaths of millions of other Russians who had been denied competent leadership during the great conflict with the Nazis.

In the summer of 1937, concurrently with the slaughter of the military, another great bloodletting also got under way. That was

Stalin's "purge" of millions of his minor "opponents," *apparatchiks* and party functionaries. For that, he dispatched his most trusted flunkies to the four corners of the land. Zhdanov was assigned to Leningrad, Kaganovich to White Russia, and Beria to the Caucasus areas, where the latter had the special assistance of Mikoyan, who performed mightily in crushing his fellow Armenians. Initially, Khrushchev was given the task of purging the Moscow party minions. He did the capital job speedily and well. As a result, he was then sent to the only part of the country that was putting up a fight, the Ukraine. On that second, more difficult, assignment Khrushchev was joined by Molotov and Yezhov, the latter backed by special NKVD troops. Beyond all question Khrushchev also did an equally fine job for Stalin on his second assignment because he was made Party boss of the Ukraine—or what was left of the party there—in January, 1938. Although party underlings were the chief victims of that purge carried out by Stalin's lieutenants, a few luminaries of a sort were also eliminated. Chief among that group was Avel Yenukidze, another of Stalin's onetime Georgian cronies, who had once been a bodyguard of his master.

In that same period, Stalin also embarked on a major campaign to eliminate foreign Communists who did not see things exactly his way as well as numbers of Soviets living abroad, chiefly espionage agents. Some of the foreigners—primarily the Germans and the Poles—were stupid enough to obey Stalin's orders to report to Moscow and thus simplify their liquidation. Prominent among that group was Bela Kun, the bloody-handed Hungarian, who had once been so rash as to establish a rival—even though shortlived—Communist state. Although it was more convenient and quieter to inveigle the "renegades" to the Soviet Union for liquidation, Stalin was able to dispose of them almost equally well abroad, thanks to the international operations of his secret police, and thanks to the political obliviousness of many foreign governments of those times to the operations of the NKVD within their confines. For example, Trotsky's son, Leon (Lev Sedov), who had some of his father's files, died under mysterious circumstances (an obvious victim of the NKVD) in a Paris hospital in 1937. In that same year and city, Lieutenant General Yevgeny Miller, the successor of General Kutepov as leader of the White Russian emigrés, was kidnapped and disappeared without a trace, the almost identical technique used against his predecessor seven years earlier. And in 1938, again in Paris, Trotsky's secretary, Rudolf Klement, dropped from sight. Later, his headless body was found in the Seine River. There has never been a French police solution of the Sedov and Klement deaths and General Miller's disappearance, nor, of course, have any perpetrators been brought to justice. Equally unsolved were the elimination of numbers of Soviet spies living abroad at that time. Particularly applicable in that category was the 1937 murder by the NKVD in Switzerland of Ignace Reiss, who was unfortunate enough to have knowledge—embarrassing to Stalin—of Kandelaki's dealings with the Nazis. At the same time, the NKVD carried out extensive "purging" of its rival and subsidiary organization, the GRU (Military Intelligence). A pitiful few of those GRU men managed to escape to the U.S., chiefly Alexander Orlov and General Walter Krivitsky (Ginsberg). But Krivitsky was killed in his Washington hotel room in 1941, another unsolved murder with no killers brought to justice. Especially vulnerable were any GRU men involved in the Spanish Civil War. Yan Berzin, chief of the GRU in Spain, was shot. The same fate met his successor.

Although that special purge of foreigners, Soviet citizens living abroad and others impossible to put on "trial" seemed to have reached its peak with the 1940 murder of Trotsky in Mexico, it actually continued, although to a lesser degree, throughout the remainder of Stalin's lifetime. And subsequent information gives strong indication that many other personalities who dropped from sight or died suddenly, although seemingly healthy, during that 1937–53 period, may also have been purge victims. Murder victims would be the better term. Chief among those is Krupskaya, Lenin's widow. On February 27, 1939, her seventieth birthday, she was about to make a speech—anti-Stalinist in tone—to a group of teachers. The text of her talk, of course, was not approved, but Stalin's minions made no issue of that. Instead, within moments of having been given a cup of coffee by her NKVD she-watchdog, Krupskaya died. Again, officially the cause of death was "natural."

Earlier, Stalin had staged the third and last of his great "legal" performances. Known as the "trial of the twenty-one," it was put on in a dozen days in early March, 1938. The chief characters of that performance were Bukharin, Rykov, and Yagoda. The producer, Stalin, and the rest of the direction were the same, except that Yezhov had taken over Yagoda's role. And the script was truly the most

[215]

inspired and imaginative of the three performances. Although based on the usual "Trotskyite-rightist" tommyrot, it also had scenes involving "sabotage," "treason," and "murder," much of the last rivaling the best of Macbeth. Britain, Germany, Japan, and Poland were dragged in as supernumeraries directing the "plots" to wreck Stalin's Russia. And Stalin, Kaganovich, Molotov, et al., were cast as heros of a sort, targets for assassination by the "defendants." But the juiciest lines were reserved for Yagoda. That worthy was accused of obeying Yenukidze's orders to kill Kirov—and thereby was the liquidation of Yenukidze disposed of without further ado. Yagoda was also charged with having his "medical staff" kill off Menzhinsky, Gorky, Gorky's son, Maxim Peshkov, and Kuybyshev. Why Stalin's wife was omitted from that list supplies interesting conjecture. Perhaps her case was being saved for Poskrebyshev at some later date that never came. In conformance with the script, all twenty-one "defendants" were found guilty in the last act, and most of them were executed forthwith.

That last and grand "trial" completed Yezhov's usefulness. In the summer of 1938 he was reduced to the laughable post of Commissar of Waterways. In December of 1938, Beria took over the NKVD and ran it and its successors for most of the next decade and a half. The horrible little runt Yezhov dropped from sight—and forever—in 1939.

No one will ever know how many millions were killed, how many more millions were sent to slower deaths in slave labor camps in those awful years of the late thirties. Even the perpetrator, Stalin, who well before would have been confined to an asylum in a saner era and saner country, had not the slightest idea. Those deaths and that suffering meant no more to that mad despot than the earlier mass slaughter in collectivization and the famines. But guesses have been made. The most reliable experts believe that in 1937–8 some seven million souls were arrested. By that time, there were already about five million earlier victims in custody, so on paper the total of those held would be twelve million. However, about a million were executed, almost all summarily, a trifling few "legally" during the "purge." Additionally, allowance must be made for the other hundreds and hundreds of thousands who simultaneously died in prisons and camps of more natural causes—guards' and trustees' brutality, lack of medical care, starvation, and exposure. Therefore, it can be assumed that by the time of the climax of the purge in 1938, there were some nine million in prisons and concentration camps, "building" the internal economy or turning out cheap products for Stalin's foreign trade. Nevertheless, and horrible as was the killing and enslavement of those millions, Stalin's purpose had been accomplished. He had eliminated all rivals within the hierarchy; he had subjugated the party rank and file—even the youth organization was "purged"; he had ended all chances for the armed forces rising against him; and in the course he had also swept out his secret police. All of the Georgian's rivals or enemies, real or imagined, were out of the way.

His dictatorship thus secured internally, Stalin then turned just as cynically and unprincipledly to guaranteeing it against external threat. In the West, somewhat regrettably, Stalin's foreign policy preceding, during, and after World War II, has come to be viewed as the moves of a master diplomat. That is an absolutely erroneous evaluation and another part of the Stalin myth. The reasons that Stalin seemed to succeed where others failed were simple: before World War II, in most of the rest of the world, domestic economic problems had taken precedence over foreign affairs; where there was concern about foreign problems, most was concentrated on the rise of fascism and its Nazi counterpart, with communism either being dismissed as inconsequential or regarded as a possible counter to fascism; many of the non-Fascist Western governments were far from secure, faced by the disillusioning aftereffects of World War I, standards of value under attack or at best in flux, and discontented to fickle electorates. Stalin had none of those problems: in power for life, his word was absolute law at home; therefore he had complete freedom abroad, and, of course, never had to refer questions of foreign policy to an electorate.

In the main, the non-Fascist Western world was surprised and quite shocked by the Hitler-Stalin pact of August, 1939. But it should have seen the Russian move coming. Even though Russian-supported Communists had fought Italo-German-supported Fascists in Spain, even though there was much Communist propaganda and "popular frontism" against fascism, the Soviet Union maintained diplomatic relations with the Fascists and did business with them. And by May, 1939, Western diplomats should at least have worried about a possible Stalin-Hitler rapprochement. In that prewar spring month, Stalin dumped his Foreign Commissar, Litvinov, long the archadvocate of collective security against fascism. In Litvinov's place, the Georgian installed Molotov, the advocate of nothing except performing to the letter whatever his boss ordered.

In that fateful year of 1939, Stalin was talking publicly with the British and French about joining him in an alliance against Nazi Germany and at the same time dealing secretly with Hitler. In fact, British and French officers were in Moscow discussing military cooperation with the Russians at the very time the Hitler-Stalin "nonaggression" pact was announced. Details of the agreement—called the Molotov-Ribbentrop pact by some who like to pretend those two stooges were more than messenger boys—were secret at first. But the gist, an agreement between the Nazis and the Communists to divvy-up eastern Europe, was not long in forthcoming. Nine days after a smiling Stalin had affixed his name to it, Hitler forces blitzkrieged into Poland. And less than two weeks after that, Stalin's Red Army rolled into defenseless eastern Poland, taking two hundred thousand "prisoners"—massacring some ten thousand Polish officers in the Katyn forest in the best Ivan the Terrible tradition—and "deporting" some million and one-half other luckless Poles far to the east to slave labor camps from which few were to return.

And also in September, 1939, for the folks back home, already busy with industry converting to war production, preparedness pursuits, and rapidly expanding armed forces, Stalin decreed universal compulsory military service—one of the most hated features of Tsarist autocracy—still in effect to the day of this writing.

The Georgian had almost immediate need for that cannon-fodder. On the last day in November, 1939, he started his first military venture in almost two decades, the extremely ill-fought war with little Finland. Invasion is the exact term for that attack, the cause of which was fabricated by Stalin having his own troops fired on. When that foray ended in March, 1940, the Soviet Union "gained" chunks of territory, mainly in the Leningrad area for the Red Army's loss of thousands of troops, even an entire division in one action. And most of the returning "victors" were paraded in triumph through Leningrad and then sent off to slave labor camps as a reward for their sorry showing.

That attack on Finland, which was not only a disgrace but also even more of a debacle than the Americans were to face years later in southeast Asia, showed most of all the cost of purging the Red Army of the bulk of its senior officer corps. In the interim between the purge and the "war," an effort was made to replace the missing officers with juniors rapidly advanced or men sped from the ranks through military schools. But, when the chips were down, that new group—for all of its Stalinist purity—just could not produce.

Therefore, in May 1940, after a postmortem of the Finnish "war," Stalin shook up his high command. He made Marshal Semen Timoshenko—"hero" of the Finnish "epic" who brought that struggle to an end by using twenty-seven divisions and thousands of artillery pieces against a Finnish force that never numbered more than one hundred twenty thousand men—Commissar of Defense. And he got rid of Voroshilov by promoting him upstairs to head a newly created special defense committee.

That done, and with the Red Army barely recovered from the foray in the north, Stalin turned on even weaker and less doughty neighbors in June, 1940. He "annexed" the Baltic republics of Estonia, Latvia, and Lithuania, a ruthless grab that all the so-called "principled" nations of the world—with the sole exception of the unarmed Vatican papal state—had so far done nothing effective about nor did they seem ready to in the foreseeable future. And just weeks later, the Georgian sent his Red Army across the border of a virtually supine Rumania to seize Bessarabia and Northern Bukovina.

All those Red Army "operations" of 1939–40—the occupation of eastern Poland, the Finnish "war," and the seizures of the Baltic republics and northeastern Rumania—disclosed the "secret" details of the Hitler-Stalin "nonaggression" pact. They also showed how distant from the principles of Lenin was the Stalin who had defrauded that chief Bolshevik years earlier as his Commissar of Nationalities. But the ghosts of the tsars probably applauded.

Many apologists for Stalin and the Soviet system have tried to justify the 1939–40 and subsequent Russian expansionism by saying that those areas were needed as buffer zones to protect the Soviet Union from aggression from the West. But that just does not hold water. While Hitler was strong, Stalin admired Hitler and marveled that such a man after his own heart was kept in power by the will of the German people and not only by the secret police, as was the Georgian's miserable lot. Additionally in those days of the start of World War II, Stalin arrogantly dismissed all possibility of Hitler's attack on him, completely disregarding the advice of Sorge in Japan and other spies in the West.

Nor have the apologists shown concern for the luckless people thus brought under Stalin's thrall. Hot on the heels of the Red Army—but invariably a safe distance from the shooting—the NKVD treated its Finnish, Baltic, and Rumanian captives to much the same fate it accorded the eastern Poles before them—ultimate destruction, or pure genocide. With that infamous handler of human flesh, Ivan Serov, Assistant Commissar of the NKVD in charge, mass arrest followed mass arrest. Millions were "deported" to slave labor camps east of the Urals. Packed into railway freight cars, thousands upon thousands of those millions died before ever reaching camps. And Russian colonists were moved in to fill the vacuum. The American Indians never knew such treatment from the white man. It was only the Nazis, whose boss was so much admired by Stalin, who were later to pay back the Russians in kind.

Since the NKVD was so busy with so much new "work," Stalin felt it necessary to reorganize his secret police in February 1941. In reality, he expanded it. He split the NKVD into two commissariats, the NKVD to handle internal affairs under Beria, and the NKGB (People's Commissariat for State Security), a political police force. Vsevolod Merkulov was made boss of the latter organization. But, since he was a former lieutenant and old crony of Beria's, Merkulov was little more than a mirror-image of Beria and it was Beria who remained as overall police boss.

In April 1941, Stalin did a little more diplomatic dickering, designed—he thought—to bolster his dictatorship at home and protect his newly won spoils. He signed a neutrality pact with the Japanese, the Nazis' Far Eastern collaborators. (Interestingly, both sides to that agreement, soon to have their hands very full elsewhere, kept it until Stalin was sure Japan had been reduced to a pushover.) With the pact with Tokyo signed and delivered, the Georgian thus became in all but name a member of the Axis and believed his foreign problems of the moment were solved. But he was living in a dream world.

Early on June 22, 1941, Hitler's forces surged across the Bug River. The complacent Stalin was caught completely unawares by the attack, and his people were to pay terribly indeed for the conceit that caused his horrible errors both at home and abroad.

3. STALIN'S "WAR AND PEACE" (1941–53)

At the start of the "Great Fatherland War"—as Stalin named it— Soviet troops immediately showed the deleterious effects of the purge and the leadership of such military half-pints as Voroshilov, Budenny, and even the inept Timoshenko.

Some 150 Nazi divisions were massed for the attack into Russian-held lands along the long front from the Baltic to the Black Sea. Facing them were an even greater number of Red Army troops, with Voroshilov in command in the north, Timoshenko in the center and Budenny in the south. But, because of Stalin's bad political judgment Soviet forces were weakest in the center. Stalin had believed in his old friend, Hitler, right up to the very end, and concentrated instead on assuring his new territorial gains in the north and south. And it was in the center, of course, that the Nazis launched their major drive, to advance in alarming great leaps and bounds.

Somewhat typically, and even more arrogantly than the worst of the tsars considering the more than adequate advance warning his spies had given him, Stalin was not even minding the store when Hitler attacked. Molotov, left behind in Moscow to do that, had the task of making a radio announcement to give the Russian people their first news of the invasion. At that time, Stalin was vacationing in the south, with two of his junior underlings, Malenkov and Nikolay Voznesensky, the latter a rising economic "genius" and a protégé of Zhdanov.

The first pertinent Soviet defensive step—and a paper one at that —was not taken until June 30. That consisted of the organization of a state committee for defense, comprising those men of no military prowess, Stalin, Molotov, Voroshilov, Beria, and Malenkov.

Not until more than a dozen days after the invasion, on July 3, had Stalin enough recovered from shock to make his first radio appeal of the war to the nation. He attempted to justify the pact with Hitler as a step that gave the Soviet Union time to arm. And he pulled out all the emotional stops. He addressed his erstwhile victims as brothers and sisters, tried to arouse their patriotism by recalling glories of the non-Communist past and the defeat of Napoleon and asked them to give the same scorched earth treatment to the Nazi invaders as their forebears had given the French.

Then on July 19, the Soviet dictator of all other Russian life took an unreasonably delayed personal step. He appointed himself Supreme Commander of the Armed Forces. But it was on the following day, July 20, that he attacked realities. Apathetic to shocked, and overburdened with years of the Georgian's horrible rule, the people and the Red Army had not rallied to his radio appeal. Therefore, he gave the NKVD back its muscle, making it again a single commissariat under Beria, a status it was to retain until the tide of battle finally turned at Stalingrad. In the initial days of the war, the NKVD was badly needed as a substitute for patriotism, to see to it that peasants scorched the earth and opposed rather than welcomed the invaders and that the backpedaling Red Army finally halted its retreat. The NKVD treatment of confused and disheartened soldiers and citizenry was cruel in the extreme, but it must be admitted that it did its job well. It soon came to be feared more than the Nazis and that took some doing.

In those midsummer 1941 days of mass disorganization and wholesale retreat and surrender, Stalin was reduced to wooing other enemies, the British and the Americans. Unabashedly, he sought the impossible, direct military intervention by them. Winston Churchill's envoys conferred with him, and so did those of President Franklin Roosevelt. But the most he got for long was military hardware. Roosevelt's emissaries, Harry Hopkins and W. Averell Harriman did the most in that respect. They initiated the Lend-Lease Program under which by war's end, some eleven billion dollars of matériel, food and other supplies were delivered to the Soviets, with American troops frequently going short so that the Roosevelt-Stalin agreement could be honored.

At the same time Stalin appealed to erstwhile enemies abroad, he also practiced the expediency of scraping the barrel of onetime enemies—later to be enemies again, of course if need be—at home. From the slave labor camps, he released many surviving purged officers, such as Konstantin Rokossovsky, who later rose to be marshal and for a time ruler of "people's" (Stalin's) Poland. And from prison camps he released General Wladyslaw Anders and other captive Poles, many of whom won doughty records with Britain's Eighth Army in the Western Desert and Italy only to complete their saga by finally returning home to other prison camps run by the same Rokossovsky. Proof indeed that helping Soviet Russia in any way brings scant reward, if any.

An example of just how cynically ruthless Stalin could be with people under his control came just after he had released General Anders. On August 28, 1941, he decreed the dissolution—in perpetuity—of the Volga German Autonomous Republic. At the same time he ordered the deportation "east" of that area's 600,000 citizens, whose hardworking forefathers had been invited to settle in Russia by Catherine the Great. The expulsion of those unfortunates was again directed by that NKVD expert on genocide, Serov. He may have picked up some pointers from that job, for it was Serov who later in the war moved from their homelands in the south the Balkars, the Crimean Tatars, the Chechens, the Ingushi, the Kalmyks, the Karachai, and the Meskhetians. Some of those remote groups were little known, if at all, in the rest of the world. But, they were still people, after all. It is estimated that Serov drove out no less than a million and a half of those minority peoples during the war and that at least six hundred thousand of them died as a result. In the same period, the United States interned thousands of its citizens of Japanese origin. But, it should not be forgotten that Americans regretted that action and became very ashamed of it. Comparatively, Russians under Soviet control have no hearts to bleed for mistreatment of their minorities, not because they are more callous, but because they, too, have been subjected to the same by their Communist masters.

The opening years of the "Great Fatherland War" were also very terrible in a strictly military way for Russia and many of its people. In their greatest advances, the Nazis encircled Leningrad, fought to Moscow's outskirts, reached the Volga at Stalingrad and penetrated the northern Caucasus region. Although besieged, Leningrad held out, even though human meat reportedly became not too rare a commodity. Moscow was evacuated of all but the most essential citizens and services, with Stalin remaining on but protected from enemy bombers at a command post set up in a subway station connected with the Kremlin by underground passage. In the first eight months of the invasion, some three million Red Army men were taken prisoner. And about a half million Russian prisoners died in the last four months of 1941 alone, as a result of winter transport in open freight cars or similar mistreatment far from in keeping with the Geneva convention.

When the Nazis first rolled in, many Soviet peasants, especially those in the Ukraine, made the mistake of greeting them as "liberators." In short order, however, the truly stupid Nazis ended that delusion—and that avenue of help as well—with unspeakable cruelties, treating Soviet citizens of the occupied areas as less than human (*untermenschen* was their word) or at best using them as slave labor for their war effort.

Perhaps more than anything else, that Nazi attitude toward the

Soviet people, both civilian and military, caused Hitler's defeat in Russia. It aroused patriotism—or nationalism—that Stalin's first appeals had not been able to stir. Stalin, of course, was quick to recognize that change supplied him by the enemy. He capitalized on it by summoning up all the ghosts of holy Russia, even to the extent of letting the church play its part. Temporarily shelved in those dark hours were the Party, its policies, and the police. Instead—but only so long as necessary—the theme was holy Russia and all its past. Gulled by that, the people rallied and went on to victory. Once that was attained, of course, their expectations of Stalin were just as false as some Russians had had of their Nazi "liberators."

Much has been written of the great valor and suffering of the Red Army and the Soviet people that brought final victory in Berlin. There is a multitude of accounts of battles to the last man, of daring guerrilla action behind Nazi lines and of tremendous sacrifices of most ordinary people. And the role of Allied battles in the Mediterranean and the West, plus the value of Allied aid in matériel is well appreciated, even though those latter facets of the common struggle have been studiously disregarded in the Soviet Union. All that is lacking for a full understanding of that dreadful war in Russia—for the general public, at least—is a better explanation of German misjudgment and error than simply laying it at the door of Hitler in particular and the German people in general. For it must be conceded that even though they faced terrific odds, the Nazis came uncomfortably close to winning.

Stalin never knew the answer, though he pretended he did. A consummate actor, once finis had been written to the Nazi effort with the heroic victory at Stalingrad in early 1943, he displayed absolute aplomb and self-assurance in his meetings with Allied chieftains. At those gatherings, the Georgian dictator screened his real aim for the international spread of communism—under Soviet control—behind the purported desire for military cooperation against facism by fellow "democracies." That was the same Stalin who signed his 1939 pact with Hitler in hopes that Nazi Germany and the rest of the Western world would eliminate each other in war and permit the Soviet system to take over the exhausted strugglers at his pleasure. But once that infamous pact had been violated equally infamously, there were some hardheaded—though unheeded—statesmen in the West who hoped that the invasion of the Soviet Union would exhaust those contenders instead, and thus rid the world of the plagues of facism and communism at one stroke. That part of that—the exhaustion of Communist forces—should not happen was Stalin's prime concern at the Tehran conference of November, 1943. Churchill fully understood that underlying duplicity of the Georgian. Roosevelt, who frequently referred to that ruthless, bloody Soviet dictator as "Uncle Joe," did not. But Churchill, with forces worn by a longer stint in the war and with a disintegrating empire, had to accept Roosevelt's grandiose naïveté. Therefore, to the degree possible, Stalin's wishes were met. Anglo-American action against the Nazis in the west—and somewhat in accordance with the Georgian's specifications rather than Churchill's—was agreed upon to relieve the Red Army.

Stalin's trip to Tehran—his first venture abroad since seizing power in the Soviet Union—also gave the outer world its initial full appreciation of the elaborate security measures taken for that successor to the tsars. First of all, northern Iran, including the entire area around its capital, of course, was a Soviet fief. Early after the Nazi invasion, the Red Army had occupied that area, at first to bolster the Soviet flank against possible Nazi take-over in the Middle East, later to receive American matériel aid routed through the Persian Gulf. As result of that, plus the dispatch of NKVD bodyguard personnel, Tehran was a virtual Soviet armed camp during Stalin's visit. Nevertheless, the canard was floated—and later made Soviet "fact" by honors awarded an NKVD bodyguard of the time—that a Nazi attempt to assassinate Stalin in Tehran had been foiled. To make the cheese of that fabricated tale more binding, Churchill and Roosevelt were also said to have been targets for assassination by a group directed by none other than the redoubtable Otto Skorzeny, whose daring airborne operation had rescued Mussolini from his pro-Allied Italian guards. Years later, Skorzeny laughed off the account as false and said the Tehran meeting had been so secret he had never known of it until it was over.

Just the same, the Tehran yarn has persisted. And so have fables about other attempts against Stalin—five in all—lingered on. One concerned a 1928 attempt by White Guard emigrés against personnel in a secondary OGPU installation in Moscow. Another holds that artillery was fired from the Black Sea in 1930 while the dictator was vacationing at his *dacha* near Sochi. A third—which has been elabo-

[225]

rately embroidered by romantic writers of the Bessedovsky school in the west—claims that an attractive young woman (identified by some as a relative of Kaganovich) gained entry to the Kremlin in 1935 with intent to poison Stalin and his bodyguards. The fourth—which seems a compounding of the 1935 story to garner victims for the purges—tells of a trio of lesser Stalin bodyguards being liquidated in the nick of time in 1937 after it was discovered they were German spies. The fifth extravaganza—which enhanced Stalin's wartime image at home—spins a tale about the 1944 capture in Moscow environs of a brace of defected Red Army prisoners, plus a plethora of sophisticated equipment, dispatched by air by the Nazis to do away with Stalin. That quintet of "attempts"—as well as the Tehran yarn—are pure cock-and-bull. Except for a potshot taken at Mikoyan's car outside the Kremlin by a deranged Soviet soldier during World War II, the life of no Soviet hierarch—and especially that of Stalin—was ever endangered by such ordinary assassination while the Georgian dictator was in full command of his powers. Only Stalin's end, when he was tired, old, and sick and succession was in the air, is up for question.

The victory of Stalingrad marked not only a turning point in the war, but also gave Stalin the leeway to renege on the comparative liberties he had been forced to grant his subjects during the desperate hours. The first indication of the return to the "good old times" after final victory seemed assured was the reconstitution of the NKVD. In April, 1943, the secret police force was again split into two commissariats with Merkulov once more taking control of the NKGB and with Beria as chief of the NKVD being the overall boss.

Parallel to these two organizations there also existed the infamous SMERSH ("Death to Spies"), the armed forces security agency whose main task from 1943 to 1946 was eliminating real and imagined enemies of the regime among Soviet citizens who had been outside Soviet control during World War II. Its chief was General Viktor Abakumov, the rising star of Stalin's future bodyguard system.

Because of the turn of the tide, that dualheaded organization had much work to do in the closing years, months, and days of the war and in the unsettled period that came with Red Army seizure of eastern Europe. First there was the problem of enemy prisoners, not only Germans, but also Austrians, Hungarians, Italians, Rumanians, Bulgarians, Spaniards, defected Red Army men from the ranks of General Andrey Vlasov's army, and finally, some Japanese. The

NKVD was admirably equipped for handling the bulk of the prisoners, sending them to the same slave labor camp system so well established earlier for Soviet "enemies." Uncounted thousands died en
route or in the camps, but the lives of real foreign enemies mattered
even less. And as the Red Army fought its way west, the NKVD hot
on its heels was spared much of the trouble of shipping its foreign
prisoners east. Ready at hand it found such convenient lockups as the
former Nazi gas chambers at Auschwitz in Poland and the Nazi
concentration camps at Buchenwald, Neubrandenburg, and Sach-
senhausen in the Soviet occupied zone of Germany.

The second major problem for the NKVD in the last years of the
war and its aftermath was the millions of Red Army prisoners taken
by the Nazis and the other millions of Soviet citizens, who had either
been in territory overrun by Hitler's forces or had been sent as slave
labor to German-held areas to the west. The harshest treatment was
accorded the Soviet soldiery. Early in the war, Stalin had decreed
that to surrender was not permissible. He even let his own son by his
first marriage die as a Nazi POW, although an arrangment for an
exchange was certainly possible. But that would not have been in
keeping with the tradition of Ivan the Terrible and Peter the Great
that the Georgian aped. As a result, millions of liberated Red Army
men were sent to slave labor camps for years, often with stops at such
way stations as Auschwitz or Buchenwald. And some were summarily executed for more "heinous" crimes. Quite disgracefully,
similar lots also befell Red Army POWs liberated by American and
British forces. Under a secret agreement made with Stalin, the Allies
turned over to the NKVD the Red Army men that Anglo-American
troops had liberated from Nazi POW camps. Knowing the fate that
awaited them, some of those unfortunate Red Army men committed
suicide. Countless others of those "liberated" prisoners were turned
over to their new captors before public outcry in the West brought
the deal to a stop, although long after it had become too late for most.

Far simpler was the NKVD's task with the civilian Soviets freed by
the Red Army from Nazi thralldom. Many of those people within the
restored confines of the Soviet Union—especially the minorities—
were just deported to Siberia or elsewhere east en masse. Unlike the
Red Army POWs in Anglo-American overrun Germany, few in the
West knew about them and therefore did not care. And, as Khrushchev later said, Stalin also would have deported the Ukrainians en

masse had they not been so numerous. Because in large part they were individuals rather than groups, very little is known about the fate of the thousands and thousands of "Ost" (east) workers, the Russians that the Nazis used as slave labor. There are reports of some being channeled through the former Nazi concentration camps, but their numbers and eventual disposition are not clear. And, of course, many, many thousands of non-Russians engulfed by the advancing Red Army also fell into NKVD clutches, but again the actual number and specific fates of that category of unfortunates also remains little more than conjecture. However, that most of those also ended up in Soviet slave labor camps is a logical conclusion.

In January 1945, the Red Army launched what was to be its final major offensive. Situated at that time along a front extending from the Baltic almost to the Aegean, Soviet forces consisted of some three hundred divisions and twenty-five tank armies. Opposed to them was a Nazi force which had dwindled to about one hundred divisions, most of which were below par in strength and matériel. Those figures alone made the outcome obvious, a matter of time, not of fact.

Therefore, to no military man's great surprise, a virtually unstoppable Red Army spearhead, directed by the real genius of the "Great Fatherland War," Marshal Georgy Zhukov, drove to the Oder River, some fifty miles east of Berlin, by the end of January. At the same time, a small bridgehead was gained across the Oder and crossing it in force was only a matter of routine logistics.

That success was most opportune for Stalin, improving his bargaining position with his "allies" tremendously. Since late 1944, Roosevelt had been pressing the Georgian for another summit meeting. Stalin conceded, but specified it be held on his own ground, at Yalta, and set its date for February, 1945, when his timetable called for his troops being at the gates of the Nazi capital.

In retrospect, particularly, the Yalta meeting was a disaster for the West, eastern Europe, and to some extent, Japan, and a great political victory for Stalin and communism. At the time, Anglo-American forces were at the Rhine, well up the boot of Italy and in complete control of North Africa and the Middle East. Appreciable elements of the Western armies also could have advanced decisively toward Berlin, but they were purposefully slowed then and later. The stated reasons then were "strategic," saving Western allied lives, plus such largesse as letting the Red Army have the "glory" of capturing the German capital, since Western forces had "liberated" Paris and

[228]

Rome. Conveniently overlooked was the fact of Red Army "liberation" of such capitals as Warsaw, Prague, Budapest, Bucharest, Sofia, Belgrade, and Vienna.

A contributing cause of the Western debacle at Yalta was the political and physical conditions of its two prime advocates. Churchill was distracted by forthcoming elections (at which a capricious electorate drove its victorious wartime leader thankless from power). The long physically incapacitated Roosevelt was very tired, and though none knew it at the time, near death. Additionally, Roosevelt's weakest trait, his naïve trust in "Uncle Joe," was insuperable.

Therefore, as a result of both previous erroneous Western policy decisions and the problems of the Western leaders facing him, Stalin got practically everything he wanted at Yalta. He got hegemony over all of eastern Europe, ostensibly as a buffer zone against Germany, but a Germany then well defeated. He got chunks of Finland, Czechoslovakia, and Rumania and the Baltic States in toto—although there was to be meaningless dispute over that last acquisition until the West finally gave up. He got part of East Prussia and all of eastern Poland, giving the Poles in return part of east Germany, part of which has always been German and thereby supplies cause for possible future conflict. He got control of half of the great city of Berlin, allowing the Americans and British the other half (the French only gained their sector later as the result of accommodation made by the Americans and British). Additionally, the Western "statesmen"— who must have completely forgotten the mess caused by establishment of the Polish Corridor and the Free City of Danzig only a quarter century earlier—agreed to a much more untenable 110-mile-long land corridor through Soviet-controlled eastern Germany as a connection between the western sectors of Berlin and western Germany. As if all that were not quite a package, Stalin also got the lion's share of reparations and the manufacturing plant "spoils" from all of Germany. (That made it even more difficult later for the West, particularly the U.S., to get its portion of Germany back on its economic and political feet.)

Finally, at Yalta, Roosevelt set up with Stalin a grossly impolite as well as impolitic secret meeting from which Churchill was excluded. At that tête-à-tête between the two "greats," Roosevelt inveigled Stalin to join the aborning United Nations and participate in the war in the Pacific. The cost of that agreement was terrific and of no benefit whatsoever to the United States. Stalin allowed himself to be

[229]

drawn into the U.N., but only with the proviso that he have a triple membership, not only for the U.S.S.R, but for White Russia and the Ukraine as well. That is about just the same as giving membership to such "independent" Western areas as Washington, D.C., and the City of London. For warring with the Japanese, Roosevelt the map-maker granted Stalin undisputed hegemony in Outer Mongolia and Manchuria, a Korea open to Soviet influence, control of the Chinese Eastern Railroad, Port Arthur, and Dairen, plus outright possession of the Kurile Islands and the southern part of Sakhalin Island. Completely unconsulted, of course, by the arrogant Roosevelt were either his Chinese ally or poor little Korea, then seeking liberation from its Japanese overlords. (There are some accounts, hopefully false, that Roosevelt did not even know where Korea was.) Stalin honored the agreement about the Pacific war only when it was cost-free and the U.S. had Tokyo at the point of surrender, or as the French Communist paper of those days slanted it with a banner headline "Just forty-eight hours after the U.S.S.R. entered the war, Japan has capitulated."

In return for those sweeping, wholesale concessions at Yalta, the West got very small change indeed. Stalin let France have a zone of occupation in the West's part of Germany, but only begrudgingly. For that trifling concession, the Georgian gained vastly more than had ever been achieved by Ghengis Khan or any Tsarist predecessor.

Three months later, Berlin fell to Zhukov. Shortly before that, American troops, who had been marking time at a bridgehead on the Elbe River, had a well-photographed first meeting with their Russian allies. (Earlier in April, an American reconnaissance patrol had rolled completely unmolested into an undefended western part of Berlin, only to be ordered summarily by higher command to return to the Elbe.) But it was not until July, 1945, that the Russians allowed Anglo-American troops to occupy their sectors of Berlin, a good indication of the trouble the West was to have with the Communists in the future about that city.

More than likely, one of the main reasons the Soviets allowed Western troops into the German capital at the time they did was the fact the final "Big-Three" conference of the war was to take place at Potsdam, outside the city, at the end of July. Essentially, that gathering was little more than a rubber-stamping of Yalta agreements and a stage on which Stalin could strut among comparative pigmies. The conference had barely started when Churchill, losing at the elections at home, was replaced by the relatively ineffective Clement Attlee. And Roosevelt, dead a quarter year before, had been replaced by Harry Truman, a complete novice at dealing with the Georgian. Additionally, another drawback was the fact that the top foreign advisors of both Western leaders lacked direct experience in bargaining with Stalin and the Russians. Even more damaging to the West was the predilection of both Western leaders—but particularly Atlee —not to rock the boat of wartime Allied unity and therefore come to agreement with Stalin, with an attitude of almost no matter what the concession. The only Western "achievement" at Potsdam was a very big concession, indeed, and one that like the Berlin corridor arrangement of Yalta could supply ground for major future international conflict. That slipshod Western concession concerned the new Polish western boundary. At Yalta, it had been too loosely stipulated by the West that the Oder and Neisse Rivers should form that frontier. No Westerner seemed to note that there was an eastern and a western Neisse. Therefore, at Potsdam, Stalin's map-makers used the western Neisse, thereby giving Poland some twenty-five thousand square miles of territory that had been German for centuries and that contained the two old German cities of Breslau and Oppeln, later respectively renamed Wroclaw and Opole. When a junior American advisor drew his senior's attention to the chunk of traditional German territory thus being given away, he was brushed off with the comment, "Well, who lost the war anyway, the Poles or the Germans?"

Getting the war-torn Soviet Union back on its feet and consolidating its newly won empire were much more lengthy and arduous tasks for Stalin than had been his dealings with the West at Potsdam. More than twenty million Soviet citizens had been killed in battle or had died in air raids, from starvation, or in Nazi camps. Another twenty-five million were homeless. And thousands of buildings, especially manufacturing plants, were in ruins, while the granary was threatened by a terrible depletion of livestock and almost nonexistent farming machinery. The simplest part was the physical labor of reconstruction, since most of that was supplied by the security police and its millions of slave laborers and prisoners of war. Much of the materials and supplies were furnished by the U.N.'s relief arm, UNRRA (which got seventy percent of its support from the U.S.),

[231]

bolstered by lesser, but direct aid from Britain and Sweden. And, of course, East Germany and the rest of Red Army-occupied eastern Europe were bled white of vast amounts of industrial plant and any other equipment that could be pried loose.

Although it took a bit longer, Stalin's problem of bringing the bulk of his newly acquired Communist empire under control was somewhat simpler than the job at home. Many well-meaning but politically naïve people in those unfortunate lands had welcomed the oncoming Red Army men as "liberators." Additionally, the Red Army and the accompanying NKVD elements held the whip hand until remnants of "bourgeois," or anti-Communist political groups were executed, expelled, or imprisoned and were replaced by obedient puppet regimes, long nurtured in advance back in Soviet political hot-houses. Using those tactics, Stalin had all his satrapies in eastern Europe under firm control by early 1947. And in the Far East, with Japanese capitulation, he similarly took over North Korea. At the same time, Red Army troops entered Manchuria and seized vast quantities of Japanese arms. That matériel was turned over to the forces of Mao Tse-tung to defeat Chiang Kai-shek's Nationalists and make the Chinese mainland another Communist fiefdom by the spring of 1949.

Back at home, Stalin had a task that was perhaps even greater than reconstruction. That was keeping his newly enlightened subjects under control. Like their forefathers in the Napoleonic wars, Stalin's people had been "tainted" by contact with the much more advanced and liberal world to the west. The Georgian recognized the problem as early as 1943, after the tide had turned at Stalingrad, and put Zhdanov in charge of the ideological screws. Forthwith, that straight-laced and narrow-minded minion, who simultaneously functioned as Leningrad party boss, launched a vast Russification program that continued apace until his sudden death in August, 1948. That program penetrated into every nook and corner of Soviet intellectual life and at its worst was known as the "Zhdanovshchina." In many ways, that marked the start of the cold war between East and West, although the West only started becoming aware of the realities about good old "Uncle Joe" with the defection of Igor Gouzenko from the Soviet embassy in Ottawa in October, 1945, and the "iron curtain" speech of Churchill in Fulton, Missouri in March 1946.

Although the "Zhdanovschina" put many a Soviet intellectual out of work and sent others to prison or exile, it was much less brutal than the similarly named programs of Ivan the Terrible and Yezhov. And in some ways—if one overlooks the harm it dealt Russian advancement—it was almost laughable. That was the period when announcement followed announcement that a Russian had invented almost everything. It also was the time when it was decreed that Soviet citizens could not marry foreigners. The purpose was to keep Soviet citizens from being "tainted" by foreigners, but the local implication was that Soviet citizens were too good for foreigners. And it was the period when much official Soviet adulation was given Trofim Lysenko, the biologist who "found" that Marx was right, that environment could influence heredity.

Although Zhdanov was in charge of such Russification, he was merely the idea man. The muscle, as usual, was furnished by the secret police. During the last two years of the war, the NKVD had done a masterful job bullying Nazi prisoners and "liberated" Russians alike and as a reward Stalin promoted Beria to Marshal in July, 1945.

Early in 1946, however, the Georgian effected a major reshuffle in the police organization, and a less important nomenclature change for it and the government in general. In January, Beria was removed as head of the NKVD. That post was given to Colonel General Sergey Kruglov, deputy chief of the disbanded wartime SMERSH, an organization later considerably overglorified by postwar fiction writers. Then in March, all commissariats were renamed ministries. With that, the NKVD became the MVD (Ministry of the Interior) and the NKGB became the MGB (Ministry of State Security). Kruglov continued as head of the MVD, but Merkulov, Commissar of the NKGB, did not last long as chief of the MGB. Early in 1946, Stalin dumped Merkulov for Gen. Viktor Abakumov, the wartime head of SMERSH and an old Chekist, who had helped Tukachevsky suppress the Tambov peasants in 1922. Stalin shifted Beria away from supervising state security and the police. He gave him, instead, the job of overseeing the development of atomic energy. He profited from some historically successful spying, as was revealed by the 1945 Gouzenko defection and the subsequent exposure of such British traitors as Alan Nunn May, Klaus Fuchs and Bruno Pontecorvo, and their American counterparts Harry Gold, the Rosenbergs, and David Greenglass. Beria's program squeezed everything possible from spies and Nazi prisoners to bring the Soviet Union on a nuclear par with the U.S.

[233]

And it is somewhat ironic that all the while Beria was hard at that job—which culminated in the explosion of the first Soviet atomic device in September 1949—Stalin was loudly demanding that the U.S. share its nuclear secrets.

While Marshal Beria was thus busy at loftier pursuits, Stalin made sure that a steady eye was kept on the more ordinary police operations. As a temporary substitute, he had standing in the wings as a sort of security watchdog one Aleksey Kuznetsov, with nothing more than a Central Committee secretaryship and *apparatchik* training as apparent background. But his real importance, so far as impending events were concerned, was that he was a Leningrad trainee and as such a protege of Zhdanov. In other words, while Beria was straining to steal atomic secrets, Zhdanov and his flunkies were moving into a challenging position on the ladder to power. And probably all with Stalin's blessing, who considered his security demanded keeping his minions at each others throats.

In the same postwar period, Stalin also made sure that the military, especially the victorious Zhukov, did not get too big for their breeches. In any other country, Zhukov would have been honored for his services. But in March, 1947, he was in effect demoted instead when the veteran *apparatchik* Nikolay Bulganin was made Minister of Defense. Although carrying the title of marshal, Bulganin was really no more a military man than was Khrushchev, also once graced with high military rank.

The submersion of Zhukov, who was respected in the west as a highly capable officer, marked not only a decline in Red Army influence at home but also a halt in Soviet aggrandizement abroad. Less than a year before the appointment of Bulganin, and while Stalin was toying with the disposition of Zhukov, the Soviet Union had been forced to yield to the pressure of the atomically armed West and made the only territorial retreat of Stalin's reign, the withdrawal from northern Iran. A year later, in May, 1947, the U.S. proclaimed what became known as the Truman Doctrine which reversed Communist penetration of Greece and Turkey. And in June, 1947, the plan of U.S. Gen. George Marshall was formulated, whereby vast American economic aid was extended to western Europe, which otherwise might have fallen to Communist political expansion.

Probably out of frustration, Stalin reacted foolishly, both politically and militarily. In September, 1947, he resurrected the Comintern (buried in 1943 to appease the Western allies) under the new title of Cominform. Designed to counter the Marshall Plan, the renamed successor had the same basic tasks, the spreading of Communist propaganda and subversion, the establishment of Communist-controlled stooge groups (substituting the term "peace" organizations for the prewar "popular" fronts) and the arrangement of secret deals with non-Communist political power structures. But the Georgian made the mistake of establishing Cominform headquarters in Belgrade, whose ambitious boss, Josip Broz Tito, was to bite the hand that fed him by booting the Cominform out of his capital and telling Stalin to keep his nose—and his secret police—out of Yugoslavia in June 1948. Then, just months later, in August, 1948, Stalin fumbled militarily by blockading West Berlin, an attempt that was successfully countered by a massive Western airlift of supplies. The airlift was not only a blow to Soviet prestige, it also resulted in the establishment of the North Atlantic Treaty Organization. Stalin's subsequent formation of the Warsaw Pact grouping with his satellites was more reaction than an effective counter to the rearming of western Europe under the aegis of the U.S.

But it may be argued that distraction with events at home contributed to Stalin's Berlin bobble. Just before he took that step in the west, Zhdanov and Malenkov had been involved in a tug-of-war of sorts for the secondary power position. Then at the very start of the Berlin blockade, Zhdanov suddenly died in mid-struggle and mid-career. Like jackals, Malenkov, Beria, and Abakumov turned on his minions. They carried out a purge of Zhdanovites that far outreached their original intentions. It eventually boomeranged and was followed by a Stalin-directed purge of top echelons of the security forces themselves as well as a threatened purge of Stalin's lieutenants. Only death prevented the Georgian from cleaning house in much the same way Ivan the Terrible eliminated the Oprichniks centuries earlier.

The anti-Zhdanovites (opposed to Zhdanov in the power struggle, not in principle) struck first at Kuznetsov, whom they loathed for his role of security watchdog while Beria was busy at the atomic spy well. He was arrested by Abakumov and shot in short order. In the same initial sweep, Petr Popkov, the Leningrad party First Secretary, was also shot. And Georgy Popov the Moscow party First Secretary, was fired, to be replaced by that veteran survivor, Khrushchev. What has come to be called the "Leningrad Affair" (whose details are still far from clear and probably will never be known because its surviving beneficiaries were too incriminated to talk) reached culmination in September, 1950, with the execution of Zhdanov's chief protégé, the young Voznesensky, a safe target since Stalin's original admiration of his economic ideas had turned to scorn—and Voznesensky continued a safe target for more than two years after his death. In 1952, Mikhail Suslov, another of those veteran survivors and the party's long-time excuse for an ideologist, attacked the dead man's theories for Stalin's edification.

Somewhat simultaneously with the blossoming of the "Leningrad Affair," there were also threats to Stalin's hegemony of the Communist camp abroad. By 1949, the Soviet show of force at Berlin had failed to impress the rebellious Tito. In fact, Tito and his cronies in the Balkans dared to discuss a possible union of the Balkans and adjacent states, without bothering to get Stalin's approval beforehand. Such *lèse majesté* could not be tolerated. The first to learn that was the weakest victim, little Albania's Koce Xoxe, who was "tried" and shot under MGB direction in June, 1949. Next to be informed was Bulgaria's Georgy Dimitrov, who was reprimanded before "dying" in July in a Soviet hospital. And in the same month, Hungary's Laszlo Rajk and three of his colleagues were hanged as Titoists, again under MGB direction. Another turn came for Bulgaria in December, when Traicho Kostov was hanged. Czechoslovakia was also to play its part in that purge, but its entry onstage was to be delayed for more fanciful and encompassing MGB fabrication by Stalin.

In June 1950, Stalin made another mistake in international political judgment, and one for which his successors eventually may pay dearly. Smarting from the setback at Berlin, and with a growing stockpile of atomic bombs in his possession, he moved against the West at the opposite end of his periphery and pushed North Korea into the invasion of South Korea. Initially, all went swimmingly and the complete subjugation of South Korea seemed imminent. However, the Georgian had made two tactical errors as well. He had not appreciated the determination of the U.S. to help South Korea and he launched the invasion at the very time his "nyet"-ing minions at the U.N. had stalked out of that organization's Security Council on his instructions and thus made it possible for the U.S. to get U.N. approval and support of some of its members. Stalin did not live to see that war become a stalemate and as such a failure for him. But he did live to witness Communist China entering that conflict and thereby reestablishing a Chinese basis for hegemony in an area immediately south of Vladivostok and uncomfortably adjacent to Soviet Far Eastern territory that later was to be claimed by Peking.

Thus thwarted soon after the start of that foreign adventure, the Georgian returned to the easier pursuit of cracking down on his more directly controlled domestic and satellite minions. In the fall of 1951, he gave an indication he was about to dump Beria for good and possibly other senior flunkies as well. He fired Abakumov, who although not a Beria creature was certainly a most veteran Chekist. As new head of the police, he named Semen D. Ignatyev, a pure *apparatchik* or functionary, whose chief qualifications were that he was not a Beria-man and had no security background whatsoever. (Beria's position, however, was not greatly weakened by the Abakumov dismissal. A year earlier, Stalin had named Merkulov, Beria's chief flunky, as head of the powerful, police-controlled Ministry of State Control.)

Directly after his appointment, and on Stalin's orders, Ignatyev conducted a pair of minipurges, removing lesser Beria adherents from the MGB and eliminating Beria party apparatus supporters in the Caucasus. But the really significant move of the MGB chief did not come until the following year. In August, 1952, he branched into anti-Semitism by running a small-scale pogrom in the south. A group of Jewish party officials and intellectuals there was framed on charges of plotting to make the Crimea independent and the entire lot was shot. That action could only be interpreted as a direct threat to Beria. Not only had the police overlord long been sympathetic to Jews, but there also were a number of reports that he was of at least partial Jewish origin himself.

Two months after the executions of those Jews, Stalin's net seemed to enlarge and to be designed not only for Beria but for other hierarchs as well. That became apparent during the Nineteenth Party Congress of October, 1952, and its aftermath. The usual long-winded speeches about the economy and foreign affairs to the side, the chief business at that gathering was down-grading the power of the Politburo, which had its name changed to Presidium. Stalin accomplished that by the simple expedient of packing the renamed top party organization. He increased its membership from eleven to twenty-five. Thereby the Presidium became unwieldy and cumbersome and so much less effective than the ten-man Central Committee Secretariat, run by Malenkov, Stalin's mooted successor. Eight of the Georgian's longtime stooges, Molotov, Malenkov, Beria, Voroshilov, Kaganovich, Mikoyan, Khrushchev, and Bulganin—and of course Stalin as well—were retained in the new Presidium. But the majority was new blood, fourteen younger party *apparatchiks*. As a result, Stalin could have carried on without the help of his old stooges any time he chose. Next at the Central Committee session that followed the congress, Stalin lashed out at most of his old stooges, accusing them of almost any "crime" or deviation that came to mind.

But it was in November, 1952, that the handwriting on the wall was made very apparent—to Beria, in particular. In that month, Stalin took two more actions against Jews. At home, he had a group of Jews in the Ukraine shot for so-called economic "crimes." And abroad, the Czechoslovak Communist hierarchy got its well-overdue purge. But, the action against the Prague Communists differed considerably and pointedly from that taken two years earlier against party chiefs in other satellites. Of course, "Titoism" was included in the charges against Vladimir Klementis, Rudolf Slansky, and the other nine victims executed. But the primary accusation against those unfortunates was trafficking with international Jewry. And almost all of them were Jews. The obvious conclusion drawn by other anxious Communists was that the "crimes" of the Czechoslovak "clique" could not have been committed without the support, or knowledge at least, of Beria and his cohorts. In that way, the Czechoslovak production was a dry run for a trial of Beria and his supporters.

However, a homegrown dress rehearsal for elimination of the beady-eyed police overlord had been scheduled to precede Beria's actual "trial." On January 13, 1953, Stalin used his press organs to advise his minions, and the world in general, of the so-called "Doctors' Plot." That frame-up involved nine Soviet doctors, most of them Jews. The arrested—and chained and beaten—"defendants" were charged with killing a high army political officer in 1945, murdering Zhdanov in 1948, and trying to kill several other top military officers. For good measure, the medical men also were charged with working for American and British intelligence. And of course, they were accused of being the agents of international Jewish groups. As in the prewar purge "trials," the chief script writer was Stalin. The producer was Ignatyev. Ignatyev's deputy, Mikhail Ryumin, handled the direction—or the interrogation and breaking of the prisoners.

In an almost hysterical press campaign that was unleashed with the announcement of the case, a crescendo of articles advised the citizenry to improve and further improve vigilance. And in a completely new departure, Stalin's press directly attacked the security police for having failed to unearth the "plotters" years earlier. Those attacks, of course, were not directed at such comparative new comers to the police as Ignatyev and Ryumin, but at Beria, Abakumov, and Merkulov, who were in charge of security at the times the "crimes" allegedly took place.

On February 17, 1953, while his flunkies were busy interrogating their prisoners and arousing the millions of dutiful pawns among the general populace, Stalin diverted himself with a meeting with the Indian ambassador. No great expression of opinion or policy resulted from that session. Its only importance lay in the fact it was to be the last meeting with a foreigner the Georgian dictator would ever have.

And on the very same day of that meeting, Major General Petr Kosynkin, the deputy commandant of the Kremlin guards, suddenly died of a "heart attack." That sudden seizure was rather unusual, to say the least. A fanatic admirer of Stalin, Kosynkin had been in the prime of life and health. Enthralled by his own fabrication, the Georgian dictator had reshuffled the top Kremlin guards and his personal physicians—making certain there were no Jews in the latter group —almost upon announcement of the "Doctors' Plot." The extremely careful physical examinations regularly undergone by all such appointees as Kosynkin automatically presupposes that the guard leader was in top condition and certainly not suffering from any heart trouble.

In light of events that followed—there is good reason to give credence to reports that Kosynkin was killed under orders of Beria, Bulganin, and Malenkov, aided and abetted by Ignatyev, who was working both sides of the street.

All that is known, however, is that on February 22, five days after Kosynkin's "heart attack," the press campaign ceased as suddenly as it had started. With that, the "Doctors' Plot" likewise was swept from the boards. And a curtain of silence dropped around what Stalin was doing, if anything.

Then ten days later, all the world suddenly learned what may have been happening to Stalin in at least part of that interim. A brief statement of March 4, 1953, announced that the Georgian had suffered a stroke on the night of March 1–2. Next, on March 6, another announcement reported that the dictator had died on the evening of March 5. As with the death of Lenin, there were medical announcements, bulletins, and statements. But the exact circumstances under which Stalin died are a mystery and probably will remain so. Whether his first seizure happened in the Kremlin and he was moved to his *dacha* outside Moscow or the entire final illness occurred in the *dacha* where he died has been purposefully confused. After she fled to the U.S., his daughter, Svetlana, told of being summoned to Stalin's bedside in his last hours, but even she had knowledge of little more than the final death throes. Therefore, whether Stalin's death—like so many of the other autocrats before him—may have been speeded and abetted, if not caused, by underlings who felt threatened by the "Doctors' Plot" will also probably remain an unanswered question.

4. STALIN'S SUCCESSORS (1953–)

Stalin's chief underlings probably had been meeting and conniving well before his death. Many a stupid member of the Russian and satellite masses actually cried when Stalin died, but to be sure that some unknown, intelligent man or group could not capitalize on the situation, thousands of police tank troops, loyal to Beria, rolled into Moscow the night after the dictator died and set up controls around approaches to the Kremlin.

The following day, in such an armed camp, the late Georgian's successors made their earlier secret negotiations formal and announced reorganizations of the government and party. The Presidium was reduced from twenty-five to ten members. The new body included the eight veteran stooges—Malenkov, Molotov, Beria, Voroshilov, Khrushchev, Bulganin, Kaganovich, and Mikoyan—plus two new figures, second-rate party *apparatchiks* both, Mikhail Pervukhin, a piece of industrial deadwood, and Maxim Saburov, who specialized in that mumbo jumbo the Soviets call planning. And the MVD and MGB were reincorporated into a single ministry with Beria at its head. In the process, Ignatyev was ousted, but given lesser posts rather than liquidated in the Stalin fashion. Poskrebyshev simply dropped from sight the moment Stalin died. Although he was reportedly seen later here or there by not very reliable sources, what happened to that hatchet man has never been determined. In the first post-Stalin reorganization, the only blood actually known drawn —at first only figuratively—was that of Ryumin, Ignatyev's deputy. He was almost immediately arrested. The following month the hierarchs announced what they had long known—that the "Doctors' Plot" was pure fabrication, and in 1954 they had Ryumin executed for his part in that frame-up.

Perhaps in keeping with a possible Stalin last testament, Malenkov initially inherited the late Georgian's dual posts of party chief and government leader, at least until the obsequies, held on March 9, had been celebrated. Malenkov, Beria, and Molotov made appropriate funeral speeches before the embalmed and berouged dead Stalin was installed alongside the corpse of Lenin in that primitive Soviet holy-of-holies, the Kremlin mausoleum. Those rites were marked by one minor good result: Klement Gottwald, the chief Czechoslovak stooge, caught pneumonia at them and died soon thereafter.

A bare dozen days after the funeral, Malenkov lost the first—and most important—of his top posts. Khrushchev took over as party leader, leaving Malenkov as government chief, and thereby starting the fiction of "collective leadership." In the same period, Beria started reasserting his control of the police. In the south, he purged the Georgians who had purged his Georgians, installing his friend and erstwhile "diplomat," Vladimir Dekanozov, as head of the Georgian MVD. And in the Ukraine and the Baltic areas, he made similar appointments of trusted cronies.

For several months, all seemed to be smooth sailing for the "collective leadership." But actually, there was a secret and desperate struggle for supreme power being waged between Khrushchev and Beria. Why Beria lost that struggle, with the all-powerful police under his control, is somewhat baffling. No Russian before him with similar forces at his command, had ever failed to come out on top. Most likely, Beria lacked political sagacity and was no more than a top cop. For lose, he did. Possible contributing factors were the East German rising of June, 1953, and riots in Vorkuta and other slave labor camps that lasted from 1952–54, but peaked in 1953. The world first learned —but not very much—about the outcome of that Khrushchev-Beria struggle on July 10, 1953 when it was announced that Beria had been ousted some two weeks earlier. Khrushchev did much to muddy the picture of that outcome by giving at least two different personal reports about it, and both not true. One of his yarns had it that he and other Stalin successors inveigled Beria to the Kremlin on July 26 and shot him. Another Khrushchev account has the same worthies strangling Beria. The facts, however, were that Khrushchev was not able to dispose of Beria until December, 1953, when the Georgian policeman was secretly tried and just as secretly executed immediately thereafter. Beria was accused of almost everything, except the horrors he had perpetrated under Stalin, with Khrushchev and the rest of the survivors, of course, looking on. Beria was charged with violations of such a nebulous matter as Soviet "legality," bourgeois nationalism (by that was meant a policy of a little more freedom for East Germany, the other satellites and the Soviet minorities), trying to put the security police above party and state, hindering (the ever woeful) agricultural development, and (ridiculously) having been a Western agent since the days of the civil war.

Naturally, Beria's downfall was followed by the elimination of his chief lieutenants in a series of other "trials." Six of his close cronies, including such small-time butchers as Dekanozov and Merkulov, were executed. And Abakumov was shot about a year after Beria for framing the so-called "Leningrad Affair," from which the "court" conveniently forgot that Khrushchev also somewhat benefited.

For some reason—yet to be learned—not until Beria was actually dead was Kruglov renamed head of the MVD. Once he had the job, he immediately proceeded with a purge of lesser Beria underlings in security ranks.

But Kruglov's "revenge" was quite short-lived. Long fearful, with reason, of the power of the security police, and supported by other Stalin survivors just as fearful, Khrushchev went through the motions of downgrading the MVD in March, 1954. He created a new organization, the KGB (Committee of State Security, nominally responsible to the Council of Ministers), as the top security organization. In that switch, the MVD was virtually castrated and left with control over little more than prisons, slave labor camps, and municipal police. And none other than Serov, Khrushchev's crony and genocide expert, was made first chief of the KGB.

No sooner had Soviet security thus been "downgraded" than the world in general got a view of the KGB being no more than just another name for the Cheka, the OGPU, and the NKVD. In Berlin, in April, 1954, KGB agents kidnapped—and later exterminated—

[242]

Alexander Trushnovich, a leader of NTS (National Labor Union), an emigré organization. And there were many subsequent examples, in many countries, of the true character of the KGB. To name a few, there was the case of KGB Captain Nikolay Khokhlov, who defected in West Germany rather than assassinate NTS Frankfurt leader Georgy Okolovich and whom the KGB later tried to assassinate in turn. And there was the case of KGB agent Bogdan Stashinsky, convicted in West Germany of assassinating Ukrainian emigré leaders Lev Rebet and Stepan Bandera.

At home, Khrushchev's reorganization of the security under his direct control was followed by his further accretion of power. By February, 1955, he had the strength to boot out Malenkov as government chief, accusing him of having master-minded the "Leningrad Affair." In that fat man's place, he installed the deceptively fatherly looking Nikolay Bulganin, who later openly admitted to a shocked Tito that he had killed off a number of World War II army officers. That new "collective" team of Khrushchev the seeming clown and Bulganin, the handsomely white-haired and goateed "statesman," then proceeded to barnstorm an overly fascinated world. Launching his unsuccessful Siberian "virgin lands" program at home and making peace with Austria and Tito abroad, Khrushchev took his erstwhile teammate to a meaningless "Big-Four" conference in Geneva and tricked some of the world into believing his "peaceful coexistence" propaganda, under which he started Soviet penetration of the Middle East, Southeast Asia, the Far East, Africa, and Latin America, all the while making no concession whatsoever about Germany.

In February 1956, at the Twentieth Party Congress, Khrushchev further delighted the non-Communist world—and sowed the seeds for the future disruption of the Communist orbit—with his so-called secret speech denouncing Stalin. That was followed by the rehabilitation of some minor Soviet figures and some major—but dead—personalities in the satellites. No Soviet man of real importance, however, such as Trotsky, was restored to good standing. Additionally, the roles played by Khrushchev himself, and his current "collective" colleagues, in Stalin's atrocities were not even mentioned, of course.

Such "de-Stalinization" as that under his belt, Khrushchev next further hoodwinked the West by disbanding the Cominform, before departing in April, with Bulganin, for a visit to Britain. That junket was somewhat marred, however, because the British, at least, balked at allowing Khrushchev's top security dog, Serov, to attend the festivities.

The first sign of trouble from the denigration of authority implicit in the attack on Stalin came in June, 1956, in Poland with the Poznan riots. Khrushchev, however, was able to trot out a Stalin victim, Wladyslaw Gomulka, from prison and thus the day was saved. First mistakenly welcomed by the Poles as a "liberator," Gomulka followed Kremlin policy obediently for Khrushchev and his successors until the Polish party threw him out in 1970 after a wave of economic disturbances.

The next reaction to de-Stalinization—again based on the mistaken belief that the Twentieth Congress declaration meant Moscow was being more liberal—came in October, 1956, with the valiant, but unsuccessful attempt of the Hungarians to break loose from Kremlin control. Khrushchev's Western image suffered severely as he crushed that rising with brutal force. But in his own orbit, that action was approved by Peking especially, and even by Tito, albeit grudgingly. In charge locally with bringing the Hungarians to heel was Yury Andropov, Soviet "ambassador" to Budapest, a party *apparatchik* with some speciality in foreign affairs, later to become chief of the KGB and, still later, General Secretary.

In the spring of 1957, the MVD was further weakened—and Khrushchev's Serov thereby strengthened—by the return of frontier and other police to the control of the KGB. That, and the Communist world's acceptance of Khrushchev's firmness within the orbit —East Germany, Hungary, and elsewhere—greatly bolstered the rotund little man's position. As a result of that, plus smart political maneuvering, in June, 1957, he was able to get Central Committee approval of the ousting of his rivals and potential rivals from the Presidium. Labeling them the "antiparty group," he was able to dump into oblivion Molotov, Kaganovich, Malenkov, Dmitry Shepilov, Foreign Minister and onetime editor of *Pravda*, plus those two newcomers, Pervukhin and Saburov. Then in October, 1957, Khrushchev's—and the Soviet Union's—repute hit a new high with the launching of the Sputnik, the world's first man-made global satellite. Thus ahead in the still undeclared space race with the U.S.— Eisenhower was foolish enough to deprecate the Sputnik as no more than an orange—Soviet nationalism soared. And although Soviet scientists—and what they had garnered from German POWs—were responsible for that success, Khrushchev saw to it that he could bask in the reflected glory.

With a new aura of respect thus generated around him nationally and internationally, Khrushchev made his big power play in March 1958. He ousted the aging dodderer, Bulganin, and so reached the pinnacle attained by Stalin before him, that of both party and government chief. In December 1958, however, he made a move that still is unexplained and probably cost him his leadership. He dismissed Serov and sent him to head the GRU and to control Zhukov and the Armed Forces. It is true that Serov's intelligence quotient was not of the highest and his past activity in the genocide field was somewhat of a handicap. But it is also true that Serov, despite his obvious drawbacks, was intensely loyal to Khrushchev, and that is something that cannot be said about Alexander Shelepin, the young and ambitious propaganda and Komsomol *apparatchik* Khrushchev put in place of Serov at the head of KGB. Why Khrushchev violated such a prime prescription of Soviet power, by replacing a trustworthy and obedient security chief for one who could betray him, still needs an answer. But it may be that the little man was not as astute as he was touted to be.

On the surface, though, the appointment of Shelepin looked like a good thing, both at home and abroad. Shelepin had no police background and thereby accorded a new—but fraudulent—look to the KGB, letting some wishful thinkers believe that Soviet security was becoming more liberal. And the same—doubtlessly purposeful—misunderstanding at first applied to the new penal codes instituted in the Soviet Union and its subsections in 1957–58. Under those revisions, a political crime as such no longer was listed. Ergo, there were no more political prisoners, a hypothesis that was just one gigantic lie. But, in the place of political crimes, the new codes mentioned such misdeeds as "anti-Soviet agitation and propaganda" and "antisocial parasitism," convenient catchalls for those considered offensive to the regime and its leaders. Nor was there any amelioration of that veteran Soviet "legal" standby—economic "crime." From the time of Stalin's death until 1964 alone, some three hundred Soviet citizens had been shot for economic "crimes."

In September, 1959, Khrushchev reached the high-water mark of his career, both nationally and internationally, with a state visit to the U.S. He conferred with President Eisenhower and toured the host country from coast to coast. In the course of the trip, he met and talked with ordinary Americans of all classes—farmers, industrial workers, and businessmen—and pretty well succeeded in his primary objective of ending the cold war that Stalin had started between the two powers. Many Americans swallowed his initiative, practically without question. One result was the increase of American tourists of all categories to the Soviet Union. Another was the telling psychological victory of getting the average American to take a more sympathetic view of the Soviet Union and of persuading many a short-memoried and ostrich-headed American analyst to stop using the term satellite when referring to the states of Soviet-controlled eastern Europe.

But those successes were attained in the West at perhaps too great a price. Peking, long suspicious of Khrushchev's "friendly" approach to the West, and especially to the U.S., started countering Moscow directly. Mao Tse-tung started nibbling at the Himalayan frontier of India which was a beneficiary of Soviet technical aid in great quantity. Khrushchev retorted by halting Soviet assistance to Communist China. Thereupon the situation between the two great Asiatic nations degenerated more and more and was marked by clashes between troops along their mutual frontiers, direct Peking demands for Chinese territory seized by Tsarist imperialists and by thinly veiled Russian threats of massive retaliation. Khrushchev never managed to extricate himself from that mess with the Chinese, nor, as of this writing, have his successors succeeded in doing so.

In May 1960, Khrushchev dumped his newly won "friendship" with the U.S.—and in the course showed himself less than a statesman—when a high-flying American intelligence plane was shot down over the Soviet Union. Khrushchev knew that such planes had been flying over his nation during and well before his visit to the U.S. And he also must have been aware that such an observation technique was almost obsolete and that soon both the U.S. and the Soviet Union would be monitoring each other by earth satellites. Enough had been accomplished by shooting down the American plane. But Khrushchev chose to make much of Eisenhower's awkward reaction and used the incident as an excuse to stalk out of a "Big-Four" meeting in Paris. That tempestuous gesture may have paid some minor dividends in Peking. But it gained him no advantage in the West and little, if any, at home, where the Soviet man was struggling to change his image from that of an uncouth fellow in bell-bottomed trousers to that of a polished and cultured gentleman. And later that year, the Soviet Union's top man was uncouth, indeed. During a visit to the U.N. in New York—but studiedly not to the U.S.—the bald-headed, fat little man embarrassed diplomats, including his own, by removing a shoe and banging it on his desk to show disapproval of a speech.

Perhaps in continued pique at the West, perhaps in hopes of buttering up Peking, Khrushchev struck at the West in August, 1961, at one of its most vulnerable and defenseless points, Berlin. He sealed a longtime breach in the Iron Curtain. He had his East German satellite—backed by the Red Army—erect that primitive monstrosity, the Berlin Wall, to divide the Soviet and western sectors of that great German city. The Wall was followed by a plethora of Communist explanations, excuses, and attempted rationalizations, none worth repeating. Whatever benefits Khrushchev and the Communists said accrued from the Wall were more than countered by the gross picture of the Soviet system in general it gave the West and millions of Western visitors. Unfortunately, however, the Soviets, so long inured to such devices, are basically incapable of understanding the effect the Wall has made on the civilized world, a world they try to ape with more operas and ballets. Khrushchev, himself, posed for photographers at the horror.

With the Berlin Wall as his personal monument, Khrushchev next drew attention to himself at his party's Twenty-second Congress. Once more he denounced Stalin. But he gave no pertinent new information. His discourse was little more than a rehash of what he had stated five years earlier. Nor were any significant personalities rehabilitated as the result of it. Its only effect was to eliminate what Western wits called the "gruesome twosome" in the Kremlin mausoleum by having Stalin's corpse removed from its viewing place alongside Lenin's.

Stalin thus further de-sanctified, his successor then turned to tidying up his security situation at home, but not wisely. In November 1961, he allowed Shelepin, who had long groused about his political future being limited by dead-end work as KGB chief, to leave security work and become a Secretary of the Central Committee. As new boss of the KGB, he installed Vladimir Semichastny, a Shelepin toady and fellow Komsomol *apparatchik*, whose chief recommendation seemed to be that he was a friend of Khrushchev's son-in-law, Aleksey Adzhubey, another Komsomolchik. Although extremely ambitious, Semichastny was not too bright a young man. That defect was countered by the appointment of the professional Zakharov, chief of the Guard Directorate, as KGB Deputy Chairman. Although he could not have known of it at the time, Khrushchev's use of the politically ambitious Shelepin and Semichastny as his security chiefs, and the professionally apolitical Zakharov, stripped him of the police protection that Stalin had always had and that his successor could not do without in time of political crisis. Khrushchev was to learn that later—but too late. At the time of the Semichastny appointment, however, his attention seemed riveted on further downgrading the police arm. To do that, he disbanded the MVD (but its elimination proved only temporary) and replaced it with the MOOP, or the Ministry for Preservation of Public Order.

At the end of 1961, Khrushchev's loud mouth and uncontrolled tongue led him into another foreign policy error. He called Albania's Enver Hoxha a Stalinist. By that expression of opinion, he opened the first crack in the Soviet monolith since Tito's defection. Albania switched from the Soviet to the Chinese orbit. Although Albania was a triflingly small country in area and population, its defection sealed the schism between Moscow and Peking.

As a result of that and increasing Chinese intransigence, by 1962 Khrushchev may well have been getting desperate and in fear that Soviet hegemony was about to crack wide open at the seams unless he took some major step. Whatever the cause, he made a bold but losing gamble. In October, using the same type of plane the Soviets had shot down in 1960, the U.S. caught Khrushchev red-handed installing missiles in Cuba on the very doorstep of America. For anxious hours, the world tottered on the very brink of a massive global conflict until Khrushchev obeyed the demands of President John Kennedy and agreed to remove his missiles from Cuba.

That showdown as good as finished Khrushchev. But, except for a few Chinese sneers, he paid no immediate penalty. His party and nation had been shocked into temporary immobility by the defeat of its leader's stratagem. But from then on, Khrushchev kept his nose out of major foreign policy matters. Instead, he concentrated on home-bred culture. In November, 1962, he allowed Alexander Solzhenitsyn—the finest Soviet writer of the post-Stalin era and perhaps an all-time great literary figure—to publish "One Day in the Life of Ivan Denisovich." Publication of that fictionalized account of the horrors of slave labor camps rocked the Soviet Union and many people abroad. And its effects at home proved to be like the ripples from a stone cast into a pond, everexpanding, and for the Soviet leadership dangerously so. Earlier, Khrushchev had refused to let another outstanding Soviet author, Boris Pasternak, accept the Nobel Prize. But he probably viewed writing of the Solzhenitsyn genre as a cathartic of sorts that he could prescribe or halt as the occasion demanded. After all, he had a stable of such "tame" writers as the poet, Yevgeny Yevtushenko. However, be that as it may, the temporary freeing of Solzhenitsyn's work let loose a long pent-up intellectual flood that continued, albeit "illegally" in Soviet terms, long after Khrushchev. And it may well be that such courageous new intellectuals who dare prison terms, slave labor camps, and even death in their opposition to the injustices of the Soviet regime, may be the forerunners of the same kind of ground swell that caused the downfall of the comparatively less oppressive tsardom. Only time will tell that. But, as the tsars before them, Soviet leaders may come to find the threat of overthrow by the masses a greater danger than the internecine palace revolts and struggles for power. However, looking at the historical record, one may well believe it will take another millennium for that to come to pass. Odds for a Soviet leader surviving are still greater than for many a motorist on American, European, and Japanese highways.

Khrushchev's image suffered another severe blow—but at home, primarily—in the spring of 1963 with the trial and execution of Colonel Oleg Penkovskiy, a veteran GRU intelligence officer. From the disclosures that accompanied that, the Soviet Union, and the world in general, learned that the West had long been aware of many major Moscow policy decisions. And they made Soviet intelligence a bit of a laughing stock. Khrushchev was probably too shaken and too worried to come up with one of his usual offhand reactions. Instead, he waited almost a year, or until March, 1964, before dismissing and sending off into relative oblivion his old crony, Serov, the GRU chief. But, by that time the fat little party and government leader was doing no more—to use his own earthy idiom—than closing the barn door long after his horse was well away.

Khrushchev was holidaying at the Black Sea in October, 1964, when the axe finally fell. Taking advantage of his absence from Moscow, Mikhail Suslov (like a disloyal boyar in the days of Muscovy) had convinced the majority of the Presidium that Khrushchev must go. And a hastily garnered somewhat rump majority of the Central Committee had agreed to go along with that decision. A telephone message from the Presidium—and probably at least one from a cohort still loyal to him—advised him that he was urgently wanted back in Moscow. When Khrushchev arrived at the resort airport for the trip, a special plane manned by KGB personnel, not his personal aircraft, was awaiting him. And when he reached Moscow, he was met by none other than his defecting KGB chiefs, present and former, Semichastny and Shelepin. Another surprise also awaited Khrushchev in the capital. In his absence, the personal telephone numbers of all the party hierarchs he might have called to rally to his support—as he had used the Central Committee to wrest control from the "antiparty" group in 1957—had been changed. Probably stunned on learning of that quick change, Khrushchev realized that all was as good as over. He went meekly before his "peers," who removed him from both party and government leadership at his own "request" because of "advanced age and poor health." The real reasons for his ouster, however, were his assumption of one-man rule, his major setbacks—China, Cuba, and the Siberian "virgin lands" flop—and perhaps also his uncouth conduct in public, particularly in the West.

Two uninspiring and mediocre *apparatchiks* took over. Leonid Brezhnev, whose specialties were agriculture and metallurgy, was made party leader. And Aleksey Kosygin, a financial technocrat of sorts, became chief of government. As a reward for their roles in betraying and rounding up Khrushchev, Semichastny was made a full member of the Central Committee and Shelepin was advanced to the Presidium.

Quite ironically, the day after Khrushchev's ouster, the Chinese Communists successfully exploded their first atomic device. And possibly directly connected with his overthrow was the mysterious and fatal crash in Belgrade a few days later of a Russian plane carrying the chief of staff of the Soviet armed forces.

After Khrushchev was retired to putter in his garden and publish his reminiscences—but only a carefully weeded part of them—some in the West, especially those fascinated by his admittedly interesting personality, were inclined to praise him, compare him to Peter the

Great and Catherine the Great and credit him with liberalizing and modernizing Stalin's Russia by great leaps and bounds. Some of that, of course, is very true. But also, it should not be forgotten that Khrushchev crushed the East German rising, was ready to do the same to the Poles until Gomulka took over for him, ruthlessly suppressed the Hungarian revolt and erected the Berlin Wall.

Until spring of 1966, the new Soviet regime muddled along in the guise of another "collective leadership." But then in March and April, at the Twenty-third Party Congress, Brezhnev got himself advanced to "General Secretary" of the party, a title held before only by Stalin. That marked the end of the "collective leadership" in fact, although for political and psychological reasons the term itself was not discarded.

Brezhnev's slow and careful move to the top was also marked by an ever-so-gradual shift to re-Stalinization. Some of that erosion may have been caused by a wish to curry favor with the Chinese Communists who have never removed Stalin from their pantheon. But in the main, it seems to have been caused by Brezhnev's realization that at least some of Stalin's techniques are necessary for retaining top power under the Soviet system. In that way, although dull in the extreme as a personality, Brezhnev has shown himself as more· astute than his predecessor. And in keeping with the new-old fashion, the Twenty-third Congress also changed the name of the Presidium back to Politburo.

Good evidence of the return to the hard line was given even before that congress. In February, 1966, the Western world in particular was shocked at the five and seven years at forced labor given respectively to Soviet writers Yuli Daniel and Andrey Sinyavsky, for doing no more than publishing in the West, at a rigged and completely KGB-controlled "trial" in Moscow. That was only one of a number of actions taken against a small but courageous group of intellectual dissidents by the Brezhnev regime. And some of those unfortunates suffered even more arbitrary treatment. They were dispatched, without trial, to insane asylums, a practice initiated by Nicholas I, and aped by Khrushchev as well.

By May 1967, Brezhnev was well enough seated in the saddle to get along without his hand-me-down KGB chief. He dumped Semichastny by giving him the ridiculously trifling post of First Deputy Premier of the Ukraine. After all, Semichastny had betrayed Khrushchev and he could just as easily do the same to his successor. As the new KGB chairman, Brezhnev installed Yury Andropov, the same "diplomat" who had distinguished himself helping crush the Hungarian rebels. Like his immediate predecessors, Andropov had no police background. But he was made a candidate member of the Politburo, becoming the first security chief to reach that upper stratum since Beria. And a month later, Brezhnev also dumped that other turncoat, Shelepin, sending him into oblivion as Chairman of the "Trades Union" Council, a meaningless post in the Soviet Union where trade unions, as such, do not exist.

Zakharov, the security professional (whose face became familiar in the West when he served as chief bodyguard during Khrushchev's visit to the U.S.) continued for a while under Andropov as Deputy Chairman of the KGB. But he was later sent to the sticks in the Crimea and subsequently was charged with genocide by a group of Tatars.

Almost immediately after that shake-up of the KGB command, Brezhnev had his attention well diverted with foreign affairs. In June, 1967, that sector of Soviet policy suffered a stunning defeat when their Arab protégés were roundly routed by little Israel in a mere six days of battle. Only the diplomatic intervention of the U.S. —a move for which future historians may come up with a good answer, and a better one than that world war was thereby prevented —restrained the vastly outnumbered, victorious Israelis from sweeping on to Cairo and all the other Arab capitals.

Less than two weeks after that defeat, Brezhnev in effect shrugged it off by sending Kosygin to the U.S. for a meeting with President Lyndon Johnson. Absolutely nothing at all came from that get-together, either for the Soviet Union or the U.S. But a pose of palavering with the other major power did help somewhat to overshadow and assuage the Soviet setback in the Middle East.

A little more than a year later, in August, 1968, Brezhnev had his Red Army win the kind of "war" his Arab protégés could not. With the support of Warsaw pact forces—for appearances' sake—he invaded helpless Czechoslovakia because it was showing long-belated signs of becoming more liberal. The infamy of that action will be long remembered by civilized men. But in a minor way—a very minor one indeed—that invasion and brutal occupation had one beneficial effect. It removed the cobwebs, formed by Soviet propaganda, from the eyes of many Westerners. With the Czechoslovak invasion, the term Soviet satellite again became current.

The intellectual dissidence to Brezhnev's re-Stalinization, both nationally and internationally, and perhaps the shame of some Soviet citizens about Czechoslovakia, reached a peak of sorts in January 1969. And it took the form of the first publicly witnessed attempt against a Soviet leader since Fanya Kaplan shot at Lenin. The scene was the gates of the Kremlin, almost impregnable under the tsars and commissars. A cosmonaut motorcade was about to enter. Suddenly shots rang out. A KGB driver was killed and an escort was wounded. But the assailant, wearing a police uniform, had made a mistake. He had fired at a vehicle carrying a cosmonaut who looked remarkably like Brezhnev, not realizing that the party leader was farther to the rear in the motorcade. The assailant was overwhelmed and arrested on the spot. Only months later was a meager report given about him, "information" that did not even include his name. He was declared "insane," but what happened to him is not known.

However, the real importance of the incident is that for the first time in decades someone was actually seen trying to kill a Soviet leader. (In comparison, all the reports of "attempts" against Stalin seemed to be the fiction they most likely were. And in such a light, equally doubtful are the less-publicized reports of attempts against Khrushchev in Minsk, in Kiev—some accounts say Lvov—and in Archangel.) Also very important to the Brezhnev attempt is how his assailant managed to position himself where he was and how he obtained his weapon and ammunition. The approaches to the Kremlin are most severely controlled, and especially when a party hierarch is in the vicinity. Additionally, only someone with top clearance could have carried a weapon and live ammunition on such an occasion.

That attempt against Brezhnev may well prove to be the only part of his career to be accorded a place in subsequent history. So far, as compared to Lenin, Stalin, and even Khrushchev, his achievements have been slim indeed. He wasted away the tremendous lead scored under Khrushchev in the space race with the U.S. By 1969, the Soviet Union was able to do no more than watch on television as America landed the first of a series of men on the moon. Nor has he made any progress whatsoever in the great struggle with Communist China. Instead, he was only able to watch—again on television—as America's President Richard Nixon visited Peking.

CHAPTER IV

Pre-Stalin Communist Bodyguards

1. RIFFRAFF, BOBTAILS, AND BUSYBODIES

When Lenin seized power in November, 1917, the Okhrana had already been eliminated. The other government security organization, the armed forces, was at the height of disintegration. And the Bolsheviks had little concept of the requirements for the personal safety of their hierarchy. For up until that time, the SDs had had no real need to protect their leadership. The Tsarist regime, while fearing the SRs and doing its best to wipe them out, had always regarded the SDs more as harmless dilettantes, or mere word-mongers, and had somewhat countenanced them as the decided lesser of two evils. Additionally, the SDs had not used terror tactics in their quest for power and so could not readily conceive of terror being used against them once they had gained their ends.

Therefore, the Lenin in power had no more real security than he had had when in exile. And the problem was increased by the fact that he himself struck the pose of needing and wanting no personal protection. As the result then of that combination of factors, throughout his scant seven years of dictatorship he actually had less genuine personal security than most of the leaders of the decidedly more politically settled democratic states.

That did not mean, however, that Lenin had no bodyguards. In fact, he had a plethora of them. But, practically to a man, every one of those many individuals was completely inexperienced in such security work. And most of them were too lowbrow, or otherwise lacking in capacity, to have done the job well even if they had been properly trained. So, it was more or less by good fortune alone that Lenin escaped a violent end. And that despite the fact that in the years following his death Communist mythologists have ground out thousands of words about how this or that good comrade saved the sainted leader's life on one or another occasion. Every one of those accounts is exaggeration to fiction. And, realists that they must have been, subsequent Soviet police officers in charge of their leaders' personal security probably almost shuddered when they read of the "exploits" of such predecessors.

But, unqualified as they were, those bodyguards of Lenin were under the organizational control of the Cheka, GPU, and OGPU, in exactly the same way as successive bodyguards formed a part—but an elite and practically separate part—of the NKVD, MGB, and KGB.

However, under the Lenin regime, and especially its early part, the Cheka concentrated on its bloody course of wiping out the actual and suspected opponents of bolshevism throughout the length and breadth of Russia. The best Cheka brains were expended on that campaign. Relatively little attention was given to the protection of Lenin and the other hierarchs.

As a result, a veritable rabble of misfits and hangers-on was able to install itself as Lenin's bodyguards. And the selection and direction of that sorry lot was assumed from time to time by any one of the more officious of Lenin's cronies.

The guarding of Lenin's person started, of course, well before he had seized power. Immediately upon his arrival in Russia in early 1917, after the Germans had sent him home to help them by stirring up his revolt, a coterie of several dozen stalwarts gathered around him to secure his safety. After the Bolsheviks' abortive rising of July, 1917, those worthies supplied Petrograd apartments and homes to hide Lenin out from Kerensky, furnished him with false documents or otherwise aided his temporary escape across the Finnish border. Later, the Communists listed those volunteer guards in history books. Their names run from A to Z and include a few women. Some of them guarded Lenin more formally later at Smolny, after he had seized power. Many of them died as victims of Stalin's purges, but some lived on, surprisingly, to die of natural causes in the last decade. Among them was one name important enough to be included in most non-Communist history. It is that of Sergey Alliluyev, one of those who hid Lenin from Kerensky, and who, probably thanks to the fact he later became Stalin's father-in-law, survived until a peaceful death in 1945.

Once established in power, however, Lenin—like it or not—had need of more systematized arrangements for guarding himself and his top lieutenants. Immediately after Lenin and the other Bolshevik leaders took over the Smolny institute as their command post, their so-called Military Revolutionary Committee, led by a defrocked Ukrainian priest, one Nikolay Podvoysky, organized the first real Soviet bodyguard unit. It was composed mainly of Latvian soldiers. (Other Latvians participated later in the murder of Nicholas II and his family and Latvians seemed to qualify as disinterested butcher-boys for the Bolsheviks in much the same way as some Koreans served the Japanese in World War II POW camps.) That original Latvian guard unit numbered some one thousand at its height. An infantry group, it was reinforced—if that be the term—by a machine-gun detachment, a motley array of sailors and rifle-toting workers, drivers who had commandeered cars of aristocrats and wealthy *bourgeoisie*, motorcycle riders, and even bicyclists. In charge of that conglomeration, and thereby as commandant of Smolny, Podvoysky installed a Baltic seaman, one Pavel Malkov, who survived to write his memoirs in Khrushchev's time. To say the least, it was hardly an elite, or even a properly organized guard for the new ruler of All the Russias.

Part of the reason for the shoddy organization of those Smolny guards lay in the fact that too many officious Bolsheviks, completely inexperienced in security work, stuck their noses in one way or another into the bodyguard arrangements. Additionally, there were also probably a few too many Latvians mixed up in it, politically or militarily. The biggest busybody of all was a veteran but somewhat dilettante Communist and boon-companion of Lenin, who was endowed with the name of Vladimir Bonch-Bruyevich. Somehow, he was also a sort of commandant of Smolny and would give orders of a kind to Malkov, when the mood struck him. Dzerzhinsky, of course, was also around then, very much so. He, too, would give an occasional order to Malkov, but his main attention was on the Cheka that he soon formed. Besides that Pole, there was also another Russian somewhat superior to the obviously unfortunate Malkov, one Fedor Bykov, who served briefly and without distinction as commissar of

Smolny. And Sverdlov, the first Soviet president, also delighted in giving the bodyguards orders on any and all occasions. But it was non-Russians, especially Latvians, who somewhat as soldiers of fortune, managed to call most of the turns for the Smolny guards. An Armenian, Varlaam Avanesov (also called Martirosov, thereby matching Lenin and Stalin in having a revolutionary code name), used the organization of Lenin's bodyguards as the stepping-stone to the higher stratum of the Cheka and later into Stalin's entourage. But Avanesov was quite a minority as compared to a quartet of Latvians, who pushed their careers as the result of direct or indirect connections with the business of guarding Lenin. One was Eduard Berzin who joined Avanesov in Dzerzhinsky's command. Another was the somewhat mysterious Martyn Latsis, also known as Yan Sudrabs, who later led the Cheka terror in the Ukraine. Somewhat equally mysterious was Yakov Peters, the Cheka subchief who investigated the Lockhart and Fanya Kaplan cases. And there was Karl Peterson, commissar of the Latvian regiment—from which the Smolny guards were drawn—and briefly Military commissar of the short-lived first Soviet government of Latvia. Only the last, Peterson, died a natural death, of tuberculosis in the mid-twenties. The other three met their ends in Stalin's purges.

Therefore, with that mishmash of personnel and "commanders," the early Lenin bodyguards distinctly suffered from a bad case of too many generals and not enough soldiers, or in North American parlance, too many chiefs and not enough Indians.

Not really knowing what to do under such circumstances, or having much actual authority either, Malkov concentrated more on keeping house for the Lenin entourage than on guarding the leadership. He saw to the food, the heat, and the comfort of quarters at Smolny, duties which were also assumed by subsequent Soviet bodyguards, up until the present day. When not busy at that, Malkov joined fellow security men in hunting down SRs, chasing Anarchists, or raiding suspected hideouts of *bourgeoisie* or "counterrevolutionaries."

Those punitive sweeps in which the Smolny commandant participated were not much better organized than small boys' cops and robbers games. But they were still deadly serious, since the victims were either killed or imprisoned. Malkov shared those outings with three groups, which also had vaguely specified tasks of guarding the leadership: the Latvian regiment from which most of his guards had been drawn, the so-called CHON (Chasti Osobogo Naznacheniya), or units of special purpose, and a conglomeration of gun-toting, but otherwise idle Communist recruits who later were organized into what is now called the First Dzerzhinsky Division. The Latvian organization was the shortest lived. It was disbanded as politically unreliable in late 1920, after Latvia wrested itself from Soviet control and became independent. CHON, according to Communist accounts, composed only of Communists and Communist youth groups, but actually mainly made up of freed or escaped common criminals, lasted only a few years longer, or until the windup of the civil war in 1924. The Dzerzhinsky organization, however, became permanent, being forged into a more or less crack unit to bolster the Kremlin bodyguards in the event of a massive attack on the Soviet leadership. Its successor, the Dzerzhinsky Division, was signally honored in 1968 at the fiftieth anniversary of the Bolshevik seizure of power. Despite such honor, that organization has never been called upon to carry out the duties for which it was formed. But, its mere presence must be a comfort to Soviet usurpers of power who thus can count on massive protection against any possible uprising of what Communist ideologues once called the "downtrodden masses."

Because of the extremely poor organization of those early units, the Smolny guards, the Latvian soldiers, the CHON (whose chief assigned task was to guard such government installations as banks, communications centers, and railroad stations), and the Dzerzhinsky group, it is practically impossible to speak of their uniforms as such. Some had no uniforms at all and were garbed in motley assortments of civilian caps and greatcoats. A few wore outfits they had inherited or garnered from the armed forces and to those they had added the hussar-like, lateral cloth chest strips and the peculiar peaked cap affected by the early Red Army. Eliminated, of course, were the shoulder boards and other tsarist insignia of rank. For such insignia, a system of diamond-shaped collar pieces was substituted. And that system, in one form or another, lasted until World War II, when the Soviet armed forces—and police—resumed the use of shoulder boards and other internationally recognizable insignia of rank. Equally haphazard was the weaponry of the early bodyguards. Some were truly loaded for bear, weighted down with bloodthirsty-looking conglomerations of rifles with long bayonets, pistols, and swords.

Others affected sabres, which except for Budyenny's cavalry, saw no practical use beyond the hacking off of heads of defenseless victims.

For Malkov's Smolny bodyguards, basic security measures were just as hit-or-miss as were their uniforms and weapons. At the beginning, nobody entering Smolny—even those approaching the precincts of Lenin and other hierarchs—was really checked. If a person wore dirty to nondescript clothes and appeared like a worker or a peasant, he was passed. On the other hand, if he were neatly dressed and looked like a bourgeois, he was challenged. Only later was a pass system devised, but that was so crude it could have been easily counterfeited by anyone wanting to make the slightest effort. And, pass or no pass, once inside Smolny a visitor was free to go everywhere he wished without question. True, guards with bayoneted rifles stood at the doors of the quarters of Lenin and other leaders, but most of those stalwarts were so vainglorious and overcome with the honor of guarding a Soviet hierarch that more attention was centered on themselves than on the visitors.

All those drawbacks considered, it was therefore far from surprising that Lenin could have been reported shot at while driving through the streets of Petrograd in January, 1918, with no other guard than an extremely amateur chauffeur. Absolutely no surveillance had been made of Lenin's route and no units were nearby to go to the help of the Soviet leader. If that truly was an assassination attempt, rather than stray shots in a completely lawless capital, the would-be killers were just as feckless as Lenin's bodyguards.

Despite that possible attempt against Lenin, it would be unfair to be too severe in appraising his guards, knowing the handicaps under which they labored. No sooner had security at Smolny been organized to the scant extent then possible, than Lenin disrupted everything with his sudden move to Moscow's Kremlin in March 1918. For that trip, Malkov's guards and other Latvians, most decidedly organized on a catch-as-catch-can basis, "secured" the rail stations and route. Again—that time because the decision to move south was a hurried, scurried affair, a runaway from a possible German advance on Petrograd—there was no surveillance of the route. And an advance train had not been sent ahead, not only to clear the route but to make sure it was even viable. Instead, guards and commissars all packed into the same train, like schoolboys on an outing. As could have been expected, therefore, on the way to Moscow, the Soviet travelers encountered other travelers on another train. Once more, Communist mythologists seized on that trip to fabricate that purely chance encounter into a tall story about Lenin's being saved from "counterrevolutionaries" by his brave guards. However, since the Lenin entourage arrived in Moscow completely unscathed, the fact of the matter appears to be that frightened guards unnecessarily roughed-up a chance trainload of casual travelers.

Once arrived at the Kremlin, Malkov, the first Kremlin Commandant under the Soviets, got his marching orders from Sverdlov. He was told to increase the number of his Latvians, to the size of a regiment, if need be. And he was told to take over the household chores of the hierarchs, to see to their rationing, quartering, and other needs, in much the same way that successive Soviet body-guards have acted as "cradle-to-grave" housekeepers of successive Soviet leaders. Sverdlov also instructed Malkov to heed the advice of Avanesov and Dzerzhinsky. Bonch-Bruyevich was equally free with advice and again contributed to fragmentation of the Soviet body-guard chain of command. But probably feeling more secure in his position, Malkov rejected part of the advice given him, at least some proferred by Bonch-Bruyevich. When the latter told the Kremlin commandant to stop body-searching monks and nuns being expelled from quarters in the fortress, Malkov refused. He said he took orders from Lenin and Sverdlov only and told Bonch-Bruyevich to stop interfering.

Besides removing the clerics and other squatters from his new command post, Malkov also had the task of not only cleaning up the Kremlin but also of removing from it all vestiges of Tsarist rule. It was he who took down the Romanov double-eagles, crosses, and other religious devices—later replaced by Communist insignias—from the many towers. And it was Malkov who helped Lenin, Sverdlov, Avanesov, and other hierarchs personally pull down the monument erected on the spot where the Grand Duke Sergey had been assassinated in 1905. After that tour de force, Lenin had all the rest of the Tsarist memorial statuary removed as well. But he did not do those jobs personally. He left them to Malkov. But Lenin specified that one old regime statue was to be left intact, as a work of art—that to Peter the Great in Petrograd (Leningrad). To be sure, most of the Tsarist monuments removed from the Kremlin and elsewhere were later replaced with statues to Communists of note. And in the course of that cleanup, Lenin also instructed Malkov to get the clock working again atop the Spassky tower and to change its chimes from church music. In the place of that, the clock was to ring out the "International," the Socialist workingman's anthem, taken over by the Communists, music that probably will be heard from Spassky tower as long as Communist rule lasts.

When not busy at such distinctly nonguard-like duties, Malkov and his Latvians (from the Ninth Latvian regiment) spent much time in forays with the Cheka and other police units, just as they had done from Smolny. They were frequently given the job of raiding public markets, in search of "speculators." On one of those ventures out of the Kremlin, they were shot up by trigger-happy militiamen, guarding the residence of hierarchs, who thought the Latvians were attacking them. And, of course, they took part in the city-wide shoot up that followed the assassination of the German ambassador, Count Mirbach, and the ill-fated SR take-over of July 1918.

With Malkov and his men thus occupied with so many chores completely extraneous to the business of being bodyguards, it is no small wonder that a half blind, would-be SR assassin, and a woman at that, Fanya Kaplan, was able to wound Lenin seriously when he visited a Moscow factory at the end of August, 1918. On that occasion, again, a pretty incompetent chauffeur was Lenin's only pretense for a bodyguard. At least, however, the guard did manage to seize and hold Kaplan after the act, although it should not be overlooked that Kaplan probably could not see well enough to make her getaway. But so far as Malkov was concerned—and by his personal account—all he contributed was pillows for the wounded Lenin and much clucking and wringing of hands.

Despite his obvious incompetency as a commandant of bodyguards, Malkov was called upon a few days later to dispose of Kaplan, who, of course, never stood trial. All his orders regarding Kaplan— from her transfer from the Lubyanka to a Kremlin basement, to her execution—were given by Avanesov. Therefore, since Avanesov was a toady of Stalin, it is not beyond the realm of probability that Kaplan's summary execution was the Georgian's first "legal" killing of note. And some substantiation is given to that suspicion by the existence of spurious accounts—somewhat like those about Anastasia, the daughter of Nicholas II—that Kaplan was not killed, but lived on to a ripe old age. The facts about Kaplan's death however, are quite

clear, if Malkov's memoirs, published at the height of the Khrushchev era, are to be believed. That first Kremlin commandant wrote
that he, himself, shot Kaplan with his service revolver. All that
Malkov omitted was that he shot his victim in the back of the head
while she was being held by his Latvian "bodyguards."

As a result of that nearly successful attempt against Lenin, someone in the Soviet hierarchy, apparently Dzerzhinsky, finally decided
that a force better than Latvian soldiers was needed to guard the
leader. That impression is not gained from Dzerzhinsky, who left no
memoirs, but again from Malkov. In detailing, ad nauseam, how he
selected the estate at Gorki for Lenin to recuperate—and later die
in—Malkov wrote, "Dzerzhinsky chose ten Cheka men to guard
Gorki and I had to supervise them." The reference to supervision is
probably mostly Malkov vanity. In all probability, those ten Chekists
were under direct Dzerzhinsky control finally, while Malkov had no
more to do with this improved variety of bodyguard than supplying
them with rations and meeting their other needs.

Typically, within hours after the Lenin attempt, Malkov instead of
being instructed to guarantee that nothing further happened to the
leader, was given another extracurricular and relatively inconsequential assignment. Peters, the Cheka subchief, summoned him to
the Lubyanka and ordered him to make the predawn arrest of Bruce
Lockhart, the British entrepreneur. That arrest was purposefully
coincidental. Hours earlier, Sverdlov had capitalized on the Lenin
attempt by decreeing the *Red Terror* to wipe out all possible opponents at home. And the Cheka was using the same excuse to make
it appear the Soviets were also beset by international enemies. The
memoirs of Malkov dutifully give great detail of all the routine Soviet
charges against Lockhart, even though it is most apparent that the
ex-seaman had no knowledge of the facts and purpose of the fabrication against the Britisher at the time. Only one part of that incident
remains baffling: why Malkov was selected to make the Lockhart
arrest instead of the Cheka, which had plenty of men available for
the job. Perhaps he was chosen because he bore the title of Kremlin
Commandant and the arrest, therefore, would look more "official."

The Kaplan attempt against Lenin also wrote finis to the Latvians'
sinecure in the Kremlin. Doubtlessly, their inefficiency as guards was
the cause of their removal, even though it was garbed in all the usual
Communist double-talk and hiding of the truth, with Malkov quoting

Sverdlov as saying the Latvian comrades should be given an opportunity of striking at the White Guard "scum." And at first, it had been rumored that the Ninth Latvian regiment might be replaced with the Second Latvians. But the upshot was that Latvians were dropped entirely as Kremlin bodyguards in September, 1918. (And a little more than two years later, most all the Soviets' Latvian butcher men were given shorter shrift when they became politically unreliable after Latvia's declaration of independence.)

2. THE FIRST REAL COMMUNIST BODYGUARDS

Instead of Latvians, Malkov was given an odd group of Communists and workers—whose chief distinction was that most of them were Russians—or what was called the First Machine-Gun Courses trainees. Evidently the firing practice within Kremlin walls of that outfit soon got on the nerves of the party hierarchs. Within months, the machine-gun apprentices were replaced by cadets of the newly formed armed forces military academy. Those cadets remained in the Kremlin, but not long as bodyguards, until Stalin removed them to other quarters near Moscow in the thirties.

The ten Cheka men who had guarded Lenin at Gorki were assigned to the same duties at the Kremlin after the end of the Soviet leader's first period of convalescence in the country. But, even though those ten were vastly superior to the conglomeration that Malkov had first commanded, they were often almost equally ineffective. The main reason was that Lenin, despite the Kaplan incident, so persisted in the game of sneaking away from his guards that more of their effort was spent in keeping an eye on him than on those who might do him harm. Additionally, even when Lenin was accompanied by a bodyguard in travels outside the Kremlin, he would never permit another car carrying guards to join his group. Therefore, the lone guard with him had no support whatever in event of any serious trouble.

As a very natural result of that recalcitrance on the part of Lenin, the Soviet leader, his bodyguard, and his sister were waylaid by plain, ordinary bandits on a trip to the Sokolniki area (in those days, on the outskirts of Moscow) to a sanitorium to visit the ailing Krupskaya. And the bodyguard with him had to serve more as a servant than a guard. Lenin had planned to surprise his wife with a can of milk he had garnered somewhere. The can had a faulty lid. The guard had the task of holding the lid on the can so the milk did not slosh over. Therefore, when the bandits stopped the car on a snow-covered road in January, 1919, the unfortunate bodyguard was not even able to draw his revolver. Lenin tried to intervene by displaying his identity paper as ruler of All the Russias, but the bandits did not even bother to read it. At gunpoint, the bandits forced Lenin and the other occupants out of the car and drove away with it. Lenin had to walk the rest of the way to the sanitorium where he was finally found by a worried Malkov and the alarmed Cheka. Lenin's car was later found abandoned, and bandits, who may, or may not have been those who held up the Soviet leader, were caught. In his memoirs, Malkov made a rather revealing comment about that incident. He said the bandits had not known who was traveling in the car and had not recognized Lenin, adding, "this explains why Lenin escaped with his life." What it really explains is that the holdup men were not just bandits, but more likely SRs or possibly White Guards.

After the Sokolniki mishap, Malkov more or less faded into the background and devoted most of his time to Kremlin administrative and household chores. It was Avanesov who really ran the bodyguard operation until Dzerzhinsky moved into the Kremlin and made the bodyguards an integral part of the Cheka under his direct control.

Malkov's less than distinguished career as first commandant of the Kremlin for the Communists ended after the Ninth Party Congress in April 1920. He was put into the limbo of an administrative post that had nothing to do with guarding the leaders, but thanks to that obscure position he was able to survive long after Stalin. In his place as Kremlin Commandant, Dzerzhinsky put that ubiquitous Latvian, Rudolf Peterson, who held that post until dismissed by Stalin shortly after the Kirov murder in December 1934.

The Peterson appointment marked an actual downgrading in the authority of the Kremlin Commandant. From that time—until the present—that job became one of administering the bodyguards of the leadership, but not of controlling them. That task, always an offshoot of the Cheka and its successors, was given a variety of men, with an almost equal variety of titles, and titles that subsequently were made real misnomers—and purposefully so—under Stalin.

For instance, when Peterson was made Kremlin Commandant, the job of supervising Lenin's bodyguards was given to a Dzerzhinsky aide, Abram Belenky, who served in that capacity until Dzerzhinsky's death in 1926. He later became chief of the Moscow OGPU, until he disappeared in Stalin's purges of the thirties. And for the Kremlin bodyguards personnel, Belenky used members of OSNAZ (Otryad Osobogo Naznacheniya), the Cheka's "Detachment of Special Designation," a so-called armored unit, first organized in 1918, as was its sister group, CHON, for the purpose of guarding the Soviet leadership and installations. The hodgepodge of hangers-on, Latvians, machinegun trainees, and cadets, that served under Malkov was no longer deemed adequate and was in a sense replaced by professionals, although that term could hardly apply to the early CHON and OSNAZ. In June, 1924, CHON and OSNAZ were reorganized into the Division of Special Designation. After Dzerzhinsky's death in 1926, the outfit was renamed the Dzerzhinsky Detached Motorized Infantry Division of Special Designation, or OMSDON (Imeni Dzerzhinskogo). Later renamed the First Dzerzhinsky Motorized Infantry Division, the organization still serves as the security police's special, or punitive, troops, whose task is to suppress possible uprisings or rebellions against the Communist leadership.

Belenky, Peterson, and their OSNAZ personnel, although far better organized than Malkov's group, never had a chance to prove their mettle with Lenin. Ill most of the time after that reorganization, Lenin's travel was limited to nonexistent. Nor could OSNAZ' more select bodyguards, police dogs, and other security refinements save him from death by apparent natural causes in January 1924. But, had Lenin lived longer, the Soviet bodyguard system might not have become the perverse monstrosity for acquisition and perpetuation of power that it became under Stalin.

Peter I interrogates his son Alexis in Petergof.

TSARIST RUSSIA

Oprichnik's uniform.

Александрова
Слобода
Гравюра из книги
Я Улльфельда
XVI в

Oprichnik's court. *(16th-century engraving)*

Count Alexis Orlov, the kidnapper of Princess Tarakanova who was a pretender to the Russian throne during the reign of Catherine II.

General Benkendorf, chief of the Gendarmes and chief of the Third Department under Nicholas I. The Third Department was the forerunner of the modern Russian secret police.

A playing card showing Nicholas II above and Rasputin below.

General Alexandre Spiridovitch, one of the last chiefs of the Okhrana under the Tsarist regime.

The son of Nicholas II.

Aleksandr I. Ulyanov, older brother of Lenin, hanged May 8, 1887, for attempted assassination of Tsar Alexander III. Photo was taken in jail before his execution.

Lenin (left) and, to his left, Fanya Kaplan (so it is believed), who shot Lenin on August 30, 1918.

Lenin and his Swiss Communist friend Fritz Platten. During the assassination attempt on Lenin's life on January 1, 1918, Platten was wounded in the hand with which he had covered Lenin's head. Platten was arrested during the purges in 1938 and executed in 1942 on Stalin's order.

Moisey S. Uritsky, first chief of the Petrograd Cheka, assassinated August 30, 1918, in his office by right Socialist-Revolutionary Kenigisser.

Felix Dzerzhinsky in 1920.

A 1921 pass to enter the Kremlin and the Soviet government offices inside. Second signature is that of Nadezhda Alliluyeva, Stalin's wife, who worked in Lenin's office at that time.

Stalin on Red Square, Moscow, May Day 1946.

Lavrenty Beria in his marshal's uniform.

Left to right: Grigoriy K. Ordzhonikidze: Peoples' Commissar of Heavy Industry and member of the Politburo; a suicide in February 1937.

Valerian V. Kuybyshev: chairman, State Planning Commission; member of the Politburo; died from poisoning in January 1935.

Sergey M. Kirov: member of the Politburo; secretary of the Central Committee of the Communist Party; first secretary, Leningrad Party Committee; assassinated in December 1934.

Nikolay Sidorovich Vlasik (left) watchdogging his boss Stalin. Stalin's bodyguard from 1919 to 1952, Vlasik died in Lubyanka Prison in 1952.

The Smolny guards, consisting of revolutionary sailors and Red Guards, were the first Soviet bodyguards after the October Revolution.

Smolny guards examining passes at Smolny in 1917.

Kremlin bodyguards, in State Security soldier's uniform, keeping watch at the V. I. Lenin Mausoleum.

Col. Gen. Nikolay S. Zakharov, deputy chairman of the KGB and supervisor of the Soviet bodyguards during Khrushchev's era.

Part of the KGB headquarters building in Dzerzhinsky Square in Moscow. In 1953, the author had an office on the 9th floor (top right window).

Left to right: Yagoda, Kaganovich and Khrushchev, on an inspection tour of a concentration camp (ca. 1936).

Colonel Litovchenko, Khrushchev's chief of personal bodyguards.

Lt. Gen. Andrey Vedenin, commandant of the Kremlin, 1953–67.

Leonid I. Brezhnev, General Secretary of the Central Committee of the Soviet Communist Party. This 1971 painting is by Soviet artist Dmitry A. Nalbandyan, who during the Stalin era won prizes for his painting of Stalin. Resemblances between Brezhnev and Stalin are not difficult to observe in this work.

CHAPTER V

Early Stalinist Bodyguard System

At the time of the Bolshevik take-over, Stalin, like Lenin, had a coterie of hangers-on and sycophants whose chief concern was his security. Stalin's group, of course, like those of other lesser Soviet leaders, was relatively small and remained so until after the death of Lenin.

Stalin's first bodyguard of note, and the most enduring of all, was Nikolay Vlasik. That worthy was a fawning, dullminded peasant, who had no security police background or training at all and while almost illiterate, yet rose to the rank of lieutenant-general in the security forces.

Vlasik started his servitude with Stalin as a nondescript Red Army soldier, who, almost like a dog, slept outside the Georgian's door in the early days in Petrograd and Moscow. He was also a little man in physical stature, because Stalin, who was a little man, too, would not tolerate anyone of greater height in his immediate entourage. And throughout his career, despite the almost facetious misnomers of his titles and posts, Vlasik was nothing more than Stalin's chief butcher boy, but an inordinately faithful one, who was in charge of the killer-group that elimated all the Georgian's enemies of greater and lesser importance.

While Lenin ruled, Stalin had to make do with Vlasik and the occasional OSNAZ type assigned to him as bodyguards. The future dictator spent that period quietly, but very determinedly, organizing the group of toadies that would care for his security once he had gained power. For that purpose, he suborned underlings in the only two organizations Lenin allowed him to control, the window-dressing group that was supposed to help, but actually suppressed, the national minorities (Komissariat po Delam Natsionalnostey) and another group that gave Stalin greater penetration of the party organization than possibly even Lenin realized, the Inspectorate of Workers and Peasants (Raboche-Krestyanskaya Inspektsiya). Simultaneously, he developed a very close relationship with the Cheka-GPU. His advance in that sector became relatively easy when he gained the friendship of the cold and extremely dedicated Dzerzhinsky, a convergence of conflicting personalities that is yet to be explained. Nevertheless, it is a fact that Stalin managed to gain influence over that fanatic, but honest Pole and well before the death of Lenin. And that sway of Stalin's over Dzerzhinsky was great enough so that the Georgian was able to get the Cheka boss to go along with him in his brutal suppression of Nationalists in the Caucasus, an act that aroused the ire of Lenin. But, so great was the Georgian's influence over Dzerzhinsky that the latter supported such heresy against his otherwise sainted leader. And the result was that Stalin had Dzerzhinsky in his pocket.

The importance of Stalin's suborning of the personnel in the national minorities and workers-peasants inspectorate organizations, plus his control of Dzerzhinsky, lies in the fact that the Georgian had greater appreciation of the basics of supreme power under the Communist system than any other so-called Marxist leader in the Soviet Union or elsewhere. He understood both the party politics of gaining power and the security guarantees he needed to retain it. In a sense, he politicked with one hand and with the other he organized his own elite and personal police force. And, of course, with his somewhat Oriental obscurantism, he perfected the latter under such a multiplicity of guises, of both nomenclature and personnel, that he held the whip hand before the party purists realized it and when they had rendered themselves powerless to combat him.

One of the first Stalin security men to enter his service by such a back door was the Armenian, Avanesov. That campfollower of revolution, after playing a leading role in organizing the Cheka and Lenin's excuse for bodyguards, gravitated toward Sverdlov. But, when Sverdlov died prematurely and unexpectedly in 1919, he found himself at loose ends and moved into Stalin's entourage. Stalin at first found him a nook in his nationalities commissariat and then made him his deputy in the other font of the cadre of his future

[283]

security force, the workers-peasants inspectorate and member of the VChK Collegium. The Armenian probably would have risen high in the Georgian's security organization, had he not died of tuberculosis in 1930.

Another seemingly minor but important move made by Stalin after the death of Sverdlov was the sponsoring of fellow Georgian Yenukidze to replace Avanesov as Secretary of the Central Executive Committee. As Avanesov's successor in that post, Yenukidze also took over indirect control of the Kremlin bodyguards. At about the same time, Stalin also enlisted Ivan Ksenofontov, another founding member of the Cheka. As party general secretary, the Georgian was able to put Ksenofontov in the central apparatus of the party. The actual post given Ksenofontov—about whom very little is known—was that of party business manager. The real job of Ksenofontov, however, was to function as liaison between Stalin and the secret police. That somewhat mysterious early minion of Stalin also might have gone far in the dictator's personal security service, but he too died prematurely of natural causes in 1926.

The device Stalin employed to attain and retain supreme power was his secretariat. Normally, a secretariat is defined as an organization, usually administrative, headed by a secretary. In Stalin's case, the only part of that definition that is applicable is the fact that he was party secretary and thereby in charge of a secretariat. But his secretariat had far from normal functions. It did administrative work, of course, but its prime functions in the period Stalin was seeking power were to gather political intelligence and clout and to form a cadre of future bodyguards. Once Lenin had died, the secretariat's main duty became that of keeping the Georgian in power. In effect, therefore, the Cheka and its successors were bypassed. From 1924 on, the secret police, and especially the Kremlin Commandant, had no control whatsoever over the somewhat obscured, but very real bodyguards of the leader. Stalin's secretariat, and its equally misnamed subdivisions, assumed all ramifications of that task and was used to eliminate all actual and potential opponents of the Georgian, up to and including the long list of "convicted," "purged" or otherwise liquidated party hierarchs and security bosses. In sum, despite its seemingly innocent name, the secretariat was Stalin's Oprichniks, Preobrazhensky Guards, Third Section, and Okhrana combined. Others have called it Stalin's secret cabinet, but it was much more than that.

With such Chekists as Avanesov and Ksenofontov in the wings to handle police connections, Stalin needed a trusted lackey to head his secretariat. For that, he again resorted to his nationalities commissariat, taking from that organization its secretary, Ivan Tovstukha, a veteran revolutionary and a somewhat senior Communist. Official Soviet sources list Tovstukha as working in the apparatus of the CCCPSU in 1921–24 and 1926–30, as assistant director of the Lenin Institute in 1924–26 and as deputy director of the Marx-Engels-Lenin Institute after 1930. Actually, however, during most of the period 1921–30, he was organizing and running Stalin's secretariat and also serving for a time after 1924 as head of the secretariat's secret department, the latter being another name for the top command of the Georgian's Okhrana. Tovstukha's institute jobs were merely nominal sinecures that did not distract him from his main duties. His only drawback was that he was tubercular and by the late twenties frequently could not report for work. By 1930, he was virtually retired. But when he died of his ailment in 1935, some understanding of his earlier importance and work was gained by the fact he was buried near the Kremlin wall and was mourned officially by an imposing list of high secretariat members, bodyguards, and security bosses.

In its formative years, Stalin's secretariat always moved cautiously, secretly and often in a conspiratorial manner that probably was more a reflection of the Georgian's orientalism than strictly necessary. Even though Stalin had great influence over Dzerzhinsky, he awaited that Pole's death in 1926 before improving on the bodyguard organization. But once Dzerzhinsky's assistant and fellow Pole, Menzhinsky, ailing even then and a mere functionary to boot, took over command of the OGPU, the secretariat made a refinement in the bodyguard system by organizing a special operational department, called the OPEROD.

Nominally, the OPEROD was an offshoot of the OGPU and its function was to guard party and government leaders. Actually, however, it was run by the secretariat and its duty was to guard Stalin and keep an eye on the other party hierarchs, rather than guard them.

Dzerzhinsky's death not only gave Stalin the chance to organize an effective bodyguard, it also put the Georgian in full control of the OGPU—and its successors—from that time and until Stalin himself died in 1953. In fact, even before Dzerzhinsky died, Stalin had his hands on the actual reins of the security police in the person of Yagoda, who had obeyed all behests of Stalin and had given little more than lip-service to Dzerzhinsky. As a result, under Menzhinsky, Yagoda was the actual if not the nominal boss of the secret police.

Therefore, the reorganization of the bodyguard and the formation of OPEROD, presented few if any difficulties. Belenky was eased out of the job of overseeing the guards and into the comparative oblivion of the Moscow OGPU. In that opportunistic but relatively able man's place, Stalin put the Hungarian, Karl Pauker, as first chief of OPE-ROD. In Dzerzhinsky's lifetime, such a veritable joker as Pauker would never have been tolerated for such a post, and thereby is some conception gained of the complete control Stalin had attained over the OGPU. Pauker was one of the most worthless carpetbaggers of revolution. In the twilight of the Austro-Hungarian Empire, he had worked in Budapest as a barber for actors and opera singers. During World War I, he was mustered into Franz Josef's forces on the eastern front where he deserted to the Russians, probably taking his first safe opportunity to do so. Exactly how he wiggled his way into Stalin's entourage is not clear, although some accounts say he was a sidekick of Vlasik. No matter what the route, Pauker was a true horror, a bit like some of the Oprichniks with whom Ivan the Terrible consorted and a marked example of the bureaucratic degeneracy of the Stalin era. A complete toady, that Barber of Budapest once drove Stalin into gales of laughter by aping Zinoviev begging for his life. But, not only was Pauker a source of amusement to Stalin, he was also trusted by the Georgian to the extent he allowed the Hungarian to shave him.

With the establishment of OPEROD, Stalin's bodyguard system took form. And, in fact, except for amplification and changes in titles and personalities, the system retained that form throughout the reign of the dictator. The power of those bodyguards was second only to Stalin's. Through them, the Georgian controlled the complete party and governmental scene, including, of course, the security police. And through that elite guard, he was able to remove from office, arrest, imprison, exile, or execute any Soviet citizens he pleased, no matter what their ranks or positions.

Despite the emergence of OPEROD, Peterson continued on as commandant of the Kremlin. But the Latvian's real authority, earlier

[286]

well whittled away under Belenky, was reduced to practical zero in 1926. And never, during the lifetime of Stalin, were Peterson and his successors more than administrative and logistic commanders of the guards. All those Kremlin Commandants took their orders from the chiefs of OPEROD and its successors.

At about the same time as the organization of OPEROD, a very important development was under way in the bodyguards control organization, the secretariat. Tovstukha's illness was becoming progressively worse and severely limited his activities as chief of the secretariat. The gap was filled by Poskrebyshev, who fulfilled more and more of Tovstukha's duties by 1927 and all of them by 1930. Information about Poskrebyshev's background is scarce to nonexistent. About all that is known is that he came from Central Asia and became a member of Stalin's secretariat in the mid-twenties, probably as a protégé of Tovstukha. His most distinguishing characteristic was discretion. Somewhat naturally, therefore, he was also extremely laconic. During his long tenure as Stalin's man Friday and alter ego, he was encountered by many foreigners of distinction, who had business with Stalin. Some of those personalities later described their visits with Stalin, but none of them were able to recount any more of an impression of Poskrebyshev than they were of the doorman. He never allowed himself to be photographed with the dictator, although Vlasik was an omnipresent amateur photographer.

Within OPEROD itself, there were also two other men most important to its structure and functions. One was Pauker's deputy, Volovich, and the other was Vlasik. For a time, Volovich specialized in handling Stalin's problems with opponents abroad—he played a leading part in the kidnapping of White Russian General Kutepov in Paris in 1930. But, after that "success," he was returned to Moscow and served chiefly as Stalin's chauffeur, until he and his boss, Pauker, were eliminated by a purge in 1937. Vlasik, however, who remained in good standing despite a passing squabble with the Georgian, played a much more significant role. Vlasik was chief of a special section of the OPEROD and its successors, an elite group called Stalin's personal bodyguards by some, but that actually served as the dictator's chief hatchetmen, or killers.

Once Poskrebyshev was in the saddle, the Stalin control-by-body-guard system was an accomplished fact. The Georgian used the by then well subservient OGPU to keep the ordinary masses of the

Soviet Union in check. And to keep the whip hand over more important persons, especially the other party hierarchs, he had ready in the wings the Poskrebyshev-Vlasik team. Nominally, the chain of command was Stalin-Poskrebyshev-Pauker-Vlasik. In many cases, however, it was not necessary for Stalin to exercise direct control. Poskrebyshev's intelligence, both native and that gained through the secretariat he ran, was such that he usually knew Stalin's wishes and intentions in advance of any order from the Georgian and had performed the jobs desired without benefit of any direct instruction from Stalin at all. In those cases, Poskrebyshev might go through the motions of informing Pauker of what action was needed, but that was only a formality, when done at all. The more usual process was for Poskrebyshev to bypass Pauker completely and give the arrest or kill order directly to Vlasik, who then would assemble his butcher boys and carry out the command. It was by use of that technique, or even the threat of use of it, that Stalin was able to kill off seemingly all-powerful secret police chiefs during the purges of the thirties and later to control Beria and his lieutenants.

But, formidable as it was, that Poskrebyshev-Vlasik team was relatively idle for several years after its formation. For, in that period, such an elite security group was not really needed. Stalin was performing most astutely in his political maneuvering, playing off Lenin's other successors against each other. Those better meaning, but almost incredibly foolish and naïve men eliminated themselves as political effectives by allowing Stalin to ensnare them in so-called factions of the right or left. And once so entrapped, they were so hypnotized by their own dialectics, they were unable to appreciate, let alone check, Stalin's surge to absolute power over their relatively politically prostrate bodies.

To keep his bodyguard from going to rust by virtue of complete idleness during those formative years, Stalin gave Poskrebyshev the diversion of preparing the script for Vyshinsky of the "trials" of the "saboteurs" of the Donbass coal basin, plus "legal" actions against engineers of bourgeois background in industrial organizations, some surviving Mensheviks and a half dozen British technicians. And in 1932, Poskrebyshev had to do a job for Stalin highly similar to the tasks Malyuta Skuratov performed for Ivan the Terrible. He had to prettify the death of Stalin's second wife, Nadezhda Alliluyeva, and clean up whatever mess was left behind by her sudden demise.

By 1933, however, the period of relative marking time came to an end for Poskrebyshev. Although his master had all the other veteran heirs of Lenin well in hand by that time, a new and much more serious menace had appeared on the political horizon. Posing that major threat was the good-looking, magnetic-to-charismatic Kirov, who was fast capturing the minds, and the support, of the party rank and file and much of the nation as well. The danger of Kirov to Stalin became most apparent at the Seventeenth Party Congress in early 1934. That party congress not only reduced the Georgian's party title from "General Secretary" to plain "Secretary," but it almost removed Stalin from the party leadership and cheered Kirov as much, if not more, than Stalin. After that near debacle, the Georgian dictator's grumblings to Poskrebyshev must have been severe, although there is no solid indication of when he decided to take action against Kirov or how.

Somewhat fortuitously in the spring of 1934, Menzhinsky, the nominal boss of OGPU and an ineffective even if consistent opponent of the Georgian's strong-arm methods, died. Within months, Yagoda, a most obedient tool of Stalin and Menzhinsky's deputy and successor, acceded to the OGPU's being reorganized into the Narodnyy Komissariat Vnutrennikh Del (People's Commissariat for Internal Affairs), or the NKVD. The most important part of that change was that it included a reorganization of OPEROD, which became the Pervyy Otdel (First Department) of the NKVD, thereby showing what division of the security police Stalin considered most vital. Pauker continued on as head of the First Department, with Volovich and Vlasik as his nominal assistants, and with Peterson as Kremlin Commandant. Over that quartet, of course, was Poskrebyshev, still the nominal chief of Stalin's secretariat, although he eventually rose to be a lieutenant-general of the security police.

Obviously, the elimination of Kirov was well beyond the Georgian's political machinations and control of mere party machinery. That was a task for the First Department and Yagoda's NKVD. And the script, of course, was prepared by Poskrebyshev, no doubt with Stalin standing at his shoulder, to make sure that major roles were given Zinoviev and Kamenov, thereby assuring that several birds literally were killed with a single stone. It is somewhat moot why Leningrad rather than Moscow was selected as the scene of the Kirov murder, but it is probable the former capital was preferred because security was more freewheeling there plus the fact there were fewer party dignitaries and practically no foreign interlopers in the northern city.

The site thus chosen, Poskrebyshev next culled lists of misfits and malcontents in the party rank and file in Leningrad and eventually selected Nikolayev as the best choice for murderer in the primitive Soviet production. Nikolayev was well examined and interrogated before his selection by Yagoda's NKVD underlings in Leningrad and one can well imagine that Poskrebyshev overheard at least one of those sessions before he gave his consent to the character who would play the role of murderer. That done, the Leningrad NKVD arranged that Nikolayev should obtain the murder weapon and brainwashed the unbalanced young man about what a great service he would be doing the party and the cause of communism in general by eliminating its archenemy, Kirov. No doubt by the time that process was completed, Nikolayev envisioned himself as another Sazonov or better. The indoctrination over, Nikolayev and his revolver were sent to Kirov's Smolny headquarters on what was no more than a dry run, although the future "murderer" thought it was the real thing at the time. His weapon was taken from him by the NKVD at Smolny, but it was soon returned by his NKVD controls, who most likely remarked "better luck next time." He needed luck, for according to some reports he was caught yet again trying to get into Smolny with his pistol and again had it returned to him.

All preparations thus completed, Stalin had to enter the picture personally so that Kirov would be in Leningrad on time for his murder. The Georgian accomplished that by first stressing his need and desire for Kirov to be at his side in Moscow and then "reluctantly" agreeing to his victim returning to Leningrad. Thereupon, practically no sooner had Kirov reentered Smolny than Nikolayev and his revolver made their appearance there once more. On that, the real time, the armed Nikolayev was allowed to make it all the way to Kirov's offices. With Kirov's guard absent by prearrangement, Nikolayev had no difficulty in shooting and killing the Leningrad leader like a pigeon.

The second act of that production followed swiftly. Stalin, Poskrebyshev, Yagoda, et al., rushed to Leningrad to handle the investigation of Kirov's murder. Their actual mission, however, was to cover any possible traces of their roles in the affair and manufacture the "guilt" of the Zinoviev-Kamenev faction and thus set the stage for the purges to come. It must be admitted that that Leningrad foray of Stalin and his Oprichniks was extremely tidy. Before he recovered from his trauma, the unfortunate Nikolayev was executed, as were hundreds of other far more innocent persons rotting in NKVD prisons in Leningrad. Kirov's absentee NKVD guard was killed in an auto "accident" while on his way to be questioned by the Stalin-Poskrebyshev team. And Nikolayev's NKVD controllers were given astonishingly short prison terms—and at least one of them was seen free before their final elimination in the bloodbath of the purges. In fact, so well did Stalin and Poskrebyshev cover their tracks in Leningrad that for more than two decades the citizenry of the Soviet Union, and that of most of the rest of the world, was convinced that Kirov had been the victim of a mere crazy malcontent. And even when Khrushchev decided to talk about the Kirov murder, in an effort to clear his own skirts by putting all blame on Stalin, he told only some of the facts.

Returning to Moscow after "mourning" at the Kirov obsequies, Stalin again reorganized his bodyguards to prepare for the great purges he had scheduled for his then unwitting nation. His first step was to enlarge Pauker's First Department by incorporating it in the all-encompassing GUGB (Main Administration of State Security) of the NKVD, a super-body he had discreetly established in July, 1934, well in advance of the Kirov murder. And in the last days of December, 1934, the Georgian also made two more moves to improve the power and effectiveness of his household troops. Within GUGB NKVD, he formed the SPU (Secretno-Politicheskoye Upravleniye) Secret Political Directorate, thereby formalizing the investigative powers of Poskrebyshev and at the same time somewhat "legalizing" the arrest and kill tasks of Poskrebyshev's minion, Vlasik. And he fired the last Latvian hanger-on, Peterson, the Kremlin Commandant. Peterson survived for several years as an NKVD officer in Kiev, before being arrested and shot in 1938. The Latvian's replacement as Kremlin Commandant, Tkalun, did not last much longer than his predecessor. He, too, was arrested in 1938, and after that all that is known about him is that he "disappeared"—permanently and violently, no doubt. And that despite the fact that Tkalun, who had been Moscow city military commandant before being sent to the Kremlin, was a protégé of Voroshilov.

The sophistication of the bodyguard setup that followed the Kirov murder gave Stalin a protective and punitive private army that was second to none. The Georgian had complete control over Yagoda's NKVD to handle rank-and-file dissidents and suspects among the benighted masses across the nation, to kill off by the hundreds of thousands those unfortunate creatures of all categories who fell afoul of the dictator or his underlings, to work millions more at earth moving, timber-hacking and mining projects, and to run the vast complex of prisons and camps established for the additional millions of lesser victims. And for his real and potential rivals of position and authority, he had Poskrebyshev's "secretariat," and under that the SPU, beefed up by Vlasik's butcher boys. Actually, although veiled by intentionally abstruse nomenclature, that top level of the household troops was not a complex organization. Wearing one hat as chief of the "secretariat," Poskrebyshev was aware of and controlled all party and government business to the nth degree. Wearing his other hat as chief of the SPU, he conducted the investigation, interrogation and/or frame-up of the particular worthy under assault at the moment. The case of the intended victim thus well settled within the confines of the SPU (it was that practice that post-Stalin Communists were talking about when they demanded "Socialist legality"), Poskrebyshev and/or Stalin then decided whether the "culprit" should have the luxury of a show trial, for which the SPU prepared the script, or be quietly rounded up and dispatched. Most of the dispatching, usually by a bullet in the back of the head, although sometimes by "suicide," "heart attack" or some other "illness," was handled by Vlasik's picked troops. Very occasionally, however, Poskrebyshev himself would conduct the liquidation of a particular veteran or otherwise special worthy, by persuading the victim that suicide, to be followed by an official declaration of death by natural causes and full funeral rites, was the best solution.

Russia, and indeed the world, had seen no such organization of personal henchmen since the days of Ivan the Terrible. And that mad tsar's Oprichniks were comparatively but a pale and passing shadow. With the post-Kirov tidying up of his bodyguards, Stalin's autocracy had advanced an infinite distance from the naïve Lenin era when the Georgian's security had been assured by little more than a fawning, stupid Vlasik outside the door.

Those improvements in the bodyguards should be in the handbook of all members of the Communist elite interested in gaining and keeping control over such a complex and diverse empire as the Soviet Union and its satrapies. For, as the fate of some of Stalin's successors so clearly shows, there is no other route to abiding power under the Soviet system. Astute and ruthless enough to recognize those hard and perhaps occasionally unpleasant facts, Stalin was able, once his bodyguard system was perfected, to control or crush all resistance, both domestic and foreign, for the rest of his life.

Once thus well armed, the dictator placed his two chief victims of the moment, Kamenev and Zinoviev, on trial in January, 1935, but in secret. The principal charges, of course, were engineering the Kirov murder, but Poskrebyshev's group had been too rushed to prepare an adequate script so the two "defendants" escaped with prison sentences and not the death penalties Stalin had determined they should have.

But, Poskrebyshev was much more successful in eliminating another hierarch who did not see things his master's way. Almost simultaneously with the Kamenev-Zinoviev "trial," Kuybyshev, although in the best of health, suddenly died of a "heart attack." About the only truth in the official report of that liquidation was the fact that Kuybyshev's heart did indeed stop, but whether that death was caused by a bullet, poison, or the extremes of torture is not known and probably never will be. But it is well established that the Kuybyshev elimination marked the beginning of a long series of medical killings by Stalin's bodyguards. In a way that type of liquidation carried a certain amount of honor for the victim, if that were of any benefit to him. For it was reserved for those opponents who were too strong of character or too distinguished in repute either to be paraded at a show trial or to be dispatched summarily in some NKVD cellar. Among the better known persons on that list, which may become a roll of honor to more enlightened Soviet citizens of the future, were Gorky and Ordzhonikidze. But, there were also countless others, whose names probably never will be memorialized for the simple reason that they have been forgotten by all but their immediate kin as a result of the rush of events that attended Stalin's mass slaughter. And additionally, of course, those victims' liquidators were liquidated in turn.

Shortly after Kuybyshev died, Poskrebyshev arranged that Yenukidze should be dumped. There may have been some personal rivalry in that action, since as Avanesov's successor in the early Stalin bodyguard setup, that veteran Georgian Communist still had some influence over arrangements within the Kremlin. But Yenukidze's chief "crime" appears to have been his greater humanity and regard for old party hierarchs, plus a tendency to think for himself, characteristics that eminently disqualified him from further association with such a cold-blooded gang of cutthroats. Additionally, he was known to have expressed objection to Yezhov, acting under Poskrebyshev's direction, disbanding in mid-1935 societies of party veterans and seizing of their records. At first, however, Yenukidze was merely dismissed from his sinecure as Secretary of the Central Executive Committee of the USSR. His final liquidation was to await action by Vlasik's hatchet men at the height of the purges to come.

Truly though, at that time, Poskrebyshev had a much greater problem on his hands than the elimination of Yenukidze. Disappointed to baffled by the lack of death sentences given at the Kamenev-Zinoviev "trial"—and at a mid-1935 "retrial" of Kamenev alone—Stalin had ordered his chief flunky to prepare another and better session for the "Trotskyites."

For almost a year after receiving those orders, Poskrebyshev and his "secretariat" labored mightily. And so did Yagoda's NKVD, including the First Department, and the Secret Political Directorate. It was a massive force, but it had not only to prepare the script, setting, and claque for the pageant; it also had to "prepare" the victims themselves. Fortunately, however, the chief victims already were in NKVD hands. And so were many others as candidates for the roles of "co-defendants."

The setting and the claque were relatively simple tasks. The judiciary was a complete tool of the security police—as it still is. And there was a plethora of bodyguard and other NKVD personnel to jam the courtroom with antidefendant "spectators." Also press coverage was simple because there were always more than enough foreign newsmen anxious to go to any Stalin production.

It was "preparing" the "defendants" that took the major effort. Those unfortunates had to confess their "crimes" and in strict accordance with the script written by Poskrebyshev and edited by Stalin. Means were more than ready at hand to attain that: torture, promises of acquittal, threats against the victim and his family, mawkish references to party traditions and loyalty, or a combination of all those

[294]

methods. But Poskrebyshev's teammates, despite their absolute power, were still novices at such refined tactics, so it required time to establish what approach should be used toward each individual victim. Additionally, although Kamenev and Zinoviev were comparative pushovers at the hands of their "interrogators," quite a few of the others originally selected as "co-defendants," balked, even met death rather than comply with the script.

By August, 1936, all was in readiness. During a judicial carnival half a dozen days long, Kamenev, Zinoviev, and a dozen of their fourteen "co-defendants" dutifully pleaded guilty to charges of murdering Kirov and trying to do the same to Stalin and an assortment of his toadies. They were convicted in short order and executed less than twenty-four hours later.

Although seemingly vacationing at the Black Sea while that grisly process was going on, Stalin almost immediately afterwards—through Poskrebyshev—ordered Yagoda and Yezhov to strike while the iron was hot and carry out the mass executions—without trial, of course—of some five thousand prison and camp inmates also accused of being "opponents." All those unfortunates were misguided members of the Communist party. But that made not a whit of difference. Once Stalin had succeeded in killing off such hierarchs as Kamenev and Zinoviev, the party small fry counted for nothing.

Participation in those mass murders was Yagoda's last activity for the NKVD. He was demoted to postal commissar in September 1936 and thereby was started on the road to eventual liquidation as one who shared too many of Stalin's secrets. His job as head of security was given to the ugly, little Yezhov, a graduate of Poskrebyshev's "secretariat" and thus more amenable to commands from the top echelon and better versed in its ways of doing business.

Yezhov celebrated his promotion in the best traditions of Ivan the Terrible. He ordered scores of Yagoda's henchmen to entrain for new posts in the boondocks. Once they were safely out of the capital, he had them arrested and shot wholesale. Others who had not yet received their marching orders obliged Yezhov by killing themselves. In general, the bloodbath within the NKVD that marked the Yezhov take-over was no great loss for Russia. But it did have one deleterious effect for future victims of Stalin's whims and prejudices. It made the surviving NKVD men even more brutal than their predecessors.

But Yezhov was permitted only a certain measure of such self-indulgence in killing. Poskrebyshev had much more serious duties for him—"conditioning" another batch of "opponents" for the second of Stalin's great show trials. It was a difficult production for Poskrebyshev to prepare, for woven into its script were lines that gave a hint of, in fact laid the groundwork for, "trials" and purges yet to come. But, the "defendants" cooperated well with the scriptwriter. By the end of January, 1937, Pyatakov, Radek, and their fourteen fellow-victims were in shape to be trotted into "court" and "confess" their "crimes" by rote before being executed or transported to NKVD camps for slower deaths.

Despite the care that went into the production of such pageants, there were a few bobbles and slipups. Occasionally during "court," it turned out that a "defendant" had not been conditioned well enough and would muddy the script either by retracting his "confession" or ad-libbing a few lines. But those were minor matters for the producers and somewhat welcome opportunities for Vlasik's henchmen. In intervals between "court" sessions, such recalcitrants would be "persuaded" to stick to the lines Poskrebyshev had prepared for them. It is hardly necessary to describe the means that Vlasik's creatures had ready for such "persuasion." Or on other occasions, quite glaring factual errors, particularly regarding events that allegedly occurred abroad, would be found in the script by foreigners and cause much subsequent clucking of tongues and casting of doubt, but nothing more. However, Poskrebyshev and Stalin were not even slightly embarrassed by those disclosures. After all, each show trial was a one-time only production, the "defendants" were executed or otherwise eliminated and the controlled press gave the Soviet citizenry not a smidgen of information about such scriptual imperfections.

With the conclusion of the Pytakov-Radek process, the purge machinery went into top gear for all categories and at all levels. In retrospect, the selection of Yezhov for a period when mass killing was a mere matter of routine had been a wise choice. That semimidget was the proper type of psychopath for the job, rivaled only by subsequent tasks carried out by some of Hitler's fellow psychopaths. And for the top-level liquidations, there was faithful Poskrebyshev and his team.

And in his field—beside scriptwriting—Poskrebyshev was just as busy and hard pressed during 1937 as was Yezhov. That monkey-faced, often drunk man Friday to Stalin had first of all to get rid of one of his master's Georgian stalwarts, Ordzhonikidze. Unfortunately, as with so many other liquidations in that bloody period, there are conflicting reports and a complete absence of hard facts about how Ordzhonikidze was eliminated. Nobody in the top bodyguard echelon of that era was allowed to survive long enough, let alone escape abroad, to give any information about such processes. And such details were beyond the capabilities of even the fabricators and fancifiers. Additionally, any records of those events—and it is doubtful that any at all were kept—would have been destroyed long ago.

However, there is no doubt that Ordzhonikidze, although in the best of health, died shortly after the Pyatakov-Radek "trial." Officially, he had a "heart attack." It is believed that that "seizure" followed a final talk between the victim and Poskrebyshev and/or Stalin. It is possible that Ordzhonikidze shot himself, or maybe Vlasik or some member of the First Department did that work for him. There was also the chance he was poisoned, but that seems least probable, because the report of a talk with the deposed Poskrebyshev following Stalin's death, cites Poskrebyshev as saying his group did not use poison until 1940.

Equally moot is the death—officially a suicide—of Yan Gamarnik, armed forces political officer, in mid-1937. He, too, is believed to have had a final talk with Poskrebyshev and/or Stalin. The subject discussed was the forthcoming great purge—or virtual decimation—of the officer corps of the Red Army. Gamarnik refused to participate. That *lèse majesté* made his death only a matter of time and method. But again, there is not the slightest information about who in the top bodyguard echelon saw that the death sentence was carried out or how.

Somewhat simultaneously, Poskrebyshev also had to do some housecleaning of his Kremlin crew. Stalin finally realized that Pauker, despite his ability to please the dictator with mimicries of Zinoviev begging for his life, lacked the qualifications to be chief of the First Department. Or perhaps the Hungarian had made the error of imitating or joking about his master. Also ticketed for extinction was Pauker's assistant, Volovich, the onetime kidnapper and later driver for Stalin. Perhaps Stalin was displeased with Volovich's driving. But the most logical reason for the elimination of that pair is that they had been in the inner circle too long and knew too much.

Once the decision had been made to get rid of Pauker and Volovich, a new chief of the First Department was appointed without Pauker and Volovich, of course, knowing anything about it. The selection went to a General Veniamin Gulst. Very little, except for his rank and name, is known about Gulst. He was an NKVD officer. And he also must have been very well known by Stalin and/or Poskrebyshev to have been given the job. But everything else about him, his background, his qualifications, is unknown.

However, it is a fact that immediately after getting his appointment, the new chief of the First Department and some of his men went to the quarters of Pauker and Volovich and put them under arrest. It can be presumed that those visits were made in predawn darkness. And it can be envisioned, without too much imagination, that Pauker once more went down on his knees in imitation of Zinoviev, but that time begging for his own life. Actually, that begging was a bit premature, for Pauker and Volovich were not scheduled for physical liquidation until the following year. One other formality came after those arrests: Vlasik was made deputy to Gulst and the activities of that dog's-body were again and from then on limited to guarding his master's door, or indulging in his hobby—taking candid camera shots of Stalin and his cronies.

But Poskrebyshev handled that shake-up in the palace guards with little more than his left hand. His main attention was on a much more important matter, the elimination of Tukhachevsky, and thereby gaining unquestioned control of the armed forces. And that was a task that concerned Stalin, Poskrebyshev, and his SPU alone. Yezhov was excluded from it entirely, since a mere maniacal killer lacked the qualifications for a job of that importance.

However, once Gamarnik had been disposed of, the going was relatively simple. Budyenny, the only other military hierarch who might have balked, was given the simple choice of being a victim or a member of the court, and he naturally opted for the latter. That settled, the "trial" of Tukhachevsky and his fellow officers behind closed doors followed immediately. And within hours after the victims had been executed, Gamarnik's replacement, the sycophantic Mekhlis, was well embarked on the mass purge of the Red Army officer corps.

The issuance of those marching orders to Mekhlis was a signal of sorts for the purge—better called Stalin's mass slaughter—to go into high gear. Under instructions from Poskrebyshev, whose SPU had drawn up lists of the more important victims, such worthies as Yezhov, Molotov, Kaganovich, Mikoyan, Beria, plus that future "de-Stalinizer" Khrushchev, were dispatched across the length and breadth of the Soviet Union to liquidate lesser civilian party "opponents" of Stalin by the millions. That those worthies did a very satisfactory job is quite permanently established by the fact that, with the lone exception of the extreme psychopath Yezhov, all the others, including Khrushchev, survived Stalin.

That bloodletting well under way, Poskrebyshev then busied himself on the script for Stalin's final and perhaps greatest show trial pageant. Early in 1938, he had Yezhov arrest the only two surviving old Bolsheviks of note, Bukharin and Rykov, plus a score or more of appropriate co-victims, as well as a suitable number of candidate co-victims, the latter to be replacements, in case some of the intended "defendants" fell by the way during NKVD "conditioning." And added to that miserable lot, somewhat as a last-minute whim, was none other than Yagoda, whose arrest and "interrogation" must have given Yezhov's peculiar talents considerable satisfaction. The fabrications of that "trial" were speedily exposed and even ridiculed abroad. But that made not a whit of difference to Stalin and Poskrebyshev. For, before the Kremlinologists of those days had pondered out a line, the dictator's victims had long since been liquidated.

While preparations for that so-called "trial of the twenty-one" were in course, Stalin apparently came to the conclusion that he needed somebody of greater standing than the *apparatchik* Yezhov to run his security police. Or maybe he had already decided to taper off the purges and therefore wanted to improve the image of the NKVD by giving it a more important boss. So, for those, or other reasons, he summoned his fellow-Georgian, Beria, whose purge of "opponents" in the Caucasus was well completed, to the capital. And he gave him the somewhat amorphous task of being deputy to Yezhov, who was then completely unaware of the fact, of course, that he was soon to be permanently unemployed, and worse.

In another such preparatory move in the security organization in early 1938, Poskrebyshev fired Tkalun, the erstwhile Kremlin commandant. Just what wrong Tkalun did is not and probably will never be known. And all that is known about his eventual fate is that he disappeared. In Tkalun's place as Kremlin commandant, Poskreby-shev installed a Major Rogov of the NKVD. Like Tkalun, and other palace guards of that pre-Beria period, there is no record of Rogov's first name or details of his background. Other details about such functionaries in the bodyguard organization, even if available, would be far from rewarding, since the lot of them literally disappeared from the scene like ships that passed in the night. Nevertheless, all were stark examples of the fact that to be a bodyguard of the Soviet dictator in that bloody era was usually a very short-term and danger-ous business.

In late summer of 1938, once Beria had settled into his new assign-ment as deputy chief of the NKVD, Stalin suddenly gave Yezhov the seemingly additional duty of being commissar of inland waterways. There appears no doubt that the little runt was mad enough to believe that his new task was a kind of reward for the slaughters he had performed for his master. For, characteristically, Stalin kept him on as titular head of the NKVD until Beria was firm in the saddle. And, of course, by the time the facts finally dawned on Yezhov, he was powerless to do anything.

CHAPTER VI

Bodyguards of an Entrenched Stalin

Stalin's appointment of Beria as chief of the NKVD in December 1938 may have been caused in part by his desire to have a more competent security boss, rather than a mere psychopathic killer, in charge of the police as Europe rushed toward war. And a contributory factor may have been the dictator's wish to have a man who not only shared his nationality, but also his cynicism, brutality, and ruthlessness at the helm of the organization that really ran the Soviet Union for him.

Shortly before the formal announcement of the appointment, Yezhov had dropped from sight completely. No official statement has ever been made about his fate. But one can imagine that the at least half-mad Yezhov must have gone completely mad, may even have frothed at the lips, when confronted with the same kind of arrest order he had so blithely given Yagoda. Reports that he subsequently hanged himself in an asylum may well be true.

Beria's establishment of himself at the top of the NKVD was no less vindictive than his predecessor's had been. But, it was a considerably quieter and to some extent a bit less bloody take-over. Of course, Yezhov's henchmen were thrown out, "encamped," or liquidated. However, none was known to have physically thrown himself from Lubyanka windows, as did many of Yagoda's creatures when Yezhov took over. Instead, there was a discreet but steady influx of Beria henchmen from the south, a Georgian take-over of all top NKVD posts. And among those new arrivals was one crony of Beria's, who was so entranced with Cheka work that he fabricated the name of "Dzermen" for his son, thus to give honor to the father and first disciple of the Soviet security police, Dzerzhinsky (Dzer) and Menzhinsky (Men). The only parallel to that would be a German Nazi admirer of Himmler and Eichmann giving his offspring a name like "Himmeich."

Although throughout his long tenure Beria concentrated more on the strictly national and international activities of the security police, his influence was also felt by the palace guards, even though that elite group remained under direct control of Poskrebyshev.

For example, about a month before Beria had formally taken office, Rogov was dismissed as Kremlin Commandant and disappeared into some Soviet limbo. That post remained vacant until spring 1939, when it was given to an NKVD brigadier-general, Nikolay Spiridonov. A protégé of Beria's, Spiridonov rose to be a lieutenant-general and continued as Kremlin Commandant until several weeks after Stalin died. His deputy, however, Petr Kosynkin, was evidently a Poskrebyshev selection. Kosynkin was a fanatic Stalin supporter and had risen to be an NKVD major-general before he suddenly succumbed to a "heart attack" about a fortnight in advance of Stalin's death.

There was also a shake-up of major proportions in the First Department. What caused it is not known. It may have been another ripple caused by Beria's take-over of the NKVD, but that does not appear very probable. It is more likely it was the result of Poskrebyshev and/or Stalin sprucing up the palace guards in the light of the onset of World War II. Gulst was dismissed as chief of the department and probably sometime in 1943 was shot for a so far undisclosed "crime." Few of Gulst's immediate successors had any better security of post, and to some extent of survival. In the period 1940–1945 a veritable series of NKVD generals served as chief of the First Department— Andrey Kapanadze (yet another Georgian), Aleksandr Kuznetsov, Pavlov, and Vasily Rumyantsev. Like Tkalun, Rogov, and Gulst before them, little is known about these NKVD men, thrust onto the scene, virtually at the last moment, in the continuing secret struggle by Beria, on the one hand, to assert control over all NKVD personnel, and Poskrebyshev-Stalin, on the other hand, for not only complete domination of the bodyguards, but also of the NKVD itself, no matter who was its nominal or titular boss. That struggle was most pronounced in the Beria period, for the simple reason that that Georgian was far stronger and astute in character than any of his predecessors except Dzerzhinsky, and that Pole was dead before the struggle really commenced. Victims of that cross fire, Pavlov was shot in 1941 or 1942, while Rumyantsev (who had made the error of "losing" Stalin, while the Georgian was making a tour of troop positions) was dismissed to a lesser position in 1944. Vlasik, of course, continued on virtually unscathed to practically the end, first as deputy and co-chief and finally as chief.

Practically on the eve of Hitler's attack on the Soviet Union, Stalin saw fit, for some reason that is still not clear, to reorganize the main structure of his security police. In effect, he split it in two. He retained the NKVD, with Beria as its commissar, and formed another commissariat for state security, the NKGB. Since Merkulov, a Beria creature, was named commissar of the new organization, the regrouping did not whittle away at Beria's powers by dividing them, in fact, the change strengthened them. It is therefore probable that the purpose of the reorganization was to improve control of the new border areas and the captive millions the dictator had gained as a result of his deal with Hitler. That February, 1941, reorganization was just another indication of the Georgian's naïveté on the international scale, and his absolute belief in the Nazi words, despite the subsequent Soviet propaganda that Stalin signed the pact with Hitler to gain time to strengthen his defensive position.

Within a month after the Hitler onslaught, however, Stalin realized that he would have to do without his newly gained territories, at least for awhile. Accordingly, he eliminated the NKGB and put all internal and security matters back into the hands of one organization, the NKVD. Beria continued as chief of the NKVD and the somewhat deposed Merkulov reverted to being his deputy. And the First Department, which had been under the administrative control of the NKGB, was switched back to the NKVD.

In 1942, before the tide of war had turned in his favor, Stalin created SMERSH, nominally a counterintelligence organization. Actually, SMERSH, which was staffed by NKVD officers and under direct control of Stalin and not the NKVD, had two tasks. The first was to keep the Red Army, whose men had been surrendering to the then victorious Nazis by the hundreds of thousands, in line, by terror and mass killings if need be. Its second was to be a sort of supreme security force for Stalin, to protect him from attack and possible assassination by the enemy. Subsequently, that second role has been greatly exaggerated, both by writers of fiction and Soviet security propagandists. At no time during World War II was Stalin ever in danger, nor was his life seriously threatened by enemy agents, despite extensive accounts of Nazi parachutists and/or airborne agents being captured near Moscow and of a Skorzeny attempt to do in the Georgian dictator during his meeting with Churchill and Roosevelt at Tehran. Such fabrications were little more than efforts to glorify SMERSH, and with it, of course, Soviet security officers. As a matter of fact, however, the prime assignments of SMERSH were to control the Red Army while the Nazis were still advancing, and to work over captured enemy forces and liberated Soviet elements once the Nazis began retreating.

But, since SMERSH did have the stated duty of guarding Stalin, its chief, Viktor Abakumov, became a member of the dictator's inner sanctum, whose authority rivaled if not exceeded that of First Department chiefs Kapanadze and Vlasik, although Poskrebyshev's powers remained inviolate. And at the same time, Abakumov's deputy, Sergey Kruglov, also entered into a close relationship with the seat of power. Thereby Stalin, who had probably followed Poskrebyshev's suggestion in appointing Abakumov and Kruglov, gained a pair of top security officers, who although basically NKVD men, were not creatures of Beria.

By April 1943, after the victory at Stalingrad had shown that the Nazis were at last on the final run, Stalin again had new territories and new captured millions to deal with. So he again reorganized his security police in exactly the same way he had done in the first hopeful days of 1941. He split them in two, retaining the NKVD with Beria at its head and reforming the NKGB with Merkulov once more its chief. At the same time, he also made a nomenclature change in the palace guards organization. He changed the name of the First Department to the Sixth Directorate and placed it under the NKGB for administration. The reasons for that change, which was one of name only, are far from clear. One possible explanation is that the Georgian sought to disguise it and appear to downgrade it, while in fact the powers of the household guard remained unchallenged. For Kapanadze was switched to being chief of the Sixth Directorate and Vlasik continued as his deputy.

At about that time, Stalin and Poskrebyshev became increasingly concerned about the power and authority they had vested in Beria.

To meet possible threats from his fellow-Georgian, the dictator used the same tactics as employed by Ivan the Terrible centuries earlier. He advanced the influence of the chief Leningrad *apparatchik*, Zhdanov, thereby providing a more potential rival to Beria than such subservient stooges as Molotov, Kaganovich, Malenkov, Voroshilov, et al.

A by-product of that ploy of pitting the leading minions against each other, and a forerunner of greater changes impending, arrived in the Kremlin in late 1945 in the person of Aleksey Kuznetsov. Although a somewhat personable young man, Kuznetsov was a sacrificial goat of sorts. A lesser *apparatchik* through and through, his only valid qualification was that he was a faithful creature of Zhdanov. Nevertheless, to accommodate Zhdanov, Stalin was willing to grant Kuznetsov the title of Secretary of the CC CPSU, and even to let him appear to oversee the security organs—including the bodyguards. In fact, this was Stalin's and Poskrebyshev's personal domain, and he advised Abakumov not to confide fully in Kuznetsov. And when Kuznetsov—not recognizing he was a fifth wheel—really tried to muscle in, he irritated Abakumov, Poskrebyshev, and Stalin. After Zhdanov's death, Kuznetsov was the first to fall in what became "the Leningrad Affair."

The political move that made Malenkov and Zhdanov co-crown princes of a sort resulted in a tripartite division of influence within the top echelon of the palace guards. Beria was represented by Kapanadze and other holdovers from his period of unchallenged power; Zhdanov had his Kuznetsov; and in a somewhat independent position were Abakumov and his career-type underlings. Granted, such a three-way split in the control of the Sixth Directorate in no way enhanced the efficiency of that organization. But, that three-way dog-fight did provide Stalin and Poskrebyshev with the assurance that no single person or group within the guards could contemplate any arrogation of power, so busy was each with the mere struggle for survival. And that Stalin could afford the luxury of bearbaiting his own bodyguards with factionalism was just another indication of the completely undisputed and tremendous power the Georgian dictator then wielded.

Buttressed by the almost unbelievable victories of World War II— a war which he almost abysmally lost—Stalin made his first overt move against Beria. That took the form of making Beria a Marshal of the Soviet Union in the summer of 1945 and then ousting him as nominal security boss in January, 1946, under the pretext that his services were needed to steal American nuclear secrets and to obtain rocketry know-how from German prisoners. (Actually, that promotion-demotion was not completely fraudulent: in due course, Beria and his security underlings did purloin the nuclear secrets and did pummel the Germans into divulging their rocket-lore.) Beria's chief minion, Merkulov, was retained as boss of the NKGB for a few weeks until he, too, was axed.

Technically, that was accomplished by yet another change in nomenclature. In March 1946, as Peter the Great had done before him, Stalin "Westernized" his administrative organs. The Communist term commissariat was abandoned and all such organizations became ministries. Thereby, the NKVD was changed to MVD and the NKGB to MGB. Merkulov was dismissed into the boondocks of the security service and Abakumov became chief of the MGB. The NKVD-MVD post had been given to Kruglov, when Beria was ousted. And somewhat concurrent with the changes in the security police leadership, Abakumov's wartime organization, SMERSH, was disbanded and its duties returned to military counterintelligence under the MGB.

In March, 1946, another very important change was also made. The palace guard unit was again reorganized and renamed. In effect, deciding to call a spade a spade, Stalin ruled that the guards should be called exactly what they were, guards, or "Okhrana," no matter if that was the term used for the last political police of the tsardom. Accordingly, the misnomer Sixth Directorate was dropped, and the organization became the "Upravleniye Okhrany," the Guard Administration. At the same time, the new organization was split into two, becoming Guard Administration No. 1, responsible only for the protection of Stalin, and Guard Administration No. 2, which nominally protected, but actually kept an eye on all other party and government leaders. Both administrations and the post of Kremlin Commandant, the third by that time a job of diminishing importance so far as the protection of Stalin was concerned, were subordinated to the MGB for administrative purposes. And, of course, the three new units were much larger and more sophisticated than the Sixth Directorate and its predecessors had been.

Spiridonov and his deputy, Kosynkin, remained on in the Kremlin *kommandatura.* And as could be expected, Abakumov men became chiefs of the two guards administrations. (The star of the chief of the former Sixth Directorate, Kapanadze, had set with the ouster of Beria.) Leadership of Stalin's guards was given to one Aleksandr Rakov, yet another of the many security officers briefly in the fickle Georgian's entourage, about whom little is known, and who ended up as chief of a forced labor camp in 1952 after Abakumov's downfall. Boss for an almost equally short time of Guard Administration No. 2 was General Dmitry Shadrin. Earlier, Shadrin had been unfortunate enough to have had the task of organizing Tito's bodyguards. When that Balkan worthy twitted his would-be monolithic master in 1948, Shadrin's security career came to a sudden end. Nor did either Rakov or Shadrin have any real independence of action during their short tenures, even though both were backed by Abakumov. The reason was that Zhdanov's creature, Kuznetsov, was practically and literally looking over their shoulders at all times.

However, the travails of Rakov and Shadrin proved to be little more than academic, so short a time did they hold their jobs. For in February 1947, or in less than a year after their previous shake-up, the palace guards were once again reorganized by Stalin and Poskrebyshev. The comparative autonomy of the three divisions—the two guards administrations and the Kremlin *kommandatura*—was eliminated. Although keeping their identities, those three units were superimposed by the ultimate in Stalin's refinements of his bodyguards. Under the new overall top command thereby established was a really vast organization of bodyguards—far greater in strength and structured in much more encompassing detail than any other leadership, Communist or otherwise, ever had or since has been furnished. It was called simply the Glavnoye Upravleniye Okhrany[1] or Main Guards Administration.

A good indication of the power and prestige of the new bodyguard organization can be gained from the fact that like the seemingly more important security police, from the Cheka to the NKVD, it speedily gained its own acronym, becoming known as simply the GUO.

Vlasik, by that time an MGB lieutenant-general, was made chief of the GUO. He had two deputies, both Abakumov men, Vladimir Lynko and Serafim Goryshev. (Under that trio, but subordinated to

[1]See Appendix I.

them, Rakov was retained as chief of Okhrana No. 1, and Shadrin similarly continued as boss of Okhrana No. 2 until 1948, when he was replaced by a fellow MGB officer, a Moscow SMERSH man, Major General Rozanov, another of the many whose first names are not known.) The progress up the security ladder of the Lynko-Goryshev pair ended in 1952, after Stalin had fired Abakumov. Along with Rakov, Goryshev was demoted to a camp commandant. Rozanov was downgraded to the militia. Lynko was not so lucky. He was arrested and subsequently believed shot. Initially, along with his two Abakumov deputies, Vlasik also had to put up with Zhdanov's stooge, Kuznetsov. But Kuznetsov did not long survive Zhdanov.

From the viewpoint of Stalin and Poskrebyshev, the single-headed GUO they had established was a decided improvement over its tripartite predecessor. Not only was it a patently more efficient organization, but it was also a much more secure body, being once more nominally run by Vlasik, who in turn was bossed by Poskrebyshev. With the previous dual administrations and the separate Kremlin *kommandatura*, there had always been the possibility—even though remote—that some would-be rival of Stalin could suborn all or an important segment of the bodyguards. Especially vulnerable were Okhrana No. 2 and the *kommandatura*.

As a result, except for some comparatively minor organizational changes, and the aging, testy Stalin's subsequent pique with both Vlasik and Poskrebyshev, the GUO retained its basic 1947 structure until shortly prior to the dictator's death.

CHAPTER VII

The Years of Trouble

The period 1949 to 1953 became known to Stalin's Okhrana, even through its rank and file, as the "years of trouble." For that organization, at least before 1949, everything had been more or less peaceful and orderly. And that despite the ousters and eliminations of various chiefs and subchiefs, actions which had become mere matters of routine in that kind of society. But, in the four successive years, even the average Okhrana man's life was uneasy and disturbed, because no one knew what was going on or might happen at the next moment.

Several prime factors caused that unsettled era: the sudden death at the end of August, 1948, of Zhdanov, Stalin's successor; the power struggle that started among the Georgian's other underlings after Zhdanov's death; the direct effect of that struggle on the top echelon of the security forces; and the increasing querulousness, spitefulness, and unpredictability of the sainted leader himself, who was fast losing both his former physical and mental powers as senility crept up on him. The culminating factor was the death of the dictator which brought the power struggle out into the open and thereby rattled the very foundations of the Okhrana organization. Most of its membership was reduced to being guards who did not know whom to guard, an indecisiveness that could be fatal.

For Abakumov, the Zhdanov death caused a real dilemma, and one that eventually caused his downfall and execution. According to the official announcement, Zhdanov's death, even though sudden and unexpected, was the result of natural causes, but senior GUO officers were skeptical indeed of that announcement. For, shortly before the death of Stalin's chief stooge of the moment, the GUO's operational department (the successor of the OPEROD, and in a way the SPU, or the Secret Political Directorate) had received information that Zhdanov had been the victim of malpractice by his doctors and probably had been poisoned.

Although Abakumov is not deserving of too much sympathy, it must be admitted that he alone of the men that Stalin and Poskrebyshev brought into the top security echelons after the purges had no political connections, no political ambitions. His only real concern was the protection of Stalin and his regime, obeying the Georgian's various whims conveyed to him directly or through Poskrebyshev, and, of course, worrying about his own survival. In comparison, all the others had been either Beria or Zhdanov men and as such gave their first loyalty to those lesser figures rather than to Stalin.

In the course of ridding the palace guards of personnel with such divided loyalties, he had managed in 1947 to persuade Poskrebyshev and Stalin that even the stupid Vlasik was a better choice as chief of the GUO than Kuznetsov. More naïve and far less wily than Beria, Zhdanov made no objection to Kuznetsov's reverting to his party secretaryship, evidently believing that his relations with Stalin (and by his son's marriage with Stalin's daughter) did not need the security of having an agent installed in the Georgian's household.

Beria, however—out in the cold at his atomic pursuits—fully recognized the need to know every twist and turn performed or planned by Poskrebyshev and Stalin. But Abakumov made the gross technical error of almost puritanically flaunting each and every approach from the anxious Beria. Stalin had warned him of Beria when he made him chief of the MGB and Abakumov was reacting to that warning.

After that warning had been delivered, Stalin and Poskrebyshev ordered Abakumov to have more modern listening devices installed in the quarters and offices and on the telephone lines of every Politburo member, high-ranking Red Army officer, and many lesser party personalities. All the information received from that monitoring was reported daily to Poskrebyshev, who, in turn, delivered it to Stalin. It was on the basis of that listening-in that Stalin later shook up party and government organizations. And some of that information, often taken out of context, or even "doctored," was also subsequently used to send Kuznetsov, Voznesensky, and others to their deaths.

In the "good old days" when he and/or his stooge Merkulov had run security, Beria had always looked over such monitoring reports before they were delivered to Poskrebyshev and Stalin. He made frequent attempts to establish such a routing with Abakumov, but never succeeded. In fact, Abakumov even lied and told him the practice had been discontinued. Those refusals and dodges made Beria furious. Therefore, it was only a matter of time before the far more astute Beria got the relatively faithful but exceedingly unwise Abakumov.

The seeds of that process were sown at the time of Zhdanov's death. The "information" about Zhdanov being poisoned had come from a Dr. Lidiya Timashuk, a member of the Kremlin medical office. Although possessing a medical degree, she was little more than a nurse. Her actual work was that of an informer for the operational department of the GUO. She reported that Zhdanov's doctors had given him the wrong medicine and thereby caused his death.

Timashuk's first report was made while Zhdanov was still alive. On receipt of it, Abakumov started an investigation that he directed personally, but apparently he made the very bad—and fatal—mistake of not reporting the investigation to either Poskrebyshev or Stalin. However, he did arrest a medical professor connected with the case. When that unfortunate refused to confess his "guilt" he was put in solitary confinement in the Lubyanka. Abakumov also checked with the chief of Zhdanov's personal bodyguard, who informed his boss "this woman (Timashuk) is crazy." A few days later, the professor, who had been in poor health, caught pneumonia and died in his jail cell. By pure coincidence, Zhdanov died at the same time, so Abakumov closed the case. In doing so, he advised his fellow investigators: "We have to stop this investigation; otherwise we will lose our heads." Abakumov meant that very, very literally. After all, he had been at the security helm long enough to appreciate that there were groups and powers superior to him who might not welcome too much investigation. He knew that there was every possibility that Poskrebyshev and/or Stalin, acting through the GUO's independent and all-powerful operational department, may have done away with Zhdanov for reasons that were not his concern.

Somewhat concurrent with the "closing" of the Zhdanov case, Abakumov became a sort of innocent victim in another power struggle, that of Malenkov, Stalin's reigning favorite-of-the-moment, once

Zhdanov had died. That great ball of lard, and a leading alumnus of Poskrebyshev's "secretariat," struck quickly to assure his new position as heir-apparent. His immediate targets, of course, were Zhdanov adherents. The leading Zhdanov men to be eliminated were Kuznetsov and Voznesensky, the latter a fellow graduate of the Poskrebyshev "secretariat" and a winner of the Stalin Prize for his economic theories. And, of course, all of Zhdanov's Leningrad *apparat* had to go.

Evidently, Stalin fully supported and abetted those machinations of Malenkov, no doubt enjoying watching his dogs again eating one another. His daughter, Svetlana (although her chronology was in error) later described how Stalin cold-shouldered Kuznetsov out of a dinner, even though the Georgian knew full well that his erstwhile watchdog of the palace guards had been one of the invited guests.

That studied rudeness of the dictator was as good as a direct order for the MGB chief. In due course, doubtless with some personal vengeance, Abakumov himself arrested Kuznetsov. On the order of Stalin the arrest was arranged in Malenkov's office. Kuznetsov was executed in February, 1949.

Voznesensky's elimination was preceded by his dismissal from all his positions in the party and government. He was arrested a few months after that ritual and put to death in 1950. As result of Voznesensky's downfall, his brother, Aleksandr Voznesensky, also perished, although the reason for his death is not clear unless it was simply because he was a close relative. He was education minister for the Russian Republic, and prior to that a rector of Leningrad University, an institution that ironically bears the name of Zhdanov.

Abakumov's most difficult assignment, which he handled under the direction of Malenkov, was the frame-up that came to be known as the "Leningrad Affair," or in simpler terms, the elimination of all of Zhdanov's *apparat* in the northern metropolis.

That infamous business had as its background a 1948 proposal—while Zhdanov was still the undisputed No. 2 man—that the capital of the Russian Republic be transferred from Moscow to Leningrad, and that the republic's party headquarters be moved to the northern city as well. The advocates of that move were Rodionov and Vlasov, respectively chairmen of the Council of Ministers and of the Presidium of the Supreme Soviet of the RSFSR, Voznesensky, Kuznetsov, Petr Popkov, Leningrad party first secretary, and other members of Zhdanov's *apparat*. They held that such a move would increase the efficiency of the republic's party and government organs and in support they cited the fact that the Ukraine, White Russia, and other republics also operated out of their own capital cities. And almost as an afterthought, Voznesensky suggested that an international fair be staged in Leningrad.

Bearing in mind that the bulk of those proposals had already been made—and without Stalin making any known objection to them—well before Zhdanov's death, it does not seem too presumptuous to wonder if Abakumov's suspicion that Stalin really did have Zhdanov killed off was correct.

All that is known, however, is that Stalin did not see fit to vent his rage until Malenkov had assumed the role of heir-presumptive. And it is quite easy to picture Malenkov sidling up to the old Georgian, then almost in his seventieth year, and pouring poison into the dictator's ear about the Zhdanovites. Most probably, he told him that such a shift of the Russian capital would dim the luster of his power as dictator of the whole Soviet Union and might make the world pay more attention to Leningrad and the Russian people than to Moscow, where the ruler was not a Russian, but a Georgian.

Such a conversation is pure speculation, but it is a fact that Malenkov managed to arouse Stalin's anger over the Zhdanovites' proposal, which the Georgian labeled a "Trotskyist suggestion" and ordered a thorough "investigation."

That nasty chore Malenkov seconded to Abakumov, who dutifully proceeded to fabricate a case against the Zhdanovites to fit the needs of his masters. The whole affair was conducted in the strictest secrecy and it is extremely doubtful that the formality of "trials" was resorted to even behind closed doors. It was a rehash of the purges of the thirties in miniature, but without the publicity that was given the earlier sorry events.

As result of that frame-up, conducted by Abakumov, but under the direction of Malenkov and Poskrebyshev and with Stalin as overseer, Zhdanov's entire party and government organization in Leningrad was wiped out. And that purge included other areas as well. Most pertinent was Moscow, where Georgy Popov, the capital's party first secretary who was on friendly relations with the Zhdanovites, was removed and replaced by Khrushchev. Of the some three hundred Zhdanovites purged, most were put to death.

In the spring of 1949, almost directly on the heels of completion of the "Leningrad Affair," Malenkov gave Abakumov yet another dirty job, that of working over the Jews, always convenient scapegoats for Russian tsars, commissars, and their successors. Under the direction of Poskrebyshev, Abakumov unearthed—manufactured is the better word—the so-called "Jewish Plot" of "rootless cosmopolitans" allegedly acting as agents for Zionism and the Israeli government throughout the Soviet Union. The Jews who were wiped out as a result of those fabrications were more or less innocent bystanders. They were just caught in the scatter of shots directed at the real target, Molotov, Stalin's most veteran surviving flunky, and a possible roadblock in the way of Malenkov's drive to power. Molotov's wife, Polina Zhemchuzhina, and his Deputy Foreign Minister, Solomon Lozovsky, were both Jews. Molotov's wife was pretty easy pickings, because earlier she had suggested forming a Jewish autonomous republic in the Crimea and moving there all Jews in the Soviet Union, including those in the phony Jewish autonomous *oblast* in far eastern Siberia.

Naturally, of course, the chief victim, and among the earliest "punished," was Molotov's wife. She was expelled from the party, deprived of all civil rights (nebulous as such rights are under the Soviet system) and was sent to the frightful forced labor camp at Vorkuta in the far north. (Later, she was moved to a less redoubtable camp in Kazakhstan.) Regardless of the myriad of other blots on his once noble escutcheon, to his credit, Molotov did not follow long established form and denounce his wife. For that, and to be sure because of his relationship no matter what he had done, he was "relieved" of his duties as Foreign Minister in March, 1949. Molotov continued as First Deputy Prime Minister, but in name only. The conviction of his wife had ended his career and he knew it. From that time on, he scarcely ever bothered even to visit his office, let along take an active role in party and government affairs. It was a somewhat tragic finale for a man for whom the "Molotov cocktail" may assure greater continuity in world vernacular than Stalin, but one that he had seen meted out to many another, without blinking an eye.

Only parenthetically, of course, as compared to the much greater misfortunes that befell the Zhdanovites and the Jews, is the fate of their bodyguards worthy of note. But it further illustrates how that period was "years of trouble" for the Okhrana. When Stalin fired a hierarch, without punishment, that hierarch's bodyguards were also dismissed, and also without punishment, generally being reassigned to security posts outside the capital. But, when a hierarch was not only fired but was also arrested and jailed, his chief bodyguard would also be imprisoned and the subordinate guards dispersed to remote areas of Siberia. Never, never were bodyguards transferred from one hierarch to another. After Kuznetsov's arrest, his chief bodyguard was imprisoned with the master. It is not known if that guard was likewise shot, but he did disappear, and forever. The same thing happened with Voznesensky's guard. In the case of Zhdanov, since he officially died of "natural causes," his bodyguards were either assigned to other Okhrana components, or transferred to other state security offices in Moscow. A few bodyguards, chauffeurs, and other servants, continued on with Zhdanov's wife and son. And when Molotov's wife was "encamped," she was allowed to take a few Okhrana servants with her. (That assignment was kept from Stalin's knowledge, although "new class" or no "new class" among the Communist hierarchy, it is difficult to imagine those Okhrana people going voluntarily to Vorkuta.)

The persecutions of the Jews continued apace and well into 1952. They were a sort of background music or stagesetting for yet another power struggle among the increasingly anxious flunkies of the declining Stalin. The chief feature of that conflict was the gradual but steady reemergence of Beria. By 1950, that most powerful of all Communist security chiefs to date was well enough back into Stalin's good graces to wangle the appointment of his veteran stooge, Merkulov, as chief of the potent and police-run Ministry of State Control.

In doing that, Beria also ousted Mekhlis, the great prewar purger of the Red Army, and a longtime faithful servant of Stalin and Poskrebyshev, from his post as boss of the Control Ministry. Beria thereby opened the road for again gaining control of the state security apparatus as well. And shortly after that achievement, Beria himself informed the newspapers that Okhrana-man Ryumin, who had pushed the investigation of Timashuk's charges about Zhdanov's death, had been moved to Merkulov's ministry.

At the time, that was a seemingly innocent and unimportant transfer. Eventually, however, it turned out to be a move that not only demolished Stalin's extremely sophisticated and well-organized

[315]

Okhrana, but also one that thereby may have hastened the dictator's death.

For Ryumin was a complete bureaucrat from head to toe, a sort of Soviet version of the Tsarist types depicted in Gogol's *Inspector-General*, Abakumov's halting the Zhdanov poisoning investigation in mid-course apparently had disturbed him to the very bottom of his petty, bureaucratic soul. He was literally almost aching to continue the probe. His opportunity came, it seems, after his transfer to Merkulov's staff. Whether Beria purposefully had Ryumin moved to the Ministry of State Control to unburden him of his knowledge about the Zhdanov death inquiry, or whether Ryumin voluntarily told Merkulov and/or Beria about it after his arrival there is not known. But beyond all doubt, that insignificant bureaucrat, then no more than a security lieutenant-colonel, must have had very powerful backing, probably Beria's, even to have considered sending, let alone actually sending, a letter to Stalin in midsummer of 1951.

In that letter, Ryumin made the devastating charge that Abakumov had not only halted the investigation of Zhdanov's death, but had even covered it up. Within hours the axe fell. Abakumov, about to leave Poskrebyshev's Kremlin office after having delivered a routine, nighttime report, was arrested by members of the Okhrana's operational department. He was taken to the Lubyanka and put in solitary confinement. Seven of his deputies and several dozen senior state security officers were arrested along with him. And his chief bodyguard, Lieutenant-Colonel Kuznetsov (no relation to Zhdanov's stooge) was arrested a few days later and charged with lack of vigilance for not reporting the "evil deeds" of his master.

Interestingly, the charges brought against Abakumov at that time were that he had not recognized the enemy of the people during his handling of the "Leningrad Affair," basically a treason charge. No mention whatsoever was made then of the Zhdanov death case. That would have upset Stalin's future plans.

As could be expected, the arrests of Abakumov and his fellow officers caused decided qualms and another and quite serious flurry of unrest among the Okhrana rank and file. In September, 1951, none other than Khrushchev was ordered to calm the worries of Okhrana party activists and explain the situation. In his speech, the little man echoed Stalin's charge to the letter—that Abakumov and his officers had failed to recognize the enemy of the people in the northern city's party apparatus. Few of the Okhrana men, however, accepted that mimicry of Khrushchev's. It was common knowledge to most of them that Abakumov had been axed on the demand of Beria who was seeking revenge for the number of his stooges who had been fired by Abakumov. But they also accepted the supplementary charges against Abakumov of misconduct, moral degeneration, and misuse of government funds. They knew only too well about their boss' many mistresses and the government funds he had squandered in entertaining them.

A few days after Abakumov's downfall, Beria attempted to strike while the iron was hot. He proposed to Stalin that Merkulov again be installed as chief of state security. But the dictator disregarded that ploy and appointed Lieutenant-General Sergey Ogoltsov, the only one of the few Abakumov deputies who had escaped arrest, as acting chief of state security.

Still not quitting his attempt at a comeback, Beria then stressed Abakumov's crimes and the woeful state to which the security organization had been reduced during his administration. As a result, Stalin agreed to appoint a commission to investigate, not only Abakumov, but also the entire state security apparatus. That commission was composed of Beria, Malenkov, Bulganin, and Ignatyev. In December, 1951, after that investigating body had started its work, Ogoltsov was eased out and Ignatyev, up to then no more than an inspector (functionary) of the CC CPSU, was appointed boss of the MGB. And the real boss, the partially reestablished Beria, helped by furnishing him with a few deputies, all, of course, faithful stooges of Beria.

However, Ignatyev's most active deputy was the ardent bureaucrat Ryumin, the betrayer of Abakumov and the "expert" on the Zhdanov death case. Stalin, by then quite psychotic, if not actually approaching madness, regarded Ryumin and his "revelations" as a prized windfall. In time, he virtually brainwashed the submissive and doubtless terrified bureaucrat and made him aid and abet a vast, fabricated enlargement of the Zhdanov death case. That enlargement eventually became the so-called "Doctors' Plot," a patent lie that a number of doctors—and the number varied—had poisoned Zhdanov and Aleksandr Shcherbakov, a former Secretary of the CC CPSU, and were scheming to similarly do away with Stalin, selected members of the Politburo, and Red Army leaders. And, of course, most all of those "evil" but completely innocent doctors were Jews, caught in yet another Russian pogrom.

In the course of that horrendous fabrication, the female Okhrana creature, Timashuk, was awarded an Order of Lenin, an award accompanied by much nauseating biographical bilge in the controlled press. It is a moot point whether that woman, who triggered the whole mess in 1948, did so of her own volition, or was acting under orders of Stalin, laying the groundwork for another, but much more complicated, Kirov case.

But, since Stalin had intended the "Doctors' Plot" to surpass the great show trials of the purge era, it was an exceedingly long time in production before any announcement was made about it. The arrested doctors must have been brave men, for they long proved difficult. Khrushchev mentioned that years later in his partial revelations when he quoted Stalin as telling Ignatyev (and Ryumin), "If you do not obtain confessions from the doctors, we will shorten you by a head." And after those two worthies had forced the doctors to confess—by techniques better left to the imagination—we again have Khrushchev's revelation that Stalin told the Politburo: "You are blind like young kittens. What will happen without me? The country will perish because you do not know how to recognize enemies."

Meanwhile, Beria's commission had been hard at work. Ostensibly that body was only supposed to make a financial examination of the Okhrana, but it far exceeded its terms of reference. On a strictly financial plane, it determined that the Okhrana was costing the state the vast sum of three billion rubles a year. It also recommended that economies be made by eliminating the heads of several departments of state security. But that done, it then proceeded—and with the fullest cooperation of Malenkov—to cut Stalin's bodyguards to the bone and thereby put him under control. By that time, the dictator was so engrossed with his "Doctors' Plot" aborning that he had thoughts for almost nothing else.

As a result, Beria purged the Okhrana, the very bodyguard organization that Stalin, when in full command of his powers and senses, had so labored to perfect. Dozens of generals and colonels were imprisoned or transferred, and about seven thousand men were dropped from the original Okhrana force of some seventeen thousand. Beria sent most of those eliminated from the Okhrana to other state security organizations, keeping them in reserve for the time when his try to seize power should come.

Others, he completely reorganized. The street traffic section was restored to control of the local Moscow militia. The supply department which ran the farms and slaughterhouses for the use of the hierarchs was returned in part either to the trade ministry or to state security's main supply directorate. And the Okhrana's *sovkhozes* and *kolkhozes* were turned over to the agriculture ministry. The ubiquitous Okhrana plainclothesmen, once so familiar a sight on Moscow's main arteries whenever Stalin or his lieutenants were traveling to or from the Kremlin, were subordinated to state security's surveillance directorate.

Before making that last cut, Beria spoke openly to a group of ex-Okhrana chiefs to whom he had given other posts in the capital. He asked them: "Why do we need 3,000 plainclothes agents on Moscow's streets? Do you think that thirty-five years after the revolution there is anyone who would want to kill our dear Comrade Stalin? Everybody loves Comrade Stalin. There is no need for such a big Okhrana."

Not all of the Okhrana chiefs thus made redundant were pleased with the reductions, but all obeyed Beria. Therefore, when the slashing was finished, Stalin's personal bodyguards, Okhrana No. 1, had been cut to half strength, leaving the dictator guarded by not only a small group of officers, but also a group that had little security experience, especially as bodyguards, and one that was headed by a mere major. Only the Okhrana personnel that staffed Stalin's household were left unchanged.

One day in early May 1952, at the height of Beria's campaign to whittle away his fellow Georgian's personal security, some two hundred fifty dismissed officers of Stalin's bodyguard gathered at state security's central personnel office looking for reassignment. For a few of them, Beria had arranged retirement. But most were given the simple choice of going to a remote camp or post in Siberia, or being fired.

The majority not lucky enough to have been given retirement was completely unaware of the wholesale nature of Beria's campaign and believed that some bureaucrat must have made a mistake. So later they gathered again in front of state security headquarters on Dzerzhinsky square. They blocked Ignatyev's doorway and demanded to see him. Alarmed, Ignatyev telephoned Beria, who advised that sorry excuse for an MGB boss to placate the protesters by having their names put on a list for consideration for future assignment. That ended the first known demonstration of a Russian leader's bodyguards since the days of the tsars. The following day the group was summoned to the personnel office and flatly given the same choice —go to Siberia or be fired. Within the week all of them had disappeared from Moscow.

Beria's concentration on eliminating the effectiveness of the Okhrana did not hinder him from being fully informed about developments in the "Doctors' Plot" fabrication. After all, unlike Abakumov, he had Ignatyev well under his thumb and Ignatyev had a plethora of information about the "poisoners" from his deputy, the "expert" Ryumin.

Therefore, the Beria commission, when making its report in May 1952, not only told Stalin about such comparative trifles as Abakumov's embezzling and the staggering costs of the Okhrana, but also reported that Abakumov was not the only one who had not informed him about the "poisoning"—Vlasik and Poskrebyshev had known as well.

Of course, the claim about that pair of longtime faithful servants was a bald and most complete lie. But Beria took the calculated risk that Stalin's mental condition was near to that of Ivan the Terrible before him and that the dictator's suspicions of enemies being all about him would permit separating this fellow Georgian from his most trusted adherents.

And things worked out as Beria had gambled. Stalin, long such a great liar that he once knew a lie when he heard one, had lost that faculty. He flew into one of his finest furies. He called Poskrebyshev "Vlasik's drunken companion, who has sold himself out to Vlasik for a bottle of vodka." He called Vlasik "a drunk and a *darmoyed* (parasite)." And he fired them both on the spot. His suspicions next turned to the head of the Kremlin medical department Professor Petr Yegorov, and to his longtime personal physician Professor Vladimir Vinogradov, and he ordered that pair arrested. Subsequently, his rage swung to his bodyguards, whom he also called *darmoyedy*, and whose chiefs, Rakov, Rozanov, Lynko, Goryshev, he dispatched into oblivion, thereby himself completing the destruction of his bodyguard organization and, albeit unwittingly, aiding Beria in his

[320]

labors. The *Götterdämmerung* of the Stalin era had begun.

Vlasik, once the faithful doormat outside the then insignificant Stalin's rooms, was not only fired, he was also expelled from the party and sent to Sverdlovsk, not as commandant, but as deputy commandant of a forced labor camp.

When Vlasik left for the Urals (or should it be western Siberia?), a group of officers went to the train to see him off. Among them was Stalin's son Vasily, Vlasik's old drinking companion. Vasily was drunk as usual and when the train pulled out he screamed: "They are going to kill him, they are going to kill him." By "they," he meant the other members of the Politburo, and by "him" he meant his father.

The handful of Okhrana officers that had joined Vasily in saying farewell to Vlasik were all fired upon return to their offices in the State Security Building.

The treatment accorded Poskrebyshev was not so severe. He was placed under house arrest in his *dacha* outside Moscow, with Ignatyev-Beria guards posted about.

In midsummer of 1952, Vlasik, not much younger than his master and by then a rather pitiful wreck, took French leave from Sverdlovsk, and went to Moscow. He tried to see Poskrebyshev, but the Beria guards at that *dacha* chased him away. Next he went to the Kremlin in an attempt to see Stalin. Again he was turned away by Beria guards. Later, he was picked up near the Kremlin gates and put into the Lubyanka. Two weeks later he died there of an "illness."

Sometime after Vlasik's death, Poskrebyshev was released from house arrest and brought back to the Kremlin. That did not mean that Stalin had relented or had had a change of heart. The recall was due only to the fact that nobody else was qualified, nobody else so knew the queer twists of Stalin's mind necessary to help the dictator with preparations for the Nineteenth Party Congress, scheduled for October, 1952, and the packing of the Politburo. It does not seem logical that the Georgian also used his rehabilitated alter ego in perfecting the fabrication of the "Doctors' Plot." That was too much the peculiar specialty of Stalin himself and his newly found disciple Ryumin. Nevertheless, there are some accounts that Poskrebyshev not only assisted completion of the final phase of the "Doctors' Plot," but also resumed his role as the untitled chief of Stalin's personal bodyguards. But, those accounts are not correct.

As a matter of fact, so far as the bodyguards were concerned, the firing of Vlasik and his subchiefs and Beria's paring down of the strength and efficiency of the Okhrana resulted in the last reorganization of the palace guards that was to take place in Stalin's lifetime. In the spring of 1952, the GUO, or the Main Guards Administration, was phased out of existence. It was replaced by the Guards Directorate, a single-bodied organization. Eliminated were Okhranas No. 1 and No. 2, which meant that Stalin no longer received any special, individual protection, but only the same kind that was given to other members of the Politburo and similar hierarchs. With the dismissals of Vlasik and his subchiefs, MGB chief Ignatyev himself also served as chief of the castrated Okhrana for several months. Later, the down-graded palace guards, which probably should be called the Beria-Malenkov Okhrana, got a chief of their own, MGB Colonel Martynov, who had previously served without distinction as head guard at the building of the CC CPSU. But while at the party headquarters, he had become personally acquainted with such lesser hierarchs as Khrushchev and Malenkov. It was on Malenkov's recommendation, and of course with Beria's approval, that Ignatyev made Martynov chief of what remained of the Okhrana.

Stalin did not turn to Poskrebyshev (who must inwardly have been pretty well disgusted by that time) to again organize his security, nor rely either on Martynov or others of those latter-day Okhrana chiefs. Instead he gravitated toward the original guard setup of his more youthful days, the Kremlin *kommandatura*. However, he did not put his trust in the Kremlin Commandant, Spiridonov, aware that he had become a caterer to the whims of Beria and Malenkov. So he entrusted himself to the Deputy Kremlin Commandant, Kosynkin, whose intelligence quotient was not much higher than Vlasik's had been, but who literally adored Stalin and worshipped the very ground on which he trod.

That Martynov's Okhrana existed in little more than name only became very apparent at the Nineteenth Congress. Previously at such gatherings, Vlasik and his lieutenants had stalked officiously through the hall, checking scores of subalterns, examining papers and documents, and assuring the security of entries and anterooms. But at that October, 1952 meeting, what security there was was run by Ignatyev and Martynov, supervised by Beria. And Stalin spoke from a podium, theretofore almost surrounded by masses of guards, that was protected by a mere sprinkling of bodyguards of his own.

In effect, he was a prisoner of the Politburo and the reconstituted Okhrana and there was nothing he could do about it. Nor did that Okhrana even have the strength to do the job properly. It had to be reinforced in the hall by several hundred MGB officers on detached service from other state security units. That made a force strong enough to carry out the usual procedure—to station plainclothes armed guards at every table of a dozen to twenty handpicked delegates as well as to have an armed guard for almost every person in the gallery. But, only an insignificant few of those officers were Stalin's men.

Despite that lack of the personal security of his prime, Stalin was able to control the congress and weaken the Politburo—renamed the Presidium at that time—by packing it with new blood. He managed that, despite his failing health and faculties and despite his mistake in letting his Okhrana be virtually disbanded, because figuratively at least he was still head and shoulders over his underlings who dared no more than connive behind his back. Shortly after the end of the congress, his latest plaything, the "Doctors' Plot," the instrument with which he intended to settle the score with the connivers once and for all, had reached perfection. At that time, the fabrication was still a somewhat privileged matter. The Okhrana rank and file only learned that it was in the offing after arrests in the Kremlin medical office. Comparatively, Beria and Malenkov, through their control of Ignatyev, were very well informed, as were other Politburo old-timers allied with them. And some of that information thus gleaned bothered Beria and Malenkov to a high degree. Particularly worrisome to them was the fact that they were not included on the list of those the doctors allegedly planned to poison. The implication to all those omitted from that carefully prepared list was obvious— Stalin had excluded them from his inner circle and therefore they were in extreme jeopardy.

On January 13, 1953, the "Doctors' Plot," which had been in manufacture for well over a year, was finally completed and announced to the world in general. The announcement puzzled only the non-Communists, who although agreeing that it was yet another example of Russian anti-Semitism, had various subsidiary explanations—that it was a thinly veiled attack on Israel or that it might be the prelude to a wave of anti-Semitism among the Soviet satellite states. Only a few Western Kremlinologists made the correct assumption—that it was the introduction to yet another Stalin-directed purge. His intended victims among the Soviet hierarchs knew that, of course, full well, and some by then were so frightened they might have supplied the names, had any Western analyst bothered to ask.

A small and comparatively unimportant, but actually quite significant, occurrence took place immediately after the announcement of the "Doctors' Plot." Zhdanov's former chief bodyguard who had regarded Timashuk as crazy and had been in a sort of retirement in Moscow, a retirement that was carefully watched, suddenly disappeared from the capital. After several weeks' intensive and frantic search on the part of Ryumin's men, he was found in Stalingrad and returned forthwith to Moscow and the Lubyanka. That sealing of the lips of one of the few honest men in the case did not escape the attention of the connivers and increased their worries.

However, the accompanying Stalin-controlled flurry in the Soviet press soon made that aspect of the "Doctors' Plot" clear to all. In a crescendo of calls for vigilance on the part of the helpless and ignorant average Soviet citizen, and other such common Communist hokum, the first direct attacks ever by the Communist press were leveled against the security apparatus for having failed to have discovered the "plot" earlier. No names were named, but it was obvious then to even the *lumpenproletariat* that Beria and Merkulov and their cohorts, and even the arrested Abakumov, were in very bad trouble, indeed. For it was they who had been running security at the time the doctors had started their "machinations."

Somewhat concurrently, and doubtless as a result of the double warning of being omitted from the doctors' list of intended victims and of the press attacks on state security, Beria made the final changes of the Stalin era in the Okhrana setup. He had Ignatyev fire Martynov and dump him in a minor MGB job in the capital. At the same time, he also completed the emasculation of the Okhrana. The most important steps in that move, which was well disguised by other strictly administrative measures, were the final and outright transfers of the operational department, the plainclothes agents and the Kremlin *kommandatura* from the Okhrana to MGB control.

As new chief of the Okhrana, Beria gave Ignatyev a Colonel Nikolay Novik, an experienced MGB counterintelligence officer, and a protégé of Suslov. Stalin, who had well seen what a failure his Okhrana was at the Nineteenth Congress made no objection to Martynov's dismissal, nor, does it appear, to Novik's appointment. Perhaps he did not understand that previously Novik had been chief of the very MGB Secret Political Directorate to which the Okhrana's once-powerful operational department was transferred.

About the only significant step taken by Novik in his comparatively short time in office was to send a group of MGB Secret Political Directorate officers to China to arrest a Soviet doctor who was treating Mao Tse-tung. The doctor not only was accused of being a member of the "Doctors' Plot," but claims were also made that he was trying to poison the Chinese leader.

Except for the stridency of the press campaign about the doctors and the laxity in the state security, a sort of calm before the storm settled over the Kremlin and the rest of the Soviet Union during the month following the announcement of the plot. Then, on February 17, 1953, there came the report, generally overlooked at the time, that the Deputy Kremlin Commandant, General Kosynkin, the only surviving guard that Stalin could trust, had suddenly died of a "heart attack." And on February 21, a most significant change was made in the army high command. General Sergey Shtemenko was replaced by Marshal Vasiliy Sokolovsky as Chief of Staff of the Soviet armed forces. Shtemenko had worked very closely with Stalin during World War II as chief of the operational department of the general staffs, and the Georgian not only trusted him completely, but truly adored him. His removal was very important for the Beria-Malenkov coalition, and particularly so for that pair's coat hanger, Bulganin, who was also glaringly omitted from the doctors' list. And concurrent with Shtemenko's replacement, the Okhrana bodyguards were removed from the general staff and their places taken by army counter intelligence officers.

That completed the process of stripping Stalin of all personal security, except for the comparative window dressing of the minor Okhrana officers in his office and household. It had been a studied and very ably handled business: the framing of Abakumov, the dismissal of Vlasik, the discrediting of Poskrebyshev, the emasculation of the Okhrana and its enforced subservience to the MGB, Kosynkin's "heart attack," the replacement of Shtemenko, and the removal of the general staff from the last vestiges of Okhrana control. And certainly not to be forgotten at that juncture was the dismissal of the Georgian's personal physician followed by MGB control of the Kremlin medical office. With state security and the armed forces under their command, the connivers were finally in the driver's seat. And ironically, much of the whole process had been aided and abetted by Stalin, a most telling indication that he had lost the capability to run the Soviet system. Ivan the Terrible, whom Stalin so admired, mad though he was, had run his terror machine to the last moment while Stalin surrendered his protective weapons before his death.

Five days after the death of Kosynkin, the press campaign about the "Doctors' Plot" ended as suddenly as it had started. What brought that pet project of Stalin's to a halt is not known. The surviving connivers refrained from disclosing such details, no doubt since they were too directly involved in the last days of their master. Nor, so denuded of effectives had been the Okhrana by that time, were there any bodyguards, later defecting to the West, in an authoritative enough position to know. And even those Okhrana men still with the dictator in his last days are no longer extant to furnish any enlightenment.

Overlooking the red herrings and fabrications manufactured by his successors, it is logical to presume that once Kosynkin and Shtemenko had been disposed of, the connivers mustered up the courage to confront Stalin. They knew that for their own very survival they had to quash the "Doctors' Plot," or later be brought to "trial" themselves, either individually or as a group. The allegations hurled back and forth would have been horrific. And it seems reasonable to presume that at the height of that scene the by then apoplectic Georgian suddenly staggered and fell to the floor of his Kremlin office, the victim of a heart attack and probably a stroke.

At that, it would seem from the accounts of terrified Okhrana subordinates on the periphery of that set-to, the connivers, terrified themselves at the sudden collapse of the master, scurried like rats from the Kremlin. The Okhrana men, even more frightened, probably had already made themselves scarce. Poskrebyshev may have been bustled out even before the confrontation started, for his whereabouts became unknown after the "Doctors' Plot" was quelched.

The attack Stalin suffered was not fatal, and did not become so for some days. It would appear that after the connivers and guards had departed, the Georgian recovered enough to struggle to his feet and take a chair at his desk where he collapsed again. From that point on,

[326]

supposition is no longer needed. Okhrana men supplied the rest.

Later—just how much later can no longer be determined—an Okhrana underling dared to peek into the dictator's office. He saw the Georgian unconscious at his desk. He sounded the alarm and went through the form of notifying other members of the Presidium.

But it was not until early the next morning—and in the utmost secrecy—that the ailing dictator was moved to his *dacha* at Kuntsevo, some seven miles away, on the outskirts of Moscow. And only after Stalin had arrived at Kuntsevo were doctors summoned to his bedside. They were MGB functionaries all, not much better professionally than Timashuk. No call was made for the able Vinogradov. As could be expected, the MGB men could (or would?) do nothing to help the stricken Stalin. So, they called in the Minister of Health, who administered the last medical rites. Officially, Joseph Vissarionovich Dzhugashvili (Stalin) died March 5, 1953.

With that death, the so-called "years of trouble" of the bodyguards of the Soviet leadership came to an end. But, they were to be followed by many long months of trouble that proved even more critical to Okhrana survivors.

Bodyguards of Stalin's Successors

1. THE END OF BERIA

Once Stalin was dead, Beria evidently thought that all he needed to attain supreme power was the same sort of control of the bodyguards and other security forces as had been exercised by his fellow Georgian in maintaining his rule.

But Beria, actually a Mingrelian, a lesser Georgian group, completely overlooked the fact that Stalin, a master politician in the Communist sense, had first played off one potential rival against the other and had kept his bodyguard organization relatively innocent-appearing and arcane until he had achieved political control. Only when that had been accomplished did Stalin use his security organization, which he had been perfecting simultaneously with politicking, to keep himself in the saddle. And there is little doubt that years of unquestioned authority as a police autocrat must have warped Beria's power of judgment. Also, in the confusion that accompanied the death of the dictator, his fellow connivers were at first too anxious to secure their own positions to pay attention to, or evaluate immediately, Beria's moves.

Therefore, even before Stalin's body was cold, Beria ordered the MGB troops, primarily the First Dzerzhinsky Motorized Infantry Division (of Special Designation) and its sister Second Motorized Infantry Division, into Moscow from their quarters in the environs of the city. Within hours, those units not only set up controls and halted traffic, including pedestrian, on every principal capital thoroughfare, but had also ringed the Kremlin. The city, the party, the government, and the army leadership were under virtual siege.

With his troops thus in command of the situation, Beria permitted the formality of a quick division of the spoils. Malenkov, the heir-apparent, took over leadership of the party and government. Security reverted to Beria, the armed forces to Bulganin, and foreign affairs to Molotov.

Even before that division became official, politicking was rampant among all the connivers, except Beria. He was too busy reasserting his control over the security forces. He merged the MVD and the MGB into a single ministry, of which he was the boss. In doing that, he made what later proved to be his greatest mistake: as deputies, he retained Kruglov, the former MVD chief and a Malenkov man, and Serov, Khrushchev's creature from the Ukraine.

And almost as afterthoughts, he sent the former MGB chief, Ignatyev, back into the obscurity of the party apparatus, arrested Ignatyev's chief deputy, Ryumin, the fabricator of the "Doctors' Plot," which Stalin's successors had exposed almost immediately as the fraud it was, and saw to it that the Minister of Health who had tended Stalin in his last moments disappeared, and forever.

Nor did Beria overlook reorganizing the Okhrana, the leadership's bodyguards. He reduced that once elite and independent group to the status of a mere Ninth Directorate of the security forces. For him that denigration served two purposes: it made the Okhrana seem far less formidable to the general public to whom Beria was then catering as a prelude to his eventual bid for supreme power; and it put the bodyguards of the rest of the successors under his direct control. He obviously believed that he, himself, needed no bodyguards as such, since he ran the whole security organization. That was poor judgment. In the same category of sloppy thinking fell his dispatching back to their barracks, and without first having gained top control, the security divisions with which he had taken over Moscow after Stalin's death. In retrospect, it is now very apparent that from the moment Kruglov was retained and the security divisions were sent out of Moscow, Beria's days were numbered.

As it was, all the while Beria concentrated on regrasping the security reins, the other connivers, especially Khrushchev, were busy at what proved to be the more important infighting. Less than a week after the last rites for Stalin, Khrushchev had "persuaded" Malenkov to surrender his post as party boss to him and thus form the first of the phony "collective" leaderships. Just what persuasion Khrushchev used is unknown. It could have been threat of exposure of Malenkov's role in the "Leningrad Affair." Or, since Khrushchev himself was a party to much of the dirty work that went on during the Stalin era—a neglected aspect in the de-Stalinization speech he made later—he could have threatened with many another of the horrible skeletons in the Soviet closets of the thirties and forties still to be made public. But whatever it was, it must have been formidable, for Malenkov gave in with hardly a whimper.

There is no doubt that Beria, too, knew many a terrible secret. But instead of capitalizing on them, he became involved in the luxury of playing chief cop once again. Thereby he also gave the Okhrana and the other security forces, which at first had welcomed his resumption of power as a return to the "good old days," more months of trouble and unrest.

First, he embarked on a wholesale purge of all security officers associated with Abakumov or Ignatyev, as well as those who worked behind the scenes for Malenkov, Bulganin, Molotov, or Khrushchev (with the notable exceptions of Kruglov and Serov). That purge was about the worst to hit state security since the late thirties. And it involved not only senior officers at Moscow headquarters, but also security subchiefs and subalterns throughout the length and breadth of the Soviet Union.

Reinstated in high positions were all his own supporters who had been ousted since 1946 by Abakumov, Poskrebyshev, et al. Novik was fired almost immediately (thereby giving some indication of Beria's low regard for Suslov) and a Beria crony, General Sergey Kuzmichev, was released from prison and made chief of what was left of the Okhrana. At the Kremlin *kommandatura*—by that time little more than a ceremonial post—the long tenure of the cautious Spiridonov ended with his replacement by one of the few nonpolitical security officers, General Andrey Vedenin, who was installed on the insistence of Khrushchev.

At his headquarters, Beria installed his longtime confidant, Colonel General Bogdan Kobulov, as his chief deputy. All the other top posts went to other henchmen, including Lieutenant General Mikhail Zhuravlev, appointed deputy-at-large despite the fact he had been dismissed from the MVD in 1946 as an alcoholic. And, as he made those appointments, the police boss also ordered Lieutenant Colonel Karasev, chief of the Second Technical Support Department, as the wiretappers were euphemistically named, to install bugs in the offices and residences of all Politburo members and other hierarchs, just as had been done in Stalin's time.

The appointment of Zhuravlev was by no means an exceptional case. The only qualification necessary to be a member of the Beria organization was to have been a loyal Beria man. As a result, obscure and long-forgotten officers, many of whom had been dismissed for drunkenness, graft, and worse, were virtually pulled out of the woodwork and put into positions of authority. And members of minority national and racial groups—Letts, Byelorussians, Caucasians and Central Asians—were put in charge of security installations in their respective areas, a step that did not endear Beria to the Russians who formed the great majority of the security apparatus.

In making all those changes, Beria also gathered many other enemies. He never bothered to go through the form of getting the approval of the respective Central Committee concerned. Rather, he interfered directly in party appointments on all levels throughout the country. And at the same time he gave each area's security officers orders to keep a close watch on all party officials in their districts.

One of those who received such a surveillance order was Major General Timofey Strokach, security chief in the Ukraine's Kamenets-Podolsk *oblast*. By chance, the general was on very friendly relations with the local party secretary, and he told his party friend: "There is something I cannot understand at all. Today, I received orders by telephone from Moscow, from Beria himself. He told me to keep a running check on—of all people—you."

Neither could the party secretary understand. He telephoned the party *apparat* in Moscow. Comparatively unimportant as that functionary was, his call marked the beginning of the end for Beria.

Although some three and a half months had passed in apparent calm for the "collective" leadership, activity beneath the surface had been intense, indeed. All the other connivers were fully aware of almost every detail of the Georgian police boss' efforts to consolidate his position for an eventual take-over of supreme power.

That knowledge had not been gained by any political astuteness, but by well-established Soviet technique. Kruglov, although ostensibly a deputy of Beria's, had sold out to the police boss' opponents even before his appointment. And Serov was much better informed about security operations than Beria believed. Using trusted technicians from his former MVD headquarters, Kruglov had bugged the offices and residences of Beria and his henchmen just as efficiently as Beria had wired those of his rivals.

Evidently, Kruglov's monitoring equipment was superior to the devices of Beria. And Serov's information must have complemented it. For on the night of June 26, 1953, Red Army tanks of the Kantemirovskaya Division rolled into Moscow and took up much the same control positions as had Beria's troops in March. And the tanks were supported by infantry from the Byelorussian military district. At first, the general populace had been curious about the sudden appearance of troops in the city. No parade had been planned for the following day. But that curiosity soon gave way to the opinion that some transfer must have been going on among army units in the capital environs.

Once the troops were in place, Beria was asked to go to the Politburo conference room in the Kremlin, to answer what were said to be some routine questions. As Beria entered the room, Voroshilov walked in directly behind him. A warrant in his hands, the little "general" said: "In the name of the Union of the Soviet Socialist Republics, Lavrentiy Pavlovich Beria is hereby placed under arrest."

Despite Khrushchev's subsequent fabrications about that moment, there was no violence and Beria made no resistance. Instead, he sat down at the table and argued for hours with his onetime fellow connivers. But they had outsmarted him and he was trapped, and he knew it. The presence of Red Army leaders in the conference room told him the whole story.

Thanks to Kruglov's wiretapping, Beria's questioners had learned that the police boss had planned his coup for the following day, June 27. In preparation for that, he had "neutralized" Colonel General Pavel Artemyev, commander of the Moscow military district, to the extent that that Red Army officer had sent the entire Moscow garrison off to Byelorussia on maneuvers. Thus, theoretically, Beria's security troops were again in command of the capital.

However—and completely unknown to Beria despite his wiretappers—Bulganin, acting on instructions of the rest of the Politburo, had called in the Kantemirovskaya Division, an armored command that was not subordinate to Artemyev. And in support of that armor, Bulganin had also summoned some of Marshal Semen Timoshenko's troops from the Byelorussian military district. Thus, Beria's *Putsch* had been defeated before it started.

At the end of the confrontation in the Kremlin, Beria was formally arrested by some of Kruglov's men and sent—not to the Lubyanka where some of the guards might have been loyal to him, but to Lefortovo prison, also under MVD administration, but one run by Kruglov men. Later, both for greater security and to involve the Red Army politically in the case, the former chief cop was transferred to the Moscow military district headquarters, part of whose basement was made into a jail for the purpose.

As soon as Beria had been safely put away, Kruglov personally saw to the arrests of Merkulov, Kobulov, Dekanozov, and another pair of Beria's top lieutenants. Foreign observers—who make most of their political evaluations on the basis of head counts of Soviet hierarchs appearing at public gatherings—noted that Beria was not among party and government dignitaries at a Bolshoi Theater presentation that evening, but were unable to draw any conclusions.

So secretly and suddenly had the axe fallen that even the Okhrana was not immediately *au courant.* Only the next morning did a routine change of his bodyguards learn that something was amiss with their master, when they arrived at Beria's residence and were confronted by GRU officers who told them to report back to their headquarters (by then, Kruglov's) for new orders. (As usual, since their master had been dismissed in disgrace, the security careers of those bodyguards came to a sudden and complete end.)

Cautiously, Khrushchev and his fellows waited until the Red Army had matters fully in hand and the last vestiges of Beria's control of security had been eliminated, before making the arrests public. Then, on July 9, the Central Committee was used to announce that Beria had been dismissed as "an enemy of the party and the Soviet people." As could be expected, the "press" pulled out all the stops called for by the "collective" leadership in denouncing the once feared police overlord. And party hacks did even better when informing the rank and file about the "reasons" for Beria's downfall.

[333]

For almost half a year, Beria and his henchmen were interrogated. At one time the Georgian went on a hunger strike and had to be fed intravenously. At another, he told his questioners what was almost the truth: "If I am guilty of anything, the rest of the members of the Politburo are also guilty." And to keep the Red Army involved, Marshal Konev was made one of the interrogators. Then on December 23, 1953—just three days after the thirty-fifth anniversary of the founding of the Cheka—Beria and his henchmen were sentenced to death. A few minutes later, they were marched from their cells and shot—not by the military, but by Kruglov's men.

2. THE RISE AND FALL OF KHRUSHCHEV

Ironically, Khrushchev's mistake in his struggle for power was just the opposite of Beria's. While Beria had given all his attention to security and practically none to politics, Khrushchev concentrated on politicking and showed little real concern for security. If those basic converging characteristics of the two men had been combined in a single person, the world might have seen another and even more fearful Stalin. To that degree, at least, the *muzhiks* of the Soviet Union have been fortunate.

Not so fortunate, however, after the downfall of Beria were the Okhrana and the security forces. Their time of troubles was accented by the Beria ouster and continued for some time thereafter. A mini-purge, directed at all supporters of the former police overlord, especially at security men, followed as a matter of course. Initially, some of them were inclined to welcome the departure of Beria as meaning an end to the influence of his minions who were Georgians or were from other minorities, but developments soon divorced them from their illusions.

With the elimination of Beria, Khrushchev as party leader became the unquestioned boss of the Soviet Union, despite the brief appearances on the horizon of such "collective" colleagues as Malenkov and Bulganin, and despite the government roles and titles of them and others, since, under the Soviet system, a government leader is little more than a messenger boy and at best a mere functionary and figurehead. In that position of power, his first step was to weaken the security forces to keep them from again posing a threat such as they did while in Beria's control.

Khrushchev took his first moves in that direction almost immediately after Beria was arrested. He kept his chief wiretapper and disloyal Beria deputy, Kruglov, on as MVD chief until March 1954 although that worthy was not formally given the post until after Beria's execution. And he maintained the Okhrana as a mere Ninth Directorate of the MVD, but sent its chief, Kuzmichev, back to the prison from which Beria had released him, replacing him with a creature of his own, Aleksandr Lenev, a former Khrushchev underling in the Moscow party secretariat. As deputies, Lenev brought along with him other party *apparatchiks*, a practice that was aped in general in the other security forces as well. Lenev was kept on as Okhrana boss through the initial phase of the Khrushchev-Malenkov conflict, but was replaced in 1954 by another member of the Moscow party organization, Vladimir Ustinov, who served until 1957.

The shake-up that Khrushchev[1] effected in the Okhrana and other security organizations was quite wholesale and relatively long lasting. And after he had completed it in 1956, there were only a few men left in the security forces in Moscow, the rest of the Soviet Union, and abroad, who had worked for either Stalin or Beria. In the Okhrana about the only officer not removed was Vedenin, the Kremlin Commandant. But that post had become so virtually ceremonial that Vedenin was retained for another dozen years and well after the ouster of Khrushchev. And, of course, Khrushchev did not rely at all on Vedenin for his personal security. For that, initially, he had a Colonel Litovchenko and a Colonel Stolyarov, who had been his bodyguards when he ran the Ukraine, and whom he brought to Moscow as chiefs of his personal bodyguard in 1949.

The appointment of Khrushchev's stooge, Lenev, as Okhrana chief, bothered Malenkov, worried that that gave his rival too much control of security. Therefore, in the days when he still swung some

---

[1] To correct the somewhat too folksy and "man-of-the-people" image Khrushchev attained during his visits to the U.S. and elsewhere abroad, note should be made of the personal Okhrana, more than three score strong, with which he was supplied in 1953, before he had grabbed total power. At that time, his Okhrana force consisted of two cooks, four waiters, one housekeeper, one lady's-maid, one barber, two caretakers, three charwomen, three chauffeurs for his personal use, two chauffeurs for his wife, and forty-five guards officers. And that staff was soon enlarged, because it was not considered adequate in view of the internecine struggle then going on with other Politburo members.

weight, Malenkov got one of his men, Nikolay Shatalin, another Secretary of the CC CPSU, named as MVD deputy to Kruglov. But even that did not balance Khrushchev's influence over the security, because he already had his crony, Serov, ensconced as Deputy Minister of the MVD. That imbalance in Khrushchev's favor became even greater when the party boss inveigled the appointment of yet another of his underlings, Konstantin Lunev, as an additional Deputy Minister of the MVD, allegedly to counter-balance Malenkov's Shatalin. And the Lunev appointment came in quite handy for Khrushchev, for it just so happened that Lunev was the only MVD representative to sign the Beria death sentence.

However, those security posts of both Shatalin and Lunev were quite short-lived, not outlasting 1954. Shatalin was booted back to the party *apparat* and soon was transferred to the provinces and oblivion. Lunev, too, was sent to the provinces as a security man, before gradually disappearing from the scene for good. But the importance of those two functionaries lay more in their elimination than in their work.

For the replacement of that pair marked the start of Khrushchev's surge to total power, a drive in which he aped Stalin to a considerable degree, by not only politicking, but also making the security completely subservient to him. The latter objective was attained by yet another of those changes of names, so common under the Russian systems, both Tsarist and Communist, whereby Khrushchev not only pretty generally fooled the public, both national and foreign, but also captured the security to use for his own advance.

In March 1954, Khrushchev went through the ploy of reconstructing the former MGB *apparat*, a ministry and organization that carried not only the foul odor of Beria tactics, but of its predecessors as well. In the place of that ministry, he created a "mere" Committee for State Security, or what has been thenceforth known as the KGB. However, despite the comparative innocence of the term "committee," the KGB from its very inception was much more powerful than a ministry, and in fact was a super-ministry of sorts. Concurrent with the creation of the KGB, the MVD was divested of its brief post-Beria power, reverting to a more actual ministry of interior, while the KGB was strengthened by being given control of the internal and frontier security forces that for a while had been subordinated to defense and other ministries. Kruglov was continued at the helm of the debili-

[336]

tated MVD, being allowed to linger on there for a few years, before being fired by Khrushchev.

Since the security organization had been "demoted" to a committee, its boss was no longer a minister, but a chairman. As first Chairman of the KGB, Khrushchev appointed his old crony, Serov, certainly no longer needed as his watchdog at the MVD after that organization's powers had been slashed. Once Serov was installed, Khrushchev then proceeded to organize a "Mafia" of his own, much as Stalin had done earlier. The fat little man's personal force might have been called the "Granovsky Street Gang," since it was formed from and operated by his stooges who were concentrated at a hierarch apartment house at that Moscow address. Serov lived there, as did another Khrushchev henchman, Roman Rudenko, the procurator-general, or chief prosecutor of the Soviet "legal" system. As Penkovskiy disclosed, Serov and Rudenko used to meet at Granovsky Street over drinks in the evenings and decide what "enemy of the people" (by that, read Khrushchev's opponent) should be shot or merely imprisoned. All such "Socialist legalities," of course, were pursued without benefit of trial. So, in a way, it is somewhat a pity that Penkovskiy did not give more details of those "processes" and thus help deflate the favorable image of Khrushchev the "anti-Stalinist," created by his admirers, both Soviet and foreign. And it was probably at Granovsky Street sessions that the decisions were made for the 1954 executions of Karasev, Beria's wiretapper, Ryumin, the scapegoat of the "Doctors' Plot," and the luckless Abakumov and his cohorts.

Despite the refinements of control furnished him by Serov, Rudenko, and their cohorts, Khrushchev, as noted earlier, was expert at politicking but failed to follow Stalin's example by giving proper emphasis to personal security, especially personal security in the Russian and Soviet sense. That is shown most markedly by the fact that although he had a plentiful coterie of security officers that functioned as personal bodyguards, and although he had full control of the security organs, he never had a Poskrebyshev or even a Vlasik of his own. True he had one Grigory Shuysky, a party newspaper-man-*apparatchik* he had encountered during his days in the Ukraine, who served as a sort of secretary and accompanied him during meetings with heads of state in the U.S.A., Paris, and Vienna. But Shuysky was not much more than a pale image of Khrushchev's son-in-law Adzhubey, and was certainly not his "man Friday" or alter-ego.

Therefore, with such basic predilections about personal security, Khrushchev let the Okhrana muddle along with much the same deficiencies it had when he inherited it. It remained a mere Ninth Directorate of the KGB. Nor was its chief anyone of particular security ability at first, although some improvement was made in this area in the later Khrushchev era. The first Okhrana boss under KGB control was yet another Moscow party *apparat* underling of Khrushchev's, one Vladimir Ustinov, concurrently also a Deputy Chairman of the KGB, who ran the bodyguards without any distinction whatsoever from 1954 to 1957, later served as Ambassador to Hungary and was fortunate enough to die in bed in 1971.

Ustinov's Okhrana successor, Nikolay Zakharov, was another indication of Khrushchev's concentration on top security control to the detriment of the bodyguard structure. An alumnus of the old Okhrana No. 2, Zakharov was another member of the "Granovsky Street Gang," with a probable original leaning toward Malenkov rather than Khrushchev. In Stalin's last years, he had been chief of the guards at the No. 3 Granovsky Street building, where Bulganin, Khrushchev, Malenkov, Suslov, and other Politburo members were quartered. A major in those days, Zakharov was promoted to colonel shortly after Beria's arrest and made Deputy Chief of the Ninth Directorate, a position he held until Malenkov's fall from grace. Soon after that, Khrushchev, on the apparent basis of no more than the recollection of a genial bodyguard at his former apartment building, and with little concern about determining the personal loyalties of his appointee, named Zakharov chief of the Okhrana and promoted him to major-general.

Despite his probable original Malenkov propensity, Zakharov was an able courtier, who speedily ingratiated himself with the boss of the moment. Khrushchev reciprocated by taking his Okhrana chief along with him on his trip to the U.S.A., where Zakharov seemingly spent as much time smiling for photographers as he did in checking security with his secret service counterparts. Shortly before that trip, and most likely in preparation for it, the chief bodyguard had been promoted to lieutenant-general.

Then, in 1961, Khrushchev further rewarded that pale, but smiling, shadow of what Soviet chief bodyguards once were by making him a Deputy Chairman of the KGB as well as Okhrana boss. And in 1963, Zakharov—who was soon to be completely ineffective when his boss was in dire need of a real and less genial bodyguard—reached the peak. He was made a general-colonel and at the same time the First Deputy Chairman of the KGB with control over the Ninth Directorate, the Kremlin *kommandatura*, and other security forces. Never before in Soviet history had a security officer been advanced so high and so rapidly for doing so little except smiling on the right occasions. And it evidently must have been a winning smile, indeed, for that officer's career continued for several years after Khrushchev's fall, in fact until old age caught up with him.

During the period of Zakharov's meteoric rise, Khrushchev made what proved to be his ultimate mistake, that of relying on the KGB command, rather than a well-organized bodyguard, for his personal security. In the mid-fifties, with Serov at the KGB helm, he could get away with such indiscretion, since that deporter par excellence was, despite his other unfavorable characteristics, extremely loyal to Khrushchev.

But, in 1958, evidently heady with his success over his rivals, Khrushchev made the error of not only dumping Serov, but also of replacing him with a complete no-account, so far as security, integrity, and loyalty were concerned. Granted it had been embarrassing when the British had refused Serov entry for the Khrushchev-Bulganin state visit of 1956. And granted that the image of the Soviet security forces needed improvement, and then some, both at home and abroad. (The assumption that Khrushchev transferred Serov to the top command of the GRU to keep the armed forces in rein did not appear justified at the time the change was made, nor has it been justified by later information.)

All such rationalizations aside, it subsequently became evident that Khrushchev was most careless in his selection of Shelepin as Serov's successor. True, there are many accounts of daily security conferences between that Komsomol toady and Khrushchev. And true, Shelepin had the attraction of his youthful years and carried no reek of a security background. But therewith ended his qualifications. Against them consider his drawbacks—a career checkered with sycophancy, welshing and political knifings of every opponent who stood in his way. And a loyalty to no one but himself; a perfect example of the "new" Soviet man. Despite the decimation of the security forces that followed Beria's downfall, and despite the political isolation that Khrushchev had attained by that time, there must have been a better choice.

Although security problems most certainly were discussed at the daily Khrushchev-Shelepin sessions, it appears that the ambitious KGB chief used those meetings more to promote his own political future than to help his boss retain power. For in late 1961, he was able to persuade Khrushchev not only to relieve him of his unwelcome KGB task and give him a politically promising post of a secretaryship on the CC CPSU, but also to appoint his personal henchman, Semichastny, another Komsomol *apparatchik*, as his successor as security boss.

In agreeing to that, Khrushchev compounded his error of placing security in questionable hands. Semichastny was such a complete toady of Shelepin's that every security move that Khrushchev took with his new KGB chief was beyond all doubt speedily relayed to Shelepin for him to use in his wheeling and dealing on the Central Committee. What made Khrushchev take such a fallacious step as appointing Semichastny is not clear. In taking it, he belied all the political sagacity with which he was credited. He not only gave an untrustworthy man a top Central Committee post, but also supplied him with a channel of security information to which nobody under the Soviet system, except Khrushchev and his closest adherents, should have been privy.

From an ex post facto viewpoint, the only explanation seems to be that Khrushchev was so confident and so giddy with success that he had lost sight of Soviet realities whose chief principle was, and is, that a Soviet leader in addition to being a most astute political infighter, must also have unquestioned control of security. And Khrushchev was supplied none of the latter by the Shelepin-Semichastny-Zakharov team. Additionally, it appears Khrushchev's mistake may also have been the result of his near mania to downgrade the image of security, no matter what the cost. For shortly after the appointment of the unreliable, incapable Semichastny, he prettied-up the MVD again by disbanding it in name and replacing it with a ministry for the preservation of public order, which bore the rather ridiculous acronym of MOOP.

Even that creation of a "new" ministry for internal affairs represented a further loss of security control for Khrushchev. In 1956, the fat little man had dumped his wiretapper, Kruglov, as chief of the MVD, replacing him with still another of his Moscow party *apparatchiks*, Nikolay Dudorov. A building trades and industrial "expert" in Stalin's labor camps, Dudorov had only little security background, but at least he was loyal to Khrushchev—the main reason he was given the job. However, when MOOP was formed, the loyalty factor seemed no longer to count to Khrushchev when making a security appointment, for the post of MOOP chief was given to one Vadim Tikunov, another Komsomol sidekick of Shelepin's. Thereby was Shelepin, who had had rather excessive security powers before, placed at the reins of all security in the Soviet Union, a most dangerous amassing of authority and one to which Khrushchev appeared blithely oblivious.

And in early 1964, the fat little man had been forced to get rid of Serov, the GRU chief, and the only security officer truly faithful to him, because of the Penkovskiy case.

And that was not as if Khrushchev had not had prior warning, and aplenty. Even back in 1959, when Shelepin was the actual KGB boss, that ambitious man had dared to make political hay and embarrass his master by arresting and expelling an American diplomat in Moscow at the very time of the Camp David rapprochement between the Soviet leader and President Eisenhower. Having gotten away with that with impunity, the Shelepin-Semichastny pair next figuratively, at least, stabbed Khrushchev in the back by having KGB agents manhandle three American military attachés (and a British colleague) in a Siberian hotel room while Khrushchev was trying to assuage President Kennedy in an attempt to mend the Soviet-American fences damaged by the Cuban missile affair. There were other incidents of less publicized KGB insubordination as well, but the crowning case came in September, 1964, when a KGB agent sprayed a poison gas on a West German diplomat attending a church service in the Moscow environs as a counter to Khrushchev's attempts to improve relations with Bonn. Khrushchev apologized deeply for that, but he should have saved his breath and thoroughly thrashed his security chiefs, who were probably by then fully committed to the plot for his downfall.

Instead, still supremely—and by that time foolishly—self-confi-

[341]

dent, he went off to the Black Sea for a vacation. To thus absent himself from the capital at that time proved to be the last straw on the back of his well overweighted security camel. For Suslov and his fellow plotters, Khrushchev's overthrow was a cinch. They had easily suborned the ambitious and treacherous Shelepin-Semichastny pair with promises of advancement. And Zakharov was just as willing to cast his genial and shallow smile on them as on Khrushchev.

Khrushchev wriggled briefly after being taken in tow at the Moscow airport by his chief betrayers and onetime subordinates, Shelepin and Semichastny. But he made no major fight for survival. For he realized—at last, and when it was far too late—that without security, he was finished. And the Russian people—far more powerless than they had been under the tsars—had been bystanders at another palace revolution, albeit a bloodless one.

3. UNDER BREZHNEV

From the time he took over as party secretary after Khrushchev's ouster in 1964, Brezhnev waged a low-key but extremely careful and persistent battle to not only continue but expand his power. An unusually phlegmatic man—as compared to his flamboyant predecessor—he attracted relatively little attention to himself, no doubt purposefully, as he first secured and then improved his position.

From the outset, he appeared to model his tactics after those of Stalin rather than Khrushchev, and to the extent that his control has been frequently referred to as "neo-Stalinistic." His political mills ground slowly, indeed, but they also ground very, very fine. He resumed the fiction of "collective leadership," abrogated by Khrushchev, in fact soon made it an apparent triumvirate, with his powers split with Kosygin as Premier and with Nikolay Podgorny as the equivalent of president. Actually, however, that collectivism was mere fiction and his fellow triumvirs relatively powerless, especially after he elevated himself to party "General-Secretary," a post held previously only by Stalin.

As Stalin had learned before him—and Khrushchev did not—he recognized that leadership under the Soviet system demanded a most careful balancing of politics and security, with the first being used to attain power and the second to retain it.

In retrospect, when Brezhnev was first named party secretary, his position was not particularly enviable, either politically or from a

[342]

security standpoint. He not only had to pay off—and thereby elevate —Shelepin and Semichastny for the betrayal of Khrushchev by putting the first on the Politburo and making the second a member of the Central Committee. But he also had those two ambitious and ruthless men in charge of all Soviet security, including his own. In effect, therefore, the existence of the Shelepin-Semichastny team was quite analogous to that of Beria and his men after Stalin's death. And additionally, Shelepin was a very real and potent—although undeclared—political rival. Brezhnev was the beetle-browed, dull, well past middle-age and completely uncharismatic technocrat-*apparatchik*. Shelepin was young, much more attractive, comparatively urbane and worldly, a "smooth operator" who already enjoyed some popularity at home as well as abroad, and was touted by some as the leader, in the future at least, of Soviet Russia.

Faced with such odds, Brezhnev played his opening moves slowly and very cautiously. At the same time that Shelepin was elevated to the Politburo, the party boss saw to it that a pair of his henchmen were also appointed to that top organization, one as a full, the other as an alternate member, as a countermove against the Shelepin advancement. He also provided that Shelepin's name should come rather low in official listings of hierarchs and that second-rate rather than first-string dignitaries should do the welcoming and seeing off of Shelepin at airports. Then, in 1965, he "retired" the president, the unreliable little Armenian, Mikoyan, onetime sycophant of Stalin and Khrushchev alike, but who had not been loath to sign Khrushchev's ouster papers. In Mikoyan's place as president, he secured the appointment of Podgorny, who thus lost his secretaryship on the CC CPSU and the possibility to help his potential ally, Shelepin. Next, in December, 1965, Shelepin's sails were trimmed even further. The powerful Party-State Control Committee, which Shelepin headed and might have used as Stalin once employed his workers-peasants inspectorate, was abolished.

Evidently satisfied that he had drawn enough Shelepin blood by that time, and probably concerned lest he be accused of acting dictatorially against his younger opponent, Brezhnev then waited until well into 1966 before making his next and decisive moves. First, he fired Tikunov, the pro-Shelepin chief of MOOP and replaced him with Nikolay Shchelokov, a longtime personal friend, fellow metallurgical institute graduate and former party colleague from Dnepropetrovsk. (And two years later, MOOP was changed back to MVD, with Shchelokov continuing at the helm and with its power restored by the transfer of internal and escort security troops back to its control.)

So girded with at least partial control of security, Brezhnev evidently felt strong enough to finally bring the KGB into line. And Shelepin, probably outplayed politically behind the scenes by that time, had made no open moves against the changes in the interior ministry. Therefore, in May, 1967, the party boss dismissed Shelepin's stooge, Semichastny, as head of the KGB, and replaced him with a reliable functionary, Yury Andropov. Proof of Andropov's reliability was the fact that as Ambassador to Budapest in 1956, he had fully cooperated with the crushing of the Hungarian uprising by the Red Army and the KGB, a brutal action that was one of the most Stalinist steps of the "anti-Stalinist" Khrushchev. Additionally, so far as Brezhnev was concerned, Andropov was also attractive because he had no political tie-ups with other hierarchs or the KGB. And to help Andropov, who had no security background, Brezhnev supplied him three lieutenants, or deputy chairmen, trusted implicitly by the party boss and the real chiefs of his security, Viktor Chebrikov, a fellow *apparatchik* from Brezhnev's hometown, Georgy Tsinev, a former SMERSH man, and Semen Tsvigun, who had worked under Brezhnev in Moldavia. The last, Tsvigun, was made first deputy chairman, and it was he who really ran the KGB, despite Andropov's nominal title. Although thus demoted to being another deputy chairman, the smiling and ineffective Zakharov was kept on for a while before being transferred to a security post in the provinces and the end of his lackluster career.

In the course of that violent shake-up of the KGB's top command, Vedenin was relieved—but without dishonor—from the Kremlin *kommandatura*, being replaced by yet another Brezhnev man, Sergey Shornikov. But Shornikov was completely subordinate to Tsvigun, who not only ran the KGB, but also controlled the Ninth, or Guards Directorate, and thereby watched over both Brezhnev and his possible opponents as well.

That was quite a radical departure in the technique of top Soviet security control. Although Tsvigun was somewhat screened by the title of first deputy chairman, vested in him was the authority once exercised by Beria, Poskrebyshev, and Vlasik combined. And, although the pretense that Andropov was the boss of the KGB was improved by making him a candidate member of the Politburo, the facts were that the comparatively untitled Tsvigun was the most powerful man after Brezhnev and unquestionably the most powerful security chief Imperial or Communist Russia had ever had. But, his highest apparent position—as of this writing—was only that of an alternate member of the CC CPSU. Well prior to his take-over of the KGB, Brezhnev had quietly secured control of the armed forces. He accomplished that by long association with, and thereby control of two key officers, General Aleksey Yepishev and General Petr Ivashutin. Yepishev was an alumnus of Poskrebyshev's "secretariat," had been seconded to Abakumov by Poskrebyshev, and was a Deputy MGB Minister in Stalin's last years. By Brezhnev's time he had advanced to being chief of the main political administration of the Soviet armed forces and Brezhnev saw to it that he was elected to full membership of the CC CPSU. Ivashutin, whose official title was that of Deputy Chief of the General Staff of the Soviet Armed Forces, had an extensive NKVD, MGB, MVD, and KGB counterintelligence background and also had been a SMERSH chief in the Ukraine, Austria, and East Germany. Actually Ivashutin was head of the military and strategic intelligence services (GRU), the KGB's sister military and subordinate arm. He was appointed to that post in 1963 following Serov's dismissal as the result of the Penkovskiy disclosures, an appointment made during Khrushchev's decline, and seemingly at Brezhnev's instigation.

Concurrent with his struggle to wrest control of security from the Shelepin-Semichastny pair, Brezhnev also had the problem of eliminating Khrushchev adherents from top security positions, although that task had been made somewhat simpler for him by the Shelepin-Semichastny efforts in the same direction. In that area, one cannot overlook the "accidental" (and according to experts in Belgrade at the time, completely unexplained and unnecessary) crash of a Soviet airliner in Yugoslavia within less than a week after the ouster of Khrushchev. Aboard were six top Soviet military chiefs. Of particular interest, among them were Marshal Sergey Biryuzov, Chief of Staff of the Soviet Armed Forces and a known Khrushchev man, and KGB Lieutenant-General Nikolay Mironov, a strong campaigner for

Khrushchev's program for "Socialist legality" and chief of the administrative department of the CC CPSU, the euphemism for the party's watchdog over the security organs. There is a possibility that Shelepin and/or Semichastny knew the real reason for that air crash; and there is also a likelihood that Brezhnev may have been a party to its cause. That removal of surviving Khrushchevites from the woodwork of the security structure continued spasmodically but well into the next decade. In June 1970, Major General Boris Shulzhenko, Deputy Chairman of the KGB in the Ukraine, "died suddenly" although only fifty-one years old. And in the same month, the longtime KGB Chairman of the Ukraine, General Colonel Vitaly Nikitchenko, was relieved and transferred into limbo, being replaced by Lieutenant General Vitaly Fedorchuk, a World War II Brezhnev associate. Both Shulzhenko and Nikitchenko were Khrushchev men.

The peak of tension in Brezhnev's struggle for power in the Kremlin, especially in his fight for control of security, appears to have occurred between May and July of 1967. Beyond doubt, the battle was precipitated by the ousting of Semichastny and the final tussle with Shelepin. No firsthand reports of that struggle are yet available, although it was marked by a pair of seemingly unrelated developments that may have been directly related to it.

The first sign was given by a series of sudden and unexpected deaths among KGB, MVD, and military leaders, reported in terse announcements in the press. At least fifteen senior officers thus died, among them, KGB Major General Vasily Lukshin, chief of military counterintelligence, KGB Major General Sergey Vishnevsky, three KGB colonels, and a militia colonel.

Next, on June 26, 1967, announcement was made that an award had been given to the Kantemirovskaya Armored Division by the Supreme Soviet of the Russian Republic. No reason was given for the award, nor within the previous decade had there been even the least incident in which that outfit was known to have distinguished itself. But that was the very same division the Politburo had called out against the Beria coup exactly fourteen years earlier. If its 1953 action had been the reason for the award, some statement, at least a guarded one, to that effect would have been made. Therefore, since the reason for the award was kept secret, the assumption, at least, can be made that the Kantemirovskaya performed some special feat for

Brezhnev, perhaps aborted a Shelepin attempt to seize power a la Beria.

However, all that is known is that by the end of summer 1967, Shelepin had been railroaded into the politically meaningless job of chairman of the trades union organization. And at the same time, he was relieved of his chores as a Secretary of the CC CPSU. That dismissal was the one that really counted. For Shelepin's secretaryship had been that of party supervision and control of the entire security *apparat*. With that dismissal, Brezhnev finally had won unquestioned control of the KGB, the GRU, the militia, and all security supporting forces, and, of course, his own personal security as well as security control of his possible rivals.

Even before he had attained final victory in that palace upheaval, Brezhnev had made much progress in perfecting his own Mafia—or, in effect, elite bodyguard—of state, security, and party *apparatchiks*.

Brezhnev had known most of them since his early days, when he was a student in Dneprodzerzhinsk and later a lowly party official in Dnepropetrovsk. (In Moscow, the group was called the "Dnepropetrovskaya Banda.") The first members given positions of influence were such worthies as Shchelokov, Tsvigun, Tsinev, Chebrikov, Yepishev—all from Ukrainia—and Ivashutin. Nor should it be overlooked that four of that sextet—the sole exception was Shchelokov—had all been security officers under Stalin.

Directing that Mafia in matters of high policy, the beetle-browed party boss outdid Stalin. Brezhnev had not just one, but two alter egos. The first—and probably less important—who posed as a diplomat but actually was a covert intelligence officer, was called Aleksandr Aleksandrov-Agentov. (Probably Agentov was his original name, but since that means agent in Russian, the Aleksandrov was tacked before it.) That hyphenated diplomat had served from 1966-69 as Soviet Ambassador to Sierra Leone with distinction, in fact with such distinction that in 1971 Soviet "instructors" were called to Freetown by Prime Minister Siaka Stevens to serve as his bodyguard after that African leader had had some trouble maintaining himself in power. Aleksandrov-Agentov held much the same position with Brezhnev as Count Ciano did with Mussolini, but to foreigners he was identified only as a "personal aide" to the party leader.

Brezhnev's men were Georgy Tsukanov and Konstantin Chernenko. Tsukanov had worked for Brezhnev since 1958. After Khrushchev's ouster, he was made chief of the party leader's special headquarters, the so-called "secretariat." Much as Poskrebyshev once did for Stalin, Chernenko coordinated all business for Brezhnev. And to continue the comparison between Poskrebyshev and Brezhnev's two-man team, both Aleksandrov-Agentov and Tsukanov held the title of Assistant to the General Secretary of the CC CPSU, the same as held by Poskrebyshev, and Chernenko in due time became CC CPSU secretary and Politburo member.

Although Brezhnev had achieved uncontested control of the Kremlin and security and had organized his *banda* to protect him from palace upheavals, his personal security was still inferior to that of Stalin. That was proved to him—and no doubt quite frighteningly —in January, 1969. An assailant—never identified as more than one Ilyin—was able to take potshots at his motor cavalcade at the very gates of the Kremlin. Something like that had not happened since the Grand Duke Sergey was assassinated in 1905.

The gunman was arrested on the spot, of course, But not before he had killed one bodyguard and wounded others. That Brezhnev had not been hit was only the result of the gunman's mistake, and certainly not because of any sterling action on the part of the palace guards. In fact something was very wrong indeed with the guards organization for an armed man ever to have been that close to the Kremlin or to a Soviet hierarch.

A plethora of rumors followed the shooting—that it had been engineered by some other member of the Politburo—that the armed forces had been behind it—or that it had been organized by disgruntled intellectuals. No official explanation was immediately forthcoming. Only months later was it announced that psychiatrists had adjudged the assailant insane and that he had been committed to an asylum, the favorite dumping ground for dissidents with brains enough to think. The determination of insanity relieved the leadership of giving any explanation for the attack.

However, what may have been an indirect explanation was made in April and May 1969. In those two months alone, there was another great dying-off of high-ranking Soviet officers, some "tragically, while performing their duties," others "unexpectedly." Among that lot were eight generals, including Valentin Penkovskiy, onetime deputy minister of defense, commander of the Byelorussian military district, and great-uncle of Oleg Penkovskiy. (He was never involved in his relative's case.)

And in 1969, the usual May Day military parade was cancelled.

To this day, neither the sudden flurry of deaths among the senior officers, nor the abrupt cancellation of the May Day show, has been explained. In lieu of such clarification, assumptions must do. There may have been a major accident involving the military in the April-May period, even assassination by accident. Perhaps the dead officers were regime supporters killed in conflict with opponents, and, if so, the names of the latter, of course, would not have been mentioned. Or, since it is known that the invasion of Czechoslovakia did not receive the full support of the Soviet citizenry and military, there may have been serious reaction to that Warsaw Pact action on the part of the Soviet armed forces. And finally, there is the possibility the military may have been directly involved in the shooting at the Kremlin gate, since the assailant was said to have been a member of the armed forces. That possibility is heightened by the exclusion of the military from the May Day festivities. If it had been established —or even feared—that the military was connected with the shooting, the interval between that incident and the parade was too short for authorities to have made a wholesale enough purge of the armed forces to assure that other attacks would not be made on the leadership assembled in Red Square.

Despite all the obscurity about the facts behind the Kremlin shooting, the incident was followed by very definite changes in the security organization. Almost immediately, the smiling Zakharov, the senior official responsible for the affair since his authority included supervision of the Guards Directorate, was booted to the provinces, where he should have been sent much earlier. Tsvigun, who had had overall control of the directorate, formally took over direction of the bodyguards.

And after a small rash of dismissals, imprisonments—and possibly a few executions—of bodyguard subordinates who had not prevented the gunman from gaining his position at the Kremlin gate, the Guards Directorate was returned to much of its original strength and effectiveness. Apparently, at last, there was an awareness in the leadership that, as in the final era of the tsardom, assault could as easily come from without the palace as from within. After all, dissent among the intellectuals, at least, was by then a well-established fact.

As a result, Brezhnev beefed up the Guards Directorate to about fifteen thousand men. And liaison was strengthened with the two standby divisions of state security troops as well as with the Kantemirovskaya Armored Division in Moscow's environs, although the latter was nominally under defense ministry command. Closer ties were also made with the militia and security troops under Shchelokov, even though that was hardly necessary since Brezhnev and Shchelokov shared adjoining apartments and thus were in frequent unofficial as well as official contact. With that tightening up completed, it would be a long time, indeed, before another armed assailant would get close enough to the Kremlin or a Soviet hierarch to do any shooting.

That strengthening of personal security notwithstanding, there was another tussle for power among the hierarchs in April and May 1970. So far as is known, it was a scuffle rather than an all-out fight, nor did Brezhnev's leadership appear to have been directly threatened. But it was serious enough to cause postponement of the Twenty-fourth Party Congress.

The other outward signs of that infighting were the appointment of a new Moscow city commandant, the dismissal without future assignment of his predecessor (who had held his post since the Beria coup was thwarted), and the minor purge—mentioned earlier—of Khrushchevites remaining in the KGB command in the Ukraine.

However, the struggle of which those changes formed the aftermath could not have been very serious. For in the last week of June 1970, Brezhnev had a bust of Stalin, his apparent model to some extent, at least, unveiled with honors near the Lenin mausoleum on Red Square.

And by 1971, Brezhnev's political and personal security appeared almost as assured as Stalin's had once been. The only untoward event of that year was the flurry within the KGB when the British finally expelled more than a hundred of its representatives posing as diplomats and/or trade agents. But, comparatively that was a mere bobble within the foreign intelligence structure rather than a security defect that affected the leadership. Therefore, with his Guards Directorate, the armed forces, and other security organiza-

[350]

tions under the control of his *banda* and his political opponents rendered supine, the beetle-browed successor to Stalin was not afraid to make a state visit to Paris and be extended the pomp of Pompidou's France. And in 1972 he could even afford to grant a relatively favorable welcome to the visiting President of the U.S.A., Richard M. Nixon.

Finally, in fact, Brezhnev managed to hold on to power longer than any Soviet ruler except Stalin—and if his health had permitted, he could have gone on to exceed Stalin's record. He had learned his lesson well. His security and bodyguard system, like Stalin's and unlike Khrushchev's, worked as it was designed to work.

Through his last decade of life he continued to advance his own loyalists, the Dnepropetrovsk Mafia. Counted in the West (where data were inadequate), they occupied about sixty key positions in the party and state apparatus.

Also, Brezhnev continued to get rid of those who did not depend on him, charging his security service with this task. Petr Shelest, a Khrushchev appointee, continued to rule over the Ukrainian party apparatus. In 1970, to undermine Shelest, Brezhnev and Andropov sent a tough KGB professional named Vitaly Fedorchuk to the Ukraine to replace Shelest's KGB chief, Vitaly Nikitchenko. Two years later, the ground prepared, Brezhnev ousted Shelest and put his own man, Vladimir Shcherbitskiy, in his place. Fedorchuk stayed on in the Ukraine for ten more years before getting his own reward: the chairmanship of the KGB (replacing Andropov) and, later, the Ministry of Internal Affairs, where he is still active in 1984.

As his power solidified, Brezhnev accumulated new titles—the presidency in 1977, and Supreme Commander in Chief of the Soviet Armed Forces—and his "cult of personality" grew apace. He accumulated even more decorations than Stalin: four times Hero of the Soviet Union, seven times Order of Lenin, every order of all the satellite countries, down to the newly devised Sun of Freedom of Afghanistan. Stalin's ghost must have applauded Brezhnev's literary awards. His sycophantic critics extolled his books about Leninism and internationalism—uninspired jargon pasted together for him in the CC apparatus from standard formulations, printed in gigantic editions, and discussed solemnly in conferences and meetings throughout the country. His four volumes of memoirs (*Vospomina-niya*) won similar praise; its fourth volume, appearing just before his seventy-fifth birthday, was serialized on radio and television and won him the Lenin Prize for Literature. His statesmanship won him great praise: "the most outstanding political leader of our time...architect of détente...resplendent defender of peace." Public celebrations of his birthday were built up for weeks; statues were erected and Bulgaria honored him with a giant bust in Sofia. He promoted family members and in-laws to high posts: his son Yuri to First Deputy Minister of Foreign Trade, his daughter's husband, former policeman Yuri Churbanov, to First Deputy Minister of Internal Affairs.

Brezhnev's KGB continued to protect the leadership from the people. With the help of internal troops and militia, the KGB put down dozens of local uprisings and strikes, and prevented everything but a few whispers of hearsay from leaking to the West about them. Dissidents were silenced, jailed, put away in psychiatric hospitals, or exiled to the West; dissident movements—like the Helsinki Watch groups monitoring their government's observance of its own commitments— were crushed and dissolved. Brezhnev's Polish flunkies (counseled and shouldered by Soviet advisors) coped with a dangerous explosion of freedom in Poland, which, under the name of "Solidarity," threatened for nearly two years to sweep the Polish Communist party into oblivion. And Brezhnev's regime helped create and preserve bloody pro-Soviet regimes in Afghanistan, South Yemen, Ethiopia, Angola, Mozambique, and many other states—and perhaps tried to murder the Pope.

All the while, Brezhnev's regime kept its secrets so well that it could still posture as peace-loving and democratic. In fact, the image it projected to the outside world was not unlike that of the man himself: square, stolid, slow-moving, stable—and stultified. And old—the top leadership aged visibly and by the early 1980s averaged over seventy. Seated there together in their tiers at the Supreme Soviet, these old men projected an image of dour gerontocracy.

Starting in 1975, however, time began to catch up with Brezhnev. His health—not his personal security—began to weaken. In December 1977 he fell seriously ill after addressing a Central Committee Plenum and thereafter repeatedly cancelled meetings with foreign visitors, postponed trips to the West, failed to appear at sessions of the Supreme Soviet, and disappeared for weeks from public view. When he did appear during these last years, he sometimes stumbled and often had to be held up. Rumors of his death spread several times in both East and West. This could not fail to heat up the power struggle underneath the dense foliage of the secret jungle.

That struggle had never ceased, of course; it never does. The initial post-Krushchev division of top responsibilities among Brezhnev, Kosygin, and Podgorny did not last long. Already by 1971 Kosygin's role had been curtailed; in 1976 he suffered what was variously rumored as a heart attack or stroke following a near-drowning—but only after several unexplained absences and signs that his first deputy, Nikolay Tikhonov, was already taking over some of his functions. When Kosygin finally retired for ill health in 1980, Brezhnev gave the job of Prime Minister not to a younger up-and-coming potential rival but to his old colleague, Tikhonov ("old" colleague in more ways than one—Tikhonov was then seventy-five). In 1977 Brezhnev ousted Podgorny unceremoniously from the Politburo, and a month later took over his title of Chairman of the Presidium of the USSR Supreme Soviet—in a session when Podgorny was not even present.

Andrey Kirilenko appeared to be the heir apparent in 1976-78, but he apparently jumped the gun, misjudging the seriousness of Brezhnev's ailments. He seems to have acted as if he were already in charge during Brezhnev's illnesses. In November 1976 he appointed a friend, Yakov Ryabov, to the CC CPSU Secretariat, apparently to oversee the administrative organs (including the KGB). In late 1977 and early 1978 he made himself prominent with speeches and other public appearances. But then Brezhnev came back to full health, apparently irritated, and dropped Kirilenko from favor and Ryabov from office. Another candidate, Fedor Kulakov, Politburo member and CC CPSU Secretary overseeing agriculture, ended up dead (having cut his own wrists in his bathtub, according to rumor) in July 1978.

But another man was rising: Yury Andropov. A full member of the Central Committee since 1961, Secretary of the CC CPSU since 1962, Andropov was already selected in 1964 to give the Lenin anniversary speech. In 1967, within weeks after being appointed Chairman of the KGB, he was promoted to candidate member of the Politburo, and became a full member in 1973. His selection to give the Lenin anniversary speech again in 1976 (unheard-of for a State Security chief in office) showed that he had the support of Mikhail Suslov, the party's chief ideologist, and made him a prime candidate to succeed Brezhnev. Other signs suggested that Andropov was being prepared to return in 1976-77 to the Secretariat, no doubt as a potential successor to Brezhnev. Among these signs was the unusual prominence given to his first deputy at the KGB, Semen Tsvigun (husband of Mrs. Brezhnev's sister). Tsvigun was awarded Hero of Socialist Labor in September 1977 and published large-circulation books about security matters, as well as an article on Dzerzhinsky in Znamya in late 1977; eventually (in September 1981) he had the unprecedented honor of having an article featured in the Party's highest ideological organ, *Kommunist*. Andropov's candidacy—unlike the others—remained constant: he again made the Lenin speech in April 1982, just before making the move back to the Secretariat, which had been foreshadowed six years earlier.

Konstantin Chernenko, too, became ever-more prominent as the other candidates dropped by the wayside. This drab bureaucrat, with no major accomplishments or executive positions on his record, was hard to take seriously at first; he seemed nothing more than a bag carrier for Brezhnev. But he enjoyed Brezhnev's confidence and occupied a formidable position, not unlike that held by Poskrebyshev under Stalin. Brezhnev had eschewed a large private secretariat, choosing instead to use for that purpose the General Department of the CC CPSU. At its head, Chernenko coordinated and arranged Brezhnev's appointments and priorities and sat athwart all the incoming reports and outgoing commands. He came to know where the skeletons were buried and how the system really ran and perhaps, too, he enjoyed the self-interested and powerful support of Brezhnev's large and well-placed Mafia.

Brezhnev's regime seemed unable to come to grips with any of its internal problems (except dissidence) but none of its failures threatened its (nor Brezhnev's personal) hold on power: not gross inefficiency, waste, or corruption, not production failures or declining growth, not slumping agriculture (and growing dependence on grain from the capitalist world), not even the infirmity of the leader. These leaders were not running for election and they could count on the coercive power of the KGB.

Brezhnev's State Security system played its role in the power fight. Normally invisible to the outside world and even to the Soviet people, that role could be detected by subtle signs from time to time. For example, after Brezhnev dumped Podgorniy in 1977, a spate of awards, promotions, and appointments in the party, KGB, armed forces, and other institutions followed, suggesting that as in the past, loyalists were being rewarded after a victorious struggle against internal rivals.

The honors heaped on the forces of State Security in 1976-78 represented much more than a further build-up of their image. They certified that the KGB was really responsible for holding on to power for Brezhnev—and for the whole leadership. Here are just a few of the signs of that time:

—In February 1976, at the Twenty-fifth Party Congress, Brezhnev paid homage to State Security before even mentioning the armed forces.

—That same party congress appointed as an alternate member of the Politburo former career KGB officer Geidar Aliyev (then head of the party in Azerbaijan). It reelected four active KGB officials to the Central Committee: Andropov as a full member, Viktor Chebrikov, Semen Tsvigun, and Georgy Tsinev as alternate members. (The latter were all to be made full members at the next party congress, in 1981.)

—In April 1976, KGB Chairman Andropov (a full Politburo member since 1973) made the principal address at the anniversary of Lenin's birth, traditionally a great honor and one for which any of the other members of the Politburo and secretaries of the CC CPSU could have been selected. It was the first time in the history of the Soviet state that a Chekist leader was given this honor.

—In September 1976, Andropov was appointed to the rank of Army General, violating a decree of the Presidium of the USSR Supreme Soviet dated October 23, 1973, limiting the top KGB rank to Colonel-General. The only peacetime precedent was Ivan Serov. In wartime, Lavrentiy Beria had been a Marshal and his man, Vsevolod Merkulov, at the head of State Security had Army General rank.

—In May and September 1977, two of Andropov's deputies, Tsvigun and Tsinev, were made Heroes of Socialist Labor—as no KGB men except Andropov had been before and few who were not members of the Politburo.

—In December 1978, three KGB deputies—Tsvigun, Tsinev, and the Border Guard Troops commander V. Matrosov—were promoted to Army General. Until Andropov, only one peacetime chairman had ever held this rank; now three of his deputies did.

By 1980-81 Brezhnev was tottering about like a zombie, and not even the ministrations of the special Kremlin clinic could hold him up much longer. Now the underground fight for his succession began to seep out into the open—and KGB instruments came into play.

In late 1981 and the first half of 1982, strange events were brought to the attention of the western public. In December 1981, in this land of meticulous censorship, a Moscow theater was allowed to present a play about the last months of life of the enfeebled Lenin. No one could fail to notice the parallel with Brezhnev's condition, but in case anyone missed the point, rumors were floated to westerners to explain it. Also, a Leningrad magazine issued a special edition consecrated to Brezhnev's seventy-fifth birthday; its seventy-fifth page (the number would be noticed and also called to western attention) satirized Brezhnev's literary pretentions and his extended old age. Within the week (again according to rumors) the police (probably KGB) by extraordinary coincidence uncovered stolen diamonds in the home of a singer—a close friend of Brezhnev's daughter.

Then on January 19, 1982, Semen Tsvigun died suddenly—probably violently, perhaps by his own hand. It was a startling occurrence; this was, after all, the day-to-day operating head of the KGB, a man given extraordinary prominence, and a brother-in-law of Brezhnev. Again rumors floated to western sources: Tsvigun had committed suicide because he had been unable to quash the jewel theft scandal to protect Brezhnev's family.

But then something equally surprising happened: Brezhnev failed to sign Tsvigun's obituary notice—although, at about that same time, he signed those of lesser functionaries with no personal connection. Even more astonishing, neither did a single military officer except Defense Minister Ustinov. This can only have been purposeful and malevolent: Tsvigun's official biography in the Soviet Military Encyclopedia describes him as an Army General who took active part in the defense of the country. The newspaper account of Tsvigun's death failed even to name the cemetery where he was buried.

Then immediately Mikhail Suslov disappeared, too. Two days after Tsvigun's death—and on the very day Tsvigun's strange obituary appeared—Suslov suffered a "stroke" and four days later (on January 26) died. The ways of fate are extraordinary: here, in the midst of a power struggle, disappeared the man who would probably arbitrate the succession struggle.

Three days after that (again, the West was privileged to learn of things it normally never hears) the police arrested Boris Buryatia (called "the Gypsy"), the singer implicated in the jewel affair of December. Now a scandal broke, involving performers and managers of circuses, theaters, and dance groups who, on trips abroad, had been smuggling gemstones. They enjoyed the corrupt collusion of the authorities who granted the exit visas, OVIR, whose chief, MVD General Konstantin Zotov, was fired. So were some of the performers and managers, of whom some were reportedly friendly (and as rumors implied, criminally involved) with Brezhnev's son Yuri as well as his daughter Galina (wife of MVD First Deputy Minister Churbanov). These smuggling rings are known, routinely watched, and penetrated by the KGB; clearly someone chose to close this one down with a bang—at this particular moment.

Hardly two weeks later the Soviet authorities—normally hypersensitive to such things (one remembers their later reluctance to allow photographers to snap Andropov in the months of his decline, before his disappearance)—permitted the dissemination to foreign television of film showing Brezhnev weak and weeping at the funeral of his friend General Konstantin Grushevoy.

On March 3—Tsvigun and Suslov dead, scandals erupting around them—eleven members and candidate members of the Politburo, headed by Brezhnev, trooped off together to the theater to demonstrate their unity in crisis as their predecessors had done after the death of Stalin and again after the arrest of Beria. In case someone should fail to get the point, *Pravda* the next day published a photo of the theatergoing leaders on its front page, alongside a prominent editorial about party unity. Then the leaders spoiled the happy picture by revealing their disarray: they postponed until May the Plenum of the Central Committee, which had been scheduled for late March or early April.

During this extraordinary time (as in 1967) the KGB leadership was being changed. On February 27, 1982, Georgy Tsinev, a longtime military security specialist, a onetime military-political officer, and an old associate of Brezhnev, took over the place liberated by Tsvigun's demise; but five weeks later he got an unprecedented companion in the job of First Deputy KGB Chairman: Brezhnev's fellow countryman Viktor Chebrikov. On April 22 KGB Chairman Andropov again made the key ideological speech on the occasion of Lenin's birthday, and on May 26 left the KGB and returned to the post of Secretary of the CC CPSU. He was clearly preparing to take over from the failing Brezhnev.

One might think that the leaders were wary of the eventual role of the Army in the forthcoming changes. Andropov's replacement was Vitaly Fedorchuk, who for three decades in military-security work had watched over the army's conformity to party discipline. So had his first deputy Tsinev, a longtime veteran of military security and of military-political work. For the first time in the KGB's sixty-five-year history, two military-security specialists occupied the KGB's top two positions. And the old party leader and onetime State Security officer Aleksey Yepishev remained as head of the armed forces' political administration, and the old military-security specialist Petr Ivashutin remained atop the GRU.

No one in the West can say with confidence what lay behind these events or their purposeful exposure to the West. The explanations that have been put forward (some of them accepted) are too facile; too many bricks are missing to build a sound edifice of deduction.

But there is a pattern, even if it may be misleadingly obvious: someone apparently set out systematically, using KGB facilities, to discredit Brezhnev and, by association, his Mafia and his close associate Konstantin Chernenko. Someone took pains to explain this to westerners—no doubt to insure replay from the West. Whoever could do this must control some capabilities of the KGB. The finger points inexorably at Yury Andropov.

But Semen Tsvigun was supervising the KGB's day-to-day operations. What was his role in all this? We need not believe the inspired rumor that, unable to protect Brezhnev from the circus scandal, Tsvigun committed suicide. This would not explain the hostile reaction of Brezhnev or of the armed forces leaders, reflected in their failure to sign his obituary. Did Tsvigun lend himself to the operation to discredit his boss, who had hitched his wagon to Andropov's star rather than to Chernenko's? Or, to the contrary, did he and Suslov oppose Andropov and his anti-Brezhnev operation, and get murdered to clear the path? How did Tsvigun die? Heart attack? Suicide? Murder?

And what was Suslov's role? How did he really die? It is not sensationalism to reject the story that he died of a stroke; the long line of strange deaths in Soviet history—Menzhinsky, Kuibyshev, Frunze, Ordzhonikidze, Zhdanov, to name a few—reminds us of that. Suslov—Stalin's helper in the great purges of the 1930s and astonishing survivor of Stalin, Beria, Khrushchev, the antiparty group, the overthrow of Khrushchev, Brezhnev's takeover and power consolidation, and the downing of Shelepin and other rivals of Brezhnev—had supported Andropov in the past. Did he now try to speed Brezhnev's exit, and concur in the subtle public denigration of Brezhnev? Or did he set out to oppose Andropov's course, and pay the price?

There are no answers to these questions, only guesses. What remains is a mystery, evidence that in Soviet power politics, things never change. Secret conspiracy and bloodshed remain the rule, and the bodyguards and other facilities of the State Security apparatus continue to play their central role.

[358]

Leonid Brezhnev appeared atop the Lenin Mausoleum at the November 7 parade, and three days later was dead. With a minimum of delay, the Central Committee met, Konstantin Chernenko proposed that Yury Andropov be named as General Secretary, and for the first time in Soviet history, the head of State Security became overall boss of the country.

It was as if Count Benckendorff, head of the Third Section, had succeeded to the throne of the Tsar he protected, Nicholas I.

4. ANDROPOV AND CHERNENKO

Yury Andropov must have prepared his way to the top by skillful maneuvering and by using the capabilities of the KGB he commanded. But he was not the new broom, the vital new force, that western journalists sought to make of him. On the contrary, he steadfastly pursued Brezhnev's course, the only possible line left to Soviet leaders.

The western press tended to ascribe to this tough and "efficient" KGB leader the crackdown on shirkers, the calls for work discipline, the fight against corruption, the suppression of dissidents, and the firm policy abroad (the war in Afghanistan, the crushing of the Polish labor union Solidarity, and the aid to anticapitalist regimes wherever they gained a foothold). They dismiss Brezhnev as almost paralytically incapable of action. Yet these were all Brezhnev's policies, which for many years he had been carrying out through the KGB under Andropov. Andropov's speeches, far from being original, sounded like carbon copies of Brezhnev's.

It was Brezhnev who exalted State Security; Andropov's succession to Brezhnev's throne was but a logical consequence. It is often written in the West that a secret agreement lay behind Andropov's "willingness" to give up his CC CPSU secretaryship and take the "stigma" of commanding the KGB—an agreement to appoint him to the Politburo. Indeed, within days after his nomination to the KGB in 1967, Andropov was appointed a candidate member of the Politburo, and in 1973 a full member. But this was less a personal arrangement than the certification that State Security is an inseparable part of the central party leadership. Not only were all those State Security deputy chairmen raised to the Central Committee and given the unheard-of rank of Army General, but in 1978 the KGB itself was taken away from even nominal subordination to the Council of Ministers and made "USSR KGB." If one needed more evidence, it was provided in 1983 when Viktor Chebrikov, new chairman of the KGB, was moved

[359]

up within weeks, like Andropov before him, to the Politburo as a candidate member.

Andropov's vaunted campaigns to improve the economy had, like Brezhnev's before, already begun to run out of steam even before Andropov himself disappeared from public view, to die over a six months period. In his short time in power he shot a few corrupt functionaries (as Brezhnev had), raided public baths and movie houses to collar shirkers, talked about vague structural changes, and exhorted and threatened to make people work more and better, as every Soviet leader before him had done. But he changed nothing. How could he? The Soviet economy depends for its survival on the very corruption he pretended to fight and its only hope for real improvement would involve freedoms the regime does not dare grant.

It did not matter that it was the old guard Brezhnevite Konstantin Chernenko who took over from Andropov. Nothing can be changed, not by the youngest candidate, Mikhail Gorbachev, nor by some whiz kid still unknown outside his party organization. The system itself prevents any fundamental reform. As this is written, there sits Chernenko, confidently surrounded by the familiar faces of people he helped Brezhnev raise to high office—even his KGB Chairman, Chebrikov, was a party official in Dnepropetrovsk and for fifteen years a deputy to Andropov in the KGB. The auguries are for continuity, for better or worse.

Chernenko's successor, in turn, will depend for his survival (and the survival of the system he heads) on the system of bodyguards close at hand, repression throughout the land, and military force (carefully controlled by party and KGB) for protection against the pressures from abroad.

Appendixes

The Main Guards Directorate or Stalin's Okhrana

1. ORGANIZATION AND TOP COMMAND

The Main Guards Directorate (GUO) was probably the most perfect and sophisticated body ever organized for the personal security of a government and ideological leader. Comparatively, the bodyguard systems of other rulers of both past and present, and of all political complexions, prove relatively inefficient and ineffective.

In support of this premise, take, for example, the Secret Service group whose duty it is to protect the person of the President of the U.S.A., his family, and certain other governmental and foreign dignitaries. Without denigrating the dedication and ability of the men of that service, their built-in and apparently permanently established handicaps must be considered. They are not members of a basic law-enforcement organization but are subordinate to the Department of the Treasury, whose chief functions are the administration and collection of monies and the prevention of counterfeiting of the national specie. For any information about potential assassins or danger areas, the Secret Service has no resources of its own, but must go through channels to a multitude of other agencies, ranging from federal investigative and intelligence organs, through authorities of the various states, and on occasion, down to the police of small towns and hamlets. Nor does it have any support organization of its own, which makes it dependent, in an emergency, on the often inexperienced assistance of any one or more of a number of groups. It is an extremely effete and antiquated system that has frequently failed chief executives of the U.S.A. and is in a way a luxury of pretension and a hangover from happier days long gone by.

Stalin's Okhrana—at its peak—suffered no such drawbacks. It was his personal security organization, bossed by him and subordinate to nobody else. It was not only a security organization, but also, as needed, an enforcement and punitive agency. It was supreme over all other security groups and received from them all pertinent information, not on occasion, but routinely and as a matter of course. And, although its strength was more than a dozen times that of the Secret Service, it had always at hand trained and experienced support organizations. Additionally, it had authority equaled by no other bodyguards of past or present. For it, unlike similar groups elsewhere, had the dual duty of not only protecting the leader, but also of eliminating his opponents, real and potential. In a way, that second facet of its task was also a luxury one that can be afforded only under a Communist or other dictatorial system. There is, of course, no room for that in free societies, but it is a way of life to which Russia and its subject people have long been inured. And it secured Stalin safety of life and limb and tenure of rule.

As a matter of fact, there was no real security reason for Stalin to have organized the Main Guards Directorate in 1947. His earlier security groups, although not as strong, polished, and well directed, had acquitted themselves well of their double job of guarding him and eliminating his rivals. The explanation for the formation of that super organization most likely is that Stalin's suspicions, like those of Ivan the Terrible before him, burgeoned irrationally as he entered the twilight of his long and bloody life. Likewise, irrationality is the probable cause of his permitting his bodyguards, once they had been so perfected, virtually to be emasculated by his conniving underlings in 1952.

At its peak of perfection, the Directorate's chain of command ran from Stalin to Poskrebyshev (both of them had similar control of state security) to Vlasik, the Okhrana chief. Under Vlasik's control were a secretariat, which had purely administrative duties, party and Komsomol committees, whose functions were the usual and continuing political indoctrination of the guards, four departments, termed service, personnel and security, communications, and operations, eight subdirectorates, the Kremlin *kommandatura*, Okhrana No. 1, Okhrana No. 2, one each for the North Caucasus, the Black Sea and the Crimean resorts, supply and the Kremlin medical and sanitary service, plus such lesser units as the guards school, a physical and weapons training section, an arms and ammunition supply office, and a sanitary section.

To assist him in running that complex, Vlasik had four chief lieutenants. One was at the head of Okhrana No. 2 (Vlasik himself directed Okhrana No. 1), another in charge of personnel and security, a third for operations (the euphemistic term for the hatchet crew), and a fourth for supply, which gave some indication of that last group's importance to the organization.

For assistance and support, Vlasik was able to call on—and at a moment's notice—security ministry organizations, such as the state security troops, the Terror or "T" department, the internal counterintelligence staff, the operational and investigation units and, of course, its records and files sections. Likewise, he could have also summoned the armed forces to his aid, but that was never necessary during Stalin's rule.

The strength of the Main Guards Directorate varied from time to time, and also was a closely guarded secret. But at its best, it numbered some sixteen thousand officers and men (and women) in Moscow alone. That figure did not include those at the Okhrana subdirectorates at the southern resorts, provincial guard units, plus several thousand contract workers, hired on a permanent or parttime basis. And as standby units, the divisions of state security and internal troops should be included as part of the total. The First Dzerzhinsky Motorized Division and the Second Division of Internal Troops each had a strength of some ten to twelve thousand men. That gives a grand total, therefore, of almost fifty thousand men who were serving as bodyguards in one way or another for Stalin during the period 1947–52.

The duties of that mighty Okhrana were many and varied. Most were of public knowledge in the Soviet Union. But a few, especially those concerned with eliminating the dictator's rivals, were of top secret classification. The chief declared function of Okhrana No. 1 was guarding Stalin. The principal tasks of Okhrana No. 2 were to guard other Soviet hierarchs, visiting foreign dignitaries, and leaders of other world Communist parties as well as important installations of the party and state.

The chief Soviet personalities guarded by Okhrana No. 2 (kept under surveillance would be the better term) were: the other members and alternate members of the Politburo, the secretaries of the CC CPSU (some of those were not members of the Politburo), the ministers of defense, state security, internal affairs, foreign affairs, the chief of the general staff, and some half dozen of the leading marshals of the armed forces.

On a less lofty level, Okhrana No. 2 also supervised the protection provided by local state security organs to regional Communist party leaders and chiefs of government. The local hierarchs whose protection was thus "supervised" included the first and second secretaries, the presidents and the chairmen of the Council of Ministers of the fifteen union republics, plus the first secretaries of the *oblasts, krays* and autonomous republics. Lower level (district) party secretaries did not have special bodyguards. Nevertheless, the local state security offices bore the responsibility for their "safety."

Installations under the shield of Okhrana No. 2 included: offices of the CC CPSU and the council of ministers, the general staff building, the foreign office, the academy of sciences and such top-secret laboratores as K-R and 100 (plus the persons of some chief scientists), apartment buildings reserved for high officials, hospitals, sanitoriums, rest homes, and resorts in and around Moscow and in the Caucasus and Crimea. About the only sensitive installations at which Okhrana No. 2 did not stand guard were the MGB and MVD offices. Those places were guarded by their own personnel by day and by internal and security troops by night. However, Okhrana had plenty of other street work in the capital in the period 1947–52. For one of its tasks at that time was the direction of ORUD, or Otdel Regulirovaniya Ulichnogo Dvizheniya (Department of Traffic Regulation) of Moscow.

To fulfill its assignment of watching over leaders of foreign parties (in power), Okhrana No. 2 had men in all the satellites, East European and Asiatic, then under Stalin's aegis. Advisory staffs were furnished to the bodyguard units of the satellite leaders. And in most cases, those advisors were actual supervisors.

[365]

Such a listing of the duties of Okhrana No. 2 may make it appear as if that subdirectorate did most of the work while Okhrana No. 1 guarded Stalin and did little else. That most certainly was not the case.

Such a misconception arises from the anomaly of Vlasik's wearing two hats, one as chief of the Main Guards Directorate, the other as boss of Okhrana No. 1, plus the fact that although exceedingly loyal he was a very stupid and barely educated man. The seeming plethora of guarding done by Okhrana No. 2 was in almost every case merely a watchdog operation. That subdirectorate had no further powers. Those rested not with Vlasik, little more than a dog's body, but with Stalin and/or Poskrebyshev, who then directed Vlasik to use his departments and units as deemed necessary.

A typical case of such mutation in the chain of command as established on paper would involve the disloyalty or opposition, real or imagined, of some Soviet official (or foreign Communist), whose position might range from party hierarch to provincial *apparatchik*. Under ideal circumstances, the disturbing "facts" about that individual would be reported through channels to the chief of Okhrana No. 2, who would bring them to the immediate attention—not of Vlasik, his nominal chief—but of Poskrebyshev and/or Stalin. Only after that, and only if the situation were deemed grave by Poskrebyshev and/or Stalin, would Vlasik be made aware of it, when the case was turned over to his operations department for "disposition." Awkward as that arrangement may seem to admirers of tables of organization, it served Stalin well. For it not only compartmented the activities of Vlasik and his deputies, but it also kept them from taking any independent steps, up to and including a take-over of the palace guards. And it also meant that the system could function despite Vlasik's stupidity, since Poskrebyshev, in addition to his other duties, was the real chief of Stalin's guards.

Stalin also did much to improve the morale and status of his palace guard —and other guards organizations nominally independent, but actually subordinate to it—by the mere change of nomenclature in 1947. Despite the lingering hatred for the Tsarist term, he decreed that the "one word, Okhrana, would give more authority to the service." With that, not only the palace guards became the Main Guard (Okhrana) Directorate, but also such other security groups as the railways and waterways guards, the border troops, the internal troops, and even the Moscow subway guards, were likewise entitled "Okhrana." And at the same time, titles of the individual guards were changed to fit. Those once called "Starshy Razvedchik" (Senior Agent), "Razvedchik 1-oy Kategorii" (Agent First Category) or "Razvedchik 2-oy Kategorii" (Agent Second Category), became simply "Ofitsers Okhrany" (Okhrana Officers) of varying ranks.

The physical and personal security of the Okhrana was quite intense. There were no signs on Okhrana buildings to reveal their identity. Armed guards were posted immediately inside the entrances. Identification papers, with photographs, were required of all visitors, none of whom were allowed in except under escort.

The principal headquarters of the Okhrana was at Dzerzhinsky (formerly Lubyanka) Square No. 2, on the second floor of the state security headquar-

[366]

ters. Those were the offices of Vlasik, who was usually too drunk to appear there, although he generally managed to position himself at the doors of the dictator's Kremlin office or *dacha*, even though far from sober. And there were other Okhrana installations at Dzerzhinsky Street No. 12, as well as offices and safe houses throughout Moscow and its suburbs. The party and Komsomol committees and the Okhrana officers' club were on Zhdanova Street, across from the Peking (formerly Savoy) Hotel.

The plethora of Okhrana and other security forces virtually made two cities out of the Soviet capital. The first was the visible metropolis of some six million people, familiar to travelers and newspaper readers as the home of the Bolshoy, Intourist, the Moscow subway, Red Square, Saint Basil's, the Mausoleum, and, at that time the outside only, of the Kremlin. A visitor would have been justified in assuming that the second city, the half-visible center of Soviet authority, began and ended within the Kremlin walls.

But that assumption would have been wrong. The second city was far larger and more tightly organized than the visitor would have imagined. It was the most alert, suspicious, and intricate system ever devised for the insulation of a ruling caste from the life around it. It could be seen on a map of Moscow, starting at the complex of streets within the Sadovaya Ring, with Red Square and the Kremlin at its heart. Not far from the Kremlin itself was the hive of state security buildings on Dzerzhinsky Square, Dzerzhinsky Street, Malaya Lubyanka Street, Kuznetsky Most Street, with the MVD headquarters farther off on Ogareva Street, only a few pirouettes from the Bolshoy. Then there were the streets leading out from the Kremlin, like the spokes of a large wheel, along Gorky Street, past the special Okhrana living quarters, along Mozhayskoye Chaussee, Mira Prospekt, Arbat Street. Next came the open spaces in the suburbs, along Dmitrovskoye Chaussee, where Khrushchev, Voroshilov, and their *compères* once lived. Pencil in a few dots elsewhere, a house on Bolotnaya Street, other houses at Sirotsky Street No. 11, Yeropkinsky Street No. 3, and at the corner of Staropansky Street, the buildings at Leninsky Prospekt (formerly Kaluzhskoye Chaussee), where a special Okhrana group watched the academy of sciences. Then extend a line out to Pokrovsky Boulevard to the barracks of a security division, kept at constant alert for possible support of the Okhrana in Moscow.

That was the secret city of the Okhrana Directorate. It was complete unto itself. It had its own power plant and its own communications system. On the capital outskirts, it had its own farms and slaughterhouses, whose produce was brought into the Kremlin daily along well-defined routes. Those farms also supplied the secret city's thirty-odd private houses and apartment buildings, the residences of members of the Politburo, the guest houses of foreign Communist visitors, and the homes of families of departed Communist hierarchs still in the official history books.

The secret city had its service personnel as well, and aplenty. It had a small army of plumbers, electricians, doctors, cooks, valets, handymen, almost every variety of professional and domestic help. (Only lawyers were not needed.) There was no end to the categories of those service troops, whose female ranks ranged from charwomen to specially paid prostitutes. But, despite their variety, all had one thing in common—a small Okhrana or state security identity card.

2. OPERATIONS

The Operations Department was the eyes, ears, brain, and heart of Stalin's bodyguard system. As such, it was the most important and the most secret part of the Okhrana. It was under the close supervision of Poskrebyshev and had at its helm only the most experienced and trusted security officers. At Stalin's will, it conducted surveillance, investigations, arrests, and executions. Therefore, it was the special arm that makes Russian bodyguard systems differ from leadership security organizations common in most of the rest of the world—it was the arm that physically eliminated the leader's enemies.

The department was divided into several sections. Its chief components handled the Kremlin, the Central Committee, the Council of Ministers, Red Square and its environs, investigation, surveillance, and execution. It also was responsible for security checks (clearances) of all civilians working in the Kremlin, the CC of the CPSU, and the Council of Ministers.

The surveillance section had, besides its own teams, a large network of more than three thousand subagents, deployed primarily in sensitive party and government installations, as well as in areas frequented by Stalin. Those subagents were recruited by the usual methods—threats, promises of special privileges or bribery. Once recruited, however, those informers were kept at arm's length by their OPEROD case officers, who were liable for punishment or dismissal if they established more than working relations with their agents. The subagents were so concentrated along the streets and areas through which Stalin traveled that it was impossible for a visitor to arrive in a protected zone without being reported. And in those special zones, not only the subagents, but also every resident was required to report immediately on every outsider, including friends and relatives, who entered the areas for visits.

OPEROD Okhrana surveillance teams not only kept tabs on party and government functionaries and other persons under suspicion, but also on Okhrana personnel as well. Such periodic checks of the personnel of both Okhrana No. 1 and Okhrana No. 2 were to acquire "character information," or in plain words every detail about the officer's personal life, friends, and inclinations. If the officer were found to be associating with suspicious persons, or if the information about him proved otherwise unfavorable, he was immediately transferred from bodyguard work to other security functions as fuller investigation of his activities got under way.

However, the bulk of the Okhrana teams' surveillance work concerned possible direct threats to Stalin. For that, a special group worked closely with Poskrebyshev, reading, analyzing, and classifying all letters sent to Stalin and those Politburo members in the Georgian's favor at the time. The great majority of letters requested some boon or dispensation, but even such

[368]

innocent communications were most rigorously checked. Letters that were considered to be threatening in any way received most special treatment. Work on those was coordinated with the "T" (Terror) department and the special investigation department of state security. Of course, under the Soviet system and during Stalin's rule especially, almost anything constituted a threat. Additionally, both Poskrebyshev and Stalin were incapable of believing that there were no terrorists, no threats to Stalin's life. It was a sort of mania, so, if there were no terrorists, OPEROD and state security invented them. As a result, card files on people with terrorist tendencies numbered in the thousands. Names of such "terrorists" were not only garnered from letters to Stalin and other hierarchs, but also from anonymous accusatory letters, routine surveillance work, subagents and regular police. And some worthy citizens volunteered information about threats—all of it false and most of it malicious. The OPEROD first "isolated" (arrested is the proper term) such fingered "terrorists" and then "investigated" their cases. Those deemed less serious were investigated first and isolated later. But the outcome for most usually was the same: five years, without trial, in prison or forced labor camp. And those really believed to be "terrorists" got much longer terms or were simply shot, also without trial.

To carry on its work with the subagents and against the "terrorists," the surveillance section had its main office in state security headquarters as well as operational stations scattered all over Moscow, but so located as to provide the best possible coverage of the capital's populace. All those teams were in direct telephone communication, not only with each other, but also with the city militia and the Okhrana officers in militia uniform who controlled Moscow traffic. In that way, they were overseers of security for Stalin and his cronies as they traveled in Moscow, or between Moscow and their *dachas*. And when Stalin went south for rest or vacation, half of the surveillance staff went with him.

The surveillance teams also had the chore of keeping some of the hard and disagreeable facts of life from the eyes of the leader. One such task concerned a legless veteran of World War II. For a number of evenings during 1947, that unfortunate used to roll his wheelchair to the sidewalk outside a Georgian restaurant near Arbat Street, where Stalin passed, and cadge money and cigarettes from the clientele by yarning about his war exploits and displaying his Red Star medal. In time, a surveillance plainclothesman tried to shoo the cripple away, fearing he might make a bad impression on Stalin. But the cripple was deaf to persuasion, so other OPEROD officers arrested him. The veteran soon disappeared for good, but not before he had called his interrogators Oprichniks of Stalin the Terrible and had thrown his medal in their faces. Lest such a "threat" disturb the leader's peace of mind again, Vlasik then issued an order "for more vigilance and the removal of all beggars from the streets" that Stalin and his underlings would travel.

The investigations section interrogated all persons detained and, if there were enough "compromising" material or an actual offense had been committed, made arrests. But one of its most demanding and continuing tasks was compiling lists of "suspect" persons and turning those lists over to state security for formal record. It was enough to "dirty-up" a man—or get him listed at state security—if he were careless enough to enter protected areas two or three times, for periods of more than half an hour. For that, the "suspect" would be card-filed at state security under such an entry as "detained in a special service zone," or "appears frequently near areas under special protection."

Comparatively, the investigations section's job of interrogating "suspects" was quite simple. That was due to a precept handed down by Lenin himself that "the judicial processes should not do away with terror. To do this would be self-deception. Instead, the process should be based on terror and should legalize it as a matter of principle, clearly, without any shamming or attempts to make it look better." And since the OPEROD interrogators were the elite of the security forces, there was no question but that they excelled in the techniques recommended by the sainted leader of the past.

Therefore, OPEROD interrogators employed to the fullest the device of the forced, "voluntary" confession, that nice combination of the revival meeting, the Inquisition and the third degree so common to the Communist way of life. For long, the outside world swallowed such "confessions," but even the most average Soviet citizen had fully understood the process. He appreciated that any prisoner, whatever his background, had his breaking point. And the Soviet citizen had been conditioned to expect such confessions as the normal outcome of arrests.

The technique was the combined result of the Lenin precept and the motive of the interrogator. Under the Soviet system, the case officer was committed to secure conviction from the moment he formally opened a case file. Additionally, under the system, the Okhrana "never arrests anyone who is not guilty."

The need of a confession, however, sprang not only from the interrogator's desire for promotion and survival. There was also the practical need to protect the security's own agents and informers, who were responsible for opening the case in the first place. If the investigating officer had to rely on his agents for witnesses, he automatically destroyed a good intelligence network by bringing them into court. The accused may have recoiled in surprised horror when he heard the "evidence" his interrogator accumulated against him and when he learned or suspected the identity of the informers. But the interrogator, by means of the extracted confession, kept such information from becoming general knowledge.

The interrogator also conducted his investigation behind the shield of being a representative of the Soviet state. And the Soviet state never makes mistakes. In the Soviet context, it is only individuals who make mistakes, by willfully "distorting" or falsifying" the clear precepts of communism. The interrogator had had that "principle" well drilled into him long before he ever approached the prisoner in his cell or the interrogation room. But many, in their zeal to prove its "truth"—and at the same time get a promotion to senior case officer or deputy section chief—often ended up by brainwashing themselves as well as the prisoner.

It is that final factor—the likelihood that psychological pressures were so intense that they frequently exhausted the interrogators as well as the prisoners—that has caused a considerable reduction in the use of raw terror since the death of Stalin. But, the starting premises of the investigation technique have changed not a jot or tittle, despite the various political "relaxations" of the Georgian dictator's successors.

For Poskrebyshev and Stalin, OPEROD's most arcane and important arm was the executions section. Of course, it did not have that name, but was screened by the term "special" unit. However, and whatever the terminology, it was the group to which the dictator and his man Friday turned when they had decided to get rid of someone.

The chief executioner in the heyday of the Directorate was a Colonel Okunev, an exceedingly unsalubrious character, who was regarded by his fellows as an "outstanding" Chekist. Besides his propensity for killing, he was also an advanced alchoholic when he took over his "duties" in 1947. Doubtless a true psychopath for years earlier, his drinking not only became extreme, but he had also developed a speech defect, a sort of combined stammer-stutter, by the time he was "retired" in 1952. Then a fifteen-year veteran of executions, he tried, but unsuccessfully, to get employment at the notorious state security laboratory, called the *kamera* (chamber), a worthy rival of the Nazis' concentration camp medical horrors, where experiments were carried out on living people—prisoners and persons about to be executed—to determine the effectiveness of various poisons and injections, as well as the efficacy of the use of hypnotism and drugs in advancing interrogation techniques. (Although not an integral part of the Directorate, that *kamera* was an acknowledged and useful tool of the guards organization.) Throughout his service as chief executioner of the Directorate, Okunev lived in a little world of his own. Other guards officers shunned him, not in revulsion to his duties, but because it was common to encounter him lurching down the corridors of the Dzerzhinsky Square headquarters with vodka and saliva dripping from his mouth.

One of Okunev's first major jobs for the Directorate was the elimination of the prominent Jewish actor and director, Solomon Mikhoels. Although Mikhoels had been of much help to the Russian cause in World War II by enlisting Jewish and other sympathy in the U.S.A, Stalin not only deemed his usefulness as terminated, but had decided for internal political and other reasons to conduct another minipogrom. Part of the scheme was both to close Mikhoels' Yiddish theater in Moscow and to initiate a swipe at Mikhoels' chief Jewish supporters, Molotov's wife, the former foreign minister Litvinov, and Lozosky, Litvinov's deputy. As for Mikhoels himself, Poskrebyshev felt that the usual Soviet elimination procedure—staged trial, "confession" and a sentence to a forced labor camp or death—would arouse too much unfavorable reaction, not certainly in anti-Semitic Russia, but in the West. Instead, Okunev was ordered to stage a "tragic and regrettable auto accident." So smoothly was that assignment carried out that Okunev and his teammates were later singled out for special awards by the security arm.

More routine tasks for Okunev were the eliminations of Kuznetsov, Voznesensky, and Rodionov, the last chairman of the Council of Ministers of the

Russian Republic, in 1949–50. Kuznetsov was taken straight to the Lubyanka, where he was not even interrogated. After about three weeks in solitary confinement, he was taken to the inner court of the prison, where he was shot in the back of the head by Okunev. "Legalities" were maintained by having an Okhrana doctor issue a death certificate, signed by Abakumov and witnessed by Okunev. The completed certificate was delivered straight to Poskrebyshev. The only alteration in the disposition of Voznesensky was that he spent several months under house arrest, followed by another several months in solitary at the Lubyanka, before being trotted out to be dispatched by Okunev, who again forwarded the usual death certificate directly to Poskrebyshev. And Rodionov's execution was much the same as Kuznetsov's.

Not all of the auto "accidents" staged by Okunev were as fatal as that of Mikhoels'. A particularly benign mishap was one he produced for Stalin in the winter of 1949–50, when Red Chinese guests Mao Tse-tung and party were quartered at Lipki on the Dmitrovskoye highway outside Moscow, in one of the Georgian's *dachas*. In the course of his wheeling and dealing with the visitors, Stalin considered it necessary to have an hour or two private talk with Mao and without the presence of Liu Shao-chi, the Chinese Communist No. 2 man of the era, who had been virtually glued to his boss' elbow at previous meetings. Okunev solved that problem by having an Okhrana garbage truck collide with Liu's Okhrana-chauffeured limousine, while the honored guest was en route to the Mao-Stalin meeting. So perfectly had Okunev organized the job that the "accident" did not even awaken Liu from his sleep in the rear of the limousine. But it took two hours to complete police formalities and clear the highway, thereby giving Stalin his private lesson with Mao. Even the aftermath was faithfully played out. Liu's chauffeur was "dismissed" and the garbage truck driver was given a year in jail. Subsequently, however, the Okhrana chauffeur returned to driving foreign dignitaries—but other than Chinese—and the Okhrana garbage man was released and given a better job elsewhere in the Soviet Union.

In that same period of the Directorate's supremacy, the Dmitrovskoye highway was the scene of another incident that supplied good proof of the virtually unchallenged power of the OPEROD. The highway was used almost daily by a major general in travel between his private house about twenty kilometers outside Moscow and the general staff offices. That officer had little patience for the speed limits imposed on that route used by Stalin and other hierarchs, and invariably ordered his chauffeur to break the regulations. For those infractions, OPEROD officers, who worked for surveillance units in militia uniforms along that "critical" route, had frequently remonstrated with the army officer's chauffeur, only to have the general tell his driver to disregard the complaints of lowly police. So matters went until one trip, when the speed-happy general told his driver to pass a limousine puttering along at the legal limit ahead of them. But the occupant of the passed vehicle happened to be Voroshilov, who used the same route to his *dacha*. The next day, a squad of OPEROD "militiamen" stopped the general's car, arrested his driver and sent him off for questioning, leaving the general stranded without a vehicle. In the interchange that followed, the general

[372]

called the "militiamen" dirty names and demanded respect for his rank, while one of the OPEROD officers told him that the morrow would tell whether the Comrade General was still a general or a simple soldier. In short order, Vlasik was informed of the incident. The Directorate chief ordered Marshal Aleksandr Vasilevsky, then chief of the general staff, to reprimand his general most severely for speeding on the highway used by Comrade Stalin. Vasilevsky called in the general, chewed him out, and ordered him to apologize personally to the chief of the Moscow traffic department (then under OPEROD control). The general balked at first at apologizing to a mere "militia" officer, but Vasilevsky warned him he could lose his general's rank. With that, the general made apologies to the traffic department chief, who reciprocated by giving him a long lecture about the proper behavior of a general. Not long after that, the general was transferred from Moscow to the boondocks and oblivion.

Although the Main Guards Directorate was emasculated in 1952, the OPEROD certainly did not go out of existence. In 1953, it was transferred to state security control as the Secret Political Directorate (SPU) and then was combined with Department "T" (Terror), with the joint organization getting the comparatively innocent title of the Fourth and Fifth Departments, SPU. Later, it became part of the Second Chief Directorate (internal counterintelligence) of the KGB.

3. PERSONNEL

Without exception, the officers of the Main Guards Directorate were chosen at the initiative of the leaders of the organization, and not at the request of the individual. Nor were the persons selected taken into the Okhrana against their will, but welcomed the opportunity to serve because of party and Komsomol pressure (discipline), high pay, prestige, and other benefits.

The general practice was for the Okhrana to accept nominations for officers from the party and Komsomol organizations and from employees of its own service. Some candidates were also chosen from such paramilitary services as the internal and border troops, and from the Kremlin *kommandatura*, but only after they had completed their usual three years of military service. And some officers—not candidates—were sent to the Okhrana directly by the CC of the CPSU or by the security minister from other components of the state security forces. And there were some candidates, practically all of them specialists, who were drawn from the universities and institutions of higher learning. Finally, as exceedingly rare additions to those candidates selected by the Okhrana, there were a few instances in which the individual solicited consideration by the Okhrana, through and because of personal contacts with the Okhrana.

Before acceptance, the candidates had to meet certain requirements, including good health, records of good behavior, acceptable backgrounds, must have had no relatives living abroad, and, of course, must have membership in the Communist Party or the Komsomol. Sometimes—but only very exceptionally—the Okhrana accepted nonparty members sponsored by either three state security officers or by three party members—and those exceptions were made only for specialists, never for guards officers.

Annually, usually, at the request of the security minister and the chief of the Guards Directorate, the CC of the CPSU issued a decree signed by Malenkov for the enlistment of Communist Party and Komsomol members in the security services. The number needed varied from some five hundred to twelve hundred.

From Malenkov, the decree went to the Moscow city party committee, which relayed it to the capital's district committees for action. The number of candidates each district was required to deliver varied according to the size of the district and the strength of the district's party membership. The greater number was generally drawn from industrial areas, such as the Stalin district, where the automobile factory of that name was located. The least came from such capital center areas as the Sverdlov district, peopled mainly by government workers and "intellectuals." Selection of candidates went on throughout the year and monthly meetings were held at the Moscow party committee to discuss progress. The capital committee's second secretary—at that time Yekaterina Furtseva—was usually in charge of those sessions.

Once the selections had been made, the list of candidates was turned over to the Personnel Department of the Main Guards Directorate, which not only checked the candidates' qualifications, but also their security status. Thus was the personnel office also the security office of the Okhrana. The security of all candidates was closely checked, while that of potential bodyguards, especially bodyguards for Stalin, was most rigorously investigated.

Normally, the security procedure for all candidates was as follows:

a. Recommendations
   1) For a party member: a statement signed and stamped by the first secretary of the district committee declaring: "The _____ Party Committee of the City of Moscow has agreed to recommend _____, a Party member since ____ (Party membership card No. ____.) to serve in the organs of the State Security."
   2) For a nonparty member: affidavits from three party members, stating how long each had known the candidate, that he was of good character and that he was recommended for "secret" or "special" work in the organs of state security.
   3) For military personnel: a recommendation from the Political Section (Politodel) of the unit.
b. Personal history:
   1) The district party or Komsomol committee furnished the complete party record of the candidate. His employer supplied his complete work history.
   2) If there was nothing classified about the candidate's potential assign-

ment, or if his task was to be quite secondary, then his employer had been informed of it and had therefore written on his file "to be presented to state security."

3) If, for security purposes, the employer was to be kept in the dark about the candidate's proposed use, the district party committee simply demanded the file without giving any reason.

4) And, in highly classified cases, when the district party committee was also to be kept in the dark, the district first secretary alone was informed, and was ordered to get the file "in the normal course of his work."

  c. Declaration by candidate:

Before being accepted into the Directorate, the candidate had to sign a statement that he had asked state security to accept him for a job. That was done to assure that he could make no future claim he had been forced or pressured.

  d. Relatives:

No one could be hired who had relatives abroad, or whose wife had relatives abroad, even if those relatives were Soviet citizens working as diplomats, trade representatives, newspapermen, etc. Nor, of course, was anyone accepted who had any relatives in prison or labor camps.

In addition to meeting such requirements satisfactorily, every candidate had to submit to very careful rundowns on his social origin (peasant, worker, or aristocrat, bourgeois, *kulak*), on his date and place of birth, and on his close relatives (what their work was, their attitude toward the Soviet regime, etc.). Also closely examined were his characteristics, his work and personal habits, his ability to hold liquor, his friends, his moral qualities, his possession of appropriate party and work character sketches (*kharakteristika*). And, of course, he must have had no record of party or administrative investigations. Simultaneously, the candidate was also put under surveillance—a procedure which he undergoes routinely ever after, if he were accepted. By the time of completion of all that checking and surveillance of a candidate, and that of his friends, associates, and neighbors, personnel usually had accumulated at least some three hundred pages of information on the individual.

Personnel also called on field stations and other state security organs for help with candidate investigations. That frequently resulted in vehement protests from local security organizations, who complained that the Directorate's demands hindered their own work. When such disputes became extreme, the State Security Minister, himself, would instruct his subordinates to fulfill the Directorate's requests within deadlines of ten days or less. On receipt of such orders, all other security work halted until the Directorate's requests had been met.

Those security investigations not only kept Personnel very busy indeed, but also severely pared the lists of candidates. It was quite common for the Department to interview more than two thousand persons in the course of conducting security checks on some five hundred candidates. The reverse proportion was also quite usual in amassing the required number of candi-

[375]

dates. In 1950, for example, the personnel officer assigned to the Sverdlov district of Moscow approved only five on the candidate list of twenty. And in the same year in the capital's Komintern district, where theaters and other government offices were located, the ratio of unwanted "intellectuals" was so high that only seven candidates were approved from a list of twenty. But, when such shortages existed in Moscow districts, the vacancies were filled with candidates from suburban areas, generally those containing small plants and factories. (The severest shortage of qualified replacements for bodyguards occurred immediately after World War II. Abakumov overcame that problem by direct transfers to the palace guards of several hundred officers from the security surveillance services of counterintelligence and from the transportation guards.)

And in very exceptional cases, when the Moscow area was not able to supply sufficient candidates for recruitment, the Directorate resorted to border troops, internal troops, the Kremlin *kommandatura*, and even to republic and *oblast* party and Komsomol committees in the rest of the country. Clearances on border, internal, and Kremlin *kommandatura* personnel were relatively simple, since all had been security-checked by their own organizations. Likewise was the checking of candidates from the other republics and the *oblasts* not too difficult, since the chief of state security in those administrative areas was almost always a member of the top party organization of the republic or *oblast* concerned. However, there was one major drawback facing recruits from the republics and *oblasts* and from security organizations stationed in outlying areas—the Moscow housing shortage. As a result, only those who were not married or those who had Muscovite wives with living quarters in the capital were taken. And the single men invariably had great difficulty in finding accommodations. (Therefore, with the exception of those outlanders fortunate enough to have married a Moscow woman supplied with living quarters, the palace guard was mainly a Moscow outfit. And although that made security clearances simpler for the personnel officers, it also was a very definite built-in security flaw of the bodyguard organization. Nobody in authority bothered about that weakness at the time, nor was any concern shown about it by their successors.)

Extreme security checking, of course, applied especially to personnel assigned as bodyguards. The rest of the Directorate's manpower, ranging from technicians and specialists in medicine and communications and experts in transportation and construction down to domestic help, were more easily cleared, and were either transferred or co-opted from universities and technical institutes or from government establishments.

As with most paramilitary organizations, age was an important consideration in recruitment for the Directorate. The bulk of the candidates approved were between the ages of twenty and thirty. That was because physical stamina was required for the duty of the majority of the Okhrana officers, namely standing long hours, either as militia or plainclothesmen, in all kinds of weather outside buildings and along streets and byways. That was called "outdoor service" *(naruzhno-postovaya sluzhba)*, a career one-way street that offered practically no chance of promotion and whose future amounted to little more than eventual retirement or dismissal with flat feet. Since discipline, in addition to good physical condition, was required for that boring task the preferred candidates for that "specialty" were men from the armed forces or the reserves, who had completed their compulsory service and would not be called back to the ranks. In exceptional cases a candidate who was under twenty and had had no military service was accepted, but those cases applied only to specialists not otherwise available. For operations work, the recruiting age ranged from twenty for men on physically active duty to thirty-five for those destined for desk jobs. The age level for true specialists, such as engineers, doctors, communications, and administrative personnel, extended up to forty. And there were a few medical men, with very special qualifications, who were enlisted up to the age of fifty-five.

Education was another important basic factor, but ironically in a rather reverse ratio. In other words, candidates with any advanced education at all (except of course, in special fields) were quite unacceptable for the simple reason it was feared (and probably correctly) they would be less amenable to discipline and more liable to balk at some of the dirty work assigned them. The situation had improved over the years, but not very much. Before World War II, the average palace guard had completed no more than seven years of schooling. Under the Directorate, however, no recruit was accepted unless he had eight or nine years of schooling. But there the improvement halted, because as Vlasik's deputy, Goryshev, said: "The education of our officers should not go beyond high school. A person who is better educated thinks too much." Nevertheless, by 1950 there was a sprinkling of officers with higher educations, but only in the operations and other upper echelon departments. Of course, another reason for the low educational level was probably the fact that the Directorate's chief, Vlasik, had completed only three years of elementary school and could hardly sign his name. Despite that high level disapproval of "high level" education, the Directorate's party and Komsomol committees encouraged the guards officers to use their spare time in improving their schooling. But, again, Vlasik objected; if officers were found taking evening courses at the universities, he would say: "We hire people to guard our leaders, not to give them higher education," or "We don't need the rotten intelligentsia." But education of another sort the guards did get, and aplenty. Daily, they received their political indoctrination, including such required items as the history of the Soviet Communist Party, biographies of the leaders of the USSR, elementary courses in Marxism-Leninism, and questions of political propaganda. For that, they had the services of top-notch party activists as well as professors from the University of Marxism-Leninism and other party institutes in the capital.

Although the Directorate decried education for its rank and file, it was very demanding about the health of the bodyguards. All candidates had to be physically fit for active duty in the Red Army. And all had to go to the Central Medical Expert Commission of state security to obtain certificates of such fitness. The examinations were quite severe, since the commission was fully aware the applicant was a potential member of the Directorate,

[377]

even though the candidate knew no more than that he might work for some state security organization. However, the degree of fitness required depended upon the future assignment slated for the candidate, or specifically, whether he would be a guard, a surveillance or outdoors operations officer —which required the most stamina—or was scheduled for such less physically demanding tasks as operations desk work, an administrative job, housekeeping duties, driving, motor mechanics, communications, or medical chores. With such advance knowledge, the commission was able to qualify the recruit for more than one job. For example, if a candidate were not fit for duty as a chauffeur because of poor eyesight, he could qualify as a mechanic or for some administrative job. Or, if flat feet forbade outdoor work for the candidate, it was possible for him to do operations work behind a desk. To be sure, candidates suffering from such afflictions as syphilis, tuberculosis, schizophrenia, and nervous disorders, or who had had a serious operation, were not accepted. Likewise rejected were those with such physical defects as loss of limbs and with family histories of contagious diseases. Those who fell in that category were turned down without even being given an examination. Some with defective vision corrected by eyeglasses were accepted, but only for inside operations and other specialized work, never as guards. Females (used only as technical, service, and housekeeping personnel) also had to pass similar rigorous physical examinations. Once the candidate had qualified physically and otherwise, his health was pretty much in the hands of the state security medical commission during his entire tenure of service, for it was that commission that sent Directorate officers to health resorts for rest and cure, that approved their discharges from state security hospitals and clinics, and that determined their fitness, or disability, when they were being fired or retired.

It may seem rather odd that Stalin, a Georgian, whom Lenin had once singled out to care for Russia's national minorities, should have had pronounced nationality prejudices about his bodyguards, but that certainly was the case. Of course, there were no written regulations about the nationality of Directorate candidates. Nevertheless, very strictly enforced unwritten regulations gave overwhelming perference to Russians and to such an extent that only a most unusual representative of another nationality would be accepted. During the thirties there had been a number of Ukrainians in the palace guard, but that was stopped after World War II. The reason for rejecting the Ukrainians as candidates was that their land had been occupied by the Germans. And that proscription was so severe that it applied even to a person who had been a boy of no more than ten at the most during German occupation. Nor, for similar reasons, were any taken from the Baltic republics (Estonia, Latvia and Lithuania), even though Latvians had once guarded Lenin and had had some representation in the palace guard until the purges. Likewise there was a ban against Kazakhs, Uzbeks, Turkmen, Tadzhiks, and other minority groups of Soviet Central Asia. And when the Directorate was formed, Stalin also decreed that none of its members should be Georgians, fearing that one or more of them might be suborned by Beria. As result of such wide-ranging "unwritten" proscriptions, the Directorate was all-Rus-

[378]

sian, except for token numbers of Ukrainians, Byelorussians, Armenians, Tatars, and Mordovians.

Of course, the group that came to be the most stringently outlawed was the Jews. Up to 1949, there had been some one hundred fifty Okhrana officers of Jewish origin. But, they were summarily dismissed and after 1950 there was an unwritten regulation banning Jews, too. In keeping his personnel officers on their toes about rejecting candidates from Jewish and other proscribed groups, Goryshev used to say: "We accept everybody. . . . (then he would smile) . . . preferably Russians, some Ukrainians, and nobody else."

Despite those instructions from Goryshev, some personnel officers felt inclined to process the application of Jewish candidates because of recommendations (pressure) of higher officials. One such case involved a Lieutenant Schlyapintokh, whose father, a party official in Kuybyshev *oblast*, had sent his son to the state security school in Novosibirsk. On graduation, the young man had been sent to Moscow, to await assignment to some Jewish community in the Ukraine. Meanwhile, the father, who had greater aspirations for his son, advised the young man to write Abakumov and ask to join the Directorate. The letter never reached Abakumov, but was sent to an officer in the personnel department. Although fully aware of the proscription against Jews, that officer processed the application because of the position of the candidate's father and of the letter sent Abakumov. After some two months, the final papers were completed and sent to a deputy state security minister for signature. Instead of signing the documents, that worthy circled the candidate's name and returned the lot to the personnel department. In time, the file went to Vlasik, who circled the word Jewish and bucked the application to Goryshev for an explanation. Goryshev called a meeting of the entire personnel department and then, as a seeming joke, asked the officer concerned why Schlyapintokh had ever been considered. At the mention of the Jew's name, the other personnel officers bust into dutiful laughter and from then on called their erring colleague "Schlyapintokh." Completely unfamiliar, of course, with the proscriptions, the young Jew demanded an explanation for his rejection. All he ever got was a yarn that there was no vacancy for him and assignment as a supply officer in the Kuybyshev state security apparatus.

In addition to all the hurdles of nationality, physique, "education," residence, social and political status, and basic security, the successful Directorate candidate had to meet a number of other political and social criteria, many of them also unwritten. Of course, he had to establish unquestioned loyalty to the building of communism, a Marxist-Leninist educational background, proper political activity (at least, on the surface), and unbridled love of the Soviet leadership (meaning Stalin). Likewise he should be a born Soviet citizen, of the majority nationality, of worker or peasant origin, not from the intelligentsia and definitely not from the classes "destroyed" by the October Revolution. All that was duly made clear in his answers to the "Anketa Spetsialnogo Naznacheniya" (special questionnaire). That was the positive side, after that came the negative. He must not have been the child or close relative of high officials in the party, government, and armed forces.

He and his relatives must not ever have been members of another party (especially genuinely Socialist ones), or of any foreign party. (Preference was given party, Komsomol, and "trade union" members, particularly those active in such organizations.) He must not have lived at any time, including childhood, outside the Soviet Union. (Children of Soviet diplomats were politely, but positively, avoided. Soviet army officers, who had served abroad, could be accepted, but with many reservations, chief of which was that they could never be the personal bodyguards of any member of the Soviet leadership.) And not only must he have never been under German occupation, he must also never have been encircled or otherwise cut off by German forces during World War II. Finally, there was the little matter, but far from a trifling one, of just when an applicant had joined the party or Komsomol, naturally applicable only to certain age groups. He must not have become a member any later than 1943. Applicants who joined later were regarded at the least as "opportunists" and were generally suspected of having been pro-German during the war.

Personnel had considerable experience with candidates who ran afoul of one or another of such unwritten criteria. In 1949, for example, the son of the finance minister was recommended for the Directorate by his district party committee. He, of course, was rejected. But that was done in a most politic manner. Enough about the applicant's character had been established for it to be apparent he was averse to hard work. So the explanation was made that the only Directorate openings then existing were for "beat-pounders," or militia and plainclothesmen for Moscow's streets. That scared the dignitary's son away. And Goryshev underlined the case to his staff, saying, "We don't need mothers' boys—the sons of ministers and generals."

Earlier, just after the Directorate had been established, there was the unfortunate case of Doctor D____, who had been accepted after prolonged checking and sent to Stalin's resort near Sochi to work as a food taster. When she was enlisted in 1947, the military counterintelligence records were still in disarray (data about the thousands of military units disbanded after the war's end had yet to reach the central card files). As result, it was not until 1948 that it was discovered that Doctor D____ and her unit had spent almost two months in German encirclement in 1941. Upon that, she was immediately subjected to reinterrogation. She said she had not mentioned the encirclement because she had regarded that as incidental to her service in the Red Army. And she emphasized that she had not been captured. Just the same, on a charge of concealing facts, she was drummed out of the Directorate, advised to go to Siberia or Kazakhstan and expelled from the party. The personnel officer responsible for approving her enlistment was severely reprimanded and transferred to a less sensitive position in state security.

Another case of temporarily missing wartime records involved an army reservist, Captain B____, who had applied for enlistment in the Directorate as a physical training instructor. During processing of his candidacy, it was found that he had been given an eight-year jail sentence for desertion during World War II. (The sentence was commuted to three months in a disciplinary battalion (shock troops). Later the jail sentence was annulled because of bravery and outstanding performance that won him decorations while with the shock troops.) Later, he had joined the party and had been serving as a physical education instructor at a Moscow institute before applying to the Directorate. Naturally, once his desertion record became known, he was rejected, despite the distinguished service he later rendered the army.

The cases of Doctor D—— and Captain B—— were not cited to show that it was common for candidates to lie or withhold information. What they do show is the complications caused candidates by the war, complications of which the applicants were usually innocent or unwitting bystanders. And that especially proved the case when a candidate had many relatives, any one of whom might have violated one of the written or unwritten regulations. As a result, personnel officers, anxious not only to simplify their work, but also avoid bringing trouble down on themselves, were prone to prefer candidates who were single and had families no larger than parents and one brother or sister. For there was a better than average chance that a married man, with many kinfolk, would have at least one relative whose past would bar the applicant from the Directorate.

Once the annual batch of some five hundred candidates had passed the final qualifying barrier, the completed files of most were sent to a deputy minister of state security for ultimate inspection and approval. However, in the cases of those being processed for Stalin's entourage, whether as guards, doctors, or mere domestics, the final approvals had to be given by the security minister, and then only after he had reviewed them in great detail with Vlasik and Poskrebyshev.

Then after the candidates had been accepted, running investigations of them were maintained by personnel throughout their service. The same process applied to the more veteran Directorate members as well, thereby enlarging personnel's work to the surveillance and security fields as a matter of ordinary routine. To facilitate that, every Directorate member was obliged to report immediately to personnel about all changes in his family life, marriages, court convictions, even illnesses of relatives. Special checks were made on such reports, both to verify them and, if negative in character, to decide the employee's future. For incorrect reports, the least punishment was demotion to a lesser post and they could result in transfer to other state security organs or even summary dismissal with a *volchy bilet* (wolf's ticket).

Actually, "wolf's ticket" was a figurative term, but it was very real just the same—a bad character reference, attached like a leech to the holder for the rest of his life. It was given to those fired as security risks, for flagrant misbehavior, for lack of vigilance, or for merely demanding to quit the Directorate (the last "offense" evidence of the fact that the employee did not want to guard "dear Comrade Stalin").

Receipt of a "wolf's ticket" from the Directorate also meant expulsion from the party or Komsomol, again with a bad character reference. Such a person was reported to state security, which specially advised Department "T" to keep him under surveillance as an "anti-Soviet element" with possible "terrorist tendencies." Additionally he was blacklisted at his former place of employment. Nor could he find work in government offices or industry, since all Soviet institutions and enterprises would be afraid to hire him because he had been fired by security, as well as because of the fact that the chiefs of personnel in all Soviet government and industrial outfits were either staff members of state security or had been co-opted by state security.

As the result of such virtually insuperable handicaps, a number of persons given "wolf's tickets" by the Directorate committed suicide. There were a few such incidents in Okhrana No. 1 and Okhrana No. 2. Particularly grim were the fates of the bodyguards of Kuznetsov and Voznesensky, who had the alternative of posts at forced labor camps in Siberia or dismissal with "wolf's tickets." Not all went to Siberia and few of those who did not survived for long. But the majority of such suicides occurred in other components of the Directorate, no doubt because many of those officers, being "better" educated, finally realized what kind of service they had entered.

The great majority of the officers, however, since they had not been forced into the Directorate and could not resign from it, just trudged along woodenly, keeping out of trouble and minding their own business. They kept their eight-hour watches on the darkened streets of Moscow or along the lonely approaches to the *dachas* of the hierarchs. Year after year, they waited at machine gun posts under the Lenin mausoleum for the "triumphant masses" to march through Red Square and they stayed away from liquor on the job, and never talked about what they did, in hope of attaining twenty-five years of service and being allowed to retire gracefully from the service on pensions amounting to about eighty percent of their salaries. It was more probable, however, that at earlier dates they would be given false medical discharges (the Soviet government dislikes dispensing too many pensions) and sinecures checking hunting rifles, caviar, or television sets in the Supply Section's branch that services Politburo members and their families. Nor could they count on any noticeable improvement in rank by the time they were discharged or retired. Guards seldom attained the rank of major and those that did were very few.

If, prior to the twilight of his career, a guards officer ran into trouble and was dismissed for it, he had no hope of appeal. Such action would merely make his situation worse, as was well known by all. Nevertheless, one Lieutenant Matveyev made the error of appealing his dismissal, and worse. His troubles started when it was found that his wife was in correspondence with an aunt, who lived in Belgium. That was automatic grounds for dismissal and Matveyev was so advised. For two months after that, he not only looked unsuccessfully for other work, but also made continuing claims to both state security and party authorities that his wife's letter writing was no concern of his. All those protests were ignored, of course, so at his wit's end and actually near starvation, he went to the American Embassy and asked for help, if not asylum. Perhaps that was one of the periods when American high policy was again toying with a rapprochement with the Soviets, or perhaps the embassy official somewhat justifiably suspected the Okhrana officer's appeal was an entrapment. Whatever the reason, the embassy refused to do anything for Matveyev. He had been trailed there by surveillance officers and the moment he stepped into the street he was arrested. Within short order, he was imprisoned for five years.

Another case of a relative causing expulsion for a Directorate member was even more unfortunate because the officer had known nothing of the relative's "crime" at the time he was enlisted—nor had the personnel investigators learned of it then, either. Later, however, the officer—and subsequently the Directorate—found that his brother-in-law had been a prisoner of the Germans. As a result, and despite the fact that he had an excellent war record himself, he was fired immediately on a charge of withholding information. (Ironically, if he had disclosed that voluntarily, he also would have been fired.) He, too, tried arguing his case with security and party officials, likewise with no success. Finally, his savings exhausted and his wife in an advanced state of pregnancy, he became desperate. He stormed into the Moscow party committee offices, threw his party card down on a desk and crudely told the *apparatchiks* what they could do with it. Within short order, a representative of party control brought the ex-officer's action to the personal attention of Goryshev, who opined that a man like that could be a danger to the party and ordered him put under special surveillance. The tails duly reported that their subject continued to harp on the injustice of his case and to tell one and all about throwing away his party card. Fully aware he was under intense surveillance, the man snatched a woman's purse and let himself be caught in the act. He had committed the robbery—not for the money the purse may have contained and which he certainly could have used. His objective was to be sent to prison or labor camp, not as a political prisoner, but as a common criminal, who, of course, would receive much better treatment. And so it turned out. He got the penalty for purse-snatching—three years—considerably less than he would have been given for his other "crimes."

Even more tragic was the case of a plainclothes officer, part of a detail on a Moscow street used by the hierarchs. One day, as a group of Politburo cars were speeding through his area under Directorate escort, a man suddenly dashed into the street and was run down and killed. The plainclothesman was suspended immediately and charges of major dereliction of duty were filed against him. That charge sheet said not a whit about the man that was killed, of course; the chief complaint was that the officer had permitted an unauthorized person to cross the street at an unauthorized time. Rather than await the inevitable outcome of the case, the officer killed himself.

In addition to keeping files on all such cases as that, personnel also handled all the records of the entire Directorate staff. The dossier of each officer included all details of his enlistment, promotions, demotions, awards, punishments, vacations, and sick leaves, as well as data about his retirement and pension rights. Appended to each were two passport-size photographs of the officer—one showing him in uniform, the other in mufti. And new photographs had to be furnished each time there was a change in the officer's rank.

For administrative purposes, the Personnel Department was divided into seven main sections. The First, of course, handled Okhrana No. 1. The Second and Seventh, which were actually one and the same, were in charge of the much more numerous components of Okhrana No. 2. The Third oversaw the Kremlin *kommandatura*, the Fourth the Directorate's administrative and supply organizations, while the Fifth was responsible for the Moscow Traffic Department (Okhrana officers in militia uniforms on the capital streets).

Goryshev, who served both as deputy to Vlasik and chief of Personnel, also directed another small and somewhat secret section of that department, the Special Inspection, called the "Chernaya Kamera" by the Directorate officers. It was so known because it was the elite organization which handled all the derelictions and offenses of the guards and recommended their punishment or trials. Usually, once an officer had fallen into the hands of the "Chernaya Kamera," he was exiled from Moscow, dismissed from the guards, or imprisoned. However, all of Special Inspection's decisions had to be approved by Vlasik and the state security minister.

4. OKHRANA NO. 1

Charged with the personal security of Stalin, this was the elite arm of the Directorate. It was also the smallest of the prime security groups of the Soviet leadership. However, its size was not a prime factor, since practically its entire strength consisted of bodyguards of the dictator, plus a relative few for his son and daughter. Those guards relied on Okhrana No. 2 and other components of the Directorate and state security for logistics and any other support needed. And, comparatively small as Okhrana No. 1 may have been, it was approximately five times as large as the bodyguard units furnished the other members of the hierarchy.

Despite the extreme care and caution used in selecting and controlling personnel of Stalin's guard, strictly speaking, their task was much simpler than that of the security forces of American presidents and other Western leaders. That was due on the one hand to the status and personality of the Georgian, and on the other to the peculiarities of the Soviet system. Stalin had almost no social life and never attended social gatherings. He appeared only during party Congresses (and there was only one of them in the period 1939–1952), for sessions of the Supreme Soviet, and at the annual May Day and November 7 celebrations in Red Square, and he did not regularly attend those latter two events. He needed protection only at the Kremlin, his *dacha* outside Moscow, and during his annual vacation trips to the South. He never stayed at public places, such as hotels. He never participated in election campaigns and so escaped the travel and mixing with the public involved in such pursuits. He never attended church or sports events of any kind. He never visited relatives (except for a very well guarded lone trip to see his aged mother) or friends. He held no press conferences, made no television appearances. He took no walks outside his quarters, except inside the Kremlin walls and around his *dacha* in the woods. And even his occasional appearances in Red Square bore no real resemblance to the security risks faced by Western leaders on their ceremonial rides in open cars through unusually large crowds. When Stalin did deign to review proceedings from atop the Lenin mausoleum, every right file of the ranks parading before him—be they workers, sportsmen, youths or troops—was a security officer, machine guns bristled from screened apertures beneath the mausoleum and in the Kremlin walls and sharpshooters were posted atop and within every salient building. And, of course, his bodyguards were ranked about him on the reviewing stand, although to casual observers they may have seemed no more than military officers.

Likewise were no chances taken at semipublic gatherings. Even when the dictator was inside the Kremlin at Party Congresses or at sessions of the Supreme Soviet, the building and grounds were combed for possible inter-lopers for hours and days before those meetings took place. And after such painstaking searches from cellars to roofs, guards were stationed at every strategic position.

To handle its assignment, Okhrana No. 1 had, at its peak, a total strength of 406 persons. Ranks of its officers ranged from general to junior lieutenant, although most were majors or captains. More than two hundred of those officers were bodyguards, pure and simple. The others were chauffeurs, cooks, waitresses, gardeners, maids, janitors, cleaning women and other ser-vice personnel. Although in an exact sense, such service persons were not bodyguards per se, in addition to their regular duties they did function as the eyes and ears of security around the person of the leader. (Free-world dip-lomats, posted to lands under dictatorial rule, forced to obtain their domestic help from agencies controlled by state security, can attest to the security service rendered by such seeming domestic help.) In addition, of course, to the personnel that came into daily contact with Stalin and bore first responsi-bility for his protection, there were hundreds of other persons concerned with his security, ranging from civilian teams, canine squads, supply and administrative officers, to security and transportation workers, servicing his *dachas* and resorts and securing his travels. All of the latter were furnished by Okhrana No. 2, or other units of the Directorate and state security.

Equally complex was the top command of Okhrana No. 1. Its unques-tioned real boss was Stalin himself, who had Poskrebyshev as his chief lieu-tenant. Subordinate to Poskrebyshev was Vlasik, the nominal chief of the Directorate. And Vlasik had his lieutenant, Colonel Rakov, at the helm of Okhrana No. 1, but only after the approval of Stalin and Poskrebyshev. Additionally, Vlasik, although chief of the entire Directorate organization, actually spent most of his time—when sober—with Poskrebyshev, or at Sta-lin's door mat, in much the same fashion as he had done before the Georgian had made himself dictator. In that way, Vlasik was also a boss of sorts of Okhrana No. 1.

Mainly because Stalin lived the life of a grand seignior—in addition to his Kremlin quarters, he had seven *dachas* in Moscow's environs and a half dozen resorts in the south—Okhrana No. 1 was divided into a number of *kommands* (lesser departments). At each of those estates, there was a com-mandant and staff, charged with running the place and supplying food and other necessities for the dictator and his family. Each commandant was an independent chief of section, responsible to Rakov. But, none of those commandants was responsible for guarding Stalin—that was done by the bodyguards from the home establishment, the Kremlin or the Kuntsevo *dacha*, who traveled with him wherever he went. And there were also commandants responsible for the safety of Stalin's children, Vasily and Svetlana. Both young people had special bodyguards, familiarly called *podveski* (pendants) or *khvosty* (tails) by Okhrana personnel. Those officers followed the children everywhere and were charged not only with their safety but also with supplying them with companionship and entertainment. And so, of course, were all the nurses for Vasily and Svetlana, their housekeepers, and their entire household staffs, members of the Okhrana who drew very fine salaries and exceptional fringe benefits.

All the *dachas* and resorts serviced by those commandants, guards officers, and domestics were called state *dachas* and resorts, even though they were for the private use of Stalin only. The upkeep, payrolls, and services were supplied by Okhrana funds. Some of the places were almost never used by the Georgian, others he visited only once a year at the most, and at still others he occasionally entertained his closest associates, or select Soviet writers, artists, or scientists. But whether Stalin used those establishments or not, the entire staffs stayed there around the clock, year after year. There were, however, rare instances in which the Soviet state gained a little from the multiplicity of establishments maintained for the dictator. One occurred in 1949–50, when state security installed some fifty microphones at Stalin's *dacha* at Lipki that had been set aside for the use of Red China's Mao Tse-tung and party.

The commandants of Okhrana No. 1 tended to come and go in much the same fashion as did their seniors in the Directorate and other security organizations, except for the commandant of Stalin's household, one Sergey Yefimov. He managed to survive almost as long as the dictator. After World War II, he was promoted to general, was given the rank and title of chief of department of state security for pay and retirement benefits, and lived like a minister with his own apartment in Moscow and a private *dacha* in the capital environs. But, when Beria started gnawing away at the Okhrana in the dictator's last year, Yefimov fell from favor. As Stalin's daughter, Svetlana, wrote later, he was "removed and 'eaten alive' by his colleagues, the other generals and colonels of the police who constituted a peculiar kind of 'court' around my father."

Other lesser Okhrana No. 1 personnel very close to Stalin were his drivers. There were five in all, three permanent and two reserve, with the rank of major, or at least captain. And they were very well compensated, perhaps because Stalin appreciated that they, more than most others, had the safety of his life and limb in their hands. The senior chauffeurs drew five thousand rubles a month, and, of course, were supplied with uniforms, board, and lodging, making their total incomes equivalent to that of a full army general. For that, they really did comparatively very little. Stalin usually made two round trips between his Kuntsevo *dacha* and the Kremlin every twenty-four hours. Some time after eleven in the morning, he would be driven to the

Kremlin, returning at about six in the evening to Kuntsevo for rest and dinner, the latter occasionally with associates. Then about eleven in the evening or midnight, he would be returned to the Kremlin for work until about four in the morning, when he would be taken back to his *dacha*. For safety reasons, the drivers were not allowed to remain on duty longer than eight hours. Even with that limitation, any two of them could have handled the daily routine. But Stalin, despite his set habits, liked to have a driver always available. As a result, those who did drive him spent most of their time waiting, while the others did nothing at all except sit outside the door at the Kremlin or Kuntsevo.

As noted earlier, Okhrana No. 1 was a small organization primarily because of the great numbers of other state personnel it could call on for logistic support. That permanent corps of standby help included not only the personnel to keep Stalin's households in operation, but also collective farmers who produced livestock and agricultural goods for his table, workers in the Moscow factory where his private cars were built and maintenanced, tailors who made his uniforms and other clothes (and those who furnished his children with clothes), the carpenters, electricians, plumbers, masons, roofers, and glaziers who serviced his *dachas* and resorts, down to the tobacconist who supplied him with tobacco and pipes and the jeweler who cleaned his watch and kept it running. Just as vast was the assistance available to the bodyguards to help them with their job of protecting the leader. The counterintelligence forces and all the technical equipment of state security were at its beck and call, not only in Moscow, but all over the Soviet Union. Around the Kremlin and other establishments frequented by Stalin, the Directorate's operations department had large networks of subagents whose information was always available to the palace guards. And, of course, they were also assisted by the Okhrana militiamen posted everywhere along the route between the Kremlin and Kuntsevo, as well as by the Railroad Okhrana Directorate and the Transportation Department of the Okhrana every time the dictator desired to travel by rail.

The support Okhrana No. 1 received for those rail trips was so great that it almost had to be seen to be believed. Upon advice that Stalin intended to travel south, normal instruction would come to a halt at the various schools for internal, border, and other security troops. Some twenty-five to thirty thousand young officers would be dismissed to take up positions, within sighting distance of each other, along the entire stretch of track from Moscow to the Caucasian or Black Sea resort selected by the dictator. Every switch was locked and guarded until Stalin had passed, every crossroad and every station was secured, and all other rail traffic, both passenger and freight, was shoved off on sidings.

Those junkets of the Georgian required three fully equipped trains. The first was the "Golovnoy" (head train), occupied by the minister of railroads, technicians and mechanics, and a few palace guards. Only when that train had passed, did the "Osnovnoy" (main train) proceed, bearing Stalin, Vlasik, the state security minister and guards, and servants of Okhrana No. 1. Finally came the third train, the "Khvostovoy" (tail), carrying the bulk of the palace guards, militia and railroad police, and hundreds of subagents in civilian clothes, the last to be posted around all approaches to Stalin's southern establishment. And upon arrival, the militia would supersede the regular police in the area and control all traffic (although, in truth, in those times, there was little automotive activity, except for an occasional truck and state or collective farm tractor).

Equally elaborate, but not quite as extensive because of the shorter distance involved, was the security help furnished Okhrana No. 1 for Stalin's daily trips between the Kremlin and Kuntsevo. At least fifteen hundred plainclothes agents and militia would be posted along the route that ran from the Troitsky Gate, down Kalinin Pospekt to Arbat Street, across the Moscow River to Bolshaya Dorogomilovskaya Street, to Kutuzov Prospekt and Kuntsevo, then by private and completely restricted road to Stalin's *dacha* "Blizhnyaya" (a name which meant that establishment was the closest of the Georgian's many suburban homes, a name, interestingly enough, of basic German origin).

When Stalin left the Kremlin—or started back from Kuntsevo—a special signal was flashed to the militiamen (guards officers) in the booths controlling the traffic lights along the route. All the lights were immediately switched to yellow, remaining so until the dictator's equipage had passed. In the event of a signal failure to the traffic light booths, Stalin's cars blew their horns, of a type available to nobody else, and the militiamen put their light on the yellow.

When traveling by car, Stalin also always used three vehicles, the "Golovnoy" car, the "Osnovnoy" car, and the "Khvostovoy" car. The head car usually contained the deputy chief of the palace guard and a few Okhrana No. 1 officers. In the main car, Stalin rode in the back seat, up front with the driver was Vlasik, Rakov, or another top man of the palace guards. The third car carried Okhrana No. 1 officers, armed with pistols and submachine guns, and a reserve driver for Stalin's car. Because of the Georgian's preference, that equipage usually swept along the streets at fifty miles per hour, although the capital speed limit at that time was only twenty.

In the capital area, since all of Stalin's movements were most highly classified, the only warning to the ordinary citizen of the dictator's approach would be a sudden blinking of yellow lights at the street corners, followed by the scream of tires and the roar of high-powered vehicles. At the rear, in the tail car, would usually be a palace guards officer, shrieking obsenities and often spitting in the faces of bystanders he deemed too close to the motorcade.

But those thus spat upon at least had the good fortune of surviving Stalin's passage, for the Zises stopped for no one. Nor did they care whom they injured or killed. A fine example of that ruthlessness was the case of the pedestrian killed by a Stalin motorcade, the case that resulted in the Okhrana plain-clothesman responsible for the area committing suicide. That pedestrian's body was sent off to the morgue by other Okhrana officers along the street. No attempt was ever made to identify him or notify his relatives. At about the same time as that pedestrian's death, there was also an incident involving four army officers. Probably slightly tipsy, they drove their jeep into an intersection at Kalinin Prospekt, despite the fact the yellow light was blinking. They caught a spray of submachine gun bullets from Okhrana No. 1 worthies riding in the "tail" car. All four army officers were killed instantly. Stalin's motorcade never stopped, of course, but in five minutes, the officers' bodies and their jeep had been removed from the area.

Probably fortunately for other aircraft and any civilians careless enough to be wandering around on the ground below, Stalin almost never traveled by air. In the late thirties, the CC CPSU had issued an order banning General Secretary Comrade Stalin from air travel for "safety" reasons, but there were reports that the real reason was that the onetime Georgian peasant was just as fearful of airplanes as any other peasant. The only time the dictator violated that ban was on a flight from Baku to Teheran and return for the Three Power Conference of World War II and, so far as is known, there were no other aircraft or innocent bystanders close enough to his plane at that time to get shot down.

Because of their privileged position—and also due to the aloofness of Stalin and the connivance of Poskrebyshev and Vlasik—the palace guards escaped the rigid standards of public conduct set for other members of the Okhrana and state security officers. And their rather exalted rank also kept them almost immune from the usual discipline. As a result—like Ivan the Terrible's Oprichniks—they were very prone to brawling, street fighting, drunkenness, bawdiness, and general hell-raising.

A typical case happened in Sochi in the summer of 1950, when some of the guards were "relaxing" from their far from arduous duties. Strolling into the town market area after a spree of heavy tippling, those representatives of the Kremlin's finest chose to annoy women selling fruit and vegetables. A local man made the mistake of trying to help the women. For his pains, he received a blow to the neck that killed him instantly from one Kolbasin (Sausage), a six foot, six inch tall brute of a guard with bearlike hands. Later, Vlasik had to "investigate" the incident. After hearing Kolbasin's version, the Directorate chief warned the guard he could face most serious penalties for the death, then added: "But, you did kill him with a single blow. We need men who are that good with their fists."

A couple of years earlier, another tippling bout among the Okhrana, also in the Sochi area, resulted in the needless—and similarly unpunished— deaths of four guards officers. That no innocent civilians were killed too was just a matter of good fortune. That incident occurred after the chief of the plainclothes agents and the chief of transportation drove to a restaurant on a mountaintop to celebrate the birthday of a friend. Of course, while there, they drank far more than they could hold. But that did not deter the transportation chief from deciding he wanted to drive back. Traveling at high speed, he failed to negotiate a hairpin curve. The car plunged into a canyon, killing the chief of the plainclothesmen, two other officers, and the regular driver. Only the drunken driver, the transportion chief, survived. When he had sufficiently recovered, he was found guilty of negligence and drunken driving and Stalin, himself, ordered him jailed. But, because the transportation chief was a crony of Vlasik, that sentence was never carried out.

Stalin probably overlooked Vlasik's disobedience because similar problems with drunkenness arose every time the dictator entertained close associates at his *dacha*. On those occasions, the *dacha* area would virtually burst at the seams with bodyguards, the regular officers patrolling the grounds with submachine guns, the canine squads, the reenforced plainclothes units, and the Okhrana No. 2 men who accompanied their masters. Himself somewhat abstemious, Stalin enjoyed watching his sycophants get drunk and make fools of themselves. So, most of those parties usually ended with the bodyguards literally sorting out their respective masters, picking them up and taking them home.

Despite the sorry conduct while off duty of many Okhrana No. 1 men, a most careful and cautious process had preceded their selection as bodyguards of Stalin, in fact a weeding-out process that was much more extensive than that used for other members of the Directorate. And almost always, they were chosen from other components of the Okhrana. Officers, even waitresses, in other units would be watched on and off duty for anywhere from three to five years before enlistment into Okhrana No. 1, for work around Stalin. Additionally, most usually had first to pass personal interviewing and questioning by Vlasik, and, in important instances, also by Poskrebyshev. Even then, there would be another several weeks of surveillance before the final decision. And after enlistment, Stalin's guards were put under surveillance for several days to a week every three months. Greatest watch was kept on the guards when they were on vacation, and especially if that took them outside of Moscow.

A good example of the overweening care employed in selecting a bodyguard for Stalin was the case of Lieutenant L____, an Okhrana No. 2 plainclothesman on Arbat Street. Upon becoming a possible candidate for Okhrana No. 1, he was put under round-the-clock surveillance at work and off duty. Nothing at all was found wrong with his duty, and he passed interrogations and investigations of his wife, mother-in-law, and neighbors with flying colors. But, he got black marks for apparently harmless off-duty activity. He lived about fifteen miles outside Moscow and used to take a local train to and from work. Surveillance noted that on his way home, he invariably would go to the station bar and have a shot of vodka, followed by a tomato juice chaser or a pickle. Other bar customers were the usual railroad station transients, none of them known to the surveillance agents. In making their reports on Lieutenant L____, the "tails" duly noted that he had only one drink at the station bar, but then added that in so doing he would "mingle with suspicious and questionable people." That "discovery" ended all chances of the young officer's enlistment in Stalin's guards. He was allowed to continue developing the plainclothesman's usual case of flat feet at his Arbat Street post, but was warned not to go near the railroad station bar again.

For doing absolutely nothing that might be regarded as a security risk— or, at the most being an innocent victim of a sort of psychopath—another Okhrana No. 2 plainclothesman likewise had his candidacy for the palace guards abruptly overruled. That hapless fellow not only had a faultless record in Okhrana No. 2, but also had good marks from earlier service in the Kremlin *kommandatura*. Additionally, he himself had dutifully reported to Personnel the "offense" that caused his rejection. His troubles started while he was pounding his beat near Krymsky bridge. A young girl, with nothing else to do and obviously not sought after by young men, used to watch the guard from the window of her nearby apartment. She would wave at the officer as he walked up and down below and finally he waved back. Over-joyed at such progress, the girl hastily wrote a note suggesting the officer meet her at a subway station and had her younger brother deliver the note. At the end of his watch, the plainclothesman informed his superiors of the incident—the only break in an otherwise boring routine—and turned the note over to them. The plainclothesman did not know, of course, that he was under consideration for Okhrana No. 1, but his seniors were fully aware of the facts. As a result, they speedily converted a trifle into a major security investigation. The girl's apartment was put under observation, she was put under surveillance, and the young officer was instructed to reply favorably to her note. When the lovelorn girl finally appeared at the rendezvous, the Okhrana No. 2 man was not there, but Directorate officers in militia uniforms were. Arrested by them, during lengthy interrogation the girl said she felt only friendship for the plainclothesman and had become sorry for him as she watched him patrol his beat in all kinds of weather. Since the girl's statements seemed true and investigation had revealed nothing unfavorable about her family and associates, she was told the plainclothesman would contact her, if he so wanted, and she was warned not to write any more notes. After that, the Okhrana No. 2 man, again acting on instructions, called on the girl and told her there was no question of even establishing a "friend-ship" since he was married. Despite all that cooperation and his good record, the young man's experience with the girl resulted in his summary rejection as a candidate for the palace guards. And for good measure, he was trans-ferred to another plainclothes beat. Somewhat ironically, the case ended with the girl gaining from the incident. During interrogation, it was found that she was also a congenital busybody as well as lovelorn, so she was recruited by Operations as an informant, or subagent, to spy on her neigh-bors.

Perhaps even more cautiously handled than the enlistment of palace guards was the selection of service personnel for Stalin's households. That was apparent in the case of Zina, a waitress in a state-operated restaurant in Moscow. She was singled out because she was quiet and courteous, was neither ugly not too attractive, lived in a small Moscow apartment with her widowed mother (her father was killed in World War II), and, best of all, had no brothers or sisters or any other relatives. She also had a top recommenda-tion by her local Komsomol committee and support of two party members. When first approached, Zina was told only that she had been selected for work in state security. That did not impress her, because she wanted no interference in her schedule which included studies at night school. But, she changed her mind when advised that her pay would be tripled, for she needed money to help her mother, who was in very poor health. Her starting work was as a waitress in an Okhrana officers' restaurant, where she spent two years, again under steady surveillance, before she was deemed qualified for Okhrana No. 1. Then she was told that she was to be transferred to some place outside the capital. (Those selected for such jobs were never advised of the exact location or specific work until the last moment.) At that, she again objected, saying she could not leave her ailing mother and wanted to complete her night school studies. But, finally, she agreed, after being assured that her current pay would be doubled and that she would be given a chauffeured car to take her to and from work, her mother's, and school. Thereupon, not long after starting work as a domestic in one of Stalin's *dachas* in the Moscow environs, she fell in love with and married one of the Okhrana guards, one stationed not within the house, but outside the fence surrounding the *dacha*. Because of the marriage, even though Zina's husband was not a guard close to Stalin, or stationed near the dictator's person, he was transferred elsewhere to other Okhrana work, due to the regulation that no close relatives, husbands and wives, brothers and sisters, fathers and sons, were allowed to work for the Okhrana in the same component or in the same area. And transfer along with her husband was refused to Zina, not only because she was in close and regular contact with Stalin, but also because no suitable replacement for her could be found. Zina was also cautioned to avoid having children for as long as possible. If pregnant, she would have been banned from working in the dictator's household and dismissed from the Okhrana, or at least transferred to some place other than where her husband was working. Only in very exceptional instances were female Okhrana service personnel permitted to return to work in a Stalin household after pregnancy. Those exceptions applied only to truly irreplaceable persons, or to those rare few in whom the dictator had a personal interest.

Although, as in Zina's case, the overwhelming majority of Stalin's Okhrana was always tested in and then recruited from some other element of the Directorate, there were some guard units from which the palace guards were absolutely never drawn. Particularly proscribed in that respect were men who had served as guards of other hierarchs, for the simple reason that they may have developed some sort of loyalty or other close connection to such a potential rival of the Georgian. For example, if an officer had served as a bodyguard of Molotov, he would never even be considered for the palace guards.

Likewise did dismissal from the palace guards place an Okhrana No. 1 member in a position ranging from the unpleasant to one of jeopardy. If he were fired for minor misconduct or misbehavior, he usually was assigned to an Okhrana supply office or transferred to the Moscow militia. If, however, he was discharged for lack of vigilance or some more serious or suspicious fault, he would be transferred to some state security job or the militia in the provinces and placed under permanent observation. And all who were dismissed, for whatever reason be it minor or major, were black-listed by having their names given to the state security's "T" department for constant surveillance. Additionally, all those fired were prohibited from ever visiting their former places of work again or from maintaining any contact with their former colleagues. Violation of the latter ban, even an accidental one, would result in the offender being put under intense investigation and possible arrest.

As with Stalin's drivers, the same boring routine, the same sitting around and waiting on the dictator's whim of the moment, was the lot of the bodyguards of Okhrana No. 1. But as a matter of fact, they were no worse off than the hierarchs attached to the Georgian's court. All members of the Politburo were obliged to mirror-image their work hours with Stalin's afternoon and nighttime Kremlin stints. Likewise did the ministers follow the same pattern, and after them the chiefs of departments, then the senior employees, and finally the lowest on the totem pole, the bodyguards, dutifully aped the others. There may have been some excuse for such extended duty for the dictator's personal guards—unlike the drivers, they were not limited to eight hour shifts. But there was absolutely no reason whatsoever for keeping on the other Okhrana personnel. However, stay they did, well into the wee hours, doing nothing more than staring at walls, or reading, playing chess, and telling jokes. Thus occupied, the most junior officers finally left shortly after midnight, supervisory officers at about three in the morning, while Vlasik and his deputies waited until Stalin actually left for Kuntsevo around four, before departing for their homes or other pursuits—the latter usually drinking bouts. The only break for the office staff of Okhrana No. 1 in such a waste of time and boredom came when the dictator went to the Caucasus or the Black Sea. Left behind in Moscow, those officers were able to enjoy life by leaving their offices not later than midnight. For the bodyguards who went along with Stalin, however, the same routine continued, although it was not always as lengthy as when the Georgian was at the Kremlin.

5. OKHRANA NO. 2

Compared to the elite palace guards, Okhrana No. 2 was a much larger organization. It had bodyguards, too—some 1,000 for the rest of the Soviet leadership, plus about half that number for party and government installations—but the bulk of its membership were the foot soldiers who supported the palace guards as well as the much greater number of service personnel needed for the households of the rest of the hierarchs.

It was divided into four departments, which actually were two pairs of units complementary to each other. The First Department supplied the bodyguards for the lesser hierarchs and other party dignitaries deemed worthy of protecting—although watching would be the better term. The Third Department also consisted of guards assigned to party and government installations and, of course, their top personnel. The Second Department was made up of some two thousand plainclothesmen assigned to the Moscow streets, and especially those thoroughfares used frequently by Stalin and his subalterns. The Fourth Department, almost three thousand strong at its peak, comprised the Moscow militiamen (all actually Okhrana guardsmen) who not only policed the capital but also directly cooperated with the plainclothesmen of the Second Department.

In the Directorate's five-year span of life, Okhrana No. 2 had two chiefs, both major generals and both of whom came to bad ends. The first was Dmitry Shadrin, the veteran state security officer earlier assigned to organize Tito's bodyguards at the end of World War II. Shadrin did that job so well that after Stalin broke with Tito in 1948 Soviet agents were unable to penetrate the Balkan leader's guards. For that overzealousness, Shadrin was charged with "Titoism," lost his *dacha* built with Tito money outside Moscow before being exiled to the boondocks and barely escaped with his life. Kuzmichev, the Beria crony who bossed the Department, later became an outlaw with Beria's downfall and was executed shortly thereafter.

The First Department was organized into sections, which were the individual bodyguard units assigned to the lesser hierarchs. Ranks of the section chiefs ranged from general to senior lieutenant, although most were generals or colonels. Usually, the more veteran Politburo members had senior officers as chiefs of their bodyguards, although that was not always the case. For instance, Kaganovich's chief was a general, Molotov's was first a general, succeeded by a colonel, while those of Beria and Khrushchev were colonels. And the general who led Molotov's guards for several years was also deputy chief of the department. However, the number of Okhrana No. 2 personnel assigned to the respective hierarchs did reflect their position in the current pecking order. As examples, Molotov was furnished some one hundred twenty people, Beria about one hundred, Bulganin, Malenkov, and Khrushchev seventy-five to eighty each, while Marshal Zhukov had less than a score and Abakumov just about a dozen.

Likewise did the actual number of bodyguards assigned vary in direct accordance to the importance of the lesser hierarch being protected and watched. The more exalted would have about sixty bodyguards, while those of less importance were allowed to get along with thirty-five at the most. But the number of Okhrana No. 2 service personnel was usually the same for each of the lesser hierarchs, regardless of their comparative importance. That meant that in addition to the bodyguards, each was furnished with a commandant (chief of the bodyguard section and chief of the household), a female housekeeper, yardkeeper or janitor, and a furnaceman, one to two gardeners, cooks and waitresses, two to three maids, and three to four chauffeurs.

Generally, the First Department personnel were posted at the Serafimovich and Granovsky Streets apartment buildings or at the few former private homes in Moscow reserved for Politburo members and other lesser hierarchs. But when those worthies under their protection and watch chose to go to the *dachas* in the woods or beside streams and ponds outside the capital, the Okhrana No. 2 staffs went along with them. Once there, plainclothes officers, armed with a pair of pistols and a small dagger, called a "Finka" (Finnish knife), and canine squads would support the submachine gun-toting regular guards by day and night patrols of the *dacha* areas and all roads leading to them

Besides the living dignitaries and their families, the First Department was also charged with the families of defunct party greats, of course, only those in current good standing. An Okhrana No. 2 chauffeur and household staff was supplied to the widow of Dzerzhinsky, the sainted founder of the Soviet security services. Similar assistance was also furnished the families of Zhdanov, Shcherbakov, Kalinin, Ordzhonikidze, and others. Interestingly, however, those relics were not given bodyguards. No doubt that oversight was because they represented no challenge whatsoever to Stalin, rather than because they were less prone to assault than the extant toadies of the Georgian and their families.

In addition to those various sections that cared for the lesser hierarchs, the First Department also had a rather unusual unit, called the "reserve group." That outfit had the dual task of surveillance of areas visited by politburo members and other Soviet citizens under the eye of Okhrana No. 2, and of "protecting" the leaders of foreign Communist countries. And that "protection" also extended to foreign Communist leaders not in power, such as those of Italy, France, and Germany, when they visited the Soviet Union. "Reserve group" officers were not only the eyes and ears of Stalin, but at times, his long arm, never hesitating, when the Georgian deemed it necessary, to interfere directly in the affairs of such satellite puppets as East Germany's Ulbricht, Hungary's Rakosi, Czechoslovakia's Gottwald and others.

As compared to such operatives, far less secure were the fortunes of the chiefs of bodyguards—and the bodyguards as well—assigned to Stalin's top Soviet underlings. Not only did their lots vary as did the political fates of those they were guarding, but also they could be victims of quirks of personality of the hierarchs in their care and even of pure misadventure. In those respects, the guards of Voroshilov and Molotov, and Marshals Zhukov, Timoshenko, and Rokossovsky had, perhaps, the most difficulty. In a few rare cases, however, the hierarchs of better character went to the assistance of their guards when the latter ran into trouble.

Cases involving Molotov are the best examples of such rarities. While that erstwhile foreign minister was away at the U.N. conference in San Francisco in 1947, one of his bodyguards was fired and transferred to his home district and a relatively low-paying state security post there. One evening, shortly after his return from the U.S., Molotov asked the whereabouts of a guard with whom he usually played billiards. Informed that his cue companion had been fired in his absence, Stalin's most veteran intimate became enraged. The following evening, the officer was back again matching shots with Molotov.

Even more magnanimous was Molotov with his chief personal bodyguard, Major General Vasily Pogudin. That Okhrana man became a chronic alcoholic, and was often so drunk that it was Molotov who guarded Pogudin, rather than the other way around. Molotov saw to it that Pogudin was retired out honorably in 1951 and given a good Moscow apartment. But, a Colonel Aleksandrov, Pogudin's successor, had a more difficult and typical experience. Aleksandrov had been given his assignment at just about the time Molotov fell badly out of favor with Stalin. Preparing for the ultimate, Vlasik's deputy, Goryshev, said: "Well, if they fire Molotov, we will fire Aleksandrov" and then ordered a subordinate to go over Aleksandrov's dossier to unearth enough "evidence" to dismiss the hapless fellow on charges of "Trotskyism," if need be. However, Molotov survived, and so did Aleksandrov, but just barely.

Far less lucky, as the result of a misadventure in which he was blameless, was a chief of Voroshilov's bodyguard in 1948, even though Voroshilov did his best to intervene. At year's end at Voroshilov's *dacha* about twenty miles outside Moscow, a fire had started during children's games around the New Year's tree, a fire started by none other than Voroshilov's grandchildren. Since it was in the dead of a more than usually severe winter, the water froze in the pumps and hoses, and fire fighting equipment sent from Moscow did not arrive unil the *dacha* had burned to the ground. Destroyed with it were all of Voroshilov's medals, honorary sabers and swords, and awards given him by the Soviet and foreign governments. Stalin was outraged at the loss suffered by his most obedient toady and had the chief of Voroshilov's bodyguards, the Okhrana's chief of administrative supply and the Okhrana's fire inspector given three to seven year jail terms for negligence, despite the fact that none of them had been at the scene at the time the fire started. But, some three years later, on Voroshilov's instigation, and apparently without Stalin's knowledge, the three "culprits" were freed and returned to the Directorate, but in minor jobs.

Even though no bodyguards came a cropper, the most difficult man for Okhrana No. 2 to "protect" in those times was Marshal Zhukov. Fearful of that wartime hero, and doing his best to denigrate him, Stalin had dumped him first in a minor job in Odessa before moving him to an equally insignificant post east of the Urals, in Sverdlovsk. When Zhukov first had been given bodyguards he had been naïve enough to have thought that it was yet another mark of distinction bestowed upon him by a grateful Stalin. In due time, though, he disabused himself of that misconception and recognized his Okhrana No. 2 staff for what it was—watchers and controllers rather than guards of his person. And with that, he became nervous and crusty and frequently flailed out at his bodyguards, even though he knew they respected him, bore no ill will and were only doing their duty. He complained —with justification—that his guards could travel back and forth to Moscow, while he, a Marshal of the Soviet Union, could not. He turned suddenly on a waitress in his mess and shouted "What are you watching me for?" He complained when his Okhrana motor pool officer was unable to furnish enough cars for his many girl friends. (That outside companionship was probably necessary since the Okhrana chambermaids had repulsed his advances.) And on a cooked-up charge of insubordination, he had one chief of his bodyguards transferred, a transfer the chief welcomed and for which he suffered no penalty. Then in 1950, Zhukov suddenly decided to appear at a provincial party meeting in Sverdkovsk and make a little speech. The speech was of no importance, but the war hero's appearance at even such a semipublic gathering certainly was. Disobeying orders of their party *apparatchiks*, the delegates gave him a five-minute standing ovation. When a report of that reached the jealous Stalin—and be assured the report got

[396]

super-priority transmission to the Kremlin—Zhukov's chief of bodyguards was in very serious trouble indeed. However, since all most fully appreciated the difficulty in handling the marshal and there were no ready candidates to replace him, the chief of bodyguards escaped with a reprimand. Zhukov was flatly instructed to make no more such public appearances and from then on his bodyguards saw to it that that instruction was obeyed to the letter.

The bodyguards had no such political problems with Marshal Timoshenko, who more gracefully swallowed the fact that it was Stalin and not the Red Army who had won the war for the Soviet Union. But that marshal tended to compensate for his postwar lot under the Georgian by taking to the bottle. His prolonged vodka sessions became notorious and guards officers assigned to him needed a very great capacity since they were invariably commanded to participate. Some of the sessions lasted for days. And one guards captain had to be hastily transferred to Moscow after hitting Timoshenko's aide with a bottle during an all-night bout.

Again the problem was not political, but the First Department also had a most difficult time "protecting" Marshal Rokossovsky. The chief nonmilitary characteristic of that latter-day proconsul to Poland (and, like Dzerzhinsky and Menzhinsky, Rokossovsky was a Pole) was lechery. That much bemedaled officer not only had numerous "wives," but also had to be supplied with endless relays of girls to share his quarters. That proclivity was so pronounced that reports of it eventually reached the party control commission and Stalin was asked to intervene. But, since Rokossovsky was of much less political concern to him than were Zhukov and Timoshenko, the Georgian just leafed through the report and tossed it aside saying "I have no Suvorov, but Rokossovsky is my Bagration." (Any comparison of Rokossovky with those Russian immortals of the Napoleonic wars is pure military heresy, but after all Stalin was certainly no military expert.)

The Second Department, the plainclothesmen, was the flat-footed infantry of the Stalin guards system. But, comparatively lowly as their jobs may have been, they were also the eyes and ears, and occasionally the arm of the Directorate. Far from unobtrusive to any but the most naïve tourist, they were positioned at all street corners, outside all buildings, parks, and recreation areas, and especially prevalent in front of all post offices, stores, restaurants, cafes, and barbershops throughout Moscow. But the capital's populace, far more habituated to Communist security operations, was very much aware of who was a plainclothesman and who was a respectable citizen. Therefore, it was necessary to move those agents frequently, generally from the city to the suburbs, or vice versa. Those posts were manned day and night by three full shifts of plainclothesmen.

All were proficient in marksmanship and well trained in jujitsu and wrestling. They were armed with pistols and knives, but they were instructed to use only the knives, if circumstances permitted, to avoid noise.

From those posts, they kept a constant eye on the public, paying particular attention to anyone entering a sensitive zone (an area frequented by Stalin and his hierarchs). When the latter occurred, and a person remained in the area for more than thirty minutes, the plainclothesman would have the nearest militiaman (a member of Okhrana No. 2's Fourth Department) demand the "suspect's" identity papers for inspection. Over the years, a real "suspect" was never unearthed. Nevertheless, the "intruder," even though completely innocent, was warned away. In that way, the sensitive zones were kept completely inviolate. About the only other actual duty of that plethora of Okhrana eyes came in the evenings when most buildings and shops closed. The agents on duty then were required to enter those establishments, check them from cellars to garrets and stand by while employees closed and locked the doors.

Daily, before leaving their headquarters for their beats, the plainclothesmen were shown photographs and given descriptions and résumés of people suspected or wanted by state security and generally for reasons that had nothing to do with the security of the hierarchs. Thus did Stalin keep the capital clear of suspects and undesirables of all categories. And the plainclothesmen made a further contribution. Returning to headquarters before going off duty, they had to make detailed written reports of all untoward incidents and "suspects" encountered during their tours.

Later, the undesirables they reported were usually moved elsewhere in Moscow, or to the suburbs. And their work of spotting unwanted citizens in the sensitive zones was supported by informants among the occupants of buildings in those areas. Additionally, all street cleaners in the sensitive zones were out-and-out informants of the Second Department.

The Second Department was divided into thirteen sections. Each of those units handled a specific area of the city. For example, officers of the First Section stood around the Kremlin walls and Red Square, while those of the Second and Third Sections were posted along Arbat Street and out to Kutuzov Prospekt, the latter Stalin's invariable route to his *dacha*. The Twelfth Section was an exception to that strict geographical placement. That unit, called the *Podzemnoye i nadzemnoye khozyaystvo* (below ground and above ground housekeeping) group, examined all attics, cellars, telephone booths, water, sewer and electric systems, and manholes of Moscow's streets. That section had to give a prior approval for all new construction, as well as maintenance and repair work contemplated for buildings and utilities. It was the Twelfth Section that ordered and supervised major work on Arbat Street in the late forties, work that consisted of a heavy concrete surface along that thoroughfare's entire stretch, designed to protect Stalin from any possible mining of the route.

Despite its exacting work, the Second Department decidedly did not have distinguished chiefs. The first was an exceedingly heavy drinker and was among those killed in a drunken drive down a mountain road near Sochi in 1948. The weakness of his successor, Colonel Georgy Komarov, was women, and in 1951 he was demoted to the militia for moral degeneracy. The same charges also resulted in the dismissal of Komarov's successor, Colonel Vasily Shatalov, in 1951.

Even though the Directorate was well versed in procedures for getting rid of personnel on security or political grounds, it took quite a bit of doing to catch up with Komarov. Lecherous as he was, the department chief had done nothing to warrant dismissal until he made the error of mixing his failing with his work. That occurred when he became so enamored of an attractive young woman that he had to see her by day as well as by night. To do that he advised Personnel about the girl's remarkable capabilities and said she would be a great asset to Okhrana headquarters. In due course, the girl had cleared all enlistment hurdles and was installed in a secretarial post. However, in investigating her for clearance, it had been found that she was Komarov's girl friend of the moment. And later, after she had been accepted into the Okhrana office, routine surveillance showed that wherever the young woman went after work, Komarov went also. That coincidence, plus the initial clearance information on the girl, was reported to Goryshev, the Personnel chief. After studying those papers, Goryshev called in an aide and said "Komarov is a stupid son-of-a-bitch, and I want to get rid of him. He is married, you know, so this is the way we will do it." The aide was ordered to make a complete report of the off-duty activities of Komarov and the girl, giving the most intimate details of their carryings-on. The report was completed with great dispatch and several nights later, sometime after midnight, the terrified girl was arrested and taken to Goryshev's office at headquarters for a confrontation with Komarov. In no time at all, both admitted their liaison. With that, the girl was dismissed, after being warned to keep her mouth shut about where she had been and why. Then Goryshev turned to Komarov and said "Now, suppose I telephone your wife and bring her down here, to. . . ." Komarov's pleas for mercy were considered to some extent, because he could have received far worse than being dumped in the militia.

The routine of the Third Department was even more boring than that of the Second even though its officers wore the smart uniforms of the state security and therefore did not attract so much derision from the general populace as the plainclothesmen.

Nevertheless, although listed as bodyguards, officers of the Third Department were little more than exalted doormen, watchmen, and concierges. They were posted at and in all important party and government installations, ranging from the CC of the CPSU on Staraya Ploshchad and the Council of Ministers on Marx Prospekt down to and including the Academy of Sciences, special nuclear research institutions and the K-R Laboratory (the last being where a husband and wife team, Doctors Nina Kluyeva and Grigory Roskin, searched unsuccessfully for years for a cancer cure, with Okhrana officers looking over their shoulders all the while). Each of those installations had a Third Department commandant and staff. Duties of those officers were to operate pass systems and to patrol on foot all corridors, basements, lofts, washrooms, and unoccupied offices by day. By night, some were assigned to keep an eye on the cleaning women and other service personnel at work.

The Fourth Department, the militiamen, was incorporated into the Directorate and its Okhrana No. 2 more as a precaution than by deliberate design, or need for its personnel as bodyguards. In 1947, there was a flurry of reports that a group of officers of the militia—then an independent unit under the MVD—was plotting an attack against some Politburo members, especially those who traveled along Arbat Street, the route used by Stalin. All those reports were false in the extreme, but nevertheless the militia underwent a gigantic purge during which some twelve hundred men were imprisoned, or at least dismissed. And in the course of that action, the militia in the Moscow area, or the ORUD (Street Traffic Regulations Department), were transferred to the Directorate's Okhrana No. 2, while the rest of the militia in the country were removed from MVD command and put under control of the MGB.

By the time that shake-up had been completed, militia morale was low, but the Directorate bolstered it in the capital by making all the policemen Okhrana offiers and thereby boosting their salaries and improving their living conditions and fringe benefits. What did not work out so well, however, was the inclusion in the newly formed Fourth Department of many regular Okhrana officers, who somewhat understandably resented what they regarded as reductions to mere policemen. That resulted in bad blood between some Okhrana-militia and militia-Okhrana men, bad blood that spilled over onto the general populace since the organization became quite mean and spiteful. For instance, although at that time especially traffic was much lighter in Moscow than in other world capitals, a far greater proportion of traffic citations were given for any and all violations, ranging from drunken driving and speeding down to jaywalking and the most minor infractions. As a result, many an average Muscovite soon came to shake his fist and scream obscenities at the militia, caring not a whit that they were Okhrana men as well. And in that way the effectiveness of the Fourth Department as an arm of the Directorate was considerably reduced, since it was more inclined to squabble with the citizenry than concentrate on protection of the leadership. Additionally—and rather incidentally here—that running fight between the citizenry and the police continued long after the Directorate was disbanded and the militia went under other command. In fact, compared to the term "pigs" hurled at some police in America, the epithets used against many militia in the Soviet Union are—so far at least—unprintable.

That built-in handicap of the Fourth Department was somewhat screened by its cooperative work with the plainclothesmen of the Second Department. The militia, with such indirect supervision, functioned adequately at its prime chores of performing the formalities with "suspects" picked up by the Second Department and turning the traffic lights to yellow whenever Stalin and his cronies chose to seep through the city. Their other duties were pure traffic administration, with very little security involved: controlling drivers' licenses, regulating regular traffic, handing out tickets, and bringing violators to trial. Its chief was about the only distinction possessed by the Fourth Department. He was Colonel Nikolay Borisov, a likeable veteran of a quarter century of militia service, who knew his capital city so well that historians frequently resorted to him for advice.

[400]

6. SUPPLY

The Supply subdirectorate was the administrative guts of the Main Guards Directorate. It looked after all the earthly needs of Stalin, his family, his underlings, and their families, literally from cradle to grave. And it made the Soviet hierarchy, not just the "New Class" described by Milovan Djilas, but truly a world apart, completely separate and existent unto itself.

During the heyday of the Directorate, Muscovites used to chortle, with considerable bitterness, at an imaginary television skit entitled "A Day in Moscow." The opening scene showed the capital at seven in the morning, when the sidewalks were teeming with thousands of drably dressed, tired looking people rushing to work. "Those," said the announcer, "are the masters of the country—the people." The next scene was staged at ten in the morning, when the same streets were filled with plush, chauffeur-driven ZIS-110 limousines, carrying scores of fat men in fur hats and coats. "And those," the announcer advised, "are the servants of the people." Hackneyed and escapist to the unfortunates living under Communist domination as such stories are, that one supplied absolute truth as well as amusement. It was imaginary only in so far as it could never have been filmed. It most accurately portrayed a very small part of the fat life that Supply provided the Soviet hierarchy, which never abandoned its long-exploded pretense of being the servants of the people.

Supply was divided into six departments, food, finance, clothing, construction, transportation, and housing. None were misnomers, as was so often the case with other Directorate organizations. And it is interesting to note that food was the First Department, and finance and clothing respectively Second and Third.

The First Department ran the world's lushest commissary. It stocked literally everything in the lines of food and drink, champagne and caviar, fine wines and liquors domestic and imported, all types of meats, fowl and fish, fruits and vegetables both in season and out of season, groceries of all descriptions, even special products required for the diet regimens of individual members of the hierarchy. All was freely supplied the privileged clientele. Nor were there any limits, except those imposed by metabolisms, constitutions, and stomach capacities.

To keep that voracious maw filled, the department operated farms and slaughterhouses outside Moscow, fisheries at Sovkhoz lakes, plus collective farms in the south. (Some of the last were in the Abkhazia region, home of the world's reputedly longest lived people, the longevity of some of whom may have been improved by their dutiful supply of viands for the tables of Stalin and his cronies.)

The department's main outlet was on Berezhkovskaya Naberezhnaya, near the Kiev railroad station. From there, the Okhrana chief of household of each hierarchical family drew the kitchen requirements, never the hierarch's wife or any member of his family. Actually there was a regulation forbidding hierarchical families from shopping at state stores and markets, as did the ordinary citizenry, the "masters of the country." Nevertheless, some gluttons could not refrain from buying and carrying home the rare specialties sold at the peoples' establishments. But when that happened, the Okhrana staffs had standing orders to see that those purchases never reached the table.

Another First Department outlet was the "Kremlin," located not within the walls of the old fortress but on Kalinin Prospekt, near the Granovsky Street apartments of many lesser Soviet leaders, a dietary restaurant of sorts. From the "Kremlin," when it was cook's night out (which never really happened), or the lord or lady of the household so pleasured, it was routine to dispatch meals prepared in accordance with the prescriptions of each individual's personal (Okhrana) physician. Or when the lords and ladies wanted to go out on the town, or were entertaining guests, they would go to the "Kremlin." It was a frequent occurrence for several Politburo members, ministers, even deputy ministers, to dine there together, and when they did, each received his prescribed special dietary dishes. The "Kremlin" was well equipped for handling such fastidious and particular clientele, for it was a huge place and had among its plethora of personnel at least thirty cooks on duty in the kitchen at any given meal. The cooks were furnished with lists of the exact dietary peculiarities of the hierarchs, in fact prepared weekly menus for each. And those menus could be changed by a telephone call, if need be. Nor were the stomachs of the Okhrana officers forgotten. Free meals were served them at kitchens and restaurants at offices and headquarters.

To keep the hierarchs' stomachs safe as well as full, the First Department also had a staff of microbiologists, chemists, and toxicologists. They had a laboratory on Kuznetsky Most where samples of everything supplied the hierarchs first were analyzed or tried out on guinea pigs and other animals. Not one segment of fruit, bottle of wine, slice of meat, or piece of bread was delivered to the tables of Stalin and his cronies before it had been thoroughly tested by those technicians—or poison experts.

As could be expected, the chief of the all-important First Department was a close friend of Vlasik and Poskrebyshev. After all, from him Vlasik received his endless supply of liquor, although Poskrebyshev was more discreet about the perquisites for his taste buds and alimentary canal. And they took good care to protect his party status and "moral standing," despite his being three times a bridegroom and an inveterate woman chaser. Lust caught up with that fellow, however, when he caught syphilis in 1949 and he was removed from any contact with provisions supplied the hierarchs. First, that worthy was sent to the provinces as a deputy chief of state security. However, life away from the capital's bright lights was not for him and after a personal appeal to Vlasik and Poskrebyshev he was taken back into the Okhrana. But Poskrebyshev forbade him assignment in Moscow or Sochi and made him deputy commandant of the resort in the Crimea, an establishment Stalin never visited. There that erstwhile glorified mess-sergeant remained until well after the dictator's death.

For a long time, the Second Department was a seemingly bottomless treasury for the hierarchs, dispensing them unlimited funds for their personal use. However, after the crackdown in the spring of 1952, those giveaways were "slashed" to a mere 30,000 rubles monthly (3,000 at the new rate) for unforeseen expenses, a handout called *na karmannyye raskhody* (pocket money). At that time, the average Soviet worker earned some seventy to ninety rubles a month, and with no fringe benefits at all. But those pocket money cuts could not have been too great a blow for the hierarchs. For all their boring speeches, propaganda pamphlets and brochures were published in millions of copies with all the proceeds of such "literary works" being deposited in their personal bank accounts. Additionally, they paid no income taxes nor did they have to subscribe to regular and extraordinary "loans" to the regime, as required of the average Soviet citizen. Nor should it be forgotten that the hierarchs received everything they needed or wanted absolutely free of cost—special private state schools for their children, food, clothing, apartments, *dachas*, cars, medical services, travel—everything. And, of course, every time they went on vacation to the Caucasus or the Crimea the Okhrana furnished them with additional household staff and bodyguards so they could make their journeys in grand ducal ease and style.

The Third Department was the hierarchs' equivalent of Bond Street for the men and Paris for the women, but with the notable exception that its civilian styling for both men and women in the Stalin era was deplorable to ridiculous. That was due to Stalin's affection for military garb. However, all was modishly correct with the uniforms and shoes and boots with elevated heels furnished the little dictator himself. The same also applied to the Okhrana uniforms which were styled after those of the Red Army but of the finest material and usually individually tailored. And in addition to the outerwear produced by tailors, dressmakers, and bootmakers, the department also carried great stocks of underwear, toweling, bed and table linen, and, of course, children's garments of all description. By dint of using the Third Department and its companion First Department, the hierarchs obtained the services of the finest department store and an imperial supermarket, and all for free and without being forced to rub elbows with the peasants.

The most varied work was done by the Fourth Department, the construction section. It built no Versailles or Peterhof for the Soviet aristocracy, but it did erect and maintain all the houses, apartments, and *dachas* for the hierarchs, as well as doing a similar job for the Okhrana itself. Its staff ranged from five hundred to more than three thousand men, depending upon the type and amount of work at hand. That small army included carpenters, plumbers, electricians, masons, roofers, excavators, nurserymen, and landscapers. It was the most conglomerate group in the Directorate, which had need for every type of service. Almost all those building tradesmen were co-opted from Moscow construction enterprises. Their pay was above the usual scale and they were given a few of the Okhrana fringe benefits. But, they were most carefully examined for security, especially those working in hierarchs' offices or living quarters, and they were also required to sign pledges not to reveal what they did.

The Fifth Department, transportation, was mainly a large motor pool, with drivers, mechanics, repair, and maintenance shops. But it also had a section that handled other modes of travel, primarily rail, the latter done in cooperation with the Railroad Okhrana. Stalin, of course, had his three-part private train. All the lesser hierarchs had to make do with no more than private rail cars. The department also handled some air travel, but, since Stalin was averse to planes, such transport was almost never furnished the lesser hierarchs except in emergency or for international purposes. Likewise the department did little overseeing of inland waterways travel, not because there was any proscription against it, but due to its slowness and the fact that most water routes were somewhat paralleled by rail lines. However, sometimes hierarchs did use waterways for vacations and inspection trips and on those occasions the department handled the voyages in cooperation with the Waterways Okhrana. Most of the department's troubles arose from supplying nonchauffeur-driven cars to hierarchs' youngsters of driving age. Not only did the young people damage the vehicles by driving them at persistent high speeds, but they also frequently wrecked them. When that happened, the wreck was hauled into the shop and exchanged for a new car. Mikoyan's sons were the most versatile in wrecking the department's cars.

The Sixth Department actually was little more than a collection of room clerks, even though the housing it dispensed and managed for the hierarchs and the Okhrana personnel was varied and far more luxurious, even at its plainest, then that available to the still downtrodden masses of Russia. And like some room clerks elsewhere, the department was always faced with a shortage of accommodations, despite the steady work of the construction department. In fact, that shortage was so severe that a special decree of 1947 required that every apartment building erected in Moscow from that time on should set aside three to five apartments for state security, which, of course, included the Okhrana. But, even that decree failed to solve the problem and many Okhrana officers and their families had to resort to single rooms in Moscow "private" houses or lodge outside the capital with collective farm groups. The hierarchs, to be sure, underwent no such deprivations. Their city quarters were assured and far more spacious than need-be, whether in the Kremlin, in the homes of the former aristocrats, or in the Granovsky and Serafimovicha Streets apartment buildings, all brave with smartly uniformed Okhrana No. 2 guardsmen at the entrances. And those apartment buildings were little cities unto themselves: within them were a theater, movie house, kindergarten, laundry and dry cleaning establishments, and a variety of shops. In those times, the Granovsky Street apartments were regarded as the more "fashionable" of the two buildings. Additionally, it was the housing department that supplied each hierarch with one or two, and sometimes more, *dachas* in Moscow's environs. It was at those places, replete with pine forests, or mixed growths of trees, and situated along streams or abutting on private lakes and ponds, that the hierarchs spent most of their time, serving the commonweal by resting, walking, hunting, fishing, or in most cases plain partying.

7. THE KREMLIN KOMMANDATURA

As the result of years of steady downgrading, by the time the Directorate was formed, the Kremlin guards had been reduced to little more than a sort of ceremonial window dressing for the ancient fortress. They were under the administrative control of the Directorate, to be sure, but, in almost all respects, their original security duties had been taken over by the Okhrana. Of course, *kommandatura* troops were quite visible at the Kremlin walls and gates and within its courtyards, but actually they were no more than reserves —and never called upon—for the officers of Okhrana No. 1 around Stalin and the officers of Okhrana No. 2 who guarded the other hierarchs living within the structure. Therefore, in most respects, they were highly similar to the Okhrana No. 2 units guarding party and government organizations, or another group of smartly uniformed, disciplined watchmen, doormen, and concierges.

Nevertheless, the organizational structure of the *kommandatura* was quite complex. Its chief components were the Otdelny Ofitsersky Batalion (Officers Battalion), the Polk Spetsnaznacheniya (Regiment of Special Purposes), the Rota Spetsnaznacheniya (Company of Special Purposes), and the Otdel Svyazi (Communications Department). It also had an arms and ammunition department, a supply department, and a pass bureau, as well as the usual administrative section and party and Komsomol committees.

The battalion's officers stood guard at the entries of every government building within the fortress. They were especially prominent around Stalin's offices, of course, and less in evidence around those of Molotov and Kaganovich. Impressive numbers of them were also posted at the Troitsky Gate, since it was used by Stalin, while fewer did duty at the Spassky and Borvitsky Gates used by others.

The other prime functions of the officers were to serve as escorts for visitors and operate the pass bureau. (In those days, no ordinary person, or tourist, was ever allowed within the Kremlin. And even those allowed in after the thaw that followed Stalin's death could not enter singly, but were required to go in in groups or accompanied by a government guide.) Officers at the pass bureau, operated at the Spassky Gate, checked all administrative (office help) and service personnel into the Kremlin each morning and made sure that they had left after working hours. For all others, even relatives and friends of hierarchs and their families, it was quite difficult to obtain a pass. In all cases, the person being visited had to confirm the request for a pass, either by telephone call or other means. And, upon receiving the pass, the visitor was escorted by an officer along designated walks and passages to the specified apartment or office. On leaving, the visitor was similarly escorted to the gate. The pass office personnel were very busy during the congresses, conferences, and other meetings frequently held in the Kremlin, with officers checking the participants in and out, escorting them, and, of course, watching them. If anything untoward or suspicious were noted, they had the right to question the visitor, no matter who he was, and in extreme cases, make arrests. Additionally, the officers at the gates had to see to it that no cameras, binoculars and similar equipment, and most definitely no arms, were taken into the Kremlin. All visitors were required to first check such equipment at an office maintained in the GUM building, on the opposite side of Red Square.

The 1,200 officers and men of the Regiment of Special Purposes were on patrol within the Kremlin around the clock. And from it were drawn the guards who stood duty within the adjoining Lenin Mausoleum, also on a twenty-four hour basis. The regiment had light artillery, machine gun and submachine gun units. The stated purpose of the artillery was to protect the hierarchs from "enemies," but all it was ever actually used for was to fire salutes on holidays. So were the machine guns, mounted in well-screened slots in the Kremlin walls, supposed to protect the leaders from demonstrators in Red Square, demonstrators who never materialized. The submachine gunners, at least, had more realistic duty: they did the nighttime patrols within the fortress.

The Company of Special Purposes was yet another of the many, many misnomers. Its only security duty was to check coal, firewood, furnaces, and fireplaces, to make sure that no explosives had been planted. Otherwise, it was sort of a twenty-four hour fire patrol that also made minor fire and accident-prevention repairs.

The Communications Department was a much more elite and worthwhile group. It operated and supervised all phone and radio networks within the fortress, and especially the "Kremlevka," the separate phone system that not only maintained intercommunications for the hierarchs within the Kremlin but also had independent lines to all prime party and government figures and offices outside the walls. (The Kremlin also had a dual electric power source. It drew electricity from the Moscow city enterprise, but also had its own generators for emergency purposes.) And the department also did all maintenance and repair work on the Moscow city phone system within the fortress, since, for security purposes, that work was prohibited to the Moscow city system's employees.

Of the *kommandatura's* lesser units, only the Supply Department was of particular interest. As its title implied, it furnished food, uniforms, and other supplies to the *kommandatura*. But it also supervised the Construction Battalion. That unit not only built and maintained *kommandatura* offices and quarters within the Kremlin and quarters outside the walls, but also kept intact the priceless historical edifices of the Kremlin. Daily, that battalion of highly skilled workers repaired and restored the palaces, churches, and other ancient buildings. And when very delicate work was to be done, the help of artists and other outside specialists was enlisted.

Finally, there was the Lechebno–Sanitarnoye Upravleniye Kremlya (Kremlin Medical Directorate). Despite its title, that unit was not part of the *kommandatura* and was not even located within the Kremlin. Its purpose was to furnish medical care to the entire Soviet hierarchy, from Stalin down to high party and government officials, and their families. It also ran hospitals, clinics, pharmacies, sanitoriums, and rest houses in the Moscow area, as well as other sanitoriums and rest houses in the Crimea, and North Caucasus, and at the Black Sea. For administrative purposes, it was a part of the health ministry. Actually, however, it was controlled by the Guards Directorate, for all its doctors, nurses, technicians and other help had to be cleared by the OPEROD (Operations).

8. LESSER UNITS

Service Department

The correct name for that unit, directly controlled by Vlasik, assisted by his deputy, Lynko, should have been planning and liaison. Although on occasions of prime importance to the Directorate, it had only a small staff of less than twenty officers, since its work was infrequent.

The department was responsible for the security planning for all travel of Stalin and other hierarchs, as well as for their appearances in Red Square and other public places. It also established liaison with foreign security organizations to assure the protection of foreign leaders and dignitaries visiting the Soviet Union. All the plans it drew up for such occasions, of course, were forwarded to appropriate Okhrana components for implementation.

The department also had one rather trifling duty— to issue passes for holiday events in Red Square.

Communications Department

As with security organizations elsewhere, the communications systems of the Directorate were complex and the most sophisticated available at the time. Six systems were used:

1. The regular civilian phone service: for all nonclassified calls. However, for security purposes, no civilian personnel, only Okhrana men, did repair and maintenance work within Directorate establishments.

2. A phone service for security organizations only: that internal network connected the Directorate with state security and similar groups. By dialing the operator, connection could also be made with the regular civilian service. But, no connection could be made from the civilian network to security phones.

3. The government's "VCH" (high frequency) radio-phones: a supposedly untappable service that linked all hierarchs and chiefs of departments, and, of course, all Directorate units, with every major area in the Soviet Union as well as with the satellite countries.

4. The "Kremlevka" of the Kremlin *kommandatura*.

5. The Directorate-Kremlin *kommandatura* phones: those were very highly secured lines and in event of emergency could have been the only connections between the Directorate and Stalin's offices and quarters in the Kremlin. And it was impossible to link them to the Moscow system or to militia and state security lines unless very high-level permission had been obtained.

6. An internal phone network connecting Directorate chiefs, top bosses of

state security, and hierarchs: that was not a dial system, nor did a bell ring to advise of an incoming call. That advice was given by a flashing light. And those phones could be interconnected to other systems.

The Black Sea Resort Subdirectorate

Because Stalin vacationed near Sochi, plus the fact that Beria liked to spend his off time nearby, the Okhrana's Black Sea detachment was the largest of its resort units. And the relatively large number of sanitoriums and villas needed for the many lesser hierarchs who preferred to bask under the same sun as their dictator also increased the need for guards in that area. That was an old story in Russia where the courtiers have always followed their leaders to the watering places, be they tsars or dictators.

Such traffic required the Black Sea Okhrana to keep always ready a large layout of luxurious estates, rest houses, parks, citrus groves and other facilities just in case the ruler and his followers had a sudden fancy to descend on the area. And when that court arrived, accompanied, of course, by large retinues of its own Okhrana staffs, the local Okhrana men were used to beef up security around the pleasure domes, as well as to keep the peasantry well out of vision.

The Crimean and Kislovodsk (North Caucasus) Resorts Subdirectorates

The tasks of the Okhrana units at those establishments were highly similar to those performed by their Black Sea colleagues. But, since Stalin never visited the North Caucasus, and only honored the Crimea with his presence twice—once for the Yalta conference with Roosevelt and Churchill (both Westerners, of course, were then under Okhrana guard)—the Okhrana staffs were much smaller. Just the same, each of those two resort areas had a permanent complement of guards. After all, it was never absolutely certain that Stalin would not drop in.

The North Caucasus resorts were used primarily by the lesser hierarchs, not for vacationing, but for taking cures. Most all of them were sources of waters regarded as healing and were so named. For instance, "Kislovodsk" meant Sour Waters, "Borzhomi" and "Yessentuki" had well known mineral waters named after them, "Zheleznovodsk" was Iron Waters, while "Mineralnyye Vody" was just that, Mineral Water.

The only frequent top level Soviet visitors to the Crimea were Molotov and his family.

The Guards School

To this establishment were sent Okhrana recruits. Training lasted from three to twelve months, depending upon Personnel's requirements and the capacities of the individual students. Sometimes, when replacements were badly needed, that training period was reduced to three weeks.

While undergoing training, the recruits did not wear uniforms, but other-

[408]

wise were treated as military cadets, getting pay and other emoluments. On completion, all those who did not already have military rank were made junior lieutenants and sent to the Second, Third or Fourth Departments of Okhrana No. 2, or any other post that did not give them close contact with the hierarchs.

The usual course included weapons technique (from machine guns to knives), combat methods, self-defense and basic state security surveillance and investigative procedures. Much time was also spent on physical training, especially jujitsu and wrestling. And, of course, studies of the history of the CC CPSU and the biographies of the hierarchs they eventually would protect were obligatory.

The school also had a special section, not for recruits but to teach Okhrana officer candidates for the canine squads how to handle dogs. The entire institution was located in Moscow and was staffed by veteran, experienced officers.

Arms and Ammunition Supply

That section not only furnished the Directorate with its weapons, but also made frequent inspections to see that they were properly maintained and kept in safe operating condition. Additionally, it supplied the hierarchs with sporting equipment and had two officers whose sole duty it was to prepare cartridges for their shotguns and keep their fishing tackle in shape.

And although it had only a dozen guards on its staff, another three of them were assigned to keeping a twenty-four hour watch on the office and supplies.

Physical and Weapons Training

The physical training part of that section would have been an interesting study for Western advocates of pure amateurism in Olympic and other international sports, who complain, with little effect, of professionalism among athletes from Communist countries.

For not only was the Directorate's physical training conducted by many Soviet champions in one sport or another, but also Directorate members participated directly in football (soccer), a sport exceedingly popular throughout the entire world, with the sole exception of the United States. In fact, Moscow's well-known "Dinamo" team was completely manned by Okhrana officers. Although those men did nothing but play football, they were secretly carried on the Directorate's table of organization for pay and allowances.

Other sports in which the Okhrana men engaged, as part of their physical training, were skiing, jumping, running, walking, volleyball, basketball, and wrestling.

Fortunately, professionalism does not prejudice participation in rifle matches and competition in other small arms. For there were also many Okhrana experts in that area. Marksmanship with the Nagant revolver, pistols and small-caliber rifles was attained at an indoor range near the Kremlin.

[409]

And there was an outdoor range in the capital environs for proficiency with machine guns, submachine guns and heavier caliber rifles.

Medical Section

That unit was still another of those incorrectly named. It actually was a sanitary group with the duty of insuring that Directorate establishments and quarters were kept clean and healthful. There were a few doctors and nurses on its staff of about twenty, but most of its personnel were sanitary inspectors. It had no connection whatsoever with the medical-technical (poison) group under the Supply Department. And its chief officer was a man who had the sole duty of checking the air that Stalin breathed.

For actual medical services, the Okhrana officers had to resort to a hospital and three polyclinics maintained in Moscow by state security. All treatment at those establishments for Directorate members and their families was free. But small fees were charged for prescriptions and drugs.

Secretariat

The duties.performed by that organization were really those of a headquarters company, although the company clerk was not an enlisted man, but a captain.

The chief administrative office of the Directorate, it controlled all incoming and outgoing papers, made copies of documents and orders, wrote orders for Okhrana officers, and periodically checked the security of top-secret and secret documents concerning various Okhrana components as well as state security organizations. And it had a pool of typists and stenographers.

The secretariat also controlled the lists of duty officers for all Okhrana units. In the absences of the various chiefs, deputies, and chiefs of sections, those duty officers assumed command.

Party and Komsomol Committees

Although in theory the party controlled everything in the Soviet Union, in actual practice in the Directorate the party had no effective say whatsoever about Okhrana operations. From time to time that was made very clear when some officious, but quite unwise party control officer would attempt —very unsuccessfully—to make the same ideological inspection of the Okhrana committees as every other organization in the Soviet Union was duty-bound to undergo regularly. Such foolish *apparatchiks* were almost literally thrown out bodily, if they had managed to get a foot within an Okhrana door.

Therefore, for all intents and purposes, the Directorate's Party and Komsomol Committees were nothing more than ideological window dressing. Stalin was the true god and Poskrebyshev and Vlasik were his chief saints. The only time the Moscow City Party Committee (to which the Directorate's Party and Komsomol Committees were theoretically subordinate) would be consulted was when an Okhrana officer was dismissed in disgrace. Then, and then only, would the city committee be allowed to intervene and complete the process of denigration by stripping the expellee of his party membership.

Despite all that, the Directorate had a purpose, beyond the ideological, in maintaining the Party and Komsomol Committees. It used them—not for dialectics and the usual Community Party blather—but to inculcate the guards with unstinted loyalty to Stalin and to further their political stability and discipline.

Main Guards Directorate
Pay Scales and Benefits

BASE PAY

Duty	Rubles per month
Okhrana Officer (Guards Officer)	1200
Senior Okhrana Officer (chief of shift)	1400
Case Officer (Operupolnomochenny)	1700
Senior Case Officer	1900
Deputy Chief of Section (otdeleniye)	2100
Chief of Section	2200
Deputy Chief of Department (otdel)	24–2600
Chief of Department	28–3200
Deputy Chief of Directorate (Upravleniye)	34–3800
Chief of Directorate	38–4200
Deputy Chief of Main Directorate	40–4600
Chief of Main Directorate	46–5000

ADDITIONAL PAY, ACCORDING TO RANK

Rank	Rubles per month
Junior Lieutenant	400
Lieutenant	500
Senior Lieutenant	600
Captain	700
Major	900
Lieutenant Colonel	1100
Colonel	1300
Major-General	1600
Lieutenant-General	1900

RATIONS ALLOWANCE

Personnel	Rubles per month
All Okhrana employees	250–300

INCREMENTS FOR LONGEVITY OF SERVICE

Years	Percentage per month
3 to 5	5
5 to 10	10
10 to 15	15
15 to 20	20
more than 20	25

INCREMENTS FOR "SECRET" WORK

Personnel	Percentage per month
Guards of Stalin	30
Guards of lesser hierarchs	20
Most other Okhrana employees	10

ADDITIONAL INCREMENTS FOR OKHRANA SERVICE

Personnel	Percentage per month
Guards of Stalin	5
All other Okhrana employees	3

PENSIONS

Personnel	For Retirement
Guards of Stalin	each year of service counted as 3
All other Okhrana employees	each year of service counted as 2

In accordance with those scales, a Politburo member's guard, with the rank of lieutenant, the (covert) duty of intelligence officer, and five years' service would receive a gross payment of 2,730 rubles a month. However, from that a tax of thirteen percent was deducted for all single employees and all married men with two children or less, although married men with three or more children paid no tax. Additionally, there were the almost perpetual government loans to which the prudent employee would always "voluntarily" subscribe from one to three months of his base pay.

Superlative as was such an Okhrana lieutenant's pay when compared to that of an average Soviet worker, it was almost small change as compared to that given the Directorate chiefs. Vlasik received some 15,000 rubles per month, not to mention unlimited expenses and free food and clothing. His deputies' salaries ranged from 10,000–12,000 rubles per month, depending upon their longevity of service.

The free clothing allowances were another very important benefit to the average Okhrana man. In fact, based only on what that equipment cost the state, even the lowest ranking guard received the equivalent of an additional 7,500 rubles yearly. And at the true price, the cost of such clothing in state stores, the figure would have ranged between 10,000–12,000 rubles a year.

All Okhrana officers, regardless of rank, received two sets of uniforms and two civilian outfits every two years. And covert (intelligence) personnel received a double set of mufti in the same period. The biennial issues were:

Military—fur cap, service cap, greatcoat, tunic and two pairs of trousers, field jacket and two pairs of trousers, two pairs of leather boots, belts, gloves, stockings, three sets of underwear. That issue not only included everything that was provided army officers but also the amounts were somewhat greater and the quality, of course, was superior. And for officers on special assignment, such articles as capes, sheepskin coats, galoshes and felt boots were also supplied.

Civilian—fur cap, hat or cap, overcoat (or the material for one), suit (or the fabric), two pairs of high or low shoes, shirts, stockings, underwear, handkerchiefs, towels. All service personnel, who did not have military rank, received only civilian clothing, in the same amount as the officers, but of slightly inferior quality.

Free housing was also provided some Directorate members, but far from all. The personal guards of Stalin and the lesser hierarchs were all supplied with quarters: the married men were furnished apartments or sets of rooms; the bachelors were given dormitory accommodations. And the Kremlin *kommandatura* officers, thanks primarily to the thoughtfulness of the commandant, plus the fact he had his own construction battalion, had the handsomest free housing of all. But all other Directorate personnel were not that fortunate. Those in Moscow had to battle—and pay accordingly—the same woeful housing shortage that confronted the ordinary capital denizens. However, they did have their relatively high salaries to ameliorate that problem in most respects.

Lesser Hierarchs under "Protection" of Okhrana No. 2 [1947–1952]

Abakumov, Viktor Semenovich—b. ca. 1900, executed 1954, Colonel-General, Chief of SMERSH during World War II, Minister of State Security 1946–51. Arrested ca. August, 1951, on charges he failed to find all guilty persons involved in the "Leningrad Affair" and because he refused to support Doctors' Plot preparations, according to account Khrushchev gave to a State Security officers' meeting in 1951. However, after Stalin's death, Khrushchev charged Abakumov with inventing the "Leningrad Affair" and sending many party workers to prison or death.

Andreyev, Andrey Andreyevich—b. 1895, d. 1971, member of CP since 1914, member of Politburo 1932–1952, onetime Secretary of CC CPSU and Deputy Chairman of the Council of Ministers of the USSR. Dismissed from all his positions in 1952 on Stalin's order and retired. One of the few old Bolsheviks to have survived the purges mainly due to the fact he was well incapacitated by failing eyesight.

Beria, Lavrenty Pavlovich—b. 1899, executed 1953, Georgian (but actually had Mingrelian father and Jewish mother), Marshal of Soviet Union, member of CP since 1917, First Secretary of Transcaucasian Party and virtual dictator and police boss of Transcaucasia 1932–38, People's Commissar for Internal Affairs of USSR 1938–45, Deputy Prime Minister in charge of atomic energy 1945–53. After Stalin's death, briefly First Deputy Chairman of the Council of Ministers as well as Minister for Internal Affairs. He was arrested as an "imperialist agent" June 27, 1953. His closest associates were executed with him.

Budenny, Semen Mikhaylovich—b. 1883, Marshal of Soviet Union, hero of the Civil War, member of CP since 1918, very popular, legendary cavalry commander. During World War II, he was very incapable commander of southwestern front and was dismissed, but retained marshal's rank for retirement.

Bulganin, Nikolay Aleksandrovich—b. 1895, Marshal of Soviet Union, member of CP since 1917, Cheka official 1918–22, Chairman of the Moscow City Council, Chairman of the Council of the People's Commissars of the RSFSR, Deputy Chairman of the Council of People's Commissars of the USSR, 1927–41, political officer and member of State Defense Committee during World War II, Defense Minister and First Deputy Prime Minister 1947–49 and 1953–55, Politburo member 1948–58, Prime Minister 1955–57, declared member of "antiparty group" by Khrushchev and ousted as Prime Minister in 1957, expelled from CC of CPSU in 1958, reportedly retired in 1960.

Choybalsan, Khorlogiyn—b. 1895, d. 1952, Mongolian. Marshal and Prime Minister of Mongolian Peoples Republic 1939–52, died in Moscow hospital. (He is included in this list since he was "protected" by a detachment of the Okhrana No. 2.)

Dimitrov, Georgy Mikhailovich—b. 1882, d. 1949, Bulgarian who also was Soviet citizen, leader of the Bulgarian Communist Party, arrived in USSR after Reichstag fire trial in 1934, Secretary-General of the Comintern 1935–43, after defeat of Germany returned to Bulgaria in 1945, Chairman of the Bulgarian Council of Ministers and General Secretary of the Bulgarian Communist Party 1946–49, held preliminary Balkan union discussions with Tito, became ill and entered Soviet hospital where he died. (Like Choybalsan Dimitrov was also under "Protection" of the Okhrana No. 2 detachment.)

Kaganovich, Lazar Moiseyevich—b. 1893, Jewish, member of CP since 1911, Deputy Prime Minister 1938–57, Politburo member 1930–57, expelled from Politburo and CC CPSU and dismissed as Deputy Prime Minister as member of "antiparty group" by Khrushchev in 1957. Reportedly retired.

Khrushchev, Nikita Sergeyevich—b. 1894, d. 1971, member of CP since 1918, active participant in Civil War, party *apparatchik* since 1925, Politburo member 1939–64, First Secretary of CC CPSU 1953–64, Chairman of the Council of Ministers of the USSR 1958–64, ousted from all posts and sent into retirement in 1964. (While he was party boss, Khrushchev, who had received no awards whatsoever from Stalin, made himself a Hero of the Soviet Union, the highest Soviet award, four times, the first for his sixtieth birthday, the second for development of the "virgin lands" of Siberia, the third for the launching of the Sputnik, and the fourth for both his seventieth birthday and for "heroism," previously unrecognized during World War II.)

Kosygin, Aleksey Nikolayevich—b. 1904, member of CP since 1927, party and industrial *apparatchik*, held variety of posts under Stalin, People's Commissar for Textile and Light Industry, Chairman of the Council of Ministers of the RSFSR, Deputy Chairman of the Council of Ministers of the USSR and was Politburo member 1949–52, but fell from favor with Stalin in 1952, his political star began rising again after Stalin's death, Politburo candidate member 1957–60, Politburo full member since 1960, Chairman of the Council of Ministers of the USSR since the ousting of Khrushchev in 1964.

Kruglov, Sergey Nikiforovich—b. 1900, General-Colonel, member of CP since 1918, Deputy People's Commissar for Internal Affairs 1938–45, Soviet chief of security at Teheran, Yalta, and Potsdam conferences, Minister for Internal Affairs of USSR 1946–53 and 1954–56, ousted by Khrushchev in 1956 and reportedly expelled from Communist Party and retired.

Kuusinen, Otto Vilgelmovich—b. 1881, d. 1964, Finn, who like Dimitrov held Soviet citizenship, Finnish revolutionary during reign of Nicholas II, one of organizers of Finnish Communist Party, a Secretary of the Comintern, Presidium member 1921–39, Deputy Chairman of the Presidium of the Supreme Soviet of the USSR 1940–58, Politburo member 1957–64, a Secretary of the CC CPSU 1957–64.

Kuznetsov, Aleksey Aleksandrovich—b. 1905, executed 1949, member of CP since 1925, started career as Leningrad party *apparatichik*, member of the Military Council of the Leningrad Front during World War II, First Secretary of Leningrad *oblast* and city committee 1945, as Zhdanov's protégé, a Secretary of CC CPSU and thus responsible for Soviet state security 1946–49, fell from favor with Stalin after Zhdanov's death and arrested on dictator's personal order in 1948, shot to death 1949. "Rehabilitated" by Khrushchev in 1957.

Malenkov, Georgy Maksimilianovich—b. 1902, member of CP since 1920, graduate of Moscow Technical Institute, Moscow party *apparatchik* 1921–34, enlisted by Poskrebyshev and Stalin to handle CC CPSU affairs in 1934, Politburo candidate member 1941–46, Politburo full member 1946–57, member of State Defense Committee during World War II, Deputy Prime Minister 1946–53, Prime Minister under "collective leadership" 1953–55, ousted by Khrushchev 1955, expelled from CC CPSU as member of "anti-party" group and made manager of East Kazakhstan power station 1957.

Merkulov, Vsevolod Nikolayevich—b. ca. 1900, executed 1953, Deputy People's Commissar for Internal Affairs of USSR 1939–43, People's Commissar for State Security of USSR February–June 1941 and 1943–46, Minister of State Control 1953, arrested with Beria.

Mikoyan, Anastas Ivanovich—b. 1895, Armenian, member of CP since 1915, active participant in October Revolution and Civil War, Politburo candidate member 1926–35, Politburo full member 1935–65, Deputy Chairman of the Council of People's Commissars of the USSR and People's Commissar for Foreign Trade 1937–46, member of State Defense Committee during World War II, Minister for Internal and External Trade 1953–55, First Deputy Chairman of the Council of Ministers of the USSR 1955–64, Chairman of the Presidium of the Supreme Soviet of the USSR (President) 1964–65, retired but retained membership in Presidium of Supreme Soviet 1966.

Molotov, Vyacheslav Mikhaylovich—b. 1890, member of CP since 1906, (as a revolutionary, he dropped the aristocratic family name of Scriabin), early *Pravda* colleague of Stalin, active participant in October Revolution, Chairman of Council of People's Commissars of USSR (Prime Minister) 1930–40, Deputy Chairman 1940–57, Deputy Chairman of State Defense Committee during World War II, Minister for Foreign Affairs 1939–49 and 1953–56, Politburo member 1925–57, fell into disfavor with Stalin who exiled his Jewish wife to Kazakhstan in 1949, charged by Khrushchev with being member of "antiparty" group and ousted from party and government positions in 1957, briefly held posts as Ambassador to Mongolia and as delegate to International Atomic Energy Commission before being retired.

Patolichev, Nikolay Semenovich—b. 1908, member of CP since 1928, made a Secretary of CC CPSU by Stalin as fulfillment of promise to Patolichev's father, who was killed in Civil War, that he would take care of his son 1946–47, Presidium (Politburo) candidate member 1952–53, Secretary of Byelorussian Communist Party 1950–56, Deputy Foreign Minister 1957–58, Minister of Foreign Trade since 1958.

Ponomarenko, Panteleymon Kondratyevich— b. 1902, member of CP since 1925, served in original Red Army 1918–21, graduated from Moscow Engineering Institute 1932, Red Army officer 1932–35, First Secretary of Byelorussian Communist Party 1938–47, officer commanding partisan warfare behind enemy lines during World War II, Chairman of Council of Ministers of Byelorussian Republic 1944–48, a Secretary of CC CPSU 1948–53, Minister of Culture of USSR 1954, on diplomatic assignments since 1955.

Popov, Georgy Mikhaylovich—b. 1906, member of CP since ?, Chairman of Moscow City Soviet 1942, First Secretary of Moscow Party Committee 1945–49, a Secretary of CC CPSU 1946–49, when replaced by Khrushchev, Ambassador to Poland 1953–54, later posts and location unknown.

Rokossovsky, Konstantin Kostantinovich—b. 1896, d. 1968, Marshal of Soviet Union and Poland, of Polish origin, member of CP since 1919, participant in World War I and Civil War, Commander of various fronts during World War II, Deputy Chairman of the Council of Ministers and Minister of National Defense of Poland 1949–56, after Poznan uprising returned to USSR 1956, Deputy Defense Minister and other Defense Ministry posts 1956–68.

Serov, Ivan Aleksandrovich—b. 1905, d. ?, Army General, member of CP since 1926, state security official 1939–40, Deputy Minister for Internal Affairs of USSR 1941–54, deporter of millions from Baltic countries, Northern Bukovina, Bessarabia, Poland, Crimea, and Caucasus during World War II, Chairman of State Security Committee (KGB) 1954–58, Chief of Military Intelligence (GRU) 1958–64, dismissed, demoted to Major General and transferred to minor military command because of Penkovskiy case 1964. Reportedly later committed suicide.

Shvernik, Nikolay Mikhaylovich—b. 1888, d. 1970, member of CP since 1905, party labor specialist, First Secretary of All Union "Trade Unions" 1930–44, Politburo candidate member 1939–52, Politburo full member 1952–53 and 1957–66, Chairman of the Presidium of the Supreme Soviet of the USSR (President) 1946–53, Chairman of the Party Control Commission of the CC CPSU 1956–66, retired 1966.

Sokolovsky, Vasily Danilovich—b. 1897, d. 1968, Marshal of Soviet Union, member of CP since 1931, active participant in Civil War, Deputy Minister of Defense 1949–60, Chief of General Staff 1958–60, Chief of Soviet Armed Forces in East Germany 1946–49.

Suslov, Mikhail Andreyevich—b. 1902, member of CP since 1921, party ideologist, economics graduate of Moscow Institute, party *apparatchik* since 1931, a Secretary of CC CPSU since 1947, editor of *Pravda*, party newspaper, 1949–51, Politburo member since 1955.

Timoshenko, Semen Kostantinovich—b. 1895, d. 1970, Marshal of Soviet Union, member of CP since 1919, active participant in Civil War, People's Commissar for Defense 1940–41, held various posts in Ministry of Defense from 1941 until death.

Vasilyevsky, Aleksandr Mikhaylovich—b. 1895, Marshal of Soviet Union, member of CP since 1938, Deputy Chief and later Chief of General Staff and Deputy People's Commissar of Defense during World War II, Chief of General Staff 1946–49, Minister of Defense 1949–53, held various posts in Defense Ministry since 1953.

Voroshilov, Kliment Yefremovich—b. 1881, d. 1969, Marshal of Soviet Union, member of CP since 1903, Politburo member 1925–60, active participant in Civil War, People's Commissar for Defense 1925–40, member of State Defense Committee and commander of various fronts during World War II, Deputy Chairman of the Council of Ministers of the USSR 1946–53, Chairman of the Presidium of the Supreme Soviet of the USSR (President) 1953–60, retired 1960.

Voznesensky, Nikolay Alekseyevich—b. 1903, executed 1950, economic planner, member of CP since 1919. Deputy Chairman of the Council of

Ministers of the USSR 1939–49, member of State Defense Committee during World War II, Politburo candidate member 1941–47, Politburo full member 1947–49, arrested on Stalin's orders 1949, shot without trial 1950.

Vyshinsky, Andrey Yanuaryevich—b. 1883, d. 1954, purge "trials" prosecutor and diplomat, member of Mensheviks 1903–20, member of CP since 1920, Deputy then General-Procurator (prosecutor) of the USSR 1933–39, Deputy Minister of Foreign Affairs, Minister of Foreign Affairs, chief Soviet delegate to U.N. 1940–54.

Zhdanov, Andrey Aleksandrovich—b. 1896, d. (possibly poisoned) 1948, one of several possible heirs of Stalin, member of CP since 1915, agitprop worker with Red Army 1919–22, Secretary of Gorky Oblast Party Committee 1924–34, First Secretary of Leningrad City and Oblast Party Committee 1934–44, a Secretary of CC CPSU 1934–48, Politburo candidate member 1935–38, Politburo full member 1939–48, member of Military Council of Leningrad Front during World War II.

Zhukov, Georgy Konstantinovich—b. 1896, Marshal of the Soviet Union, the great Soviet commander of World War II, earned (unlike Khrushchev) Soviet Union's highest award, Hero of Soviet Union, four times, member of CP since 1919, active participant in World War I and the civil war, Chief of General Staff and Deputy Commander-in-Chief of Soviet Armed Forces during World War II, Minister of Defense 1955–57, ousted by Khrushchev for "Bonapartist tendencies" and reportedly retired in 1957.

Secrecy Requirements and Penalties Applicable to the Main Guards Directorate

Decree of the Presidium of the Supreme Soviet USSR of June 9, 1947.

ON THE RESPONSIBILITY FOR THE DIVULGENCE OF STATE SECRETS AND THE LOSS OF DOCUMENTS CONTAINING STATE SECRETS

In order to establish unity in the legislation and to increase the responsibility for the divulgence of data constituting state secrets, a list of which was established by the Council of Ministers of the USSR in its resolution of June 8 of the current year,—the Presidium of the Supreme Soviet of the USSR decrees:

1. Divulgence of information constituting a state secret committed by persons to whom such information was entrusted or who could obtain such information due to their working position, and as far as these actions cannot be qualified as treason or espionage,—is punishable by confinement to a correction-labor camp for a period of eight to twelve years.

2. Divulgence by military personnel of military information constituting a state secret and as far as these actions cannot be qualified as treason and espionage,—is punishable by confinement to a correction-labor camp for a period of ten to twenty years.

3. Divulgence by private persons of information representing a state secret and as far as these actions cannot be qualified as treason or espionage, —is punishable by confinement to a correction-labor camp for a period of five to ten years.

4. Loss by officials of materials, documents and publications containing information constituting a state secret, if the nature of these actions is not legally subject to more severe punishment,—is punishable by confine-

ment in a correction-labor camp for a period of four to six years.

The same crime, if it led to serious consequences, is punishable by confinement in a correction-labor camp for a period of six to ten years.

5. Loss by military personnel of documents containing information constituting a state secret, if these actions are not legally subject to more severe punishment,—is punishable by confinement in a correction-labor camp for a period of five to eight years.

The same crime, if it led to especially serious consequences, is punishable by confinement in a correction-labor camp for a period of eight to twelve years.

6. Announcement or transfer abroad of inventions, discoveries and technical improvements representing a state secret, made within the USSR, as well as abroad by citizens of the USSR on a tour of duty by appointment of the government, if such crimes cannot be qualified as treason or espionage,—are punishable by confinement in a correction-labor camp for a period of ten to fifteen years.

7. Criminal cases affected by this Decree shall be tried by the Military Tribunal.

8. In connection with this Decree the following is declared no longer in effect:

   a) Decree of the Presidium of the Supreme Soviet of the USSR of November 15, 1943 "On the Responsibility for Divulgence of State Secrets and the Loss of Documents, Containing a State Secret";

   b) Part "a", art. 25 "Regulations Concerning Military Crimes."

In accordance with the present Decree, the supreme soviets of the union republics are invited to make the necessary amendments in the legislation of the union republics.

(signed).

Development and Structure of Communist Bodyguards, 1917-1972

Development and Structure of Communist Bodyguards
1917–1972

State Security (Secret Police)		Bodyguards (Okhrana)		
Names of the Organizations	Heads	Units	Chiefs	Commandants of the Kremlin
VChK All Russian Extraordinary Commission (Vserossiyskaya Chrezvychaynaya Komissiya) 20 Dec. 1917–6 Feb. 1922	Dzerzhinsky, Feliks E. 20 Dec. 1917–20 July 1926	VChK Armored Cars Unit. Latvian Rifles Nov. 1917–Dec. 1918 First Moscow Machine Gun Courses (Pervyye Moskovskiye Pulemetnyye Kursy) 1918–Feb. 1921	Avanesov, Varlaam A. Bykov, Fedor A. Berzin, Eduard P. Nikitin, I.I. (Chief) Borisov, Iliya I. (Commissar)	Malkov, Pavel D. (Smolny Institut in Petrograd, Nov. 1917–March 1918) Moscow Kremlin March 1918–April 1920 Assistant Martynov, Mikhail I.
GPU State Political Administration (Gosudarstvennoye		OSNAZ–Detachment of Special Designation (OTRYAD Osobogo Naznacheniya) (Feb. 1918–17 June 1924	Belenky, Abram Ya.	Peterson, Rudolf A. 1920–1935

State Security (Secret Police)		Bodyguards (Okhrana)		
Names of the Organizations	Heads	Units	Chiefs	Commandants of the Kremlin
Politicheskoye Upravleniye) 6 Feb. 1922– 6 July 1923		CHON–Units of Special Designation (Chasti Osobogo Naznacheniya) 1918–1924		
		First Combined Military School of VTsIK (Pervaya Obyedinennaya Voyennaya Shkola VTsIK) Feb. 1921–Present. Transferred from the Kremlin after Kirov murder in 1935 and seized Guards duties.	Lashuk, Petr M. 1921–1929 Yegorov, (FNU) ?–1935 Neyelov, Nikolay A. 1970	
		OSNAZ–Division of Special Designation (Divisiya Osobogo Naznacheniya) 17 June 1924–20 July 1926 Division OSNAZ became OMSDON– Dzerzhinsky Detached Motorized	Gorbachev, (FNU) 1926–1935	

State Security (Secret Police)		Bodyguards (Okhrana)		
Names of the Organizations	Heads	Units	Chiefs	Commandants of the Kremlin
OGPU United State Political Administration (Obyedinennoye Gosudarstvennoye Politicheskoye Upravleniye) 6 July 1923– 10 July 1934	Menzhinsky, Vyacheslav R. July 1926– 10 May 1934	Infantry Division of Special Designation. (Otdelnaya Motostrelkovaya Divisiya Osobogo Naznacheniya imeni Dzerzhinskogo) 20 July 1926–Present	Kozlov, A. 1967	
	Yagoda, Genrikh G. May 1934– 10 July 1934	OPEROD–Operational Department OGPU (Operativny Otdel) 1926–1934	Pauker, Karl Volovich, Vladimir V. Vlasik, Nikolay S.	
NKVD	Yagoda,			

State Security (Secret Police)		Bodyguards (Okhrana)		
Names of the Organizations	Heads	Units	Chiefs	Commandants of the Kremlin
Peoples Commissariat for Internal Affairs (Narodny Komissariat Vnutrennikh Del) 10 July 1934– 3 Feb. 1941	Genrikh G. 10 July 1934– 26 Sept. 1936 Yezhov, Nikolay I. 26 Sept. 1936– 1938 Beria, Lavrenty P. 8 Dec. 1938– 20 July 1941	First Department NKVD 1936–1938 First Department of Main Administration of State Security (GUGB) NKVD (Pervyy Otdel Glavnogo Upravleniya Gosudarstvennoy Bezopasnosti NKVD)	Pavlov, (FNU) Gulst, Veniamin N. Vlasik, Nikolay S.	Tkalun, (FNU) (1935–1937) Rogov, (FNU) (1938)
NKGB Peoples	Merkulov,	First Department		Spiridonov,

	State Security (Secret Police)		Bodyguards (Okhrana)	
Names of the Organizations	Heads	Units	Chiefs	Commandants of the Kremlin
Commissariat of State Security (Narodny Komissariat Gosudarstvennoy Bezopasnosti) 3 Feb.–20 July 1941	Vsevolod N. 3 Feb.– 20 July 1941			Nikolay K. (1939–1953) Deputy Kosynkin, Petr Ye.
NKVD Peoples Commissariat for Internal Affairs 20 July 1941– 14 April 1943	Beria, Lavrenty P. 20 July 1941– 14 April 1943	First Department GUGB NKVD		
NKGB Peoples Commissariat of State Security	Merkulov, Vsevolod N.	Sixth Directorate NKGB	Kapanadze, Andrey P. Vlasik, Nikolay S.	

| State Security (Secret Police) | | Bodyguards (Okhrana) | | |
Names of the Organizations	Heads	Units	Chiefs	Commandants of the Kremlin
14 April 1943–19 March 1946			Kuznetsov, Aleksandr K.	
MGB Ministry of State Security (Ministerstvo Gosudarstvennoy Bezopasnosti) 19 March 1946–15 March 1953	Abakumov, Viktor S. March 1946–August 1951	Guards (Okhrana) Directorate No. 1 Guards (Okhrana) Directorate No. 2 (1946–1947)	Rakov, Aleksandr M. Shadrin, Dmitry N.	
	(Acting) Ogoltsov, Sergey I. 1951–1952	Main Guards Administration– GUO MGB (Glavnoye Upravleniye Okhrany) Feb. 1947–May 1952	Chief: Vlasik, Nikolay S. Deputies: Lynko, Vladimir S. Goryshev, Serafim V. Grishkov, (FNU) Ignatyev, Semen D.	
	Ignatyev,	Guards (Okhrana) Directorate		

State Security (Secret Police)		Bodyguards (Okhrana)		
Names of the Organizations	Heads	Units	Chiefs	Commandants of the Kremlin
	Semen D. 1952–15 March 1953	May 1952–March 1953	Martynov, (FNU) Novik, Nikolay P.	
MVD Ministry for Internal Affairs (Ministerstvo Vnutrennikh Del) 15 March 1953–13 March 1954	Beria, Lavrenty P. 15 March–26 June 1953	Ninth Directorate	Kuzmichev, Sergey F.	
	Kruglov, Sergey N. July 1953–13 March 1954		Lenev, Aleksandr M.	Vedenin, Andrey Ya. 1953–1967
KGB Committee of State Security under Council of Ministers, USSR	Serov, Ivan A. 13 March 1954–	Ninth Directorate	Ustinov, Vladimir I.	

| State Security (Secret Police) | | Bodyguards (Okhrana) | | |
Names of the Organizations	Heads	Units	Chiefs	Commandants of the Kremlin
(Komitet Gosudarstvennoy Bezonasnosti pri Sovete Ministrov SSSR) 13 March 1954-8 July 1975	8 Dec. 1958 Shelepin, Aleksandr N. 25 Dec. 1958-31 Oct. 1961 Semichastny, Vladimir Ye. 13 Nov. 1961-18 May 1967	Guards Directorate (Ninth Directorate)	Zakharov, Nikolay S. Chekalov, Aleksey M. Tsvigun, Semen K. 1967-January 1982 as First Deputy Chairman of the KGB, supervised Ninth Directorate. KGB Generals in supervisory position of the Ninth Directorate: Antonov, Sergeyn, Ryalenko, Aleksandr Ya., Medvedev, Vladimir T. From late 1960s until Brezhnev's death—10 Nov. 1982	Shornikov, Sergey S. 1967-Present
KGB USSR Committee of State Security, USSR (Komitet Gosudarstvennoy Bezonasnosti SSSR) 5 July 1975-present	Andropov, Yury V. 18 May 1967-26 May 1982 Fedorchuk, Vitaliy V. 26 May 1982-16 Dec. 1982 Chebrikov, Viktor M. 16 Dec. 1982-present			

Stalin's Bodyguards [Okhrana] 1947-1952

STALIN'S BODYGUARDS (OKHRANA) 1947 – 1952

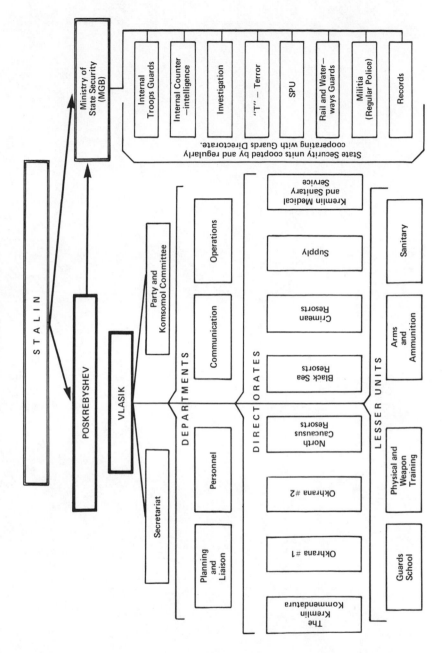

Bibliography*

ENGLISH SOURCES

ALEXANDROV, VIKTOR. *The End of the Romanovs*. Boston: Little, Brown & Co., 1966.

———— *The Kremlin*. London: 1963.

———— *The Tukhachevsky Affair*. Englewood Cliffs, New Jersey: Prentice-Hall, Inc., 1964.

ALLILUYEVA, ANNA and ALLILUYEV, SERGEI. *The Alliluyev Memoirs*. New York: G.P. Putnam's Sons, 1968.

ALLILUYEVA, SVETLANA. *Only One Year*. New York: Harper & Row, 1969.

———— *Twenty Letters to a Friend*. New York: Harper & Row, 1967.

ANDICS, HELLMUT. *Rule of Terror: Russia Under Lenin & Stalin*. New York: Holt, Rinehart & Winston, 1969.

AVRICH, PAUL. *The Russian Anarchists*. Princeton, New Jersey: Princeton University Press, 1967.

AVTORKHANOV, ABDURAKHMAN. *The Communist Party Apparatus*. Cleveland, Ohio: The World Publishing Co., 1968.

———— *Stalin and the Soviet Communist Party*. New York: Frederick A. Praeger, 1959.

BAILEY, GEOFFREY. *The Conspirators*. New York: Harper & Brothers, 1960.

BAJANOV, BORIS. *Avec Staline Dans Le Kremlin*. Paris: 1930.

BALABANOFF, ANGELICA. *Impressions of Lenin*. Benton Harbor: 1964.

*Certain books which the informed reader might expect to find listed, in the opinion of the author as expressed in the Foreword, do not sufficiently meet standards of reliability and authenticity to be included.

BARMINE, ALEXANDER. *One Who Survived*. New York: G.P. Putnam's Sons, 1945.

BEAL, JOHN ROBINSON. *The Secret Speech*. New York: 1961.

BECK, F., and GODIN, W. *Russian Purge and the Extraction of Confession*. New York: The Viking Press, 1951.

BERGAMINI, JOHN D. *The Tragic Dynasty*. New York: G.P. Putnam's Sons, 1969.

BLACKSTOCK, PAUL W. *The Secret Road to World War II*. Chicago: Quadrangle Books, 1969.

BOFFA, GUISEPPE. *Inside the Khrushchev Era*. New York: Marzani & Munsell, Publishers, 1959.

BORNSTEIN, JOSEPH. *The Politics of Murder*. New York: 1950.

BRZEZINSKI, ZBIGNIEW, K. *The Permanent Purge*. Cambridge, Massachusetts: Harvard University Press, 1956.

CHARQUES, RICHARD. *The Twilight of Imperial Russia*. Fair Lawn, New Jersey: Essential Books, 1959.

CONQUEST, ROBERT. *The Great Terror: Stalin's Purge of the Thirties*. New York: The Macmillan Co., 1969.

_____ *The Nation Killers*. London: The Macmillan Co., 1970.

_____ *Power and Policy in the USSR*. New York: St. Martin's Press, 1961.

_____ (Editor). *The Soviet Police System*. New York: Frederick A. Praeger, 1968.

COOKRIDGE, E.H. *The Net that Covers the World*. New York: Henry Holt & Co., 1955.

COWLES, VIRGINIA. *The Russian Dagger*. New York: Harper & Row, 1969.

DANIELS, ROBERT V. *Red October*. New York: Charles Scribner's Sons, 1967.

DERIABIN, PETER and GIBNEY, FRANK. *The Secret World*. New York: Doubleday & Co., 1959.

DEUTSCHER, ISAAC. *Stalin: A Political Biography*. New York: Oxford University Press, 1967.

DONOVA, K. and TRIFONOVA, N. (eds.). *Around the Kremlin*. Moscow: Progress Publishers, 1967.

DURANTY, WALTER. *The Kremlin and the People*. London: 1942.

_____ *Stalin & Co. The Politburo. The Men Who Run Russia*. London: 1949.

EBON, MARTIN. *Malenkov, Stalin's Successor*. New York: McGraw-Hill Book Co., 1953.

ECKARDT, HANS VON. *Ivan the Terrible*. New York: 1949.

ELY, COL. LOUIS B. *The Red Army Today*. Harrisburg, Pennsylvania: The Military Service Publishing Co., 1953.

ERICKSON, JOHN. *The Soviet High Command*. London: 1962.

ESSAD-BEY. *OGPU— The Plot Against the World.* New York: The Viking Press, 1933.

FEIS, HERBERT. *Churchill, Roosevelt, Stalin.* Princeton, New Jersey: 1957.

FISCHER, LOUIS. *The Life and Death of Stalin.* New York: Harper & Brothers, 1952.

———— *The Life of Lenin.* New York: Harper & Row, 1964.

FRANKLAND, MARK. *Khrushchev.* New York: Stein & Day, 1967.

GARDER, MICHEL. *A History of the Soviet Army.* New York: Frederick A. Praeger, 1966.

GOLDSTONE, ROBERT. *The Soviets.* New York: Bantam Books, 1967.

GREY, IAN. *Ivan the Terrible.* Philadelphia & New York: J.B. Lippincott Co., 1964.

GROSS, FELIKS. *The Seizure of Political Power.* New York: Philosophical Library, 1958.

GYLAND, WILLIAM and SHRYOCK, RICHARD W. *The Fall of Khrushchev.* New York: Funk & Wagnalls, 1968.

HARCAVE, SIDNEY. *Years of the Golden Cockerel.* New York: The Macmillan Co., 1968.

HENDEL SAMUEL (ed.). *The Soviet Crucible.* Princeton: D. Van Nostrand Co., 1967.

HINGLEY, RONALD. *The Tsars (1533–1917).* New York: The Macmillan Co., 1968.

———— *The Russian Secret Police.* London: Hutchinson, 1970.

———— *Nihilists.* New York: Delacorte Press, 1967.

JENKINS, MICHAEL. *Arakcheev.* New York: The Dial Press, 1969.

JESSUP, JOHN K. and the Editors of "Life." *Communism (The Nature of Your Enemy).* New York: Time Inc., 1962.

KHRUSHCHEV, NIKITA S. *Khrushchev Remembers (with Introduction and Comments by Edward Crankshaw).* Boston: Little, Brown & Co, 1970.

KRIVITSKY, W.G. *I Was Stalin's Agent.* London: Hamish Hamilton, 1939.

KULSKI, W.W. *The Soviet Regime.* New York: Syracuse University Press, 1954.

LAMB, HAROLD. *The City and the Tsar.* New York: Doubleday, 1948.

LATEY, MAURICE. *Patterns of Tyranny.* New York: Atheneum, 1969.

LEVINE, ISAAC DON. *The Mind of an Assassin.* New York: Farrar, Straus & Cudahy, 1959.

LEWIN, MOSHE. *Lenin's Last Struggle.* New York: Pantheon Avons, 1969.

LOCKHART, R. H. BRUCE. *British Agent.* New York: G.P. Putnam's Sons, 1933.

LOCKHART, ROBIN BRUCE. *Ace of Spies.* New York: Stein & Day, 1967.

MALKOV, P. *Reminiscences of a Kremlin Commandant.* Moscow: Progress Publishing House, 1967.

MARTIN, JOHN STUART (ed.). *A Picture History of Russia.* New York: Crown Publishers, Inc., 1968.

MASSIE, ROBERT K. *Nicholas and Alexandra.* New York: Atheneum, 1967.

MEISSNER, BORIS. *The Communist Party of the Soviet Union.* New York: Frederick A. Praeger, 1956.

MONAS, SIDNEY. *The Third Section.* Cambridge, Massachusetts: 1961.

MOOREHEAD, ALAN. *The Russian Revolution.* New York: Harper & Brothers, 1958.

MOSSOLOV, A.A. *At the Court of the Last Tsar.* London: Metheun & Co, 1935.

NICOLAEVSKY, BORIS I. *Power and the Soviet Elite: "The Letter of an Old Bolshevik" and Other Essays.* New York: Frederick A. Praeger, 1965.

NIKOLAJEWSKY, BORIS. *Aseff the Spy (Russian Terrorist and Police Stool).* New York: Doubleday, 1934.

ORLOV, ALEXANDER. *The Secret History of Stalin's Crimes.* New York: 1953.

OSTROUKHOVA, K.A., and others. *V. I. Lenin (A Short Biography).* Moscow: Progress, no date.

PAGE, MARTIN. *The Day Khrushchev Fell.* New York: Hawthorn Books, 1965.

PALOCZE-HORVATH, GEORGE. *Khrushchev: The Making of a Dictator.* Boston: Little, Brown & Co., 1960.

PARES, BERNARD. *A History of Russia.* New York: Alfred A. Knopf, 1951.

———— *The Fall of the Russian Monarchy.* New York: Vintage, 1961.

PAYNE, ROBERT. *The Fortress.* New York: Simon & Schuster, 1967.

———— *The Life and Death of Lenin.* New York: Simon & Schuster, 1964.

———— *The Rise and Fall of Stalin.* New York: Simon & Schuster, 1965.

———— *The Terrorists.* New York: Simon & Schuster, 1957.

PENKOVSKIY, OLEG V., *The Penkovskiy Papers* (Introduction and Commentary by Frank Gibney). New York: Doubleday, 1965.

PETROV, VLADIMIR and EVDOKIA. *Empire of Fear.* New York: Frederick A. Praeger, 1956.

PLATONOV, S.F. *The Time of Troubles.* The University Press of Kansas, 1970.

POSSONY, STEFAN T. *Lenin; The Compulsive Revolutionary.* Chicago: Henry Regnery Co, 1964.

RAMBANND, ALFRED. *History of Russia, From the Earliest Times to 1822.* (In Three Volumes) Boston: The Page Co, 1882.

RANDALL, FRANCIS B. *Stalin's Russia.* New York: The Free Press, 1965.

RAUCH, GEORG VON. *A History of Soviet Russia*. (5th revised edition) New York: Frederick A. Praeger, 1967.

RICE, TAMARA TALBOT. *Elizabeth, Empress of Russia*. New York: Praeger Publishers, Inc., 1970.

RUSH, MYRON. *Political Succession in the U.S.S.R.* New York: Columbia University Press, 1965.

SALISBURY, HARRISON. *Moscow Journal (The End of Stalin)*. Chicago: 1961.

SCHAPIRO, LEONARD. *The Communist Party of the Soviet Union.* New York: Random House, 1960.

SCHUMAN, FREDERICK E. *Russia Since 1917*. New York: Alfred A. Knopf, 1957.

SETH, RONALD. *The Executioners: The Story of SMERSH*. New York: Hawthorn Books, 1967.

SETON-WATSON, HUGH. *From Lenin to Khrushchev*. New York: Frederick A. Praeger, 1960.

SHUB, BORIS and QUINT, BERNARD. *Since Stalin, A Photo History of Our Time*. New York: Swen Publishing Co., 1951.

SHUB, DAVID. *Lenin*. New York: The New American Library, 1948.

SIMMONDS, GEORGE W. (ed.). *Soviet Leaders*. New York: Thomas Y. Crowell Co., 1967.

SMITH, EDWARD ELLIS. *The Young Stalin*. New York: Farrar, Straus & Giroux, 1967.

SMITH, WALTER BEDELL. *My Three Years in Moscow*. Philadelphia & New York: J.B. Lippincott Co., 1950.

SOUVARINE, B. *Stalin*. New York: 1939

SPIRIDOVICH, GENERAL ALEXANDRE. *Les Dernieres Annees de la Cour de Tzarskoie-Selo*. Paris: Payot, 1928.

SUMNER, B. H. *Peter the Great and the Emergence of Russia*. New York: Collier Books, 1968.

TATU, MICHEL. *Power in the Kremlin from Khrushchev to Kosygin*. New York: The Viking Press, 1969.

TROTSKY, LEON. *Stalin*. New York: Harper & Brothers, 1941.

TUCKER, ROBERT C. and COHEN, STEPHEN F. (eds.). *The Great Purge Trial*. New York: Grosset & Dunlap, 1965.

ULAM, ADAM B. *The Bolsheviks*. New York: The Macmillan Co., 1965.

UTECHIN, S.V. *A Concise Encyclopaedia of Russia*. New York: E.P. Dutton & Co., 1964.

VASSILYEV, A.T. *The Okhrana (The Russian Secret Police)*. Philadelphia: J.B. Lippincott Co., 1930.

WILSON, COLIN. *Rasputin and the Fall of the Romanovs*. New York: Farrar, Straus & Co., 1964.

WIPPER, R. *Ivan Grozny.* Moscow: Foreign Language Publishing House, 1947.

WOLFE, BERTRAM D. *Khrushchev and Stalin's Ghost.* New York: Frederick A. Praeger, 1957.

YOUNG, GORDON. *Stalin's Heirs.* London: Derek Verschoyle, 1953.

RUSSIAN SOURCES

ABRAMOV, ALEKSEY. *Chasovyye Posta No. 1* (Guards of Post No. 1). Moscow: Politizdat, 1966.

ABRAMOV, I.S. *Mavzoley Lenina* (The Lenin Mausoleum). Moscow: Moskovsky Rabochy, 1969.

AGABEKOV, G.S. *ChK Za Rabotoy* (The Cheka at Work). Berlin, Germany: Energiadruck, 1931.

———*G. P. U. Zapiski Chekista* (G.P.U. Notes of a Chekist). Berlin, Germany: Strela, 1930.

ALAKHVERDOV, G.G., KUZMIN, N.F., and others. *Kratkaya Istoriya Grazhdanskoy Voyny v SSSR* (A Short History of the Civil War in the USSR). Moscow: Politizdat, 1960.

ALEKSANDROV, G.F., and others (Comps.) *Iosif Vissarionovich Stalin, Kratkaya Biografiya* (Joseph Vissarionovich Stalin, A Short Biography). Moscow: Politizdat, 1949

AMELIN, G.K. *Petrogradsky Voenno-Revolutsionnyy Komitet i ego Rol v Sakreplenii i Okhrane Zavoevany Velikoy Oktyabrskoy Sotsialisticheskoy Revolutsii.* (Petrograd Military-Revolutionary Committee and the October Revolution). Moscow: Yurizdat, 1963.

ANTONOV, G.S., and others (eds.). *V.I. Lenin i Kremlevskiye Kursanty* (V.I. Lenin and the Kremlin Cadets). Moscow: Moskovsky Rabochy, 1969.

ARDAMATSKY, VASILY. *Vozmezdiye* (Retribution). Moscow: Molodaya Gvardiya, 1968.

ARIPOV, P. and MILSHTEIN, N. *Iz Istorii Organov Gosbezopasnosti Uzbekistana* (From the History of the Organs of State Security in Uzbekistan). Tashkent: Uzbekistan, 1967.

BELOV, G.A., KURENKOV, A.N., LOGINOVA, A.I., PLETNEV, Ya.A., and TIKUNOV, V.S. (eds.). *Iz Istorii Vserossiyskoy Chrezvychaynoy Komissii* (From the History of the All Russian Extraordinary Commission 1917-1921). Moscow: Politizdat, 1958.

BESSEDOVSKY, G.Z. *Na Putyakh k Termidoru* (On the Road to Thermidor). Paris: Mishen, 1931.

BOGUCHARSKY, V. Ya., SHCHEGOLEV, P.Ye., and BURTSEV. F.L. (eds.). *Byloye.* (magazine issues 1-10). St. Petersburg: 1906.

BONCH-BRUYEVICH, V.D. *Vospominaniya* (Memoirs). Moscow: Khudozhestvennaya Literatura, 1968.

_____*Vospominaniya o Lenine* (Reminiscences about Lenin). Moscow: Nauka, 1969.

BOZHERYANOV, I.N. *Nevsky Prospect*. St. Petersburg: 1901.

CHIKIN, V.V. *Sto Zimnikh Dney* (One Hundred Winter Days). Moscow: Molodaya Gvardiya, 1968.

DAVYDOV, L.D. (Comp.). *Partiya Shagayet v Revolutsiyu* (Party goes to Revolution [Stories about Lenin's associates]). Moscow: Gospolitizdat, 1969.

DIMITRIYEV, YURY. *Pervy Checkist* (The First Chekist). Moscow: Molodaya Gvardiya, 1968.

DUBINSKY-MUKHADZE, I. *Ordzhonikidze*. Moscow: Molodaya Gvardiya, 1967.

DVINSKY, EM. *Moskva (Fotoal'bom)*. (Moscow, A. Photo album). Moscow: Moskovsky Rabochy, 1963.

DYAGILEV, D.V., YEGORYCHEV. N.G., and others (eds.) *Istoriya Moskvy* (History of Moscow). Moscow: Nauka, 1967.

DZERZHINSKAYA, S. *V Gody Velikikh Boyev* (During the Years of the Great Battles.). Moscow: Mysl, 1964.

DZERZHINSKY, F. *Dnevnik Zakluchennogo, Pis'ma* (Diary of an Imprisoned Man, Letters). Moscow: Molodaya Gvardiya, 1966.

FIGNER, VERA. *Vospominaniya* (Memoirs). Moscow: Mysl, 1964.

FILATOVA, L. (ed.). *U Kremlevskoy Steny* (At the Kremlin Wall). Moscow: Politizdat, 1967.

FOTIYEVA, L.A. *Iz Zhizni V.I. Lenina* (From the Life of V.I. Lenin). Moscow: Politizdat, 1967.

FRAYMAN, ANTON L. *Forpost Sotsialisticheskoy Revolyutsii* (Petrograd in the First Months of Soviet Power). Leningrad: Nauka, 1969.

FRUMENKOV, G.G. *Uzniki Solovetskogo Monastyrya* (The Prisoners of Solovetsk Monastery). Arkhangel'sk: 1968.

GERNET, MIKHAIL NIKOLAYEVICH. *Istoriya Tsarskoy Tyurmy* (History of Tsarist Jails). Volumes II, III, IV and V. Moscow; Gosurizdat, 1961.

GOLIKOV, G.N., KUZNETSOV, M.I., and SHAUMYAN, L.S. (eds.). *Velikaya Oktyabr'skaya Sotsialisticheskaya Revolyutsiya—Malenkaya Entsiklopediya* (The Great October Socialist Revolution—A Small Encyclopedia). Moscow: Soviet Encyclopedia, 1968.

GOLINKOV, D.L. *Krakh Vrazheskogo podpolya* (The Failure of the Enemies Underground). Moscow: Politizdat, 1971.

GUL, ROMAN. *Dzerzhinsky (Menzhinsky-Peters-Latsis-Yagoda)*. Paris: 1936.

IOGANSON, O.N. *Dorogoy Borby* (By The Road of Struggle). Moscow: Politizdat, 1963.

IOYRYSH, A. and SERGEYEV, B. *Kuda Vedut Sledy* (Where the Path Leads). Moscow: Yuridicheskaya Literatura, 1965.

IVANOV, V.D. (ed.). *50 Let Sovetskikh Vooruzhennykh Sil* (50 Years of Soviet Armed Forces). Photo Documents. Moscow: Voenizdat, 1967.

IVANOV, V.N. (ed.). *Moskovsky Kreml'* (The Moscow Kremlin). Moscow: Sovetsky Khudozhnik, 1965.

KARAGANOV, A.V., LAVROV, P.A., and others (eds.). *Lenin* (a collection of photographs and stills). Volume I. Moscow: Iskusstvo, 1970.

KERSNOVSKY, A.A. *Istoriya Russkoy Armii, 1700-1917* (History of the Russian Army, 1700-1917). Belgrade: 1933.

KHATSKEVICH, A. *Soldat Velikikh Boyev* (Soldier of the Great Battles). Minsk; Nauka i Tekhnika, 1965.

KHIGEROVICH, RAFAIL. *Mladshy Brat* (The Youngest Brother). Moscow: Politizdat, 1969.

KLYATSKIN, S.M. *Na Zashchite Oktyabrya* (On Defense of the October Revolution). Moscow: Nauka, 1965.

KLYUCHEVSKY, V.O. *Kurs Russkoy Istorii* (A Course of Russian History). 8 Volumes. Moscow: Politizdat, 1956.

KOLOTOV, V. and PETROVICHEV, G. *N.A. Voznesensky—Biografichesky Ocherk* (N.A. Voznesensky—A Biographical Sketch). Moscow: Politizdat, 1963.

KONDRATYEV, V.A. (Comp.). *Moskovsky Voyenno-Revolyutsionnyy Komitet. Oktyabr-Noyabr 1917.* (The Moscow Military-Revolutionary Committee, October-November 1917). Moscow: Moskovsky Rabochy, 1968.

KONOVALOV, S.A. (Comp.). *Nezrimyy Front* (The Invisible Front). 1917-1967. Alma-Ata; Kazakhstan, 1967.

KONSTANTINOV, A.P. (ed.). *Piterskiye Rabochiye-Revolutsionery.* (The Petrograd Workers, Revolutionaries.). Leningrad: Znaniye, 1963.

KOPANEV, G.I. (Editor-in-Chief). *1917 Geroi Oktyabrya* (1917 Heroes of the October Revolution.). Leningrad: 1967.

KOSITSYN, A.P. (Editor-in-Chief). *Istoriya Sovetskogo Gosudarstva I Prava.* (History of Soviet State and Law.). (Vol. I, 1917-1920; Vol. II, 1921-1935). Moscow: Nauka Publishing House, 1968.

KOVALEV, A.P. *Putevoditel po Moskve.* (Moscow Tour Book.). Moscow: 1963.

KRASNIKOV, S.V. *Sergey Mironovich Kirov-Zhizn i Deyatelnost* (Sergey Mironovich Kirov—His Life and Activities.). Moscow: Politizdat, 1964.

LAVROV, P. and others. *Lenin.* Moscow: Izogiz, 1963.

LAZEBNIKOV, A. *Ikh Znal Ilych* (Lenin Knew Them). Moscow: Sovetskaya Rossiya, 1967.

LYUBOVTSEV, V.I. (Comp.). *Vsegda Nacheku* (Always on Guard). Moscow: Politizdat, 1967.

MALKOV, P. *Zapiski Komendanta Kremlya* (Reminiscences of the Kremlin's Commandant). Moscow: Molodaya Gvardiya, 1967.

MARUKHIN, V. and SLITENKO, L. *Imenem Zakona* (In the Name of Law). Leningrad: 1969.

MAZE, N. (ed.). *Rytsar Revolutsii* (Knight of the Revolution). Moscow: Politizdat, 1967.

MINTS, I.I. *Istoriya Velikogo Oktyabrya 1917-1967* (History of the Great October). Moscow: Nauka, 1967.

MIRONOV, N.P. *Ukrepleniye Zakonnosti I Pravoporyadka—Programnaya Zadacha Partii.* Moscow: Yuridichezkaya Literatura Publishing House, 1964.

_____ *Ukrepleniye Zakonnosti I Pravoporyadka V Obshchenarodnom Gosudarstve—Programnaya Zadacha Partii.* Moscow: Yuridicheskaya Literatura Publishing House, 1969.

NIKULIN, LEV. *Mertvaya Zyb* (The Death Swell). Moscow: Voennizdat, 1965.

OLDENBURG, S.S. *Tsarstvovaniye Imperatora Nikolaya II.* (The Reign of Emperor Nicholas II). Volumes I and II. Belgrade: 1939.

POLIKARPOV, V.D. (ed.). *Etapy Bol'shogo Puti.* (Along the Great Road). Moscow: Voenizdat, 1963.

POSPELOV, P.N. (Editor-in-Chief). *Velikaya Otechestvennaya Voyna Sovetskogo Soyuza 1941–1945.* (The Great Patriotic War of the Soviet Union 1941–1945). 6 Volumes. Moscow: Voenizdat, 1961–1965.

_____ and others. *Vladimir Ilych Lenin.* Moscow: Politizdat, 1963.

PUSHKAREV, S.G. *Obzor Russkoy Istorii* (A Survey of Russian History). New York: Chekhov Publishing House, 1953.

RODIONOVA, N.I. (ed.). *Geroi Oktyabrya* (Heroes of the October Revolution). Moscow: Moskovsky Rabochy, 1967.

ROZHDESTVENSKY, P. and SHKARENKOVA, G. (eds.). *Revolutsionno-Istorichesky Kalendar-Spravochnik na 1964, 1966, 1967 god* (Historical-Revolutionary Calendar for 1964, 1966, 1967). Moscow: 1963, 1965, 1966.

RYBAKOV, B.A. *Pervyye Veka Russkoy Istorii* (First Centuries of Russian History). Moscow: 1964.

SAVOSTYANOV, V.I., and YEGOROV, P. Ya. *Comandarm Pervogo Ranga* (First Rank Army Commander). Moscow: Politizdat, 1966.

SHMELEY, I.I. (Comp.). *Soldaty Nevidimykh Srazheny* (The Soldiers of Invisible Battles). Moscow: Voenizdat, 1968.

SHTEMENKO, S.M. *Generalny Shtab v Gody Voyny* (The General Staff During World War II). Moscow: Voenizdat, 1968.

SKILYAGIN A., LESOV, V., PIMENOV, Yu., and SAVCHENKO, I. *Dela i Lyudi Leningradskoy Militsii* (Events and People of the Leningrad Militia). Leningrad: 1967.

SKRYNNIKOV, P.G. *Nachalo Oprichniny* (The Beginning of the Oprichnina). Leningrad: Leningrad University, 1966.

SMIRNOV, I.I., SAMSONOV, A.M. and others (eds.). *Kratkaya Istoriya SSSR* (A Short History of the USSR in two parts). Moscow, Leningrad: "Nauka" Publishing House, 1963-1964.

SMIRNOV, M. (ed.). *F.E. Dzerzhinsky v VChk* (F.E. Dzerzhinsky in the VChK). Moscow: Pogranichnik, 1967.

———— (ed. and Comp.). *Rasskazy O Menzhinskom* (Stories about Menzhinsky). Moscow: Pogranichnik, 1969.

SOFINOV, P.G. *Ocherki Istorii Vserossiyskoy Chrezvychaynoy Komissii* (An Historical Outline of the All Russian Extraordinary Commission). 1917–1922. Moscow: Politizdat, 1960.

SOLOMENNYY, V.S. (ed.). *Geroi Grazhdanskoy Voyny* (Heroes of the Civil War). Moscow: Molodaya Gvardiya, 1963.

SPRESLIS, A.I. *Latyshskiye Strelki na Strazhe Zavoevany Oktyabrya.* (The Latvian Rifles on the Guard of Achievement of the October Revolution). Riga: Zinatne, 1967.

STARTSEV, V.I. *Ocherki po Istorii Petrogradskoy Krasnoy Gvardii i Rabochey Militsii* (An Historical Outline of the Petrograd Red Guard and Worker's Militia). Moscow and Leningrad: Nauka, 1965.

STEPNYAK-KRAVCHINSKY, S.M. *V Londonskoy Emigratsii* (In London Emigration). Moscow: Nauka, 1968.

TODORSKIY, A.I. *Marshal Tukhachevsky.* Moscow: Politizdat, 1963.

TOROPOV, L. (Ed.). *Komissary* (The Commissars). Moscow: Politizdat, 1967.

VEDENIN, A. Ya. *Gody i Lyudi* (Years and People). Moscow: Politizdat, 1964.

VIKTOROV, I. *Podpolshchik Voin, Chekist.* (Underground Soldier—Chekist). Moscow: Politizdat, 1963.

VOEYKOV, V.N. *S. Tsarem i bez Tsarya. Vospominaniya Poslednego Dvortsovogo Komendanta Gosudarya Imperatora Nikolaya II* (With Tsar and Without Tsar. Memoirs of the Last Commandant of the Palace, his Imperial Majesty Nicholas II). Helsingfors: 1936.

Voyennaya Entsiklopedia (Military Encyclopaedia). Petersburg: 1912.

VVEDENSKIY, B.A. (Ch. ed.). *Bolshaya Sovetskaya Entsiklopediya* (The Big Soviet Encyclopedia). 51 volumes. Moscow: 1949–58.

YAKIR, P.I., and GELLER, Yu. A. (Comp.). *Comandarm Yakir* (Army Commander Yakir). Moscow: Voenizdat, 1963.

YAKOVLEV, B. *Kontsentratsionnyye Lageri SSSR* (Concentration Camps of the USSR). München: Institute for the Study of the History and Culture of the USSR. 1955.

ZABELIN, IVAN. *Domashny byt Russkogo Naroda v XVI i XVII ct* (The Home Mode of Life of the Russian People in the 16th and 17th Centuries). Moscow: 1862.

ZAKHAROV, M.V. (ed.). *50 Let Vooruzhennykh Sil SSSR* (50 Years of Armed Forces of the USSR). Moscow: Voennizdat, 1968.

ZHUKOV, G.K. *Vospominaniya i Razmyshleniya*. (Reminiscences and Reflections). Moscow: Novosti, 1969.

ZILBERMAN, E., and KHOLYAVIN, V. *Pokusheniye* (Attempt). Kazan University; 1965.

ZIMIN, A.A. *Oprichnina Ivana Groznogo* (Ivan the Terrible's Oprichnina). Moscow: Mysl, 1964.

ZUBOV, N. *F.E. Dzerzhinsky (Biografiya)* (F.E. Dzerzhinsky—A Biography). Moscow: Politizdat, 1963, 1971.

OTHER SOURCES

AKIMOV, G. *Sobstvennyy Ego Imperatorskogo Velichestva Svodnyy Pekhotnyy Polk* (His Majesty's Imperial Composite Infantry Regiment). Paris: "Voyennaya Byl" #78, 1966.

ARTEM'YEV, S.A. *Sledstviye i Sud nad Dekabristami* (Investigation and Trial of Decembrists). Moscow: "Voprosy Introii" No. 2 and 3., 1970.

BEREZHKOV, B.M. *Tegeran, 1943*. Moscow: "Novaya i Noveyshaya Istoriya" No. 6, 1967 and No. 1 and 2, 1968.

DAVYDOV, L.G. *Aleksandr Ilych Ul'yanovidelo o Pokushenii 1 Marta 1887 Goda* (Alexander I. Ul'yanov and Assassination Attempt of 1 March 1887). Moscow: "Voprosy Istorii," No. 5, 1968.

DEYCH, G.M. *Konspirativnaya Tekhika Lenintsev* (Conspiratorial Techniques of Leninists). Moscow: "Voprosy Istorii," No. 9, 1969.

DUPLITSKIY, S.K. *Okhrana Tsarskoy Semi i Revolyutsiya 1917 Goda* (Protection of Tsar's Family and Revolution of 1917). Paris: "Vozrozhdeniye," 1949.

EYDELMAN, N. Ya. *Memyary Ekateriny II* (Memoirs of Catherine the Second). Moscow: "Voprosy Istorii," No. 1, 1968.

GOLINKOV, D.L. *Razgrom Kontrrevolyutsii v Sovetskoy Rossii* (The Crushing of Counterrevolution in Soviet Russia). Moscow: "Voprosy Istorii," No. 1 and 2, 1968.

KANN, P. Ya. *O Chisle Zhertv 14 Dekabrya, 1825* (About the Numbers of the Victims of 14 December 1825). Moscow: "Istoriya SSSR," No. 6, 1970.

KERENSKY, ALEXANDER. *Lenin: 'He was a Cruel Man.'* Washington, D. C., *Washington Post*, 6 December 1970.

KIRPICHNIKOV, A.N. *Vooruzheniye Rusi v IX–XIII* (Armament in Russia in the IX–XIII Centuries). Moscow: "Voprosy Istorii," No. 1, 1970.

KOBRIN, V.K. *Malyuta Skuratov*. Moscow: "Voprosy Istorii," No. 11, 1966.

KONDRASHEV, F. *Zagovor Protiv "Evriki"* (Plot Against "Evrika"). Moscow: *Moskovskaya Pravda*, 5 July 1970.

KOZLOV, O.F. *Delo Tsarevicha Alekseya* (The Case of Tsarevich Alexis). Moscow: "Voprosy Istorii," No. 9, 1969.

KRONGAUZ, ALEKSANDR. *Latyshsky Strelok* (The Latvian Rifleman). Moscow: "Ogonek," No. 16, April 1967.

KUZNETSOV, N.G. *Pobednaya Vesna 1945 Goda* (Victory Spring of 1945). Moscow: "Novaya I Noveyshaya Istoriya," No. 1, 1970.

LAVROV, A. *Post No. 1.* Moscow: "Smena," 1 January 1969.

LUKIN, ALEXANDER. *Operation 'Long Jump'.* Moscow: "Sputnik." 1966.

LURYE, S.S. *Borba za Vlast pri Preemnikakh Petra I.* (Struggle for Power after Peter 1st.) Moscow: "Voprosy Istorii," No. 3, 1968.

_____*Knyazhna Tarakanova* (The Princess Tarakanova). Moscow: "Voprosy Istorii," No. 10, 1966.

LVOV, G.D. *Karayushchy Mech Revolyutsii* (The Punitive Sword of the Revolution). Moscow: "Voprosy Istorii," No. 12, 1968.

LYUBIMOV, L. *Tayna Startsa Fedora Kuzmicha* (The Mystery of Elder Fedor Kuzmich). Moscow: "Voprosy Istorii," No. 1, 1966.

MARQUIS DE CUSTINE (Foreword by SMITH, W. BEDELL). *Has Russian Despotism Changed Much Since the Czars?* U.S. News & World Report, 14 September 1959.

MAYSKY, B. Yu. *Stolypinshchina i Konets Stolypina* (The End of Stolypin). Moscow: "Voprosy Istorii," No. 1 and 2, 1966.

MELCHIN, A. *Svyaznoy Ilycha* (The Messenger of Lenin). Moscow: "Sovetskaya Rossiya," 25 August 1970.

NEYELOV, N.A., Major-General, Chief of Moscow Higher Military Officers School of the Supreme Soviet RSFSR. *Nasledniki* (The Successors). Moscow: "Ogonek," No. 50, December 1970.

NICOLAEVSKY, B. *Gosudarstvennyy Perevorot Nikity Khrushcheva* (The State Revolution of Nikita Khrushchev). "Sotsialistichesky Vestnik" No. 9 and 10, 1957.

OVCHINNIKOV, R.V. *"Krusheniye Poluderzhavnogo Vlastelina"* (The Downfall of Semi-Ruler). "Voprosy Istorii," No. 9, 1970, Moscow.

PLATTEN, FRITZ. *"Revolutsionery Vostoka."* (Revolutionaries of the East). "Novaya I Noveyshaya Istoriya." No. 1. Moscow: 1970.

POLETAYEV, O.A. *"Kremlevskiye Kursantki"* (The Kremlin Women Cadets). "Voprosy Istorii," No. 5, Moscow: 1968.

RUSANOVA, I.B., *I.P. Tovstukha* "Voprosy Istorii," No. 4, Moscow: 1969.

SAKHAROV, A.N. *Krasnyy Terror Narodovoltsev* (The Red Terror of the "People's Will"). "Voprosy Istorii," No. 5, 1966, Moscow.

SHELOMENTSEV, LT. COLONEL F. *Kremlevskiye Chasovyye* (The Kremlin Guardsmen) "Sovetsky Voin" No. 14, Moscow: 1971.

SOLOVYEV, ANDREY. *Sentyabr Sorok Chetvertogo* (September 1944). "Smena," No. 18 and 19, September, October 1971.

SOLOVYEV, M.E. *Tsarskiye Provokatory i delo Sotsial-demokraticheskoy*

Fraktsii II Gosudarstvennoy dumy (Tsarist Provocateurs and the Case of Social-Democratic Faction of Second State Duma). "Voprosy Istorii" No. 8, Moscow, 1966.

STARTSEV, V.I. *Begstvo Kerenskogo* (The Flight of Kerensky). "Voprosy Istorii," No. 11, Moscow, 1966.

STIMSON, F.P. *Posledniy Vremenshchik Poslednego Tsarya* (The Last Favorite of the Last Tsar. Material of the Extraordinary Investigation Commission of the Provisional Government concerning Rasputin and the Decay of the Autocracy). "Voprosy Istorii," No. 10 and 12 for 1964; No. 1 and 2 for 1965. Moscow.

STUCHEVSKIY, I.A. *Neobyknovennaya Sud'ba Feodory* (The Fate of Empress Feodora). "Voprosy Istorii," No. 3, 1967, Moscow.

_____*Oktyabr v Moskve* (October in Moscow). "Voprosy Istorii," No. 7, 1967, Moscow.

_____*Ot Fevralya k Oktyabryu* (From February to October). "Voprosy Istorii," No. 5, 1967, Moscow.

VINOKUROV, N. and ZUBOV, N. *Glavkom Nezrimogo Fronta* (Commander-in-Chief of the Invisible Front). "Krasnaya Zvezda," 10 September 1967.

VOLODIN, A. *Raskolnikov i Karakozov* "Novyy Mir," No. 11, Moscow: 1969.

ZAYONCHKOVSKY, P.A. *Aleksandr III i ego Blizhayshee Okruzheniye* (Alexander III and His Closest Associates). "Voprosy Istorii," No. 8, 1966, Moscow.

YAKIR, PIERE. *Moscow Historian Demands Criminal Probe of Stalin.* "Le Monde," 16–17 March 1969, Paris.

Index